OXFORD HISTORICAL MONOGRAPHS

EDITORS

Family Structure in the Staffordshire Potteries 1840–1880

MARGUERITE W. DUPREE

CLARENDON PRESS · OXFORD

1995

Oxford University Press, Walton Street, Oxford OX2 6DP

Oxford New York
Athens Auckland Bangkok Bombay
Calcutta Cape Town Dar es Salaam Delhi
Florence Hong Kong Istanbul Karachi
Kuala Lumpur Madras Madrid Melbourne
Mexico City Nairobi Paris Singapore
Taipei Tokyo Toronto
and associated companies in
Berlin Ibadan

Oxford is a trade mark of Oxford University Press

Published in the United States
by Oxford University Press Inc. New York

British Library Cataloguing in Publication Data
Data available

Library of Congress Cataloging in Publication Data
Dupree, Marguerite.
Family structure in the Staffordshire Potteries, 1840–1880 /
Marguerite W. Dupree.
p. cm.—(Oxford historical monographs)
Includes bibliographical references and index.
1. Family—England—Potteries—History—19th century.
2. Industrial revolution—England—Potteries—History—19th century.
3. Ceramic industries—England—Potteries—History—19th century.
I. Title. II. Series.
HQ616.15.P67D86 1994 306.85′0942—dc20 94–29754
ISBN 0–19–820400–0

1 3 5 7 9 10 8 6 4 2

Typeset by Graphicraft Typesetters Ltd., Hong Kong
Printed in Great Britain
on acid-free paper by
Bookcraft Ltd.
Midsomer Norton, Avon

To My Parents

**Marguerite Louise Arnold Dupree
and Anderson Hunter Dupree**

and

To My Husband and Children

Rick, Richard, and Meg Trainor

Preface and Acknowledgements

Though the Potteries lie between, and no very great distance from, Liverpool and Manchester in the north and Birmingham in the south, though they can communicate easily with nearly any part of the country, occupying as they do an almost central position, there is something so self-contained about them and their peculiar industry that they convey a most unusual impression of provincial remoteness, an impression heightened by their odd littleness and shabbiness. You feel that nobody comes to the Potteries and nobody—except Arnold Bennett—has left them. The same firms, none of them very large though several, of course, are famous, go on from generation to generation, throughout a century employing workmen from the same families. There is something to be said for this cosy personal sort of industry, . . . but this too helps to make the district self-contained and to confirm it in whatever kind of life it has adopted or made for itself.

J. B. Priestley, English Journey, 1934

PRIESTLEY captures the distinctiveness of the Potteries, the ambiguities and paradoxes—central yet remote, an ancient craft yet an industry. Yet, to what extent do views from other perspectives confirm, contradict, elaborate, or qualify the features of his portrait—the continuity of firms and families throughout a century, the lack of immigration or emigration, the personal industry? What were the characteristics of the people who lived there? What kind of life did individuals make for themselves in this district?

Neither the Bradford of Priestley's youth nor a cotton town in Lancashire, this area of North Staffordshire in the nineteenth century was a testament to the empirical diversity and complexity of reactions to pressures for social change. It provides a clear example of how the Industrial Revolution of the late eighteenth and nineteenth centuries worked itself out differently in different areas. This is a study of the work, the people, and the general way of life of working people in the Staffordshire Potteries between 1840 and 1880 from the perspective of their family relationships.

In the making of this book I have received much generous help and support which I am very pleased to be able to acknowledge here.

Generous support from the Master and Fellows of Emmanuel College Cambridge, the Warden and Fellows of Nuffield College Oxford, Princeton University, and a Woodrow Wilson Dissertation Fellowship enabled me to complete the thesis on which this book is based. An Arthur H. Cole Grant-in-Aid from the Economic History Society provided expenses, and the President and Fellows of Wolfson College Cambridge the most congenial of atmospheres for revision of the thesis into this book. I have been able to add relevant data, recast its arguments, and relate its themes and evidence closely to recent literature. I am especially grateful to the former President, Professor Sir David Williams, for his continuing interest and support. A Postdoctoral Fellowship from the Economic and Social Research Council enabled me to undertake a closely related project from which this book indirectly benefited. More recently, in the interstices of other research projects and my duties at the Wellcome Unit for the History of Medicine at the University of Glasgow, I completed the final stages of the preparation of the book.

I have been fortunate in receiving much assistance from archivists and librarians. I am particularly grateful to Mr D. Beard and staff at the Horace Barks Reference Library, Hanley, Stoke-on-Trent; Mr F. B. Stitt and staff at the Staffordshire County Record Office and William Salt Library, Stafford; Dr I. Fraser and staff at the Archives and Mr M. Phillips at the Special Collections of the University of Keele Library; and Mr A. G. Jones at the Library of the University College of North Wales, Bangor. In addition, heavy demands on the Bodleian Library, the Public Record Office, the British Newspaper Library, the Cambridge University Library, the library of the ESRC Cambridge Group for the History of Population and Social Structure, and the Glasgow University Library were willingly met.

For access to marriage registers in their care, I wish to thank Revd P. L. C. Smith of St John's, Burslem; Revd M. G. Johnson of Holy Trinity, Sneyd, Burslem; Revd C. R. Goodley of Christ Church, Cobridge; Revd R. B. Heading of Holy Trinity, Northwood, Hanley; Revd M. F. West of St Lukes's, Wellington, Hanley; Revd L. Skinner of St Mark's, Shelton; Revd Prebendary R. A. Cason of St Peter's, Stoke-on-Trent; and Revd J. R. Williams and Revd A. D. Cox of Christ Church, Fenton. For access to the annual reports of the North Staffordshire Infirmary in his care, I am grateful to Dr C. Webster, then Director of the Wellcome Unit for the History of Medicine, Oxford.

The kind hospitality of David and Charlotte Vincent made trips to the Potteries in the later stages of the research a special pleasure.

For assistance with the computer analysis of the census enumerators' books, particularly the data-file structure and the writing of several special programs, I am indebted to Clive Payne and staff at the Research Services Unit of the Oxford University Social Studies Faculty. Further analysis would have been impossible without the aid of the staff of the Cambridge University Computing Centre and Professor J. Davis's course at the University of Essex Summer School in Quantitative Data Analysis.

I thank Cambridge University Press for permission to reprint in Chapter 3 material originally published in my essay 'The Community Perspective in Family History: The Potteries during the Nineteenth Century', in A. L. Beier, D. N. Cannadine, and J. Rosenheim (eds.), *The First Modern Society: Essays in English History in Honour of Lawrence Stone*. Also, I have used material from the Wedgwood manuscripts on temporary deposit at the University of Keele. References from them are published by courtesy of the Trustees of the Wedgwood Museum, Barlaston, Staffordshire, England, and I would like to thank Gaye Blake Roberts, Curator. In addition, I used material from the Minton manuscripts when they were on temporary deposit for cataloguing at the Department of Manuscripts, University College of North Wales (Bangor) Library. References to them are published with the permission of the Minton Archives, Royal Doulton plc, and I would like to thank Joan Jones, Curator of the Minton Museum.

I have given a number of seminar and conference papers based on aspects of this book and I want to record my appreciation of the comments of those who attended. Also, I have benefited at various stages of this work from advice, information and encouragement from Professor M. Anderson, Dr F. Botham, Miss R. Bucks, Professor D. N. Cannadine, the late Professor H. J. Dyos, Mrs S. Gater, Mr M. W. Greenslade, Dr R. Hall, Mr P. Laslett, Professor A. Macfarlane, the late Professor C. Marsh, Dr M. I. Nixon, Dr J. Obelkevich, Mr J. Oppen, Dr S. Presser, Dr D. Reeder, Dr K. Schurer, Dr R. M. Smith, Dr R. Schofield, Dr D. C. Souden, Dr S. Szreter, Professor D. Vincent, Mr R. Wall, Mr P. Waller, Dr L. Weatherill, Dr C. Webster, Professor R. Whipp, Mr P. Willmott, and Professor E. A. Wrigley.

Professor L. Stone, Dr R. M. Hartwell, and Mr J. H. Goldthorpe, in different capacities, supervised my research and read early drafts. I appreciate their comments and help. Professor W. A. Armstrong, Dr Joan Thirsk, Professor Lynn Hollen Lees, Professor Robert Woods, and two anonymous referees read the thesis on which this book is based and made many helpful comments and suggestions. Although I have not been able to follow all of them, I am enormously grateful. Particular thanks are due to my University supervisor, Professor P. Mathias, whose suggestions, example, and wise counsel stimulated and sustained me throughout the work on this project. His friendship and willingness to help have extended long after his role as supervisor ended and I am deeply grateful. Sole responsibility for the content of the book nevertheless resides with me.

In addition I would like to express my appreciation to the members of the Oxford Historical Monographs Committee and their chairmen, Mr A. F. Thompson, Mr M. Brock, and Professor C. Matthew, and to Anne Gelling of Oxford University Press for their patience.

As this is a book about families, history, and the Potteries, I cannot end without acknowledging my debt to my paternal grandparents, from whom, although they lived in the panhandle of Texas, I first learned of the Potteries and the products of Josiah Wedgwood, his contemporaries and their successors, and to my maternal grandparents, whose house and memories helped introduce me to the fascination of investigating the past. I have used the dedication to express, albeit inadequately, my thanks to those who, in ways too many and varied to enumerate, have meant most of all.

M.W.D.
July 1993

Contents

List of Figures

List of Maps

List of Tables

Abbreviations

Abst. of Brit. Hist. Stats.	B. R. Mitchell and P. Deane (eds.), *Abstract of British Historical Statistics* (Cambridge, 1962)
Amer. Econ. Rev.	*American Economic Review*
Amer. Hist. Rev.	*American Historical Review*
Amer. Sociol. Rev.	*American Sociological Review*
Birm. Daily News	*Birmingham Daily News*
British J. of Industrial Medicine	*British Journal of Industrial Medicine*
Brit. J. of Sociol.	*British Journal of Sociology*
CUL	Cambridge University Library
Econ. Dev. and Cultural Change	*Economic Development and Cultural Change*
Econ. Hist. Rev.	*Economic History Review*
ESRC Cambridge Group	Economic and Social Research Council Designated Research Centre, Cambridge Group for the History of Population and Social Structure, 27 Trumpington Street, Cambridge
Geog. J.	*Geographical Journal*
GW	Godfrey Wedgwood
Hist. J.	*Historical Journal*
Hist. Workshop	*History Workshop*
HBRL	Horace Barks Reference Library, Stoke-on-Trent City Library, Hanley
Int. Rev. of Soc. Hist.	*International Review of Social History*
J. of Econ. Business Hist.	*Journal of Economic and Business History*
J. of Econ. Hist.	*Journal of Economic History*
J. of Econ. Lit.	*Journal of Economic Literature*
J. of Fam. Hist.	*Journal of Family History*
J. of Hist. Geog.	*Journal of Historical Geography*

J. of Int. Hist.	*Journal of Interdisciplinary History*
J. Royal Sanitary Institute	*Journal of the Royal Sanitary Institute*
JRSS	*Journal of the Royal Statistical Society*
J. of Soc. Hist.	*Journal of Social History*
J. of Urban Hist.	*Journal of Urban History*
Local Pop. Studies	*Local Population Studies*
Morn. Chron.	*Morning Chronicle*
N. Staffs. J. of Field Studies	*North Staffordshire Journal of Field Studies*
N. Staffs. Merc.	*North Staffordshire Mercury*
OS	Ordnance Survey
Pop. Studies	*Population Studies*
PP	Parliamentary Papers
PRO	Public Record Office
Scot. J. of Pol. Econ.	*Scottish Journal of Political Economy*
Staffs. Advert.	*Staffordshire Advertiser*
Staffs. Arch.	*Staffordshire Archaeology*
SCRO	Staffordshire County Record Office, Stafford
SS	*Staffordshire Sentinel*
TLS	*Times Literary Supplement*
THES	*Times Higher Education Supplement*
Trans. Instit. Brit. Geog.	*Transactions of the Institute of British Geographers*
Trans. N. of Eng. Inst. of Min. Eng.	*Transactions of the North of England Institute of Mining Engineers*
VCH	*Victoria County History of Stafford*
Vict. Studies	*Victorian Studies*
WMSS	Wedgwood Papers in the Library of Keele University

Introduction

1. Industrialization, Families, and Regions: The Problem and Previous Literature

THIS book is concerned with the ways in which people both create and adapt to the process of industrialization. Yet, no study can hope to examine comprehensively such a broad theme. The aim here is to analyse how the changes associated with industrial development were experienced in one region of Britain during the nineteenth century by focusing on family relationships (between husbands and wives, parents and children, individuals and their wider kin network) not in isolation, but in the context of the workplace and other institutions in the community.

One reason to concentrate on family relationships is that they both reflect and contribute to changes in the economy and wider society and their absence or presence and their nature can be particularly important to most individuals. A long line of investigators have been concerned with the relationship between the Industrial Revolution and family life in Britain. Much of their work, however, has been preoccupied with a debate arising from nineteenth-century anxieties over whether or not factory labour led to the 'disruption' of family life associated with the view of the Industrial Revolution as rapid change driven by new technology.[1] In recent reinterpretations stressing the more gradual and uneven nature of the Industrial Revolution and the history of work, and in the outpouring of literature on family history and women's history,[2] there

---

[1] See e.g. F. Engels, *The Condition of the Working Class in England*, trans. W. O. Henderson and W. H. Chaloner (Oxford, 1958), esp. 145–6, 160–6, 233–5; for a summary of the contemporary debate on industrialism and the family, see H. Perkin, *The Origins of Modern English Society 1780–1880* (London, 1969), 149–53; M. Hewitt, *Wives and Mothers in Victorian Industry* (London, 1958); N. J. Smelser, *Social Change in the Industrial Revolution: An Application of Theory to the Lancashire Cotton Industry 1770–1840* (London, 1959); M. Anderson, *Family Structure in 19th Century Lancashire* (Cambridge, 1971).

[2] For surveys of the literature see M. Anderson, *Approaches to the History of the Western Family 1500–1914* (London, 1980); L. Stone, 'Family History in the 1980s: Past Achievements and Future Trends', *J. of Int. Hist.* 12 (1981), 51–87; L. Tilly and M. Cohen, 'Does the Family Have a History? A Review of Theory and Practice in Family History', *Social Science History*, 6 (1982), 131–79; special issue (incorporating nos. 1–3), *J. of Fam. Hist.* 12 (1987); L. Davidoff, 'The Family in Britain', in F. M. L. Thompson (ed.), *The Cambridge Social History of Britain 1750–1950*, ii (Cambridge, 1990), 71–129; T. K. Hareven, 'The

have been major reorientations in the view of the relationship between family life and industrialization.

There is a consensus emerging among historians that in England the characteristic family structure based on the principles of economic independence before marriage, nuclear family household afterwards, and late ages at first marriage, was in place before industrialization. This family structure persisted despite economic development. E. A. Wrigley, for example, argues that

it is in keeping with what might be termed the neutrality of the new sources of growth with respect to social and political context that many things should *not* have changed at the time of the gradual transfer to a mineral-based energy economy, or that they should have changed out of phase with the economic changes. It is evident that the chronology of demographic change bore little relation to that of the industrial revolution, certainly as it is normally understood. The same was also conspicuously true of familial structure, co-residential arrangements and kinship ties.[3]

Furthermore, the family structure made a significant contribution to the processes of capital accumulation, labour deployment, and social welfare.[4]

Coinciding with the theme of continuity is the idea that there was flexibility within the system. As Leonore Davidoff and Catherine Hall remark, 'the variability of family forms cannot be overstressed; there is no essential family only families'.[5] For example, there were variations in the co-residence of kin and adolescent children, differences in patterns of family employment and standards of living, and fluctuations in fertility. Conceptually there is agreement that the family and economy are not autonomous; nor is one secondary to the other. The behaviour of families

History of the Family and the Complexity of Social Change', *Amer. Hist. Rev.*, 96 (1991), 95–124; J. W. Scott, 'Women In History: The Modern Period', *Past and Present*, 101 (1983), 141–57; E. Roberts, *Women's Work 1840–1880* (Basingstoke and London, 1988).

[3] E. A. Wrigley, *Continuity, Chance and Change: The Character of the Industrial Revolution in England* (Cambridge, 1988), 116.

[4] L. Stone, *The Family, Sex and Marriage in England, 1500–1800* (London, 1977); E. A. Wrigley, 'Reflections on the History of the Family', *Daedalus*, 106 (1977), 83; P. Laslett, 'Mean Household Size in England since the Sixteenth Century', in P. Laslett and R. Wall (eds.), *Household and Family in Past Time* (Cambridge, 1972), 125–58; A. Macfarlane, *The Origins of English Individualism* (Oxford, 1978); R. Smith, 'Fertility, Economy and Household Formation in England over Three Centuries', *Population and Development Review*, 7 (1981), 595–622; D. Levine, 'Industrialization and the Proletarian Family in England', *Past and Present*, 107 (1985), 168–203; Anderson, *Family Structure*; M. W. Dupree, 'Family Structure in the Staffordshire Potteries 1840–1880', D.Phil. thesis (Oxford, 1981).

[5] L. Davidoff and C. Hall, *Family Fortunes: Men and Women of the English Middle Class 1780–1850* (London, 1987), 31.

both influences the economy and is in turn influenced by it. Furthermore, the mutual influence needs to be understood historically.[6] One purpose of this book is to explore the nature of the continuing importance and the 'flexibility' of family relationships with reference both to the economy and to wider social relationships.

A regional focus is particularly appropriate for such a study in light of the recent historiography concerning the Industrial Revolution in Britain. The former picture of rapid change driven by new technology associated with ideas of 'take-off' and 'leading sectors'[7] has given way to interpretations based on the national accounting framework with an emphasis on the slow, gradual nature of economic growth to the point where 'industrial evolution' appears more suitable than 'industrial revolution'.[8] At the same time surveys across industries and regions underline the unevenness and continuities of industrial development.[9] Recently, however, critics have begun to rescue the concept of the Industrial Revolution[10] from macroeconomic gradualism by pointing out the limitations of the current aggregate national-income estimation approach.

One line of criticism highlights the unique importance of the regional perspective in understanding the extent of fundamental economic and

[6] J. Humphries and J. Rubery, 'The Reconstitution of the Supply Side of the Labour Market: The Relative Autonomy of Social Reproduction', *Cambridge Journal of Economics*, 8 (1984), 331–46. Describing developments in population history E. A. Wrigley makes the same point when he refers to the 'logical status' of population history as both independent of and dependent on the economy: E. A. Wrigley, 'Population History in the 1980s', *J. of Int. Hist.* 12 (1981), 218. Richard Wall recommends the use of the phrase 'adaptive family economy' to emphasize the 'flexibility' of family and household patterns among different occupational groups: R. Wall, 'Work, Welfare and the Family: An Illustration of the Adaptive Family Economy', in L. Bonfield, R. Smith, and K. Wrightson. (eds.), *The World We Have Gained: Histories of Population and Social Structure, Essays Presented to Peter Laslett* (Oxford, 1986), 264–6. For a similar conclusion see also, E. Pleck, 'Two Worlds in One: Work and Family', *J. of Soc. Hist.* 10 (1976), 178–95.
[7] W. W. Rostow, *The Stages of Economic Growth: A Non-Communist Manifesto* (Cambridge, 1960).
[8] P. Deane and W. A. Cole, *British Economic Growth, 1688–1959* (Cambridge, 2nd edn., 1969); D. N. Cannadine, 'The Present and the Past in the English Industrial Revolution 1880–1980', *Past and Present*, 103 (1984), 131–72, esp. pp. 163–6; N. F. R. Crafts, *British Economic Growth During the Industrial Revolution* (Oxford, 1985); J. Hoppit, 'Counting the Industrial Revolution', *Econ. Hist. Rev.* 2nd ser., 43 (1990), 173–93; P. Hudson, 'The Regional Perspective', in P. Hudson (ed.), *Regions and Industries: A Perspective on the Industrial Revolution in Britain* (Cambridge, 1989), 6–10.
[9] R. Samuel, 'Workshop of the World: Steam Power and Hand Technology in Mid-Victorian Britain', *Hist. Workshop*, 3 (1977), 6–72; P. Joyce, 'Work', in F. M. L. Thompson (ed.), *The Cambridge Social History of Britain*, ii (Cambridge, 1990), 131–94.
[10] Classic studies with continuing relevance include: P. Mathias, *The First Industrial Nation: An Economic History of Britain 1700–1914*, 2nd edn. (London, 1983); R. M. Hartwell, *The Industrial Revolution and Economic Growth* (London, 1971).

social change from the mid-eighteenth to the end of the nineteenth century.[11] Hidden beneath national aggregates the Industrial Revolution was a political and social as well as economic process occurring in varied, somewhat self-contained regional industrial bases which added up to more than a sum of its parts, as a gradual revolutionizing of the economy and society across a broad front took place.[12] It was the regions themselves, usually dominated by combinations of 'modern' and 'traditional' industries, that were important regardless of the individual contributions of their industries either to GNP or to the role of 'leading sector'.[13]

From a different perspective another line of criticism suggests that national-income aggregates conceal the changing relative importance of the two different sets of forces, modes, or 'component types' of economic growth.[14] The first type of growth was associated with the 'advanced organic economy', characterized by raw materials drawn from the annual flow of agricultural production and by growth from increasing division of labour, all of which was growth limited by diminishing returns. Gradually increasing its contribution to growth was the second type, the 'mineral-based energy economy', based on coal and raw materials from mineral stocks providing heat as well as mechanical energy which extended the time-scale so that returns did not diminish.

Although they differ, these new perspectives on the Industrial Revolution highlight the central importance of industrial regions, especially those based on coal. The Staffordshire Potteries is such an industrial region. While playing a role in non-quantitative accounts of the Industrial Revolution, and known through the contributions of Josiah Wedgwood in the eighteenth century,[15] and the novels of Arnold Bennett in the nineteenth, the Potteries has been relatively neglected by historians,

---

[11] P. Hudson (ed.), *Regions and Industries: A Perspective on the Industrial Revolution in Britain* (Cambridge, 1989); id., *The Industrial Revolution* (London, 1992; repr. with corrections, 1993).

[12] Hudson, *Regions and Industries*, 4.   [13] Ibid. 2.

[14] Wrigley, *Continuity, Chance and Change*, 3.

[15] N. McKendrick, 'Josiah Wedgwood: An Eighteenth Century Entrepreneur in Salesmanship and Marketing Techniques', *Econ. Hist. Rev.* 12 (1960), 408–33; 'Josiah Wedgwood and Factory Discipline', *Hist. J.* 6 (1961), 30–55; 'Josiah Wedgwood and Thomas Bentley: An Inventor-Entrepreneur Partnership in the Industrial Revolution', *Royal Historical Society Transactions*, 5th ser., 14 (1964), 1–33.; 'Josiah Wedgwood and Cost Accounting in the Industrial Revolution', *Econ. Hist. Rev.* 23 (1970), 45–67; 'The Role of Science in the Industrial Revolution: A Study of Josiah Wedgwood as a Scientist', in M. Teich and R. M. Young (eds.), *Changing Perspectives in the History of Science* (London, 1971).

compared with localities based, for example, on textiles.[16] One reason for the neglect is that the region has tended to be seen as synonymous with its dominant industry, pottery, which made a relatively small contribution to GNP and did not have the forward and backward linkages to make it a 'leading sector'. Moreover, the application of steam-power and labour-saving devices in the pottery industry between the late eighteenth and later nineteenth centuries was limited primarily to processes associated with the preparation of the clay; most of the highly sub-divided production process was labour-intensive. The potteries, however, were located in the North Staffordshire coalfield and in the mid-nineteenth century there were coal and ironstone mines and ironworks as well as potteries in the same area. Thus, it has become a particularly appropriate region for study in light of recent views of the Industrial Revolution.

Both the advocates of uneven gradualism and the proponents of these newer perspectives on the Industrial Revolution call into question 'the view that the industrial revolution was a cumulative, progressive, unitary phenomenon' in which growth in a 'modern' sector was implicit in and developed out of a 'traditional' sector. The 'traditional' sectors represent 'a different path or pattern of development within the complex of industrialisation which gets lost in the aggregate studies'. They were as much 'a part of the dynamic of the Industrial Revolution as the factory'.[17] There is a picture of the diversity and irregular development of the nineteenth-century economy which challenges all unilinear ideas of change.[18]

The questioning of unilinear economic change also casts doubt on unproblematic links between changes in the economy and social, political, and cultural change. One important consequence of this perspective is to emphasize the inappropriateness of the concept of modernization, that 'check list of changes which jointly imply the transition from a traditional

---

[16] There are notable exceptions, such as: L. Weatherill, *The Pottery Trade and North Staffordshire 1660–1769* (Manchester, 1971) and *The Growth of the Pottery Industry in England, 1660–1815* (New York and London, 1986); R. Fyson, 'The Crisis of 1842: Chartism, the Colliers' Strike and the Outbreak in the Potteries', in J. Epstein and D. Thompson (eds.), *The Chartist Experience: Studies in Working-Class Radicalism and Culture, 1830–1860* (London and Basingstoke, 1982), 194–220; and 'Unionism, Class and Community in the 1830s: Aspects of the National Union of Operative Potters', in J. Rule (ed.), *British Trade Unionism 1750–1850: The Formative Years* (London, 1988), 200–19; R. Hall, *Women in the Labour Force: A Case Study of the Potteries in the Nineteenth Century*, Department of Geography and Earth Science, Queen Mary College, University of London, Occasional Paper no. 27 (1986); and a number of Keele University theses on specific topics and, for the period 1890–1920, the publications of Richard Whipp listed in the bibliography below.

[17] Hudson, 'Regional Perspective', 9.   [18] Joyce, 'Work', 151.

to a modern society', *Gemeinschaft* to *Gesellschaft*.[19] Another implication is that historians cannot assume uncritically that they can link changes in technology, industrial organization, per capita income, population, and national economic structure with changes in family structure, marriage patterns, social structure, conditions of work, determinants of wages, living conditions, religion, education, political institutions, and popular protest. Ideas of social change which are based on now questionable premises about the economy need to be reconsidered. There is a need to relate social life to a more adequate and problematic notion of the economy and work experience.[20] Similarly sociologists are warned that they cannot assume that a period is 'characterised by a mode of production, and that there is a family form which corresponds to each mode of production'.[21]

The links between changes in the economy and social, political, and cultural change that constituted the Industrial Revolution are, therefore, problematic. Thus, one purpose of this book is to demonstrate the utility of a regional and community perspective for illuminating these inter-actions. In important respects during this period individuals and their relationships with family, work, and other institutions operated at re-gional and community levels. Processes operating 'on a smaller scale to link the way in which people think, act and organise themselves through their work, daily routines and relationship to the resources of their im-mediate environment' contributed to the 'regional patterns of economic activity and cultural forms'.[22] No attempt will be made here to define what is meant by region or community. Like the region there 'is scope . . . for another book on the heuristic and other qualities' of the community 'as a dynamic concept'.[23] Attempts at definition are subject

---

[19] Wrigley, *Continuity, Chance and Change*, 99–102.   [20] Joyce, 'Work', 131.

[21] C. C. Harris, *The Family and Industrial Society* (London, 1983), 117. The complexity of the relationship between the economy and reproductive patterns, for example, is stressed in recent literature on the fertility decline: See J. Cleland and C. Wilson, 'Demand The-ories of the Fertility Transition: An Iconoclastic View', *Pop. Studies* 41 (1987), 15–16.

[22] Hudson, *Regions and Industries*, 2, 17. Recent examinations of the decline in fertility in nineteenth-century England, for example, suggest that local variation was the main source of different fertility patterns and 'these local patterns tend to be masked when counties or combinations of counties are made the framework for analysis'. C. Wilson and R. Woods, 'Fertility in England: A Long-Term Perspective', *Pop. Studies* 45 (1991), 414; also B. A. Anderson, 'Regional and Cultural Factors in the Decline of Marital Fertility in Europe', in A. J. Coale and S. C. Watkins (eds.), *The Decline of Fertility in Europe* (Princeton, NJ, 1986), 312.

[23] Ibid. 3. There is already a large literature on the uses, difficulties of definition, and methodology associated with the concept of 'community'. See e.g. C. Bell and H. Newby, *Community Studies: An Introduction to the Sociology of the Local Community* (London, 1971); M. Stacey, 'The Myth of Community Studies', *Brit. J. of Sociol.* 20 (1969), 134–47;

to the dangers of seeing the region or the community 'as a static and pre-given category',[24] to what has also been called the 'sin of pronounce-ment'.[25] Instead, communities like regions 'emerge in the course of analysis and become finite in different ways depending on where and when we place the emphasis of our study'. They are 'always historically relative and contingent';[26] moreover, it cannot be assumed 'that spatial and social relationships are identical'. In short, 'the existence of patterns of local social relations needs to be investigated not taken as given *a priori*'.[27] In the sense of region and community used here, the possible patterns of local social relations could include among others those associated with work as well as non-work activities, and institutions as well as primary networks.[28]

Despite changing views of the Industrial Revolution, the main ap-proach to topics such as the relationship between the Industrial Revolu-tion and family relationships remains the investigation of individual industries, separate occupations, or communities dominated by a single industry. Scholars are fulfilling the call for an examination of 'changes within specific occupational cultures rather than to refer to the "capitalist market place" or to general conditions of poverty'.[29] One reason for this concentration on cases of occupational isolation—both geographical and conceptual—is that the Industrial Revolution has been thought of as a series of classic industries or increasingly regionally specialized 'lead-ing sectors' which transformed the economy. Naturally investigators of women's employment and of working-class family life have been attracted

A. Macfarlane, 'History, Anthropology and the Study of Communities', *Social History*, 2 (1977), 631–52; C. J. Calhoun, 'History, Anthropology and the Study of Communities: Some Problems in Macfarlane's Proposal', *Social History*, 3 (1978), 363–73 and 'Commun-ity: Toward a Variable Conceptualization for Comparative Research', *Social History*, 5 (1980), 105–29; P. Joyce, *Work, Society and Politics: The Culture of the Factory in Later Victorian England* (Brighton, 1980); R. Dennis, *English Industrial Cities of the Nineteenth Century* (Cambridge, 1984); M. Bulmer, *The Social Basis of Community Care* (London, 1987).

[24] Ibid.   [25] Bulmer, *Social Basis*, 30.

[26] Hudson, *Regions and Industries*, 3. Dennis, *English Industrial Cities*, 285 makes a similar point.

[27] Bulmer, *Social Basis*, 30.

[28] In some literature there is a tendency to use community to refer only to non-work social relationships, see e.g. R. Whipp, 'Labour Markets and Communities: An Historical View', *Sociological Review* 33 (1985), 769. Also e.g. Martin Bulmer emphasizes the study of informal networks of primary group relations based on personal ties among neighbours, friends, and kin at the local level, see M. Bulmer, 'The Rejuvenation of Community Studies? Neighbours, Networks and Policy', *Sociological Review*, 33 (1985) 430–48.

[29] Pleck, 'Two Worlds in One', 187.

to study places and groups that fit that classic view most closely. Recently, studies of women, particularly in the sweated trades and service sector, have both contributed to and reflected the newer more complex view of the Industrial Revolution at the national level which replaces leading sectors with images of a variegated economy.[30] At the same time these and other studies have acknowledged the complexity of the occupational structure within industries. What have received little emphasis heretofore are the interactions between different industrially based occupational groups within a region.

Not only is the perspective of a coal-based region particularly appropriate, but there are also good reasons to concentrate on a region in which there was paid industrial employment for women and children outside the household.

First, looking at the availability of the 'option' of women's and children's paid employment outside the household, and at the family characteristics of those women and children who did and did not take it up, makes it possible to illuminate family decisions and to explore in some detail the relationship between families and the economy.

Second, recent studies of the experience of women in England during the nineteenth century,[31] while emphasizing the extent to which women's worlds came to be oriented around their home and family, a 'separate sphere', at the same time stress that for women there was no dichotomy between work and home or family; instead there was a continuum of women's occupations from paid industrial employment outside the home to domestic service to sweated labour inside the home to unpaid home work. 'Paid employment was usually taken up at different points in the life cycle in response to crises, as and when the family economy demanded it.'[32] Women's roles were characterized by flexibility which made it possible for families to adjust to circumstances. Unlike many other types of female occupation, paid industrial employment outside the household can be traced in the census enumerators' books, the most comprehensive

---

[30] For the classic study of women cotton textile-workers see Hewitt, *Wives and Mothers*; for a wide-ranging collection reflecting recent research, see the companion vols. A. V. John (ed.), *Unequal Opportunities: Women's Employment in England 1800–1918* (Oxford, 1986) and J. Lewis (ed.), *Labour and Love: Women's Experience of Home and Family 1850–1940* (Oxford, 1986); for a useful synthesis see S. O. Rose, ' "Gender at Work": Sex, Class and Industrial Capitalism', *Hist. Workshop*, 21 (1986), 113–31; id., *Limited Livelihoods: Gender and Class in Nineteenth Century England* (Berkeley, Calif., 1991). For visual images, see M. Hiley, *Victorian Working Women: Portraits From Life* (Boston, Mass., 1980).

[31] See e.g. John, *Unequal Opportunities* and Lewis, *Labour and Love*.

[32] J. Lewis, 'Introduction: Reconstructing Women's Experience of Home and Family', in Lewis, *Labour and Love*, 19.

source on family history available for the period.[33] As a result, if used with care, evidence is available for the mid-nineteenth century which allows systematic examination of this type of women's employment together with a number of aspects of their family life. For example, it is possible to look at women's work together with that of their children, husbands, and fathers.

A third reason to focus on women's and children's participation in the factory labour-force is that in discussions of the decline in marital fertility after 1870 women factory workers have a prominent place.[34] Paid work for women outside the home is seen as a critical variable for determining fertility. Cotton textile-workers, of whom women formed a substantial proportion, were the first occupational group within the working class to experience the decline in marital fertility which other groups eventually followed. At the same time occupational groups such as miners and ironworkers, which had few women workers and characteristically lived in isolated or homogeneous communities that did not offer paid industrial employment for women outside the home, had exceptionally high fertility. One recent commentator, however, has argued that miners and women cotton textile-workers were exceptions.[35] According to this argument high fertility was associated with family employment patterns in which male wages were low and women and children were in paid employment outside the home, while lower fertility occurred where male wages were high and women and children were not employed. As the

---

[33] For a warning about the pitfalls of using this source for studies of women's employment which recommends their use only with a knowledge of local economic and social conditions see E. Higgs, 'Women, Occupations and Work in the Nineteenth Century Census', *Hist. Workshop*, 23 (1987), 59–80.

[34] Hewitt, *Wives and Mothers*, esp. 85–97; M. Haines, *Fertility and Occupation: Population Patterns in Industrialization* (London, 1979); L. Tilly, 'Demographic Change in Two French Industrial Cities: Anzin and Roubaix 1872–1906', in J. Sundin and E. Soderlund (eds.), *Time, Space and Man: Essays in Microdemography* (Stockholm, 1979), 107–32; S. Szreter, 'The Decline of Marital Fertility in England and Wales *c*. 1870–1914', Ph.D. thesis (Cambridge, 1984); N. F. R. Crafts, 'A Cross-Sectional Study of Legitimate Fertility in England and Wales, 1911', *Research in Economic History*, 9 (1984), 89–107; R. Woods, 'Approaches to the Fertility Transition in Victorian England', *Pop. Studies* 41 (1987), 298–307; N. F. R. Crafts, 'Duration of Marriage, Fertility and Women's Employment Opportunities in England and Wales in 1911', *Pop. Studies* 43 (1989), 331–5; W. Seccombe, 'Starting to Stop: Working-Class Fertility Decline in Britain', *Past and Present*, 126 (1990), 152; id., *Weathering the Storm: Working-Class Families from the Industrial Revolution to the Fertility Decline* (London and New York, 1993), 158; E. Garrett, 'The Trials of Labour: Motherhood versus Employment in a Nineteenth-Century Textile Centre', *Continuity and Change*, 5 (1990), 121–34.

[35] Levine, 'Proletarian Family', 168–203; D. Levine, *Reproducing Families: The Political Economy of English Population History* (Cambridge, 1987), esp. 160–208.

proportion of the economy in which women and children were employed increased in the late eighteenth and early nineteenth centuries, fertility increased nationally; in the second half of the nineteenth century, as heavy industry employing mainly men increased, and ideas of respectability associated with wives and children not in paid employment outside the home became widespread, fertility declined. Close examination of an area in which one industry, pottery, offered paid industrial employment to women and children outside the home in the mid-nineteenth century, should illuminate this issue, particularly as it was an area in which there were also miners and ironworkers.

A fourth reason to examine a region with paid industrial employment for women and children outside the household is that accounts which emphasize the wide-ranging influence of the paternalism of individual factory employers in mid-nineteenth century England give a central place to family relationships both of employers and employees and particularly to the employment of family members within factories.[36] Examination of the influence of the paternalism of a factory employer in a non-textile region, the Staffordshire Potteries, with industrial employment for women and children outside the household will illuminate the limitations as well as the influence of employer paternalism.

A fifth reason for concentrating on a non-textile region with women and children's factory employment is to examine the relationships between family structure and the implementation and effects of protective legislation. Although there were limits to the paternalism of individual employers in the Potteries, employers acting together took paternalistic initiatives regarding protective legislation. This is not to question the importance of the emphasis on the relationship of the family, the workplace, and the neighbourhood,[37] but to suggest the importance at the same time of relationships among employers.[38] The initiative for the extension of the Factory Acts to the pottery industry in the 1860s came from local manufacturers. Unlike the earlier movement in textile areas, that in the Potteries was the result neither of technological change nor of a decline in the extent of child labour.[39] Moreover, the involvement of operative

---

[36] For a study based on the textile districts of Lancashire and Yorkshire, see P. Joyce, *Work, Society and Politics*, for the influence of the Courtaulds' paternalism inside and outside their textile mill in Halstead, Essex, see J. Lown, *Women and Industrialization: Gender at Work in Nineteenth-Century England* (Cambridge and Oxford, 1990).

[37] Joyce, *Work, Society and Politics*, p. xx; Lown, *Women and Industrialization*, 95–9, 214.

[38] A. C. Howe, *The Cotton Masters 1830–1860* (Oxford, 1984).

[39] C. Nardinelli, 'Child Labour and the Factory Acts', *J. of Econ. Hist.* 40 (1980), 750; id., *Child Labour and the Industrial Revolution* (Bloomington and Indianapolis, Ind., 1990), esp. 61–2, 115.

potters was minimal and those who eventually expressed their opinions were men who argued against the legislation. This is contrary to accounts based on textiles which stress the opposition of industrialists dependent on female labour, and which emphasize working-class support for factory legislation.[40] Family relationships have played a key role in accounts of working-class support for factory legislation. Support has been seen as based on the separation of parents and children in the factory due to technological changes.[41] Others suggest that working-class support was based on a threat to already low family incomes which a universal ten-hour day would protect.[42] Finally, it is argued that working-class support for factory legislation was based on the patriarchal support of male trade unionists intent on keeping women out of the competition for jobs in an attempt to raise men's wages to the level of a 'family wage' which would support themselves and their families and protect the position of the 'male breadwinner'.[43]

The consequences, as well as the movement for the extension of the Factory Acts to the Potteries, differ from the arguments which stress the role of protective legislation in the restriction and segregation of women's employment. After the introduction of the Factory Acts, rather than decreasing as might have been expected given the previous literature, the number and proportion of women employed in the pottery industry increased. This in turn raises questions about the links between protective legislation and the spread of the 'breadwinner family' and fertility decline. In addition, one reason for the increase in women's employment was that the Factory Acts also restricted the employment of children and young persons; women both took their places and provided additional labour as the output of the industry increased. At the same time, the iron industry in the region expanded and increased the competition for juvenile male labour. The introduction of protective legislation in the Potteries thus emphasizes both the importance of considering women and children together with other family members and the need to

---

[40] Lown, *Women and Industrialization*, 214. S. Walby, 'Spatial and Historical Variations in Women's Unemployment and Employment', in L. Murgatroyd *et al.* (eds.), *Localities, Class and Gender* (London, 1985) 168.

[41] N. Smelser, 'Sociological History: The Industrial Revolution and the British Working-Class Family', *J. of Soc. Hist.* 1 (1967), 27–31.

[42] M. Anderson, 'Sociological History and the Working-Class Family: Smelser Revisited', *Social History*, 3 (1976), 317–34.

[43] W. Seccombe, 'Patriarchy Stabilized: The Construction of the Male Breadwinner Wage Norm in Nineteenth Century Britain', *Social History*, 11 (1986), 55. The arguments are summarized in H. Bradley, *Men's Work, Women's Work* (Cambridge and Oxford, 1989), 45–6.

take a regional and 'community perspective'[44] rather than one based on a single industry or occupational group.

A further reason to focus on an industrial area in which there was paid employment for women and children outside the household is to illuminate ways in which family relationships, particularly women in families, provided assistance compared with other institutions and sources of assistance. In addition to the general environmental hazards of mid-nineteenth-century urban areas, such as poor sanitation and thick smoke, work in the pottery industry was among the unhealthiest, albeit better paid, in the country. In addition, miners and ironworkers were especially vulnerable to accidents at work. As a result, sickness and death at relatively early ages were prominent among the problems industrial workers and families faced. The work of women and children in the pottery industry was one way for families to compensate for lost earnings, though this had to be balanced with the need to care for the sick. The central position of women was reinforced by a differential in the mortality rates of pottery workers, with those of men higher than those of women due to the gender division of labour within the potworks. The extent to which other institutions and sources of assistance provided help in such circumstances offers a way to view families in the context of other institutions in the community rather than in isolation. It also provides evidence from an industrial region with which to examine the suggestion, based on rural areas and market towns, that the 'collectivity', particularly the Poor Law, was relatively more important than family relationships for the social welfare of the elderly in the mid-nineteenth century.[45]

This book attempts to build on the tradition of work on family relationships and industrialization in Britain, running from contemporaries such as Engels to more recent commentators such as Neil Smelser and Michael Anderson, which has concentrated on evidence from the cotton-textile industry and on issues of family cohesion and relations with other institutions. It breaks new ground not only by answering the call for

---

[44] M. Dupree, 'The Community Perspective in Family History: The Potteries During the Nineteenth Century', in A. L. Beier, D. N. Cannadine, and J. Rosenheim (eds.), *The First Modern Society: Essays in English History in Honour of Lawrence Stone* (Cambridge, 1989), 549–73.

[45] D. Thomson, 'Welfare and the Historians', in L. Bonfield *et al.*, *The World We Have Gained*, 355–78; D. Thomson, 'The Welfare of the Elderly in the Past: A Family or Community Responsibility?', in M. Pelling and R. M. Smith (eds.), *Life, Death and the Elderly: Historical Perspectives* (London, 1991), 194–221. For a valuable survey of approaches to the history of the elderly see M. Pelling and R. M. Smith, 'Introduction', in Pelling and Smith, *Life, Death and the Elderly*, 1–38.

more studies of family structure in factory towns in the nineteenth century combined with a 'conscious and systematic comparative approach'[46] and attention to the 'subtle differences between groups and industries, only a few of which have so far been fully explored',[47] but also by extending the scope of the discussion to embrace a broader, though clearly interrelated, range of aspects of family life associated with work and the communal nexus that helped maintain and structure family relationships. Subjects such as marriage, residence patterns, family employment patterns, women and work, fertility, health and mortality, family income, social stratification, individual experience, legislative reform, and informal and formal social welfare institutions, which tend to be treated in isolation and appear in somewhat discrete literatures will be examined here together in the same context. In particular, literature on work and family rarely includes social welfare as part of its subject.[48] At the same time, though recognizing the importance of the state of the economy in general and the influence of the gender divisions of the labour-market (which left women in the least skilled and worst paid jobs) on the gender division of caring,[49] studies of social welfare and family relationships have tended to relegate the economy and workplace to the background.[50] What follows reveals the flexibility of nuclear families across both work and welfare and the key position of women as wives, mothers, daughters, workers, and carers in shaping the responses of families to their circumstances at the same time that the ways in which they respond have much to do with the 'community' context. Both Smelser and Anderson offer their findings within explicit theoretical frameworks. Thus, this historical regional and local case-study, in addition to contributing in turn to the history of the Staffordshire Potteries in the nineteenth century and filling out existing sociological models providing a more rounded empirical picture, also has implications for the nature of the models themselves.

[46] Anderson, 'Smelser Revisited', 334. Also, R. Smith, 'Early Victorian Household Structure: A Case Study of Nottinghamshire', *Int. Rev. of Soc. Hist.* 15 (1970), 84; M. Anderson, 'The Study of Family Structure', in E. A. Wrigley (ed.), *Nineteenth Century Society* (Cambridge, 1972), 49, 81.

[47] Anderson, *History of the Western Family*, 80.

[48] See e.g. P. Hudson and W. R. Lee (eds.), *Women, Work and Family in Historical Perspective* (Cambridge, 1990); Whipp, *Patterns of Labour*.

[49] A. Digby, *British Welfare Policy: Workhouse to Workfare* (London, 1989); J. Lewis, 'Introduction: Social Policy and the Family', in M. Bulmer, J. Lewis, and D. Piachaud (eds.), *The Goals of Social Policy* (London, 1989), 131–9; Bulmer, *Social Basis*, 25.

[50] E.g. J. Finch, *Family Obligations and Social Change* (Cambridge and Oxford, 1989); Bulmer, *Social Basis*.

2. Theoretical Perspectives

Michael Anderson's book, *Family Structure in Nineteenth Century Lancashire*, has been particularly influential over the past twenty years. A few of the conclusions which his theoretical perspective influenced most strongly have been questioned, but there has been no sustained examination of his theoretical perspective.[51] Thus, as an introduction to the issues it is useful to examine in some detail the main theoretical ideas which underlie his interpretations of family structure alongside some more recent work.

Anderson's dissatisfaction with the basis of the larger body of sociological theory dealing with the impact of social change led him to recast the theoretical foundation of his interpretations. He shifted from Smelser's Parsonian theory of structural differentiation to a conceptual framework based on exchange theory. In other words, Anderson abandoned the question of the impact of industrialization of the family economy as a holistic social system whose primary goal was 'to generate and maintain motivation appropriate to occupational performance through the mechanisms of socialization of the child and the management of tensions of family members'.[52] Instead, he asked how important were family and kin relationships to individuals as a source of assistance available to the working classes in nineteenth-century Britain, whose goals were 'primarily those associated with survival, health and basic creature comforts'.[53]

Anderson makes three arguments to justify shifting his focus from the family as an organization on to each family member as an individual actor with his own goals, problems, constraints, resources, and alternative sources of assistance, of which family relationships provide only one potential source. He argues that the focus on each family member as an individual enables him to analyse better the problems associated with the life-cycle stages, the immense variation in family functions, and the interaction of the family and other social systems. It is worth presenting his three arguments in more detail.

---

[51] E. Roberts, *A Woman's Place: An Oral History of Working-Class Women 1890–1940* (Oxford, 1984) esp. 171–2, 185–7, and 'The Working-Class Extended Family: Functions and Attitudes 1890–1940', *Oral History*, 12 (1984), 48–55; H. Medick and D. W. Sabean, 'Interest and Emotion in Family and Kinship Studies: A Critique of Social History and Anthropology', in H. Medick and D. W. Sabean (eds.), *Interest and Emotion: Essays on the Study of Family and Kinship* (Cambridge, 1984), 22. S. Ruggles, *Prolonged Connections: The Rise of the Extended Family in Nineteenth-Century England and America* (Madison, Wis., 1987) esp. 20–3, 30, 47–57, 223 provides a critique of Anderson's exchange theory approach with specific reference to the co-residence of extended kin.

[52] N. J. Smelser, *Social Change in the Industrial Revolution*, 160.

[53] Anderson, *Family Structure*, 198.

Individual nuclear families, unlike other social organizations, have a life cycle typically advancing from courtship to marriage to child-rearing to children leaving home to dissolution. The life cycle means that it is not possible to analyse the family, only the family at a particular point in the life cycle, and the changes between these points. The life cycle also focuses attention on variations in the relationships of individual members of a family with each other at different points in the life cycle. Thus, the impact of social change will vary with the family's life-cycle stage as well as with the actor who is under consideration. Many of the variations in relational patterns that must be explained are not so much qualitative differences as variations in the timing of widespread increases or decreases in the intensity of an actor's involvement in a particular role.[54]

Also, as an organization the family, unlike most other social organizations, largely lacks both clearly identifiable boundaries and formal structure, and any one set of clearly specified functions. It lacks the conceptual bench-marks on which analysis of difference and change are usually based. A list of the functions of the family as an organization and element in social structure might include the following:

Its members bear prime responsibility for both the *timing and number of conceptions* of new members of society, and for their nurture and *early socialization*;

It is the normal unit in which resources are pooled and distributed for *consumption*;

It is the normal unit around which *residence* is organized and domestic tasks performed;

Its members are for each other the principal source of *affective and ascriptive* relationships;

To family members fall the main burden of meeting the many idiosyncratic *needs* of society's members which fall outside the scope of bureaucratically organized agencies.[55]

Instead of using these functions as analytic categories, however, Anderson argues that

the kinship system is better seen as a recruitment base, organized around blood and marriage ties, with its theoretically almost infinite expansion limited only by intermarriage. It is a base from which, in different societies and different subgroups within societies, different individuals at different periods of their lives, as a response to varying needs and constraints, come to interact with each other with varying degrees of frequency and affective content. It provides to a widely

---

[54] M. Anderson, 'Introduction', in M. Anderson (ed.), *The Sociology of the Family* (Harmondsworth, 1971), 9.
[55] Ibid. 7.

varying extent almost any conceivable function, while sharing most functions with other organizations or primary groups. As a result of this variation any one set of descriptive categories may be totally unsuited for the analysis in anything like its full subtlety of the same system at another time and of adequately exploring the intervening changes. The solution again is to focus on the individual actors, taking each dyadic relationship separately and exploring it over its normal life cycle.[56]

Thus, because of the protean character of the functions which family relationships can perform, Anderson takes as his 'basic unit of analysis individual kinship dyads at different points in the life cycle'.[57]

Finally, Anderson argues that if one is interested in the mechanisms of interaction between systems (e.g. work and family), the best way to analyse this is to take the individual as the focus.

In one sense this analysis of the mutual interaction of different subsystems is what structure-functionalist writers on this topic claim to be about. In fact, however, the consensus underpinning of their analysis is not really capable of handling the exploration of these dynamic relationships, for the consensus element of structure-functionalism and its holistic or closed-system approach to social organizations make it ill-fitted to handle the study of the mechanisms by which in different situations different compromises emerge between family and other organizations.[58]

What does Anderson's approach focusing on individual actors involve?[59] First, for Anderson, the underlying parameter is power in the sense of ability to control one's own life chances and increase one's attainment of one's goals. The issue then becomes the extent to which relations with family or kin increase one's ability to control one's life chances. Importance or significance is measured in terms of both the actor's own perceptions of the nature and significance of his kinship relationships and in terms of the historian's assessment of the extent to which the absence of any given kinsman affected or would have affected the actor's life chances or satisfactions at any period of his life in relation to the actor's own goals. Hence, Anderson concentrates on those forms of social activity most influenced by the presence or absence of kin. In confronting such forms of social activity, he poses the analytical question, 'Why should an actor want to maintain relationships with kin rather than with the myriads of other individuals with whom he could make contact?' His analysis becomes 'a network analysis heuristically focusing

---

[56] Ibid. 20.   [57] Anderson, *Family Structure*, 196.
[58] Ibid. 196–7.   [59] Ibid. 5–8.

in particular on the determinants of choices between different alternative relationship patterns'.[60]

Anderson then makes the assumption that differences in patterns of family and kin relationships between groups or between one time and another for one group have one or both of two kinds of explanation. Different patterns result from either differences in goals or in the hierarchy of goals, or they result from differences in the constraints and opportunities with which an actor is faced.

Goals and goal hierarchies, according to Anderson, can be treated as if they were relatively homogeneous within the nineteenth-century populations under study so that he concentrates on variations in 'structural constraints' (i.e. differences in constraints and opportunities), rather than goal change as a source of difference or change. He argues that the populations he considers operated at a low standard of living so that the goals were primarily those associated with survival, health, and basic creature comforts. Although he admits that some changes and differences in goals and their relative priority did occur, he assumes they are constant for the purpose of analysis. Thus, an individual's need for assistance from others is a function of goals, of conditions impeding his ability to meet these goals, and of resources available to the individual to assist him in reaching these goals, including possible sources of assistance. The principle task of research, therefore, is to specify these for any given situation.

One major problem in the application of Anderson's approach is that it is difficult to obtain independent evidence of people's goals and the alternatives open to them. In other words, it is difficult to find evidence that is independent of the behaviour to be explained.[61] Other difficulties arise from the actor-based rational-choice approach which Anderson adopts. One variant of this general approach is exchange theory, and exchange theory, as developed by Blau and Homans,[62] is the chief ingredient of

---

[60] Ibid. 197.

[61] A. Heath, *Rational Choice and Social Exchange: A Critique of Exchange Theory* (Cambridge, 1976), 101.

[62] Anderson, *Family Structure*, ch. 2. For more recent developments of this tradition of exchange theory which attempt to overcome some of the problems see e.g. K. S. Cook (ed.), *Social Exchange Theory* (London, 1987); K. J. Gergen, M. S. Greenberg, and R. H. Willis (eds.), *Social Exchange Theory and Research* (London, 1980); P. Spread, 'Blau's Exchange Theory, Support and the Macrostructure', *Brit. J. of Sociol.* 35 (1984), 157–73. It is notable that one of the most influential of the early contributors, Peter Blau, has pointed out that exchange theory is limited to 'microsociology', offering a contrasting perspective to, but not a foundation for building, 'macrosociology'. In recent years he has centred his attention on macrosociological theorizing, having abandoned his own exchange

Anderson's analytical scheme. In exchange theory interactions between people are understood as exchanges of 'activities' and 'sentiments' on a reciprocal basis with each actor seeking the maximum 'psychic profit' in return for his 'outgoings'.

Thus, the approach attributes the outlook of 'economic man' to 'social man'. It emphasizes the instrumental rather than the normative, calling particular attention to the individual rational calculation of self-interest. According to one commentator, 'rational choice theories are alike in their attempt to explain behaviour in terms of the goals that men have and the alternatives open to them'.[63] They 'attempt to explain what people will do given the existing norms and institutions. They do not attempt to account for the character of those institutions themselves', looking instead 'at the consequences of social norms rather than their origin'.[64] He points out that 'one of the important results of modern research on roles is that they leave a great deal more latitude for individual decision making than previously had been supposed'.[65] Hence, the main focus of this approach is to explore the considerable variations within the broad framework of constraints, normative and otherwise, in terms of the actors' goals and the alternatives available to them.

There are a number of limitations associated with this general approach. First, the goals or ends towards which an individual directs his action are conceptually homogeneous, separate, and independent from those of other actors. There is an assumption that actors are self-interested, preferring an absolute quantity of goods. It is 'a view of social relationships as entered into only on the level of means to the actor's private ends'.[66] It is an assumption of random wants over a group of individuals which cannot account for actors comparing themselves with others.

theory because it could not adequately cope with the properties of populations and collectivities. According to Blau, 'they deal with different aspects of social life and each seeks to explain phenomena the other assumes to be given, takes for granted, or ignores'. See, 'Microprocess and Macrostructure', in Cook, *Social Exchange Theory*, 83, 86–7. In contrast in the same volume, Jonathan Turner argues that 'exchange theory is weak at microanalysis, because it focuses on a very limited set of processes that occur during interaction among people'. 'Despite the micro bias of exchange theories, they are inadequate for understanding the full dynamics of human interaction. There are many potential avenues of convergence between exchange theory, on the one hand, and alternative formulations . . . [including] elements of interactionism, dramaturgy, and ethnomethodology; and hence, it is more prudent to see how exchange as one dynamic of interaction is related to other properties of this most fundamental process'. See J. Turner, 'Social Exchange Theory: Future Directions', in Cook, *Social Exchange Theory*, 229, 237–8.

[63] Heath, *Rational Choice*, 170.   [64] Ibid. 61, 67.   [65] Ibid. 3.

[66] T. Parsons, *The Structure of Social Action* (1st edn. 1937; edn. used here, Glencoe, Ill., 1949), 59–60, 451.

Second, the approach assumes 'methodological individualism'. The terminal, ultimate, final, or 'rockbottom' explanations of significant social phenomena must be deduced from statements about the dispositions, beliefs, and attitudes of the individuals involved. Explanations should be in terms of a series of conscious or unconscious responses by the individual to his changing situation. Moreover, the situation or context itself must be explicable in similar individualistic terms. Such an approach, however, makes no allowance for 'interaction effects' such as power, or behaviour such as rituals and ceremonies which assume other people in relationships of a different nature.[67]

Third, in the ideal-type individualist situation it is difficult to deal with more than two dimensions. What if, for example, there are five trade-offs?

Fourth, this individualistic approach is limited to revealed preferences. It asserts that the observed choice is identical with the actor's preference and well-being. When an actor's choice is observed, it does not indicate in what sense the actor rejects the other alternatives. A person could be indifferent to the alternatives, and in that case, the actor's observed choice would not indicate his preference. The relation between an actor's observed choice, preference, and state of mind or well-being is problematic. Both 'choice' and 'well-being' are primitives.[68]

Fifth, and finally, this approach assumes a reduced importance for

---

[67] For a statement of the principle of methodological individualism see J. W. N. Watkins, 'Historical Explanation in the Social Sciences', in P. Gardiner (ed.), *Theories of History* (Glencoe, Ill., 1959), 503–14. Also id., 'Ideal Types and Historical Explanations', in H. Feigl and M. Brodbeck (eds.), *Readings in the Philosophy of Science* (New York, 1953), 723–43. For criticisms of Watkins's position see among others: M. Mandelbaum, 'Societal Facts', and E. Gellner, 'Holism versus Individualism in History and Sociology', and 'Reply to Mr Watkins', in Gardiner, *Theories of History*, 476–88, 488–503, 514–15. The controversy is summarized in W. H. Dray, 'Holism and Individualism in History and Social Science', in *The Encyclopedia of Philosophy*, iv, 53–8. Subsequently, S. Lukes in 'Methodological Individualism Reconsidered', *Brit. J. of Sociol.* 19 (1968), 119–29 has confused methodological individualism and 'psychologism' which says that 'all large scale social characteristics are not merely the intended or unintended result of, but a reflection of individual characteristics'. Watkins, 'Historical Explanation', 509 makes the distinction between 'methodological individualism' and 'psychologism'. For an implicit criticism of the individualist–holist controversy as misconceived, and for the presentation of a different perspective based on semiotics, see C. Geertz, 'Thick Description: Toward an Interpretive Theory of Culture', in C. Geertz, *The Interpretation of Cultures* (New York, 1973), 10–13. For a summary of the controversy and its relation to other approaches such as that of Giddens, see C. Lloyd, *Explanation in Social History* (Oxford, 1986), 160–71. For the 'utilitarian' system's neglect of 'ritual' actions see also Parsons, *Structure of Social Action*, 57.

[68] A. K. Sen, lectures on 'Economic Concepts' given in the University of Oxford, Oct. 1977; A. K. Sen, *Choice, Welfare and Measurement* (Oxford, 1982), 1–5, 54–73.

norms. 'Behaviour that is motivated by an expected return or response from another' is distinguished from 'behaviour that is not motivated by the return but by a sense of duty or by some other internalized value'.[69] The approach de-emphasizes

the possibility of social action which is neither economically rational nor irrational, but is rather 'value-rational' or 'normative' in tenor. In other words actors may pursue a particular strategy or goal because of some 'value commitment' to it, this being derived from a source other than their perception of economic self-interest. They may act out of loyalty to friends, respect for certain religious principles, or a host of other such normative concerns.[70]

In practice, however, this distinction is often blurred when a dubious concept such as 'psychic profit' is invoked, and the 'maximand' expands to include a 'sense of duty or some other internalized value' as motivation as well as 'expected return or response from another'.[71] Nevertheless, such an approach assumes that action taken is instrumental and calculative. This assumption, however, raises the Hobbesian problem of order and Parsons's criticisms of economics in his early years.[72] If the normative system were enforced only by coercion and instrumental means it would be hard to hold together.[73] There need not be drastic sanctions. Instead, there can be internalized sanctions so that much of the strain of maintaining the normative system is absorbed by the individual and internalized. The approach underestimates the importance of internalization. Moreover, even if sanctions are imposed, other people are needed to impose the sanctions as well as the actor, thereby violating the individualistic assumptions.

In addition to these general criticisms, Anderson's application of a rational-choice approach requires more specific examination as it is reflected in his two-part argument. In the first part of his argument he suggests that family members in nineteenth-century Preston had 'instrumental'

[69] Heath, *Rational Choice*, 3.

[70] G. Marshall, *In Praise of Sociology* (London, 1990), 120, summarizing the argument of J. H. Goldthorpe in 'The Current Inflation: Towards a Sociological Account', in F. Hirsch and J. H. Goldthorpe (eds.), *The Political Economy of Inflation* (London, 1978).

[71] Parsons, *Structure of Social Action*, 65–7, discusses this problem in terms of the lack of an alternative type of norm to the 'norm of rationality' in the utilitarian position. 'Any failure to live up to the rational norm must be imputed to one of these two elements "ignorance" or "error".'

[72] Ibid. 89–94.

[73] See Turner, 'Social Exchange Theory', 232–3. 'In sociology's headlong rush to abandon the functional ship in general, and the Parsonian lifeboat in particular, it has often ignored the fact that structures are, to a great extent, held together by norms.'

orientations. He claims that family relationships were characterized by 'short-run calculative instrumentality':

> the data implied that, at the phenomenal level, both in urban Lancashire and rural Ireland some children were interacting with their parents in a manner which can only be described as one of short-run calculative instrumentality. Social relationships of any significance were only being maintained, by considerable sections of the population, in situations where both parties were obtaining some fairly immediate advantage from them; in other words where exchanges were reciprocal and almost immediate.[74]

> for both seventeenth century Clayworth, and for various areas of rural England in the nineteenth century there is also evidence of a calculative, even to our eyes callous, attitude to kin—Joan Bacon put by her son on public charity, children bargaining with poor law authorities for payment for looking after their sick or elderly relatives. How widespread this kind of behaviour was we do not yet, and may well never, know. That it would have been almost unthinkable in Bethnal Green in the early 1950s is certain.[75]

This aspect of Anderson's argument begins with a comparison between family structure in Preston and peasant family structure in rural Ireland and Lancashire. Peasant family obligations, reinforced by the economic structure and by the value-system, were lifelong, deep, and normative. In Preston the setting was hostile to the enduring obligations of the peasant family. Land was absent as an incentive, and in comparison there was rapid turnover of population, ample employment for young people, widespread economic insecurity, and various alternatives to the family as a source of assistance in time of need. Anderson's thesis, then, is that members of working-class families in these conditions increasingly governed their relations with one another by exchange considerations, by short-run calculations of individual self-interest.

There are a number of reasons why this claim is unconvincing. First, the Preston working class emerges as a group of dispassionate maximizers who would have delighted Bentham or Gradgrind. Psychological aspects of family life—love, fear, brutality, anxiety—and 'irrationality', such as working men's drunkenness, get short shrift from Anderson.[76]

Second, associated with the one-dimensional psychology of Anderson's approach is a tendency found elsewhere in recent family history to assume a linear relationship linking 'different levels of material well-being

[74] Anderson, *Family Structure*, 8.   [75] Ibid. 3.
[76] J. Obelkevich, 'Review of Family Structure in Nineteenth Century Lancashire', unpublished; H. McLeod, 'Review', *The Local Historian*, 11 (1974), 167–8.

with varying degrees of affectivity'.[77] Emotions and interests are often treated as opposites which cancel each other out so that, as in Anderson's approach, the greater the poverty, the less the affection. Instead, as David Vincent argues, poverty can intensify feelings: the problem is 'one of an evolving pattern of material and emotional considerations, neither were dominant, the balance between them varying as between classes and over time'.[78]

Third, polar opposites appear at the community as well as individual level in Anderson's approach. By comparing rural Ireland and Preston, Anderson is satisfied with the conclusion that relationships in one are relatively 'normative' and in the other relatively 'instrumental'. Despite his discussion of a normative–instrumental continuum, Anderson ends up with two polar types. This characterization is too general to be useful for describing family relationships in comparisons between two mid-nineteenth-century industrial areas. Instead, the interesting problem is to show the mix of normative and calculative elements influencing family relationships in rural Ireland and Preston. By characterizing family relations in Preston as calculative and oriented to short-term individual self-interest, Anderson breaks with the tradition that sees family relations as 'the type case' of 'communal' or 'Gemeinschaft' relationships which 'rest on various types of affectual, emotional or traditional bases'.[79] Even authors in this tradition, however, acknowledge the potential existence of both normative and calculative orientations in the same situation. Weber, for example, describes 'communal' relationships in the following terms:

the type case is most conveniently illustrated by the family. But the great majority of social relationships has the characteristic to some degree, while it is at the same time to some degree determined by associative factors. No matter how calculating and hard headed the ruling considerations in such a social relationship—as that of a merchant to his customers—may be, it is quite possible for it to involve emotional values which transcend its utilitarian significance. Every social relationship which goes beyond the pursuit of immediate common ends, which hence lasts for long periods, involves relatively permanent social relationships between the same persons and these cannot be exclusively confined to the technically necessary activities. . . . Conversely, a social relationship which is normally considered primarily communal may involve action on the part of some or

---

[77] Medick and Sabean, 'Interest and Emotion', 22.

[78] D. Vincent, *Bread, Knowledge and Freedom: A Study of Nineteenth-Century Working Class Autobiography* (London, 1981), 60–1.

[79] M. Weber, *The Theory of Social and Economic Organization*, ed. T. Parsons, Free Press edn. (New York, 1964), 137. See also 'Note on Gemeinschaft and Gesellschaft', in Parsons, *Structure of Social Action*, 686–94.

even all of the participants, which is to an important degree oriented to considerations of expediency. There is, for instance, a wide variation in the extent to which the members of a family group feel a genuine community of interests or, on the other hand, exploit the relationship for their own ends.[80]

Fourth, and most important, is that Anderson confuses an individualistic method with individualistic values. Anderson observes instances of behaviour which he interprets as actors acting in a way so as to calculate their self-interest. On this basis he adopts the rational-choice framework and assumes that individuals' behaviour is oriented towards goals associated with a low standard of living and thus primacy was given to goals 'associated with survival, health and basic creature comforts'.[81] Implicit here is the assumption that the goals were those associated with the individual's own survival, health and basic creature comforts. This assumption is questionable on two grounds. First, the assumption that the goals or ends are those associated with a low standard of living, 'survival, health and basic creature comforts' for the individual actor is not justified. Second, the instances of behaviour which Anderson interprets as actors acting so as to calculate their individual self-interest can be interpreted differently.

Turning to the first question, it is dangerous to assume that a low standard of living a priori indicates that the goals of the actors are individualistic. A central theme of studies of women and family relationships in nineteenth-century Europe and the United States with regard to migration, fertility, illegitimacy, and employment, for example, emphasizes the existence and importance of family values as an influence on women's behaviour. Authors warn that 'we must examine *their* [married women in the nineteenth century] experience in light of *their* familial values and not our individualistic ones'.[82] Family values were not necessarily limited to 'traditional', 'customary', rural life, nor was individual self-interest necessarily associated with urban industrial areas; family values could result from the interaction of customary behaviour and new circumstances.[83]

---

[80] Weber, *Social and Economic Organization*, 137.

[81] Anderson, *Family Structure*, 198 n. 14.

[82] J. Scott and L. Tilly, 'Women's Work and the Family in Nineteenth Century Europe', *Comparative Studies in Society and History*, 17 (1975), 64. See also e.g. T. Hareven, *Family Time and Industrial Time: The Relationship Between the Family and Work in a New England Industrial Community* (Cambridge, 1982), 217; Lewis, 'Introduction', 19.

[83] See e.g. Tilly and Scott, *Women, Work and Family*, 104, 232; Hareven, 'History of the Family', 115–17; Anderson, *History of the Western Family*, 78–81.

Indeed, women in this period must be studied in their family settings, for the constraints of family membership greatly affected their opportunities for individual autonomy. No change in attitude, then, increased the numbers of children whom working women bore. Rather, old attitudes and customary behaviour interacted with greatly changed circumstances—particularly in the composition of populations—and led to increased illegitimate fertility.[84]

In every kind of situation, the woman's goal, at least, seems to have been to reestablish the family economy, the partnership of economic enterprise and of social and perhaps, emotional sustenance. These women sought not sexual fulfillment, but economic cooperation and all of the other things which traditional marriage implied. That they often failed to find them, and that their attempts to establish a family took a variety of forms does not prove anything about their motivation.[85]

Anderson, himself, indicates the importance of family values, albeit in the narrow form of the maximization of family income. In his critique of Smelser's interpretation of the operatives' agitation during the Factory Movement and in his own work, he writes:

by contrast, of course, there is a body of contemporary comment which attributes agitation very clearly to the way in which technological change was further diminishing what we now know to have been desperately low family incomes, particularly among men under thirty-five. . . . Similarly, comment is quite widespread both by outside observers and by the working class themselves that the need to maintain family incomes above starvation level underlay many of these subterfuges and much of the agitation. It also seems, as I have demonstrated elsewhere [i.e. in *Family Structure*], to have underlain the willingness of mothers with young children to go out to work and the unwillingness of operatives with low family incomes to take into their homes dependent kin.[86]

But Anderson does not alter in this article the conclusion he derived from his 'heuristic framework' that short-term calculation of self-interest characterized family relationships in mid-nineteenth century Preston.

Moving to the second question, the evidence which Anderson uses to justify his assumption of a 'short-run calculative orientation' can be interpreted in terms of the persistence of family values despite poverty rather than in the individualistic terms of calculative self-interest. For example, Anderson argues that

[84] L. Tilly, J. Scott, and M. Cohen, 'Women's Work and European Fertility Patterns', *J. of Int. Hist.* 6 (1976), 452.
[85] Ibid. 473.   [86] Anderson, 'Smelser Revisited', 328.

at the phenomenal level, again and again poverty is appealed to in the literature by those who were not assisting their relatives. Thus, for example, 'Aw've three brothers, colliers—they've done their best to poo us through. But they're nobbut wortchin four days a week, now; beside, they'n enough to do for their own'.

. . .

Between 1839 and 1846, as unemployment rose and fell, so did the numbers of old and invalid persons described as completely unable to work who appeared in the relief lists. Some at least of this fluctuation must reflect changes in the willingness of kin to support those in need.

In sum, then, I would argue that an additional potent force encouraging actors to adopt a fairly calculative and short-run orientation in their relationships with kin was the extreme poverty which prevailed.[87]

Contrary to Anderson's interpretation, his evidence says nothing about the willingness of kin to support those in need. Instead, the evidence reflects fluctuations in the ability of families to support kin in need and their priorities. One's own nuclear family comes first. Ironically, his example of the man with three brothers who are colliers suggests their willingness to assist kin despite poverty until it jeopardized their own nuclear families. Not only the constraints, but the goals, ends, and values too are problematic. The goals in the case of the people Anderson describes are not solely individualistic, but family oriented, with first priority given to one's own nuclear family. Elizabeth Roberts confirms this point in her study of Preston later in the nineteenth century. She finds 'very little evidence in the later period for this "calculative orientation towards kin", but a great deal of evidence of people helping their relations at considerable cost to themselves in terms of time, energy and money'.[88] In short, it is important, as Janet Finch argues, to distinguish between 'actual assistance given to relatives and the reasons why it is given'.[89]

Anderson was too hasty in adopting the heuristic framework combined with the assumption that individualistic values characterized family relationships within the working classes of nineteenth-century Preston. Ironically, he did just what he criticizes Smelser for doing—using theory to validate data.

At the very minimum these critiques point to the need for the historical sociologist to amass and present in some detail data on the symbolic universe, motives and rationalizations of those whom he studies and to do this not merely for the

---

[87] Anderson, *Family Structure*, 164–5.   [88] Roberts, *Woman's Place*, 172.
[89] Finch, *Family Obligations*, 12 and *passim*.

ideologists and leaders of movements but also, as far as possible, for the masses. Interpretations of specific historical events which lack such elements should be treated with caution. For the reasons just stated, a model, however sophisticated, is not a replacement for data of this kind. Indeed, the danger of having a model is that if the external artifacts look as if they might fit with the theoretical predictions, one will assume they do and thus use the model to validate the data.[90]

Anderson merely substituted one version of calculativeness on the part of operatives for another. For Smelser's assumption that parents were concerned about their children's welfare, Anderson substituted his assumption that individuals were concerned only with maximizing their own income (or sometimes their family's income). Anderson ignores parents' concern for children. Was it such a calculative society that individuals were concerned only with maximizing their own income? To assume that the poor were concerned only with being poor ignores evidence to the contrary. Ballads, music,[91] and the myriad of activities described in the local newspapers, for example, indicate that individuals in the Potteries were concerned about things other than maximizing their own income. One theme, in particular, was keeping the nuclear family together. Moreover, many commentators stress the increasing importance of respectability and status based on home and family within the working class in the second half of the nineteenth century.[92]

Maintaining status was an important goal and gave a precious form of dignity to lives which had few other rewards. . . . The vitality of kin ties in giving a sense of identity is shown in the pride given to family photographs and 'memory' or funeral cards. . . . Next to providing food and shelter, the most important function of the family was in marking status through life style in the eyes of kin and community.[93]

Furthermore, working-class conceptions of respectability, while subject to local traditions, differed generally from the domestic ideal and individual instrumentality of the middle class. In the working class,

---

[90] Anderson, 'Smelser Revisited', 330.

[91] R. Kettle, *Music in the Five Towns: 1840–1914* (London, 1944).

[92] See e.g. G. Stedman Jones, 'Working-Class Culture and Working-Class Politics in London 1870–1900: Notes on the Remaking of a Working Class', *J. of Soc. Hist.* 7 (1974), 460–508; G. Crossick, *An Artisan Elite in Victorian Society* (London, 1978); R. Q. Gray, *The Labour Aristocracy in Victorian Edinburgh* (Oxford, 1976); id., *The Aristocracy of Labour in Nineteenth-Century Britain* (London, 1981); M. J. Daunton, *House and Home in the Victorian City: Working-Class Housing 1850–1914* (London, 1983), esp. ch. 11; Levine, 'Proletarian Family', 191, 203; id., *Reproducing Families*, 174–6; G. Marshall, H. Newby, D. Rose, and C. Vogler, *Social Class in Modern Britain* (London, 1988), 202–6.

[93] Davidoff, 'Family in Britain', 125.

home-centred, privatized life-styles coexisted with participation in a range of voluntary associations such as working men's clubs and trade unions linked to claims for respectability and concerned with collective self-help (albeit sectional and instrumental at a collective level), rather than solely personal or family benefit.[94] This is not to substitute one form of 'dualistic historical thinking' characterized by a nineteenth-century 'golden age' of mutual assistance for another,[95] but to emphasize that the goals and values of working-class families in the Potteries should be seen as problematic and were likely to have been more complex.

A fifth, related criticism concerns Anderson's hypothesis that 'the more calculative are orientations to relationships in a community, the more variable will patterns of behaviour be'.[96] Max Weber, however, notes that the opposite result—uniform patterns of behaviour—is more likely the more calculative the orientations.

Many of the especially notable uniformities in the course of social action are not determined by orientation to any sort of norm which is held to be valid, nor do they rest on custom, but entirely on the fact that the corresponding type of social action is in the nature of the case best adapted to the normal interests of the actors as they themselves are aware of them. This is above all true of economic action. . . . The more strictly rational their action is, the more will they tend to react similarly to the same situation. In this way there arise similarities, uniformities and continuities in their attitudes and actions which are often far more stable than they would be if action were oriented to a system of norms and duties which were considered binding on members of a group.[97]

Thus, the variability of patterns of behaviour alone is not a useful indicator of the extent of calculation or self-interested orientation. The same orientation could be manifest in different patterns of behaviour; and conversely, different orientations might be involved in similar patterns of behaviour.

Therefore, it appears that Anderson, in focusing his approach on the individual actor, failed to take both his own advice and to heed Weber's

---

[94] Summarized in Marshall *et al.*, *Social Class*, 204–5. Patrick Joyce suggests that examination of forms of 'workers' communal self-organisation' in the mid-nineteenth century may 'involve the undermining of Anderson's picture too, in the form of the extension far back into the nineteenth century of . . . the development of functional rather than instrumental kin ties and the spread of community solidarity more actively beyond the basis of kin', see Joyce, 'Work', 141.

[95] Marshall *et al.*, *Social Class*, 206. For a critique of the idea that there was a 'golden age in which family responsibilities were stronger than they are today' see Finch, *Family Obligations*, 57–85.

[96] Anderson, *Family Structure*, 13.

[97] Weber, *Social and Economic Organization*, 122.

warning that 'it is a monstrous misunderstanding to think that an "individualistic" *method* should involve what is in any conceivable sense an individualistic system of *values* [Weber's emphasis].'[98] Rather than assume *a priori* that family relationships were characterized by either wholly individualistic values or wholly family values, the assumption should be turned into a problem, so that the values, goals, and attitudes of the actors in question are problematic. The problem then becomes to collect data and to try to reconstruct the rationality behind them, i.e. the *mentalité* adequate to generate the observed empirical relations and patterns.

The second part of Anderson's argument, i.e. that family relationships were an important source of assistance to individuals compared with other sources of assistance available in mid-nineteenth-century Preston and in light of the bureaucratically provided assistance in the twentieth century, is a more fruitful formulation than the first. Although Anderson links the two parts of his argument, they can be treated separately. In the second part of his argument he considers the extent to which family relationships provided an alternative source of assistance to individuals compared with other sources of assistance. It involves describing not only family relationships as a source of assistance for meeting problems, but other sources of assistance available and the extent to which there were sanctions on individuals if they did not maintain obligations to kin.

This part of Anderson's argument offers a generally useful approach, although there are some problems associated with it. One problem is that there are difficulties in defining the 'problems' faced, and there is a tendency to assume that all 'tasks' are homogeneous and the same for everyone.[99] There are also difficulties in finding relevant information on the provision of assistance by the family and all other possible sources to meet these problems. Assuming the problems can be defined and information found, a second problem arises because it is difficult to assess the importance of the alternative sources of assistance, for the information is biased heavily towards the performance of a function. There is very little negative evidence indicating the non-performance of a service or function. A third problem occurs with Anderson's argument, because his emphasis on individual actors, rational calculation, and conceptually independent

---

[98]   Ibid. 107.

[99]   E. Litwak and I. Szelenyi, 'Primary Group Structures and Their Functions: Kin, Neighbours, and Friends', *Amer. Sociol. Rev.* 34 (1969), 465–81 suggest that neighbours can best handle immediate emergencies, kin long-term commitments, and friends intermediate needs. See also, J. H. Goldthorpe, *Social Mobility and Class Structure in Modern Britain* (Oxford, 1980) esp. ch. 6.

goals give his book a one-dimensional quality. Relevant evidence of activities in one missing dimension, the institutional level, does survive. Both trade unions and churches were sources of relief and assistance that Anderson dismisses in only a few sentences. In 1853–4 Preston was the scene of a massive strike and lockout (described by Dickens in *Hard Times*), and workers in other towns and districts sent thousands of pounds a week to support the strikers.[100] Yet, Anderson refers neither to the strike nor to the unions which on this occasion at least were a major source of assistance to working-class families. Furthermore, Anderson does not use denominational sources, thereby failing to examine churches as sources of relief or churches and Sunday schools as an influence on the goals, aims, and preferences of Preston's working people. Nor does Anderson use local newspapers which might indicate other forms of assistance. As he points out, but does not elaborate, 'the preferred relational patterns of collectivities outside the family, such as the Poor Law, which will only deal with individuals as part of a family, limit the actor's choice of relational patterns'.[101]

Despite these problems it is possible to build on this approach by using additional sources and exploring the institutional level. In what follows, evidence from the Potteries will suggest that a broad range of institutions played a more important role in providing assistance, shaping goals, and influencing family relationships than Anderson's approach allowed him to consider for Preston.

About the same time that Anderson turned to exchange theory, plundering 'the large stock of intellectually sophisticated and highly prestigious theories' of economics and game theory and applying them to the allocation and exchange of scarce social resources, e.g. the exchange of advice for status, conformity for approval, the exchange of assistance, ideas, gifts, and favours,[102] some economists turned their attention to analysing problems associated with family decision-making in terms of the allocation of the scarce resources of money and time. They took Cairncross's advice and focused on the household and family decision-making as a unit of analysis within the economic system.

In the market there is an obvious antithesis between firms and households; but the antithesis disappears when the two are looked at as administrative units. If, following Aristotle, economists had sought first to understand the activities of

---

[100] H. I. Dutton and J. E. King, *'Ten Per Cent and No Surrender': The Preston Strike, 1853–1854* (Cambridge, 1981).

[101] Anderson, *Family Structure*, 13.   [102] Heath, *Rational Choice*, 1, 3–5.

the household and then studied the firm as a special type of household, they would have been less seriously in error. They would certainly have done fuller justice to the activity which we call management. . . . The antithesis between producers and consumers has also prevented economists from conveying an adequate picture of the relationship between the two. If firms are set in sharp contrast to households, and their output is assumed to govern the standard of living, the whole maximizing process is distorted. Economists and their readers, mindful of the ultimate identity of production and consumption, come to use as the touchstone of success in an economy the volume of production which it achieves—very often, the volume of industrial production alone. They slur over the costly effort of marketing by which production is adapted to the pattern of consumer wants and rarely speculate on the correlative changes within household that go to determine whether an increased flow of goods and services from firms is of net benefit to the community.[103]

Gary Becker's article, 'A Theory of the Allocation of Time' and his subsequent book, *A Treatise on the Family*, exemplify a unified theory of economic decision-making, integrating labour-market economics and home economics in what has been referred to as the 'new home economics', making the household and family respectable subjects for economic analysis. A by-product of this approach has been a new formulation of topics such as an explanation of labour-force participation rates, patterns of occupational segregation by sex, fertility rates, the history of population, and the position of women, in terms of family decision-making and the income and time of family members.[104] The approach directed

attention to the productive aspects of non-working time and thereby opened a whole realm of non-market activities to economic analysis. Time and an individual's productivity are the limiting scarce resources in this model. Each individual allocates his or her time among many competing activities both in the market and at home in such a way as to maximize his or her total product or utility. Time can be used to earn money, which can purchase market goods, or

[103] A. Cairncross, 'Economic Schizophrenia', *Scot. J. of Pol. Econ.* 5 (1958), 16–17.

[104] G. S. Becker, 'A Theory of the Allocation of Time', *Economic Journal*, 75 (1965), 493–517; A. Rees, *The Economics of Work and Pay* (London, 1973); R. Gronau, 'The Intrafamily Allocation of Time: The Value of the Housewives' Time', *Amer. Econ. Rev.* 63 (1973), 684–91; H. Leibenstein, 'An Interpretation of the Economic Theory of Fertility: Promising Path or Blind Alley?', *J. of Econ. Lit.* 13 (1974), 457–79; T. W. Schultz (ed.), *Economics of the Family: Marriage, Children and Human Capital* (London, 1974); W. Bowen and T. A. Finegan, *The Economics of Labor Force Participation* (Princeton, NJ, 1969); C. B. Lloyd (ed.), *Sex, Discrimination and the Division of Labor* (London, 1975); M. Blaug, 'The Empirical Status of Human Capital Theory: A Slightly Jaundiced Survey', *J. of Econ. Lit.* 14 (1976), 827–55; G. Becker, *A Treatise on the Family* (Cambridge, Mass., 1981); and Cleland and Wilson, 'Demand Theories', 7–30 among others elucidate, apply, or criticize the approach in question.

can be used in the production and the consumption of commodities at home. Time and market goods are the two major categories of inputs used to produce household commodities, such as cooking, childrearing and entertaining.

Instead of simply allocating time efficiently among commodities multiperson households also allocate the time of different members. Members who are relatively more efficient at market activities would use less of their time at consumption activities (i.e. work in the home) than would other members. Moreover, an increase in the relative market efficiency of any member would effect a reallocation of the time of all other members towards consumption activities in order to permit the former to spend more time at market activities. In short, the allocation of the time of any member is greatly influenced by the opportunities open to other members.[105]

In contrast to an exchange-theory approach focusing on individual decision-making, the nuclear family is the decision-making unit in the 'new home economics'. Commentators argue that the focus on the family tends to obscure inequalities and interactions within families.[106] Economists point out that accounting for the part families play in the economy raises difficult issues requiring special assumptions about how the family functions.[107] The problems of aggregating utility curves have led to the assumption that the decisions of one family member, 'the benevolent dictator', are the decisions of the family. Another alternative is to assume that the family acts as if it were an individual. This assumption of the 'glued together family' pursuing a 'family strategy' to reach its goals has been influential in the literature on family history.[108] Critics, however, suggest these assumptions ignore the influence of patriarchy and the subordinate position of women within families. In addition, the idea of 'family strategy', while useful in 'affirming the possibility of autonomous action of ordinary people in the past', has been described as little more than an 'empirically convenient metaphor'.[109]

---

[105] C. B. Lloyd, 'The Division of Labor between the Sexes: A Review' in Lloyd, *Division of Labor*, 10–11.

[106] See e.g. A. Sen, 'Economics and the Family', in A. K. Sen, *Resources, Values and Development* (Oxford, 1984), 374, 384; D. S. Smith, 'Family Strategy: More than a Metaphor?' *Historical Methods*, 20 (1987), 118; Ruggles, *Prolonged Connections*, 16–20, 22–3.

[107] See e.g. Sen, 'Economics and the Family', 371–4; Humphries and Rubery, 'Supply Side of the Labour Market', 333–5.

[108] See e.g. Anderson, *History of the Western Family*, 78–81; L. P. Moch *et al.*, 'Family Strategy: A Dialogue', *Historical Methods*, 20 (1987), 125; Ruggles, *Prolonged Connections*, 16–20, 22–3.

[109] Smith, 'Family Strategy', 119.

In place of the idea of family strategy regarded as 'a set of normative rules that guide the action of all persons in certain groups, regions or classes',[110] Janet Finch usefully shifts the emphasis back to the individual and suggests that the sense of obligation or responsibility that informs behaviour towards kin should be thought of as a set of 'normative guidelines' with which individuals negotiate their relationships rather than as rules determining behaviour or as individuals pursuing their own self-interest narrowly defined. Such a perspective of 'negotiated commitments over time' drawing on 'normative guidelines' leaves room for flexibility and variety in relationships among different individuals and in different circumstances.[111]

It is not surprising that the line between individuals and families has been blurred in the family history literature. As Christopher Harris points out

A revolution in sociological thinking has transformed the landscape in which the study of kinship can take place. The attempt to establish the relation between different collective features of social life has been replaced with an attempt to explain the interaction between the collective and the individual. The result is a shift in the explanandum from a structural or systemic feature, e.g. the nuclear family system of family formation, to individual behaviour. Because there are no clear social rules which determine the boundaries of recognized kin who should do what for whom, the whole process of claiming kin rights is a matter of negotiation and the outcome can be represented as the product of individual action and decision. How to explain the aggregate outcomes of and patterns of free choices?[112]

Ideas of flexibility and negotiation emerge not only at the level of the relationships between individuals and families, but also in considerations of families as institutions. This is particularly apparent in the convergence of thinking among economists, demographic historians, and historians of the household about the conceptual relationship between families and the economy. Jane Humphries and Jill Rubery, for example, refer to the 'relative autonomy of social reproduction'.[113] They argue that two

---

[110] Ibid.

[111] Finch, *Family Obligations.* Continuing to emphasize the existence of family strategies, one of the first to apply explicitly the idea of family strategies to history, Louise Tilly now begins to approach Finch's position when she seeks 'to explain the adoption of one strategy or another as an outcome of bargaining among family members with unequal resources': L Tilly, 'Beyond Family Strategies, What?', *Historical Methods,* 20 (1987), 125.

[112] C. Harris, 'Kin Rights and Kin Duties' *THES,* 1 Dec. 1989, 18.

[113] Humphries and Rubery, 'Supply Side of the Labour Market', 331–46.

opposing methodologies have been used to analyse the family system across the whole spectrum of theoretical approaches from neoclassical to Marxist and feminist, and that these methodologies are inadequate. The first methodology is one of 'absolute autonomy' in which the family system is a 'given'; its development is independent of the economy. The system of production has to adapt to and operate within the constraints of social reproduction. The second, 'reductionist-functionalist', is characterized by a broader system of production which incorporates social reproduction, and turns the family system into a dependent variable within the economic system. Instead, Humphries and Rubery suggest that social reproduction and the system of production should be approached as 'relatively autonomous'.[114] 'Social reproduction develops in response to changes in the productive system but the form of this response must be understood historically. It is neither predetermined nor smoothly accommodating to the demands of the productive system, but depends on the dynamics of social reproduction.'[115] Similarly with regard to demographic history, E. A. Wrigley points to the 'logical status' of population history as both independent of and dependent on the economy.[116] As an example he describes the historically specific relationship between population growth and real wages in England during the eighteenth century. Likewise, historians of residential groups or households, have extended their investigations 'beyond the relational, age and marital status characteristics of the members of the household to include the work patterns of these persons'.[117] Richard Wall, for example, has advocated the use of the term 'adaptive family economy' to emphasize the 'flexibility' of family and household patterns among different occupational groups, though he succumbs to the danger of associating characteristics with

[114] The concept of 'relative autonomy' is also used with regard to the relationship of individuals and social structure and of the family to biological and social reproduction. Lloyd, *Explanation in Social History*, 280–1 describes a view of social structure 'as being "relatively autonomous" of individual actions and understandings but not of the structuring agency of collective action. . . . Individuals can move in and out of some social relations without jeopardizing their very existence every time they do'; and D. H. J. Morgan, 'New Directions in Family Research and Theory', in C. Harris (ed.), *The Sociology of the Family: New Directions for Britain* (Keele, 1979), 15 suggests that the notion of 'relative autonomy' combined 'with the themes of the relationships between biological and social reproduction constantly bring us back to the frontiers between the macro- and micro-' reminding us 'that there is no simple translation from the historical to the personal or back again'. See also, D. H. J. Morgan, *The Family, Politics and Social Theory* (London, 1985), 283.

[115] Humphries and Rubery, 'Supply Side of the Labour Market', 332.

[116] Wrigley, 'Population History', 218.

[117] Wall, 'Work, Welfare and the Family', 264; U. Pfister, 'Work Roles and Family Structure in Proto-Industrial Zurich', *J. Int. Hist.* 20 (1989), 83.

categories a priori when he suggests that flexibility is synonymous with a single pattern of family employment regardless of circumstances.[118] Despite the different terms, 'relative autonomy' and 'adaptive family economy', they are all being used for the same idea about the conceptual relationship between families and the economy.

With 'flexibility', 'negotiation', and 'relative autonomy' characterizing both relationships between individuals and families and families and other institutions, it is perhaps useful to see family relationships as 'having a double edged character', 'at the same time institutional and individual'.[119]

As this survey reveals, the protean nature of family life and activities covering the whole range of human activities make it very hard to create a satisfactory framework for its study compared with other institutions which have a single function or range of functions.[120] Moreover, perspectives focusing on individuals and their relations to the families as collectivities face problems in accounting for aggregate patterns of behaviour and incorporating a dynamic view of the structural context, the collective and institutional levels. Nevertheless, it is possible to explore the 'relative autonomy' of individuals and their family relationships in certain areas of social activity in a particular industrial region of Britain in the mid-nineteenth century. Individual-level information from census enumerators' books and marriage registers allows the systematic documentation of patterns of family relationships, while these and other sources facilitate the exploration of the 'relative autonomy' of working people and their family relationships as subjects, as creative actors as well as objects in the local economic, social, political, and cultural context with regard especially to work and social welfare.

In what follows documentation of patterns of family relationships suggests the maintenance and importance of these relationships in the face of the potentially disruptive processes of industrialization and urbanization. At the same time, close analysis of women's and children's paid industrial employment outside the household and its effects on the social, demographic, economic, and legal structure of family life in an area with a dominant industry reveals surprising complexity in patterns

---

[118] Wall, 'Work, Welfare and the Family', 264–6; M. Dupree, 'Social and Economic Aspects of the Family Life-Cycle: Individuals, Households and the Labour Market in the Staffordshire Potteries During the Mid-Nineteenth Century', in R. Wall and O. Saito (eds.), *Social and Economic Aspects of the Family Life Cycle: Europe and Japan, Traditional and Modern* (forthcoming, Cambridge University Press).

[119] Morgan, *The Family*, 285–6.   [120] Wrigley, 'Reflections', 71.

of family employment, fertility, family standard of living, the influence of individual employers, and pressure for factory legislation. These patterns call into question the focus on occupational groups divorced from the localities in which their members lived, or single-industry towns seen as synonymous with a single occupational group. Instead, the patterns suggest the importance of an emphasis on the region and local community and the interaction of occupational groups within the local context— even one that appears to be dominated by a single industry. They emphasize the need to see individuals in families not only as objects but also at the same time as actors or agents constructing and reconstructing their world and their 'knowledge of it through interaction with it'.[121] Moreover, they highlight both the limitations of the paternalism of individual employers and the local attitudes, structures of authority, and relations with the state which shaped the legislation affecting women's and children's employment and which also carried over to reflect and influence the problems individuals and families faced and the context within which they sought assistance in finding solutions to them. This 'regional' and 'community' perspective in turn facilitates an approach which views families as one of a number of sources of assistance—along with neighbours, the Poor Law, friendly societies, churches, trade unions, voluntary hospitals, and civic authorities—which individuals in nineteenth-century towns turned to in times of need and which played a role in shaping attitudes towards family relationships. Such a perspective is better suited both to illuminate the complexity of Victorian society and to bring family and women's history back into social history as a whole.[122]

[121] Lloyd, *Explanation in Social History*, 160–1, 308, and *passim* for a summary and synthesis of recent conceptual approaches in sociology and social history. For an eloquent exposition (influenced especially by Anthony Giddens's work) of the unity of sociology and history in seeking 'to understand the puzzle of human agency . . . in terms of the process of social structuring' and, in other words, of 'finding a way of accounting for human experience which recognises simultaneously and in equal measure that history and society are made by constant and more of less purposeful individual action and that individual action, however purposeful, is made by history and society', see P. Abrams, *Historical Sociology* (Ithaca, NY, 1982), x, xiii, and *passim*. For Giddens, see e.g. A. Giddens, *Central Problems in Social Theory: Action, Structure and Contradiction in Social Analysis* (London and Basingstoke, 1979), and D. Held and J. B. Thompson (eds.), *Social Theory of Modern Societies: Anthony Giddens and His Critics* (Cambridge, 1989).

[122] For the need to synthesize specialities and an attempt to overcome the 'balkanizing thrust in social history', see e.g. Pleck, 'Two Worlds in One', 178. For the need to integrate family and women's history into general history see, C. Degler, 'Women and the Family' in M. Kammen (ed.), *The Past Before Us: Contemporary Historical Writing in the United States* (Ithaca and London, 1980), esp. 308, 326. P. Hudson and W. R. Lee, 'Introduction', in Hudson and Lee, *Women's Work*, 34–5.

3. Choice of Locale, Period, and Sources

Reasons for concentrating on a coal-based industrial area with paid employment for women and children outside the household have been outlined above in Section 1. Yet, the areas, period, and sources chosen for detailed study need to be described more closely.

Located in the north of England, half-way between Birmingham and Manchester, the Staffordshire Potteries was the industrial area at the heart of the North Staffordshire coalfield.[123] The Potteries was made up of a chain of six towns—Tunstall, Burslem, Hanley and Shelton, Stoke, Fenton, and Longton—which were encompassed in the parliamentary borough of Stoke-upon-Trent in 1861 (Map I.1), the unit of analysis for the sample of the census enumerators' books used in this study.[124] The parliamentary borough was not incorporated under the Municipal Corporations Act of 1835, and the different towns were criss-crossed by the boundaries of numerous local government bodies.[125] Nevertheless, the parliamentary borough included nearly all of the area in which the pottery industry and the residences of its working people were concentrated as the industry expanded to 180 manufactories (called 'potbanks' or 'potworks') and 30,000 employees in 1861.[126] Moreover, as mentioned above, by the middle of the nineteenth century the potteries employed men, women, and children, while the neighbouring coal-mines and ironworks employed primarily men. So it is possible to compare the three industries, their conditions of employment, their workers and their families, and the patterns of social welfare within one area. In addition, the

---

[123] For a description of the North Staffordshire region and its neglect by geographers see S. H. Beaver, 'The Potteries: A Study in the Evolution of a Cultural Landscape', in The Institute of British Geographers, *Presidential Addresses Delivered to the Institute and Presented to the 20th International Geographical Congress 1964* (London, 1964), 1–31; and 'A Geographical Agenda for North Staffordshire', *N. Staffs. J. of Field Studies* 3 (1963), 1–16. For a discussion of the region and subdivisions within it see A. H. Morgan, 'Regional Consciousness in the N. Staffs. Potteries', *Geography*, 27 (1942), 95–102.

[124] I have taken a 1 in 15 systematic sample of the census enumerators' books for the parliamentary borough of Stoke-upon-Trent in 1861. This sample includes information on 6,700 individuals and 1,350 households which was coded, entered into a computer, and analysed. See the methodological appendix for a discussion of the process and an assessment of the reliability of census-taking in the Potteries in 1851, 1861, and 1871. The appendix also describes the procedure used to take and analyse the 1861 sample and to calculate family standards of living using it. In addition, I have taken a 1 in 24 sample of the enumerators' books for 1881 including information on approximately 6,000 individuals and 1,200 households which I use at several points but have not drawn on in detail for this book, though I hope to do so in future publications.

[125] See e.g. Map I.2, which indicates the boundaries of the parliamentary borough and the registration districts which were also the boundaries of the Poor Law unions.

[126] PP 1863 xviii, 97.

MAP I.1   The Parliamentary Borough of Stoke-upon-Trent, 1861
Sources: PP 1831–2, xl. 7–9; background map: OS (1889), scale of 1″ to
1 mile, CUL maps 34.04.123. Reproduced by Permission of the Syndics of
Cambridge University Library.

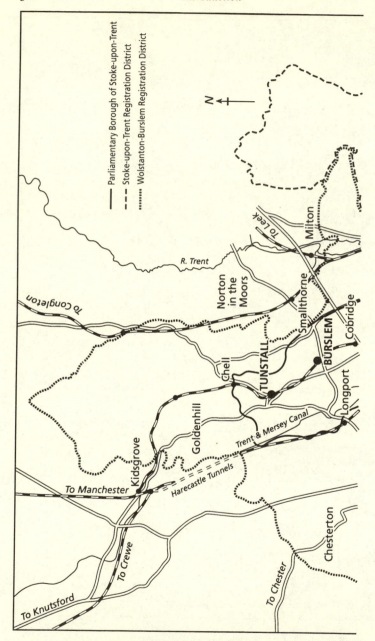

MAP I.2   The Registration Districts and the Parliamentary Borough

Sources: Census 1851, i, 55–6, 110; background map: VCH, viii, 1; maps of Staffordshire showing parishes, unions, or registration districts: CUL maps 85.88.2 (1888), 85.90.1 (1899), 31.05 (1902[28]).

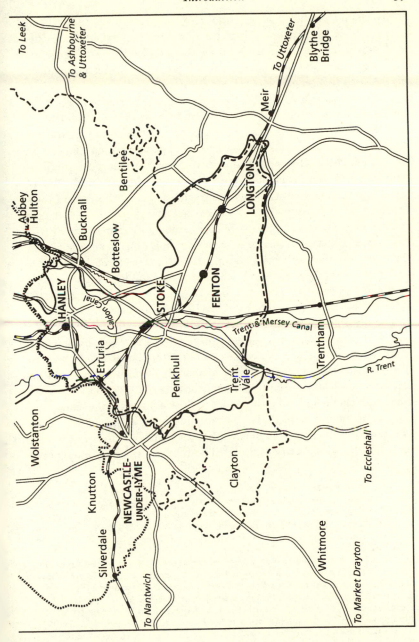

parliamentary borough was geographically, administratively, and to some extent socially and economically distinct from the borough of Newcastle-under-Lyme on the ridge to the west, the moorlands to the north and east, and agricultural land and the Duke of Sutherland's seat at Trentham on the south.

Because a sample is based on a fraction of the population selected at random, it shows nothing about relationships between the inhabitants of different houses in the same street or area. Therefore, to supplement the sample it is necessary to study the residence patterns in one area on an intensive basis.[127] The enumeration district encompassing the village of Etruria (with a population of 966 persons in 1861) adjacent to the Wedgwood factory is particularly suitable for such a study. The Potteries was made up of separate towns and villages to an even greater extent than Preston.[128] It is, then, appropriate to examine an enumeration district that was also a separate village. Furthermore, it is possible to supplement the census enumerator's book for Etruria with other sources of information, particularly the Wedgwood Company Papers and John Finney's autobiography, in order to illuminate the relationship between an employer and workforce and the families and neighbourhood adjacent to a factory.

The focus of this book is on the mid-nineteenth century, particularly the period 1840–80, for a number of reasons. First, the amount and scope of information in the census enumerators' books make them an obvious starting-point for a study of the family life of working people in a nineteenth-century industrial area. These books give the address of every household, and for each member of the household, the name, age, sex, occupation, and birthplace. From this material on certain social attributes of individuals, augmented by other source material, it is possible to infer social relationships.[129] The heavy reliance on inference is

---

[127] Anderson, *Family Structure*, 20.

[128] Anderson, however, underemphasizes the strength and influence of the neighbourhood, community, or 'townlet' around a mill. The strength of this community differs from that of the larger, undifferentiated urban unit Anderson uses. See P. Joyce, 'The Factory Politics of Lancashire in the Later Nineteenth Century', *Hist. J.* 18 (1975), 525–53 and *Work, Society and Politics*.

[129] The concern here is ultimately with social relationships including 'attitudes of mind that informed behavior' and it is recognized that 'consideration of the social attributes of individuals living in a particular geographic area is therefore *not* sociology'. Nevertheless, 'it may well be an essential preliminary to sociological analysis'. Evidence in addition to the census enumerators' books is essential. See J. C. Mitchell, 'On Quantification in Social Anthropology', in A. L. Epstein (ed.), *The Craft of Social Anthropology* (London, 1967); A. Macfarlane, *The Family Life of Ralph Josselin: An Essay in Historical Anthropology* (Cambridge, 1970), 3.

unavoidable in any argument from the census enumerators' books. Nevertheless, they provide individual-level information on the frequency and generality of patterns of co-residence, family employment, and birthplaces that is not available from any other source. However, during the period when this study was undertaken the enumerators' books with this range of information were available only for 1851, 1861, 1871, and 1881,[130] and this limitation necessarily directed attention to the mid-nineteenth century.

Second, there is descriptive material surviving for the Potteries in this period to counterbalance both the danger of overlooking attitudes, assumptions and 'mental life', and the bias towards material and outward aspects of human life often associated with the search for 'statistical facts'.[131] Sources which help to supplement and broaden the statistical picture survive for the Potteries in the mid-nineteenth century. Accordingly, I have used marriage registers, a ratebook, pollbooks, newspapers, pamphlets, autobiographies, consular papers and company papers, as well as Parliamentary Papers and the correspondence between the local Guardians and the central Poor Law authorities.

Third, the choice of the period 1840–80 is based on the argument that the descriptive evidence refers to more than one year; therefore, family structure is described not on census night but over a longer period. This implies that changes in family relations during the period were either very slow or proceeded in clearly defined and specified jumps so that the period is assumed to be homogeneous. Such an assumption seems reasonable for the Potteries in the nineteenth century, and following Anderson, I adopted a period extending roughly twenty years on either side of the census year, in this case 1861.

Fourth, this case-study of one population of working people in one particular context during one specific time-period can claim to be a study of the impact of industrialization on family and kin relationships if one accepts the arguments of sociologists who use a single sample of interviews from one time and place. They argue that the patterns of social life were already influenced by the process in question, so the effects of the process are observed at the time of investigation.[132] Applying such

---

[130] The census enumerators' books for England and Wales in 1891 became available on 1 Jan. 1992.

[131] Macfarlane, *Ralph Josselin*, 3.

[132] J. H. Goldthorpe, D. Lockwood, F. Bechhofer, and J. Platt, *The Affluent Worker in the Class Structure* (Cambridge, 1969), 51–3; M. Young and P. Willmott, *The Symmetrical Family* (Harmondsworth, 1973), 18, make a similar argument.

reasoning to this case, the patterns of social life in the Potteries by the mid-nineteenth century were already influenced by industrial development so that a description of attitudes, patterns of behaviour, and relationships in the mid-nineteenth century is a description of the effects of industrialization on family relationships. Thus, in this sense, a straightforward description of the pottery-workers and their families, set against available comparative material for ironworkers and coal-miners in the Potteries and cotton-workers in Preston, and explanation of these patterns in terms of the constraints, resources, available alternatives, values, and attitudes will be a description of the impact of industrialization in one area of Britain.

Finally, while I use information from the census enumerators' books for 1851, 1871, and 1881 I have chosen to take an overall census sample and an enumeration district in its entirety from the 1861 enumerators' books as the focus for detailed analysis. The iron industry in the Potteries was new and expanding in the 1850s, so that 1861 provides a good vantage-point for examining the workforce of a new, expanding industry for comparison with the old but expanding coal industry and the well-established pottery industry. In addition, the Factory Acts were not extended to the pottery industry until 1864. Therefore, the 1861 census provides a description of the family and workforce patterns in the Potteries immediately before the Factory Acts. No such information is available for the cotton industry due to the lack of census enumerators' books for its pre-Factory Act period. Neil Smelser's analysis of family and work in the cotton industry in which the origin and effect of the Factory Act in the industry plays a key role, suffers from this lack of information. Also, from the standpoint of sources, the Royal Commission on Children's Employment investigated the Potteries in 1862 so that more and better contextual information favours 1861.

4. General Outline

The general outline of the book is as follows. Part I is concerned with the context and structure of family relationships. For background, in Chapter 1 I describe the geographical, economic, and social conditions of the region in the mid-nineteenth century in order to determine what kinds of problems and constraints, opportunities and resources working people in the Potteries faced in their daily lives, and the frequency of various types of crises. To what extent did problems such as poverty, population turnover, uncertainty of employment, housing, and health stand out?

Evidence from factory inspectors' reports, Registrar-Generals' Reports, Medical Officers' Reports, census material, maps, newspapers, and accounts of the pottery industry are used to answer these questions.

Given the conditions in this urban-industrial area, what patterns of family relationships existed? Chapter 2 presents a detailed description of several aspects of family relationships tied to co-residence. Of particular concern are relationships between husbands and wives, parents and children, individuals and their wider kin network at different points in the family life cycle.[133]

In Part II, Chapters 3, 4, 5, and 6 are concerned with family relationships and work in an industrial area with paid employment outside the household for women and children. The patterns that emerge illuminate the 'relative autonomy' or flexibility of individual and family relationships in the mid-nineteenth century. The family and household patterns of members of the major occupational groups in the Potteries are the focus of Chapter 3. Patterns of family employment, employment over an individual's lifetime, intergenerational occupational change, intermarriage, fertility, and family standard of living of the men, women, and children employed in the pottery labour-force and the men working as miners, ironworkers, and labourers in the Potteries in 1861 are analysed and compared.

The 'relative autonomy' and flexibility of the relationship between family ties and work at the level of the neighbourhood and factory and for an individual potter are explored in Chapter 4. The enumeration district of Etruria and the pottery firm of Josiah Wedgwood and Sons can be seen as representative of the Potteries. Thus, Etruria is an appropriate place to examine the applicability to the Potteries of the wide-ranging paternalism of individual factory employers and the central place of the employment of family members in linking employer influence and employer-worker reciprocity both inside and outside the factory which appear in some accounts of the mid-nineteenth-century textile areas. The autobiography of John Finney, a potttery-worker who grew up in Etruria, not only illuminates these issues, but also gives a sense of what it was like to be a potter, his attitudes and his concerns.

Whatever the influence of individual employers in the surrounding neighbourhood, employers also acted together in the Potteries to take

---

[133] Following Stone, *Family, Sex and Marriage*, 21, the word 'family' is 'taken as synonymous neither with "household"—persons living together under one roof—nor with "kin"—persons related by blood or marriage. It is taken to mean those members of the same kin who live together under one roof'.

paternalistic initiatives which patterns of family relationships influenced
and which in turn shaped those relationships. Chapters 5 and 6 examine
the relationships between family structure and the implementation and
effects of protective legislation. Moreover, the extension of the Factory
Acts to the pottery industry not only changed the context of family
decision-making regarding the employment of women and children, but
also reflected the local structures of authority, their relationship with the
state, and the social assumptions within which individuals and families in
the Potteries sought assistance for many of the problems they might face.

A variety of problems arising from the demographic conditions, urban
environment, and industrial employment which faced individuals and
families in the Potteries emerged in previous chapters. In Part III, the
final two chapters analyse family relationships, including those of women
within nuclear families as well as with kin, together with other networks
and institutions (the Poor Law, friendly societies, burial societies, trade
unions, infirmaries, neighbours, and churches) as sources of assistance
for meeting the problems. Who provided what kinds of assistance to
whom for how long? They also consider the roles of other institutions in
shaping the attitudes of working people towards family relationships.
Although 'the limitations of the data are very apparent, and mean that
the answers . . . must be partial and to some extent speculative, rather
than detailed and authoritative',[134] the chapters conclude with an assessment of the place of family and kin in relation to alternative networks
and institutions as sources of assistance for working people in the 'mixed
economy of welfare' in the mid-nineteenth-century Potteries.

[134] Finch, *Family Obligations*, 57.

PART I

*The Context and Structure
of Family Relationships*

I

The Geographical, Economic, and Social Background

RATHER than a comprehensive portrait, the following description of the geographic, economic, and social background in the mid-nineteenth-century Potteries is oriented particularly towards specifying the kinds of problems which working people in the Potteries faced in their daily lives, including employment, poverty, housing conditions, disease and mortality, and migration into, within, and out of the Potteries.

1. Employment

Employment in the Potteries in the mid-nineteenth century was concentrated in a narrow range of industrial occupations in coal-based industries (see Table 1.1).[1] Among the industrial occupations, those concerned with the manufacture of china and earthenware clearly formed the largest proportion, but there were also significant numbers of miners and iron-workers. In 1861 coal-mining, iron manufacture, and pottery manufacture

[1] The information on occupation in the 1 in 15 sample of the Potteries census enumerators' books was coded as it appeared in the returns for each individual. There is no agreed basis for aggregating these different occupations into meaningful, mutually exclusive groups. For the purpose of a general outline of the Potteries labour-force, and to compare it with the country as a whole, I have grouped the occupations into categories following *Abst. of Brit. Hist. Stats.* 60–1 and aggregated these categories following P. Mathias, *The First Industrial Nation: An Economic History of Britain 1700–1914*, 2nd edn. (New York and London, 1983), 241. J. Foster, *Class Struggle and the Industrial Revolution: Early Industrial Capitalism in Three English Towns* (London, 1974), 75, 291–2, also follows *Abst. of Brit. Hist. Stats.* I have not, however, used his modifications of their categories. Another way to classify the occupational information in 19th-cent. censuses is to follow Charles Booth's system as described by A. Armstrong, 'The Use of Information About Occupation', in E. A. Wrigley (ed.), *Nineteenth Century Society: Essays in the Use of Quantitative Methods for the Study of Social Data* (Cambridge, 1972),191–7, 226–310. I grouped the occupations in the Potteries sample into these categories (though they are not presented here). The sample reveals a roughly similar occupational structure whether the occupations are classified according to the *Abst. of Brit. Hist. Stats.* or the Booth and Armstrong categories.

TABLE 1.1 *Occupational Structure: Great Britain and the Potteries 1861* (% of the occupied population)

		Potteries Sample	Great Britain
Agriculture (incl. forestry)		1	19
Manufacturing and processing, of which:		77	49
Pottery	(45)		
Coal & ironstone mining	(11)		
Iron	(5)		
Commerce, transport, and public services		5	7
Public Administration, forces, professions, and domestic service		17	25
N		3,325	10,523,000

Source: see Ch. 1 n. 1.

taken together accounted directly for nearly one-half of the employment of all men aged twenty and over in the registration districts of Stoke-upon-Trent and Wolstanton, which included the parliamentary borough of Stoke-upon-Trent.[2] The chronology of their development and their geographical distribution within the region differ, and even the ironmaster Robert Heath admitted that 'the potting trade is the trade of the locality',[3] yet as early as the second half of the eighteenth century the uniformity in trends in wages for potters, miners, and others in North Staffordshire suggest that a unified labour-market was already in operation at a regional level, with wages in the industrial occupations linked and agricultural wages following those in industry.[4] Thus, it is worthwhile describing briefly the development and geographical distribution as well as the employment and wages of these three trades in North Staffordshire in the mid-nineteenth century.

[2] 29 per cent of all men aged 20 and over were employed in 'earthenware manufacture', 14 per cent were 'coalminers', and 5 per cent were employed in 'iron manufacture'.

[3] PP 1867–8, xiv, 24.

[4] F. W. Botham, 'Working-Class Living Standards in North Staffordshire 1750–1914', Ph.D. thesis (London, 1982), 105.

The Pottery Industry: Industrial Development, Geographical Distribution, Employment, and Wages

The eighteenth century was the period of the establishment and most rapid development of the pottery industry in North Staffordshire. Sustained growth from the 1740s was based on a wide range of new products, sold through a developing network of dealers in markets characterized by growing consumer expenditure and international as well as home demand. Expansion was a complex process based on a wide variety of products forming highly diversified sectors, including stoneware, china, and the most dynamic sector, fine earthenware, which emerged before 1760. The different types of earthenware—creamware, tortoiseshell-ware, pearl, and printed earthenwares—accounted for four-fifths of the industry's capacity by 1780. The development of new clay bodies for china (soft-paste by the 1740s, hard-paste by the 1760s, bone china in the 1790s, and ironstone from 1800), and for earthenware, as the new white body imitating china became popular for relatively inexpensive 'useful' wares, facilitated the new products. In addition stoneware bodies such as 'jasper' and 'basalt' for 'ornamental wares' stimulated by the neoclassical revival were added. Also, there were gradual improvements in ovens, wheels, and lathes, and the development of plaster moulds allowing the creation of irregular-shaped items had begun by the 1740s, while liquid glazes and double-firing were in use by the 1750s. Moreover, there were new methods of decoration, including transfer printing and increasing expertise in painting, gilding, and an expanded range of colours. Associated with the new products and production methods were new forms of factory organization, increased division of labour, and improvements in transport and marketing techniques.[5]

During the nineteenth century the industry built on this foundation, developing new sectors without jeopardizing the prosperity of the existing sectors. Earthenware remained the dominant sector, but china production also expanded, including fine china produced by firms such as Mintons and the production, concentrated in Longton, of china and porcelain for a cheap mass market. Stoneware both for ornamental ware

[5] For accounts of the development of the industry in the 18th cent., see among others: L. Weatherill, *The Pottery Trade of North Staffordshire 1660–1769* (Manchester, 1971) and id., *The Growth of the Pottery Industry in England, 1660–1815* (New York and London, 1986); J. Thomas, *The Rise of the Staffordshire Potteries* (Bath, 1971); H. A. Moisley, 'The Potteries Coalfield: A Regional Analysis', M.Sc. thesis (Leeds, 1950); and the articles by N. McKendrick cited in the bibliography.

and that made from cheaper clays for coarse brown ware continued to be produced. In the middle of the century some firms began producing parian, a variant of porcelain for vases and statuary, and Minton's developed a flourishing business in encaustic and architectural tiles. From the later 1860s the sections of the industry producing sanitary ware and 'telegraphic' or electrical ware began to develop. For example, in 1880 there was a separate listing in the *Post Office Directory* for sanitary-ware manufacturers where there was none in 1860. Among the six firms listed separately in 1880 that of Thomas Twyford in Hanley was listed as 'sanitary-ware manufacturer', and that of Pinder Bourne and Company in Burslem appeared as manufacturers of 'earthenware, sanitary ware, telegraphic ware and enamelled tile manufacturers', while their predecessors in 1860 were listed respectively as manufacturing 'earthenware' and 'manufacturers of ironstone, china and earthenware'.[6]

During the nineteenth century the increase in the number and size of factories was modest. In 1820 there were 122 employing an average labour-force of eighty-five, in 1836 there were approximately 130 employing 155 people, and in 1862 there were 180 employing an average workforce of 167 but ranging from between 30 and 40 to over 1,000. Some firms produced only china, others only earthenware, others both, and there was a great variation in quality and price. A few of the larger firms had more than one location. By mid-century a three-tier structure had emerged with about twenty-five large firms employing over 500, including Mintons and Davenports employing over 1,000; a middle group employing 100–500; and a group of smaller potworks employing less than 100.[7]

By the end of the eighteenth century the manufacture of earthenware

---

[6] *Kelly and Co., Post Office Directory of Birmingham, Warwickshire, Worcestershire and Staffordshire* (1860), 516, 565; *Kelly and Co., Post Office Directory of Birmingham, Warwickshire, Worcestershire and Staffordshire* (1880), 58, 147, 631.

[7] For figures for 1820 see Weatherill, *Pottery Industry*, 452–3; the 1836 figures are from John Boyle quoted in F. Burchill and R. Ross, *A History of the Potters' Union* (Hanley, 1977), 23; figures for 1862 are from PP 1863, xviii, 97. The three-tier division with twenty-five firms in the élite category originates from the Report of the Children's Employment Commissioner in 1841: PP 1843, xiv, 214–15. He uses a labour-force of 50 to 800 for his second category. I have altered this at the upper end because Wedgwoods, which he includes in his élite category, had 500 employees in 1841. I have also altered the lower end because 30 to 40 hands is the lower limit cited by the 1862 Children's Employment Commissioner; also, while Burchill and Ross suggest that according to the 1851 census over 60 per cent of the pottery masters employed less than 20 men, the number employed should be raised because it does not appear to include women and children and includes potteries outside North Staffordshire which tended to be smaller.

and china was not only the main industry of the Potteries, but this area was the primary centre of pottery manufacture in Britain as it has continued to be. 'The Potteries provide a remarkable example—probably quite unparalleled in Britain—of an industry the location . . . of which has remained virtually unchanged for two hundred years'.[8] The concentration of the industry in the Potteries depended upon the high quality and variety of the local coal; it could take as much as twelve tons of coal to produce one ton of pottery. In addition, the relatively high value-for-weight of the finished products meant that their transport costs were relatively low. Furthermore, external economies associated with a single location were particularly important. These included employer co-operation in improving transport, sufficient demand for non-pottery firms to develop supporting trades such as flint and colour-grinding, the ability of dealers to visit a variety of producers without extra journeys, and most important a trained labour-force, as labour costs remained stable at approximately 50 per cent of production costs.[9] In 1862, 180 or 82 per cent of the pottery manufactories in Britain and 86 per cent of all persons employed in pottery manufacture lived in this area.[10] Another way of expressing this concentration of the industry both nationally and within the Potteries is to see how far the industry's local labour-force exceeded what one would expect given the industry's national labour-force in a town of that size.[11] Oldham, with twenty-two times more employment in cotton than the national average, has been called a cotton town. In the Potteries there was 156 times more employment in the pottery industry than the national average. The concentration of the industry has implications for migration and population turnover, affecting the availability of family and kin in the local area which will be explored further.

Not only has the concentration of the industry in this area continued, but even the pattern of distribution of the potteries within the district (Map 1.1) remained virtually unchanged from the 1830s until at least the 1950s.[12]

---

[8] S. H. Beaver, 'A Geographical Agenda for North Staffordshire', *N. Staffs. J. of Field Studies* 3 (1963), 8.

[9] For accounts of reasons for the concentration of the industry in the Potteries, see e.g. Weatherill, *Pottery Industry*, 260–3, 394–6, 423; P. W. Gay and R. L. Smyth, *The British Pottery Industry* (London, 1974), 14–15.

[10] Calculated from figures in PP 1863, xviii, 97, 103.

[11] This is calculated by dividing the industry's local ratio of labour-force to population by the national ratio: see Foster, *Class Struggle*, 293.

[12] H. A. Moisley, 'The Industrial and Urban Development of the North Staffordshire Conurbation', *Trans. Instit. Brit. Geog.* 17 (1951), 154–8.

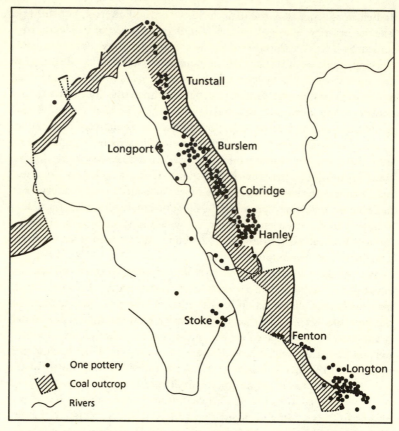

MAP 1.1　The Distribution of Potteries, 1834. Reproduced by permission of Leeds University Library.

Source: Moisley, 'Potteries Coalfield', map XV, plotted from *White's Directory*, 1834.

The potteries grew up in two groups or lines following the coal outcrops and reflecting the overriding importance of proximity to the supply of coal, though still close enough for road or tram haulage to and from a canal for clay and finished goods.[13] The first group included those potteries

---

[13] Ibid. The amount of coal necessary for fine decorated ware requiring repeated firings to set various glazes and colours could reach twelve tons for one ton of ware. The line of potteries on the Burslem–Hanley ridge was oriented along the Black Band outcrop of coal where the best long-flame coal for firing kilns was accessible. The second group of potteries (except for those at Stoke) was aligned along the Newcastle–Derby Road in Fenton and

located along the Burslem–Hanley ridge, the original site of the industry. The second line, lying at an angle to the first, was located along the Newcastle–Derby turnpike road where the number of potteries grew especially rapidly in the late eighteenth and early nineteenth centuries. A few works were built next to the Trent and Mersey Canal in the late nineteenth century and some disappeared from central urban areas, particularly Hanley, where they gave way to commercial buildings, but the distribution of the potteries retained the pattern established by 1830.

The relative distribution of potteries manufacturing differing types of ware also remained virtually unchanged. After the development of bone china in the 1790s, the china industry spread most rapidly in Longton and Fenton in the south-east of the district. The older centres of Burslem and Hanley were thriving on earthenware, while little earthenware was produced in Longton and Fenton. Although subsequently both china and earthenware were made in all six towns, the concentration of china firms in Longton persisted.[14]

During the eighteenth and nineteenth centuries the growth of the six towns closely followed the pattern of distribution of the potteries. Thus, with the lack of change in the location of the potteries, they came to be concentrated within the most closely built up portions of the towns surrounded by the terraced houses of their workers and their families.[15]

Potworks in the mid-nineteenth century tended to be built on a rectangular plan.[16] At the entrance was a porter's lodge and within there were areas 'confusedly mingled' for clay preparation, kilns, and ranges of

Longton where the Black Band coal outcrops again made coal readily available. After 1800 potters used little local clay except for making saggars to contain the ware during firing. Thus, had potteries been sited mainly for the convenience of clay supplies, they would have been built close to the canals and not near the Black Band outcrop. However, relatively few potters moved down from the Burslem–Hanley ridge to a site next to the Trent and Mersey Canal in the Fowlea Valley. There was no coal in the valley, and the marshy conditions discouraged the building of roads. The valley was crossed only in three places by turnpike roads. Where potteries were located near a canal, they coincided with the points where the canal crossed a turnpike road at Longport–Middleport, at Etruria, and at Stoke, or at the point just south of Hanley where the Cauldon Canal crossed the Black Band outcrop of coal and the main north–south road.

[14] Beaver, 'Geographical Agenda', 12, 24; Moisley, 'Potteries Coalfield', maps XV and XVI.

[15] S. H. Beaver, 'The Potteries: A Study in the Evolution of a Cultural Landscape', *Presidential Addresses Delivered to the Institute of British Geographers* (London, 1964), 14; Moisley, 'Industrial Development', 158.

[16] F. Celoria, 'Ceramic Machinery of the 19th Century in the Potteries and in Other Parts of Britain', *Staffs. Arch.* 2 (1973), 14–15. M. I. Nixon, 'The Emergence of the Factory System in the Staffordshire Pottery Industry', Ph.D. thesis (Aston, 1976).

workshops, warehouses and offices arranged either around a quadrangular area or, as in the Copeland and Garrett works in 1843, in

> a labyrinth of passages and courts, intersecting each other at all angles, and bounded by buildings. The buildings are, however, . . . divided into certain groups or compartments, according to the branch of manufacture carried on therein. One of these is the 'dishmakers' square; 'that is, an open area surrounded by buildings, in which the makers of dishes work. Then there are the 'plate-square', the 'saucer-square', the 'coloured-body square', the 'printer's- square', etc, each comprising a court or area encircled by buildings. . . . Altogether there are nearly a hundred and twenty separate workshops, in which people are employed upon almost every variety of pottery and porcelain. There are in different parts of the works seven 'biscuit-ovens', for baking the ware after it has been formed into vessels; fourteen 'glaze-ovens' for firing the ware after the glaze has been applied to it; and sixteen kilns for enamelling and other processes.[17]

Although this was an especially large potworks, it suggests the complexity of organization even in smaller scale potbanks and the highly subdivided process of production of a highly diverse range of products. This in turn led to a large number of separate occupations in a potbank. The Children's Employment Commissioner, for example, listed twenty-eight in 1841.[18]

Nevertheless, the production process in general involved a number of stages during which clay was prepared, shaped, decorated, and fired at least once.[19] During the nineteenth century changes in production methods and machinery were gradually becoming more widespread, in a few branches only after 1870.[20] Moreover, the value of the industry's exports grew, particularly between 1840 and 1873 (Fig. 1.1), the number of persons employed in the industry increased (Fig. 1.2), and wages increased, making potters one of the best-paid groups of industrial workers until 1880.[21]

Not only was a higher proportion of men aged twenty and over employed in pottery manufacture, but it offered 'employment of some kind or other to persons of every age and sex'.[22] In 1861 in the parliamentary borough of Stoke-upon-Trent, however, 52 per cent of the labour-force

---

[17] 'A Day at the Staffordshire Potteries', *Penny Magazine*, 12, no. 716 (Suppl.) (May 1843), 201–8 quoted in Celoria, 'Ceramic Machinery', 15.

[18] PP 1842, xiv, 215.

[19] The division of labour, hiring practices, supervision, and occupational life cycles of the labour-force, closely related to family employment patterns, will be described in detail in Chs. 3 and 4.

[20] Celoria, 'Ceramic Machinery', 11.

[21] Botham, 'Living Standards', 298.   [22] PP 1863, xviii, 97.

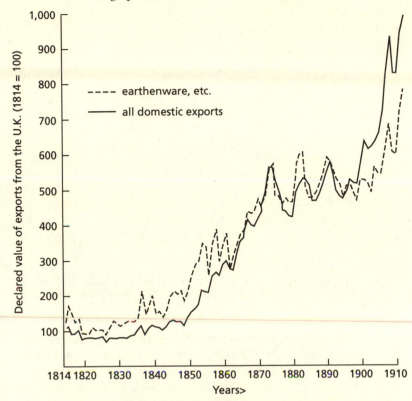

F IG. 1.1   Exports of Earthenware, China, and Stoneware compared with all domestic
exports from the United Kingdom 1814–1910

Sources: figures for Earthenware, China and Stoneware from PP 1821 xvii, 236–7, PP
1824 xvii, 232–3, PP 1826–7 xviii, 46–7, PP 1836 xlvi, 210, PP 1837 xlix, 109,
PP 1837–8 xlvii, 108, PP 1839 xlv, 114, PP 1840 xliii, 136, PP 1841 xxiv, 134,
and Wedgwood, *Staffordshire Pottery*, 213; figures for all domestic exports from
Abst. of Brit. Hist. Stats., 282–4.

employed in pottery manufacture were men aged fifteen and over, 29 per
cent were women aged fifteen and over, and 19 per cent were children
aged seven to fourteen. Moreover, 38 per cent of the employed men were
employed in the pottery industry and 67 per cent of the employed
women and 68 per cent of the employed children worked in the pottery
industry. In the Potteries, as in the cotton-manufacturing town of Preston, a large proportion of the residents depended directly on a single
industry, which offered employment to both men and women. Furthermore, an even larger section of the population worked in the pottery

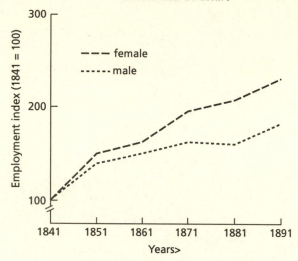

FIG. 1.2   Pottery Industry Employment 1841–1891

Source: Booth's reworking of the census occupational groups for England and Wales
following Armstrong, 'Occupation', in Wrigley, *Nineteenth Century Society*, 261.

industry at some time. In particular, there were men who had worked in
the industry as children but shifted to other occupations, and there were
women who were employed in pottery manufacture as children and
adolescents but who left the industry on marriage. As a result, the aggregate figures of employment at one time in the industry underestimate the
effect of the pottery industry on the lives of people living in this area.

The demand for the labour of children and the lack of Factory Acts in
the pottery industry before the 1860s meant that in the Potteries, unlike
a cotton town such as Preston, it was possible for children under 13 to
obtain employment—a fact which would have particular significance for
children under 13 in families near the poverty-line. In 1861 in the parliamentary borough, 28 per cent of all children aged 10 to 14 were
employed in pottery manufacture, while only 20 per cent of this age-
group was employed in England and Wales as a whole.

The pattern of employment of men over the life cycle has considerable
implications for family structure. Fig. 1.3 shows the proportion of men
in each age-group in the Potteries employed as pottery workers, coal-
miners, and ironworkers, and the proportion of men in each age-group in
Preston employed as cotton-workers. It reveals that there was some
movement of men out of pottery (the main source of demand for child

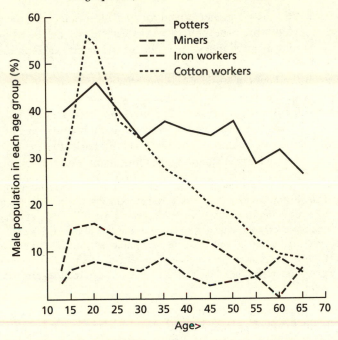

FIG. 1.3   Percentage Distribution by Occupation of Men in Different Age-groups in the Potteries in 1861 (for Potters, Miners, and Ironworkers) and in Preston in 1851 (for Cotton-Workers)

Note: Figures for the Potteries from the Potteries Sample 1861; figures for Preston from Anderson, *Family Structure*, 27.

labour) and into the coal-mines and ironworks or other occupations above the 15–19 age-group. But, there was little movement of men out of the pottery industry after the age of 30, in sharp contrast to the movement of men out of cotton and into labouring and trading after the age of 30 in Preston.[23]

Some pottery-workers probably moved into lower-paying jobs within the industry as they grew older. This was the case with John Finney, who was listed in the Etruria enumerator's book in 1851 as a 'fireman'; in the 1861 enumerator's book he was listed as a 'potter labourer'. Movement to a lower-paying job within the works was also the pattern for puddlers in the iron industry. As long as the figures for pottery workers over 30 years of age do not include many who were not employed but

[23] M. Anderson, *Family Structure in 19th Century Lancashire* (Cambridge, 1971), 25–9.

merely recorded themselves as engaged in their old occupation, then it is safe to conclude that male pottery workers were not forced to find alternative employment as they grew older to the same extent as male cotton-workers.

In general the hours of work in the potteries were from 6.30 a.m. to 6.30 p.m., with one half-hour for breakfast and one hour for dinner, leaving ten-and-a-half hours for work. The hours, however, could be longer if there were pressing orders, and workers in some manufactories observed 'St Monday' by taking an unofficial day off work after the weekend.[24] Except for the firemen attending the kilns, night work was unusual.

The usual hours of work throughout the district . . . are generally from about 6.30 a.m. to 6.30 p.m. On Saturday work ceases in some manufactories at 2 p.m., in other at 4 p.m. In some manufactories work is continued to 7 p.m. on Fridays. These hours, however, are frequently exceeded in the case of pressing orders, on which occasions children as well as adults are employed to 8 or 9 p.m.; and sometimes but I believe rarely, through the whole night. Some of the children are also liable to be worked beyond the usual hours through the irregular habits of the men for whom they work.[25]

Journeymen potters were hired at Martinmas for a year, with a notice of one month in case of either party desiring to be free. In general employment was guaranteed to those with skill and experience. When trade was bad, there would be short-time working or the employer would give his employees more time 'at play', at the time of the Christmas holidays, for example. Fluctuations in trade, such as those in the 1850s, did force some journeymen potters on to outdoor relief, but this only occurred where entire firms had gone out of business. When trade slumped, it was more usual to vary the number of young persons and children employed. In 1862 the Children's Employment Commissioner investigating the potteries observed that the number employed 'particularly those of the young persons and children, are liable to great fluctuation. Probably the above numbers are less than they would be at a time when the trade was not so depressed as it has been during the last year'.[26]

Wages and earnings in the pottery industry, even for the same occupation within the trade, are difficult to discuss because of wide variations

---

[24] For discussion of 'St Monday' see E. P. Thompson, 'Time, Work-Discipline and Industrial Capitalism', *Past and Present*, 38 (1967), 56–97; D. Reid, 'The Decline of St Monday 1766–1876', *Past and Present*, 71 (1976), 76–101; R. Whipp, ' "A Time to Every Purpose": An Essay on Time and Work', in P. Joyce (ed.), *The Historical Meanings of Work* (Cambridge, 1987), 210–36.

[25] PP 1863, xviii, 98.   [26] Ibid. 97.

among sources, the state of trade, deductions, the different pottery towns, firms, type of ware, and the skill of workers. With the exception of children , some slip-makers, warehouse workers, some firemen and placers, modellers, some engravers, and labourers who worked by the day, pottery-workers were paid piece-rates. Unlike textiles, where industry-wide price-lists for piece-work were adopted because conditions were fairly uniform and experience made it possible to make allowance in the list for every possible variation in method, product, and quality, conditions varied so much from factory to factory in the pottery industry that industry-wide price lists for piece-work that allowed for everything would be unmanageably complicated and they certainly did not exist in the mid-nineteenth century.[27] Thus, wage figures in the pottery industry are estimates of average earnings per day or week. Wage figures for the nineteenth century come from a variety of sources, so they cannot be used as indicators of year-to-year changes in wages but only of broad general wage-levels and long-term trends. Allowance must be made for the differences in figures given by employers and workmen in arbitration proceedings. Even the most reliable figures for the period 1855–83, those given in *Labour Statistics: Returns of Wages* (1887), were supplied by various chambers of commerce and private firms, making it likely that the more reputable firms are over-represented, in which case the average wages given would be relatively high. Whatever the wage-rate, the earnings of pottery-workers were subject to fluctuations with changes in the state of trade. The National Association for the Promotion of Social Science, for example, reported in 1860 that the scale of piece-work prices for that year would make wage-labour

30s per week, if the trade is brisk; but the potters' trade seems to be liable to great fluctuations, and hands are often left idle for two or three days in the week, so much so that one operative calculates the average wages actually earned during the last seven years to be not so high as 18s., if more than 16s. per week.[28]

Looking at the fluctuations in exports in the 1850s in Fig. 1.1, these variations in wages are not surprising. With the steady increase in exports in the 1860s and early 1870s fluctuations in earnings probably diminished, reappearing again in the late 1870s. Wages varied too, with

[27] H. Clay, 'Pottery Operatives' Wages: A Note on the Systematisation of Wages', in W. H. Warburton, *The History of Trade Union Organization in the North Staffordshire Potteries* (London, 1931), 249.

[28] Nat'l. Assoc. for the Promotion of Social Science, *Report of the Committee on Trade Societies and Strikes* (London, 1860), 281.

deductions for such things as machinery, artificial light, and attendants, although most wage figures purport to be net wages. There were also variations in wages geographically. Longton, for example, was a low-wage area. And there were variations among firms, with manufacturers of high-quality ware such as Mintons usually paying high wages. Finally, there was variation in wages within the same occupation depending on the type of ware produced, with quality ware, sanitary, jet, and rockingham ware being more highly paid.

Despite the variations, wages in the pottery industry in 1841 were 'considered to be the best of any staple trade in the Kingdom',[29] and there were general advances in piece-rates in the following years: 5–10 per cent in 1850–2; 10 per cent in 1866; 8.5 per cent on average in 1872. Some of the gains were offset by the increase in the cost of assistants due to competition for labour from coal-mining and ironworks and the extension of the Factory Acts to the pottery industry. In 1879 there was a reduction in piece-rates of 8.5 per cent, the so-called 'Hatherton penny', and they remained at the reduced level until 1900.[30] In the early 1860s, however, approximately 90 per cent of the adult men employed in the pottery industry earned 20s. or more per week; and those who earned less earned only slightly less. This is in sharp contrast to the cotton industry where only 50 per cent of the adult men earned 20s. or more and the rest earned not more than 15s. per week.[31] Also, it is a higher proportion than that in either the coal or iron trade in North Staffordshire in 1877, as will be seen below. In pottery manufacture boys began at a wage of 2s. to 3s. 6d. per week at age 13 or 14 for two years, and then they worked at a journeyman's wage but with a deduction of one-third to one-half to the employer. Boys 12 years and under earned 1s. 6d. to 3s. per week in the potteries. Women could earn 9s. to 10s. per week or more with overtime, while girls beginning at age 10 earned 1s. per week for their first three years.[32]

Iron Manufacture and Coal-Mining

Ironworks and coal-mines also were interspersed among the six towns, and the census enumerators in 1861 and 1871 attributed the increase in population in a number of townships within the parliamentary borough of Stoke-upon-Trent to the 'establishment of blast furnaces, forges, etc.'

[29] PP 1843, xiv, 216. Moreover, the rates reported were those which prevailed 'during an extraordinary depression of the trade'.
[30] I am grateful to Dr Frank Botham for the use of these figures from his research.
[31] Anderson, *Family Structure*, 23.　　[32] PP 1863, xviii, 102.

and 'the development of the collieries of the district' as well as to 'the prosperous state of the pottery trade'.[33] Unlike the potteries, however, the ironworks and mines in the area were not concentrated almost exclusively within the boundary of the parliamentary borough of Stoke-upon-Trent. Instead, ironworks and mines were spread more widely over the North Staffordshire coalfield (Map 1.2).

The presence of coking coal and two varieties of ironstone (clayband and blackband)[34] within the North Staffordshire coalfield provided the mineral basis for the development of the iron industry in the region from the second half of the eighteenth century. Four groups of blast furnaces came into existence at different periods in different areas (Map 1.2).[35] The first group began in 1768 with the initial furnace at Apedale. This group was located in the western region of the coalfield, where seams of coking coal and clayband ironstone were accessible on or near the surface. Other furnaces followed in this western belt at Silverdale and Kidsgrove, but ironmasters encountered numerous difficulties and the industry did not expand.[36] The second group of furnaces was established in the 1820s and 1830s in the south-eastern part of the coalfield near Fenton and Longton. Here, too, there were outcrops of coking coal and clayband ironstone. The successful demonstration of the use of blackband ores in iron manufacture in Scotland encouraged the mining of blackband ironstone[37] and the establishment of the third group of furnaces in the Fowlea Valley adjacent to the Trent and Mersey Canal and subsequently to the railway. Earl Granville began to build his first three blast-furnaces at Shelton in 1839 and other ironmasters followed with furnaces near

[33] PP 1862, l, 497; PP 1872, lxvi, pt. 2, 323.

[34] Both varieties are coal-measures ironstone. The 'clayband' ironstone occurred in 'thin seams or beds of nodules from a few inches to a few feet in thickness' within coal seams. Their iron content varied from 25–40 per cent. In contrast, the 'blackband' iron ores generally overlay different coal seams (those in the Black Band Group), and the seams of iron ore were thicker (one to six feet thick) with a higher iron content (initially 40 per cent but with calcination the figure could be doubled). The Potteries coalfield was the only one outside Scotland to have large quantities of blackband ores: Beaver, 'Potteries', 7. Moreover, one observer noted in 1855 that 'the coalfield contains a larger number of ironstone measures than any other': R. Hunt, *Mineral Statistics of the United Kingdom 1855–1881* (London, 1855–82), 45.

[35] Beaver, 'Potteries', 17.

[36] Among the problems were lack of capital, bad management, labour supply, accidents, and transport. See A. Birch, *The Economic History of the British Iron and Steel Industry 1784–1879* (London, 1967), 99–103.

[37] Before the realization of its value, blackband ironstone had been used to repair roads in the Potteries: J. Hedley, 'Mines and Mining in the North Staffordshire Coal Field', *Trans. N. of Eng. Instit. of Min. Eng.* 2 (1854), 245.

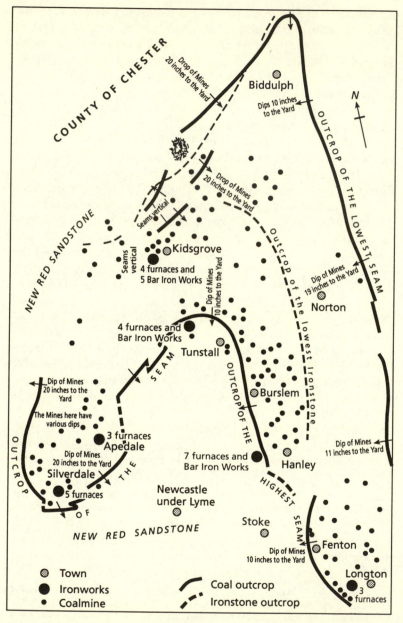

MAP 1.2 The Distribution of Ironworks and Coal-mines in North Staffordshire, 1854
Source: J. Hedley, 'Mines and Mining', insert.

Fɪɢ. 1.4   Pig Iron Output from North Staffordshire and Great Britain 1854–1900
Source: *Abst. of Brit. Hist. Stats.*, 131–2.

Tunstall at Goldendale beginning in 1840 and at Ravensdale beginning
in 1846. The fourth group of furnaces were established in the early 1860s
on the eastern side of the coalfield in the Biddulph Valley and at Norton
after the opening of the branch railway up the Foxley Valley in 1859.

The period from the early 1840s to the early 1870s was one of rapid
expansion in the manufacture of iron in North Staffordshire. The number
of blast-furnaces increased from seven in 1839 to nineteen in 1849 to
thirty-nine in the 1870s.[38] The output of pig iron also grew rapidly in the
1850s and 1860s, increasing at a faster rate than the output of pig iron in
the country as a whole (Fig. 1.4). Although ironworks in North Staffordshire included only 5 per cent of the blast-furnaces (6 per cent of the
furnaces in blast) in Britain and produced only 5 per cent of the country's output of pig iron in 1870,[39] a contemporary described it as 'without
doubt one of the most rising iron centres in the country'.[40] Much of the

[38] *VCH*, ii, 131; Birch, *Iron and Steel Industry*, 390; S. Griffiths, *Griffiths' Guide to the Iron Trade*, new edn. with introd. by W. K. Gale (1st edn., 1873; new edn., 1967), 256.
[39] Calculated from Hunt, *Mineral Statistics 1870*, 77, 81.
[40] Griffiths, *Guide*, 114.

TABLE 1.2   *Manufacturers of Pig Iron in North Staffordshire 1861*

Works	Owners	Approx. no. of assoc. collieries	Blast furnaces No.	Puddling furnaces No.	Rolling mills No.
Shelton	Earl Granville	5	8	60	6
Silverdale	Stanier	3.5	4	50	5
Biddulph	Robert Heath	5.5	3	29	3
Goldendale	Williamson Bros.	5	4	0	0
Apedale	J. E. Heathcote	6	4	0	0
Clough Hall	Kinnersley	5	4	0	0
Longton	W. H. Sparrow	3	3	0	0
Fenton Park	Lawton & Co.	3	2	0	0

Source: Hunt, *Mineral Statistics 1861*, 38–9, 66, 73, 85.

pig iron was exported to South Staffordshire, but there were puddling furnaces and rolling mills in North Staffordshire and their numbers also grew rapidly during the 1860s.[41]

Each of the eight firms manufacturing pig iron in North Staffordshire in 1861 was vertically integrated backwards with collieries, and three of them were integrated forwards with puddling furnaces and rolling mills (see Table 1.2). By the mid-1860s the number of furnaces and mills had increased and several of the puddling furnaces were independent of blast-furnaces.[42]

Two of the firms in North Staffordshire are of particular interest. Robert Heath expanded his firm especially rapidly in the 1860s. In 1867 he employed 3,500 men and boys,[43] and by 1872 it was not only the largest iron-making concern employing the greatest number of men in Staffordshire, but it was also the largest maker of ships' anchors in the country. The firm controlled the Norton, Biddulph Valley, and Ravensdale ironworks and included twenty-eight coal and ironstone mines, eight blast-furnaces, 144 puddling furnaces, and fourteen rolling mills.[44] Earl Granville's ironworks were the largest in North Staffordshire in 1861 (Table 1.2). Although by 1872 he had slightly fewer puddling furnaces

[41] In 1861 there were 139 puddling furnaces and 14 rolling mills; by 1866 there were 554 puddling furnaces and 54 rolling mills: Hunt, *Mineral Statistics 1861*, 85; *1866*, 77.
[42] Beaver, 'Potteries', 17.   [43] PP 1867–8, xxxix, 129.
[44] Griffiths, *Guide*, 114–16; Beaver, 'Potteries', 17–18.

and rolling mills than Heath's firm,[45] his ironworks at Shelton included eight blast-furnaces, the largest group of blast-furnaces in a single location in North Staffordshire, and the entire works was concentrated in a relatively small area of Hanley and Shelton in the midst of the Potteries. By 1867 1,500 men worked in Earl Granville's mines and ironworks. The Shelton works were renowned for their iron plates used in the Thames, Clyde, and other shipbuilding centres, as well as iron for rails, for engine shops, and for machinists in Manchester and Tyneside.[46]

The North Staffordshire coalfield[47] is roughly triangular in shape with its apex pointing north (Map 1.2); outcrops of the rich Middle Coal Measures[48] protrude both along the western edge of the coalfield and along the eastern side in a line roughly coinciding with the line of the six towns.[49] The coalfield is relatively small in area, covering roughly 110 square miles, but it is distinguished by the thickness and variety of its workable coal seams, as well as by the associated clay and ironstone deposits mentioned previously. The coalfield includes thirty-six seams of coal one-and-a-half feet and over in thickness with an aggregate of roughly 144 feet of coal.[50] In 1862 it was estimated to be in aggregate twenty-five feet thicker than any other British coalfield.[51] One contemporary calculated that at the rate of output for the year 1870, the North Staffordshire coalfield could supply coal for the next 1,246 years.[52] In addition to the overall thickness of its workable seams, the existence in the nineteenth century of a great variety of types of high-quality coal serving many different purposes characterized the coalfield. As well as the 'long-flame'

[45] 94 puddling furnaces and seven rolling mills, though Earl Granville also had extensive coal- and ironstone mines. Griffiths, *Guide*, 117.

[46] Griffiths, *Guide*, 116–18; PP 1867–8, xxxix, 111.

[47] Four coalfields—the Potteries, Cheadle, Goldstitch Moss, and Shaffalong—make up the North Staffordshire coalfield, but the Potteries coalfield is pre-eminent, *VCH*, ii, 70. It is the Potteries coalfield that is described here and referred to as the North Staffordshire coalfield.

[48] The coal measures are divided into the Upper, Middle, and Lower Coal Measures. The Upper series lack profitable coal; the Middle Coal Measures are approximately 4,000 feet thick and contain most of the workable coal; there are some seams of workable coal in the Lower Coal Measures: R. Meade, *The Coal and Iron Industries of the U.K.* (London, 1882), 140.

[49] For descriptions of the coalfield, see among others: J. Hedley, 'Mines and Mining', 242–3; Meade, *Coal and Iron Industries*, 140–5; H. S. Jevons, *The British Coal Trade* (1st pub. London, 1915; Newton Abbot, 1969), 90–1; W. Gibson, *The Geology of the Country Around Stoke-upon-Trent* (London, 1925); Moisley, 'Industrial Development', 151; Beaver, 'Potteries', 1–7; *VCH*, ii, 70–1.

[50] Estimates of the aggregate thickness vary from 140 to 147 ft.; estimates of the number of seams vary to a similar extent. Here I am using the figures in Jevons, *Coal Trade*.

[51] *VCH*, ii, 70.   [52] Meade, *Coal and Iron Industries*, 152.

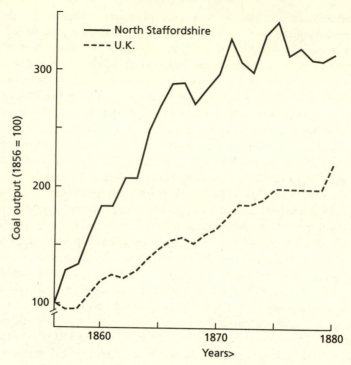

F IG. 1.5   Coal Output from North Staffordshire and the UK 1856–1880.
Sources: Hunt, *Mineral Stats.*, 1856–61; Meade, *Coal*, 146; *Abst. of Brit. Hist. Stats.*, 115.

coals used in pottery manufacture and coking coals for iron manufacture
and gas manufacture, there were suitable coals for railway fuel and domestic use. Numerous faults and steep–pitching, sometimes nearly vertical, seams, however, were also characteristic of the coalfield, making the
expansion of mining hazardous and expensive compared with the easy
accessibility of the coal seams in South Staffordshire.

Initially, the development of the North Staffordshire coalfield was
relatively gradual. Coal-mining grew along with the increasing demand
from pottery manufacturers, domestic users, and small industrial concerns. In 1840 output was hundreds of thousands rather than millions of
tons. Between 1840 and 1875, however, the growth in demand for coal
from the expanding ironworks in North Staffordshire played a large part
in encouraging the transformation of the coal industry. Output from the
coal-mines trebled between 1856 and 1870 (Fig. 1.5). Moreover, by 1871

43 per cent of the output went into iron manufacture, compared with 23 per cent in 1860.[53]

As a result of the physical characteristics of the coalfield, increased output in North Staffordshire was obtained largely through the deeper and more intensive working of the existing field rather than by extending mining to new areas as happened in the Black Country; moreover, increased output meant larger enterprises. Between 1856 and 1870, when output trebled, the number of working collieries declined from 123 to 109.[54] In 1872 Earl Granville's Deep Pit at Hanley was 1,530 feet deep and reputedly the deepest pit in the Midlands.[55] The process of expansion is reflected starkly in the explosion in 1866 which killed ninety-one miners in the North Stafford Coal and Iron Company's pit at Talk-o'th'-Hill near Kidsgrove and Tunstall. From the inquest it emerged that, although the pit had existed for some time, the company had been formed only two or three years before the explosion; furthermore, the recent deepening of the pit without adequate ventilation played a significant role in causing the explosion.[56] By 1880 there had been eight major explosions in the coalfield resulting in the deaths of 285 men and boys.[57] During this period there was also an increase in the vertical integration of collieries with ironmaking firms, thereby tying mining closely to fluctuations in the iron industry.[58] Even as early as 1861, iron-making firms owned 36 out of 128, or 28 per cent of all the collieries in the district. By 1874 approximately 32 per cent of the 157 collieries were owned by iron manufacturers.[59]

Because, as mentioned above, the increased output of coal in North Staffordshire meant deeper and more intensive working of the existing field rather than extending mining to new areas, the pattern of distribution of collieries within the coalfield changed little during the mid-nineteenth-century period of expansion. Map 1.2 indicates the pattern of distribution of collieries in 1854, and Table 1.3 presents the number of collieries in each district. Although there was a substantial number of collieries within the boundaries of the parliamentary borough of Stoke-upon-Trent, many of those listed in the Tunstall, Burslem, Hanley, and

---

[53] *VCH*, ii, 79–81; the calculations of the proportion of the output of coal which was destined for iron manufacture are based on figures in Meade, *Coal and Iron Industries*, 146–7.

[54] *VCH*, ii, 81.   [55] Ibid. 83.   [56] PP 1867, xvi, 251–81.

[57] *VCH*, ii, 93.   [58] Ibid. 83.

[59] Hunt, *Mineral Statistics 1861*, 38–9, 85; *1874*, 100, 231–3.

TABLE 1.3   *The Number of Collieries in Districts within
North Staffordshire 1861*

District	No. of collieries
Cheadle	17
Longton	24
Hanley	12
Burslem	18
Tunstall	17
Biddulph	12
Newcastle-under-Lyme	28
TOTAL	128

Longton districts were located just outside the limits of the parliamentary borough to the north and east.

Employment for men in the ironworks and collieries increased as they expanded throughout the period. Girls and women were not employed in ironworks or on coalpit banks in North Staffordshire,[60] nor were there many boys aged 12 or under employed in either the mines or ironworks.

Although the numbers were not large, there were a few boys under the age of 12 employed in the ironworks, and there is evidence that this occurred in cases of need. William Mathews testified with reference to North Staffordshire that very few boys are employed under 12 years of age 'and only those few in cases where, as far as my knowledge goes, the mother or some portion of the family is dependent upon the boy's wages and then there is sympathy on the part of the employer leading him to employ the boy'.[61]

The hours of work in the ironworks and coal-mines in North Staffordshire were not subject to extension because of pressing orders as they were in the potteries; however, both included night work. In the blast-furnaces, mills, and forges there were two shifts: 6 a.m. to 6 p.m.; and 6 p.m. to 6 a.m., with one-half hour for one meal and an hour for a second meal on each shift. The turns changed from day to night and vice versa every other week.[62] Some firms worked seven days a week, although others stopped work on Sundays. The coal-mines also had a night turn

---

[60] PP 1867–8, xiv, 124.   [61] PP 1866, xiv, 415.   [62] PP 1864, xxii, 350.

and a day turn, though the hours worked within each varied with the work allotted.[63] Five days' work per week was the yearly average in 1866 in North Staffordshire. William Mathews testified that

I should think that five days a week was quite as much as could be reckoned upon throughout the year; what with shortness of trade in the summer, accidents in the pit, and the disinclination of workmen to work on Mondays, and from various other causes, I should think that even in the best regulated collieries five days a week would be the maximum on which you could reckon all the year round.[64]

Wages in the coal-mines and ironworks were lower than those of men in the pottery industry on average. As mentioned above, the 90 per cent of adult men employed in the pottery industry earning 20s. or more per week in the early 1860s, with those who earned less earning only slightly less, is a higher proportion than that in either the coal or iron trade in North Staffordshire in 1877. Yet, a larger proportion of ironworkers earned higher wages than adult male potters; though a higher proportion of ironworkers also earned less. Adult male coal-miners also earned less on average than journeymen potters. Furthermore, although a journeyman potter could eventually earn more than a miner and many of the ironworkers, he was older when he reached his maximum earnings. Adolescents or 'lads' between 13 and 18 years of age who were employed in collieries or ironworks earned twice as much as those employed in the potteries. The few boys aged 12 and under who worked in the ironworks and coal-mines in North Staffordshire in 1865 earned 5s., 6s., and 7s. a week, which again was substantially more than the 1s. 6d. to 3s. per week earned by boys 12 years and younger in the potteries.[65]

Other Employment

In addition to firms manufacturing china and earthenware, there were flint- and bone-grinding mills, several works engaged in preparing colours or boracic acid for glazes, and engravers and crate-makers who were dependent directly on the pottery industry. Large firms would include these occupations within their works, but there were numerous smaller firms which did not.

---

[63] PP 1867, xvi, 260–1, 264, 274. Some colliers, such as Daniel Brownsword and Thomas Turnock, started the day turn at 5 a.m. and others, such as James Withshaw and John Condliff, at 5.30 a.m., others, including Francis Seabridge, at 6 a.m.; others ended work at 2 a.m. and some were still in the pit at 5.30 a.m. having worked through the night.
[64] PP 1866, xiv, 417.   [65] PP 1863, xviii, 102.

Other industries in the parliamentary borough in 1861 were on a smaller scale than pottery, coal, or iron. There were brick and tile works, a paper-mill which supplied tissue paper for the engraving process in the pottery industry, and a small engineering works owned by the same company which made paper-manufacturing machinery for a wider market. There was a railway engine works at Fenton and a number of engineering works. The British Gas Works main works were located in the Fowlea Valley. There was a copperas works (sulphur crystals were obtained by exposing iron pyrites to the action of sun and rain), and a naphtha factory which contributed unpleasant smells to the atmosphere of the area.

Although employment in the parliamentary borough depended on its industries and mines, in particular the fortunes of the pottery industry and increasingly the iron industry, a sophisticated trading structure overlay the industrial base, with Hanley serving as the commercial centre for the region.[66] A large number of shopkeepers were one-man or one-woman businesses; for example, beerhouses, provision shops, or boot- and shoe-makers were scattered throughout working-class districts, and there were butchers, potato, fruit, and vegetable dealers, and boot- and shoe-makers who were tenants of market stalls in Hanley and Burslem. In addition, there were a number of individuals with double occupations and there were some itinerant salesmen and hawkers. At the other end of the social scale, there were drapers' shops employing several assistants and attracting customers from surrounding towns. These shopkeepers were reasonably affluent and considered themselves socially removed from beerhouse owners. In addition, there were a number of professional persons and clergymen. Although the professional and clerical section was smaller than that in England and Wales as a whole, it had increased since 1851. Finally, there was a substantial proportion of the labour-force who were 'labourers' of various kinds, and would probably only have obtained casual irregular employment.

For those women who did not work in the potteries, the largest single occupation was domestic service. A significant number were milliners, dressmakers, and seamstresses, probably making a few shillings to supplement family income. Another group, probably the poorest of all, were the charwomen, washerwomen, and laundresses who made up 2 per cent of the female population over 20 years of age.[67]

---

[66] W. E. Townley, 'Urban Administration and Health: A Case Study of Hanley in the Mid-19th Century', M.A. thesis (Keele, 1969), 24–6.

[67] PP 1863, liii, pt. 2, 498, 502, 506.

2. Poverty in the Potteries

Although the previous section suggests that the wages of potters were relatively high, it is still possible that there was extensive poverty in the parliamentary borough. There is general agreement that 'poverty and the prospect of poverty were the biggest problems which working families had to face',[68] though opinions differ about the nature of the influence of poverty on family structure.[69] Therefore, it is necessary to outline in this section the extent of poverty and the experience of families in different stages of the life cycle in the Potteries.

For as many families as possible in the Potteries sample (78 per cent of the families headed by married couples) I calculated a family standard of living for a family of that size. Details of the procedure for calculating family standards of living in the Potteries are set out in the Methodological Appendix at the end of the book. This measure of the extent to which a family had the income necessary to purchase a minimum amount of food, clothing, and housing defines poverty, not in terms of overall well-being, but as a lack of food, clothing, and housing. Moreover, it gives an indication of the extent of primary poverty (i.e. those families unable to afford the minimum however carefully they spent their income) but not of secondary poverty (i.e. those families who did not in fact get the minimum due to illness, unemployment, debt, or 'misspent' income).[70]

In Table 1.4 the results from the Potteries sample are compared with those for Preston, and in Fig. 1.6 they are broken down by life-cycle stage and again compared with the results for Preston. Three points emerge from these results. First, overall, there was less primary poverty in the Potteries in the mid-nineteenth century than there was in Preston. In the Potteries 9 per cent of the family units headed by married couples for which data could be obtained were on or below the poverty-line, compared with 20 per cent in Preston. Even if the poverty-line is extended to include families less than 4s. above it the difference between the two areas remains (17 per cent in the Potteries, 31 per cent in Preston). Conversely, there is a higher percentage of families 20s. or more above the poverty-line in the Potteries (24 per cent) than in Preston (14 per cent).

Second, when the overall results are broken down by life-cycle stage, the percentage of families below the poverty-line in life-cycle stage three with most dependent children was not as great in the Potteries (26 per

[68] Foster, *Class Struggle*, 255.
[69] Anderson, *Family Structure*, 166–7.   [70] Foster, *Class Struggle*, 258.

TABLE 1.4   *Relationship of Weekly Family Income to the Poverty-Line: Nuclear Families Headed by Married Couples (for whom data were adequate), Potteries Sample 1861, Preston 1851 (%)*

	Potteries 1861	Preston[a] 1851
4*s*. or more below	4	9
less than 4*s*. above or below	13	22
4*s*.–11*s*. 11*d* above	30	32
12*s*.–19*s*. 11*d*. above	29	22
20*s*. or more above	24	14
N	960	470

[a] Figures for Preston from Anderson, *Family Structure*, 31.
Note: the 'relationship of the weekly family income to the poverty line' = the family standard of living for each nuclear family. The aggregate income was calculated for each nuclear family headed by a married couple where the income of all family members could be estimated from the figures for the earnings of the different occupations (assuming a full week's work). Information was sufficient for incomes to be calculated for 78% of the families headed by married couples in the Potteries sample. Income from lodgers was ignored and it was assumed that co-residing children gave all their income to the family. The minimum standard of family expenditure was based on Rowntree's scale of primary poverty expenditure as used by Anderson (*Family Structure*, 201) but adjusted for lower rents in the Potteries. See the Methodological Appendix at the end of the book for further information regarding the procedure used to calculate the family standards of living for the Potteries Sample 1861.

cent) as in Preston (52 per cent). But the pattern over the life cycle in both areas is the same, and it follows the poverty cycle known in all societies and well known to contemporaries.[71]

Thus, and this is the third point, in the Potteries as in Preston, few families could save to meet temporary losses in income, so that even short or comparatively minor crises could cause destitution.

3. Sanitary Conditions and Housing

Although the previous section suggests that a higher proportion of families were above the poverty-line in the Potteries than in Preston, there is no automatic correlation between income and public health.[72] Living

[71] Anderson, *Family Structure*, 31.
[72] M. W. Flinn, 'Introduction', in M. W. Flinn (ed.), *Report on the Sanitary Condition of the Labouring Population of Great Britain* (Edinburgh, 1965), 4.

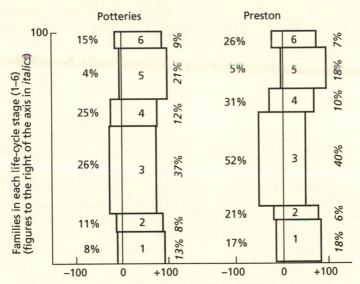

Potteries   Preston

Families in each life-cycle stage (1–6)
(figures to the right of the axis in *italics*)

Percentage of families in poverty, i.e. less than 4s. above
the poverty line (figures on the left of the axis)

FIG. 1.6   Poverty and the Family Life Cycle: Nuclear Families Headed by Married
Couples (for whom data were adequate): Potteries Sample 1861, Preston 1851

Life-cycle stages:
1. Wife under 45, no children at home;
2. Wife under 45, one child under 1 year at home;
3. Children at home, but none in employment;
4. Children at home, and some, but under half, in employment;
5. Children at home, and half or over in employment;
6. Wife over 45, no children or only children over the age of 20 at home.

Note: Figures for Preston from Anderson, *Family Structure* 31, 202 n.; the analysis parallels
Anderson. For the method used to calculate the relationship between families and the
poverty-line (i.e. the family standards of living) in the Potteries Sample 1861 see the note
to Table 1.4.

conditions deleterious to health were not incompatible with relatively
high real incomes. Other conditions which mattered to health included
both the supply of basic amenities (such as water, paving, street cleaning,
and sanitation) and housing. In this section, therefore, I shall survey
briefly these conditions in the Potteries in the mid-nineteenth century.

    The population of the parliamentary borough of Stoke-upon-Trent
grew rapidly from the beginning of the nineteenth century up to 1861.[73]

[73] The population of the parliamentary borough grew from 23,278 in 1801 to 84,027 in
1851, and 101,507 in 1861.

The size of the population of the parliamentary borough more than trebled between 1801 and 1851, resulting in an increase that was comparable to that in Lancashire towns such as Burnley, Ashton, Blackburn, Stockport, Rochdale, Bolton, and Bury, but never reaching the 70 per cent increase in ten years recorded in West Bromwich between 1831 and 1841 nor the 50 per cent increase in Preston in the same period. Between 1801 and 1851 the population of the parliamentary borough was growing at decennial rates consistently above 20 per cent and consistently greater than the rate of increase in England and Wales and the county of Staffordshire.

Public health problems grew with the growth of population. Predictably, the immediate effects of the increase in population of the Potteries are reflected in the 1850s in the deteriorating sanitary conditions described in the reports of the General Board of Health Inspectors, and many of them formed the subject-matter of the controversies over the reform of the organization of local government in the various Potteries towns.[74]

Street drainage, smoke, water supply, graveyards, food adulteration, subsidence, and house drainage posed problems for public health in the area. Throughout the period drainage was a problem despite the natural advantage of the elevated location of Tunstall, Burslem, and Hanley, in particular, on heavy clay soil. Not until the 1850s and 1860s did the towns begin to exploit this natural advantage with a system of underground drains to carry off surplus rain-water or sewage to the river.[75] Many streets were unpaved and 'the mulch of the roads is blackened blacker by the droppings from the jolting coal carts which pass along the thoroughfares to the manufactories'.[76]

Not only did a pall of smoke from the potworks and houses hang over the district but the smoke and fumes of sulphur from copperas works, a naphtha manufactory, and especially from the calcination of iron ore contributed to the dense atmosphere. The chairman of the Burslem Board of Health in 1857 remarked that 'not only owners of land, but gentlemen who have had residences in the immediate vicinity of the ironworks, have been driven away in consequence of the offensiveness of the calcining of ironstone'.[77]

Until the 1820s water came from wells. But mines affected the underground drainage resulting in the drying up of wells and at one time water

[74] Townley, 'Urban Administration'.
[75] Ibid. 77; *VCH*, viii, 96, 127, 159, 196, 216, 236.
[76] Owen, *Staffs. Potter*, 33.   [77] PP 1857, sess. 2, xi, 770.

was available only three days a week.[78] In 1847, however, the Staffordshire Potteries Waterworks Company was established to supplement the wells. By 1850 water was generally available, though its purity varied. The reporter for the *Morning Chronicle* observed in 1850 that

the water supply of Hanley and the surrounding districts is partly derived from wells, partly from the North Staffordshire Waterworks Company which conducts the water in its pipes from springs welling out in the high moorland ranges near Leek. Stand taps are common in the poorer localities, the charge to each cottage benefiting by them being generally 2*d*. a week. I presume that the inhabitants are not very punctual with their rates; for in several instances, in the course of my wanderings through back courts and unpaved alleys, I found the supply 'cut off'. In many cases, however, the ingenious defaulters, fertile in expedients, had managed to perforate the leaden pipe. Or partially to wrench open the metal lips at the place where the sides of the tube had been crushed together, and so to ensure a small but continuous dribble. In one instance the pipe had either burst or been broken below ground, and so furnished the supply of a small well which came bubbling up, not in the clearest condition, in the centre of a muddy unpaved court. The regular wells seemed to me for the most part forbidding receptacles for mere surface water. Those sunk deeper and provided with pumps yielded a somewhat purer supply.[79]

The overcrowded state of graveyards attracted public attention. For example, in Tunstall in 1856 restrictions were placed on burials in the churchyard, and in 1867 burials were restricted further. A new cemetery was opened in 1868. In Fenton, too, there were restrictions placed on burials in 1856, but the new cemetery was not laid out until 1887.[80]

Food adulteration was a problem, though for bread it was circumvented by public ovens. The *Morning Chronicle* reporter commented in 1850 that

public bakeries are common throughout the Potteries, and are mostly open at fixed hours every day. A great proportion of the bread consumed is home-made, and baked at these ovens. The charge for baking is generally 1*d*. a lot—the lot to consist of not more than four quartern loaves. I was told that it was only the most improvident among the working classes who purchased their bread at the bakers. Home-baking insures a cheaper and a more unadulterated article.[81]

Although there were also problems with sanitation and some housing, in general housing conditions in the Potteries were comparatively good in the 1850s and 1860s.

---

[78] Townley, 'Urban Administration', 78.   [79] *Morn. Chron.* 25 Jan. 1850, 5.
[80] *VCH*, viii, 96, 197.   [81] *Morn. Chron.* 28 Jan. 1850, 5.

As mentioned in the first section of this chapter, the towns grew up with the potteries in a chain of six relatively compact areas within the parliamentary borough. Thus, although the parliamentary borough was larger in area than the town of Preston (13.3 sq. miles vs. 4.4 sq. miles), it contained six relatively compact towns, each with a central core of civic and commercial buildings and a surrounding area of dense housing interspersed with potbanks, together with arms of similar development extending north and south towards adjacent towns. Even from the centre of the most densely populated town, it was less than half a mile to open countryside.

The central commercial areas were noted for their broad well-tended streets, numerous shops, and extensive market buildings. In the centre of Hanley there remained two extensive open spaces—Crown Bank and Market Square—both capable of holding large crowds on public occasions. Moreover, there were a relatively large number of public buildings, particularly town halls, erected in the 1840s, 1850s, and 1860s.[82] Despite its recent origins, however, the combination of the classical architecture of the public buildings and two-storey brick shops tightly hemmed in by surrounding potbanks and houses created a final impression of haphazard growth and variety of style.

Nevertheless, the broad paved streets with some elegant buildings in the central commercial areas of the towns, were in distinct contrast to the surrounding areas, where small terraced houses with minute backyards intermingled with potbanks eschewing any separation of housing and industrial development. The reporter for the *Morning Chronicle* described the muddle of small houses, unmade streets, and belching kilns with chapels, shops, and public houses here and there in this area of the towns.

Everywhere there stretch out labyrinths of small, undistinguished, unpaved streets, the houses generally of two stories in height, and built of smoke-grimed brick. Here you will find a new row of cottages the uniformity of the walls slightly broken by stone facings; hard by may be a cluster of old-fashioned houses with lead-latticed windows, and perhaps some attempt to cause ivy to train up the wall. Every few steps bring you in sight of a plain brown brick chapel—a Sion, or Ebenezer of Bethesda . . . and I have repeatedly seen localities in the Potteries where every fourth or fifth house was in a tavern. Diverge from the main thoroughfares—into regions of back yards and little gardens and outhouses, and waste patches belonging to pottery establishments—and you will find yourself in

---

[82] *VCH*, viii, 85, 112–13, 149, 182, 210, 228.

a curious chaos of old tumble-down sheds, littered with crates, broken crockery ware, and straw—of walls and lean-tos, built of old 'saggars' . . . diversified here and there by brick pits, clay pits, smoking engine houses, and great coal heaps, dismal wastes of muddy ground, more or less strewn with the eternal pavement of broken stoneware, the whole landscape enlivened by glimpses of barges deeply laden with piled up clay or flints, lying by wharfs, or slowly moving along the narrow canals.[83]

Near the centres of the towns, in particular, there were some congested areas where pockets of cottages had been hemmed in by potworks and later buildings. There was one area in Burslem known as the 'Hell Hole' and several areas in Hanley, Stoke, Fenton, and Longton with shared, rarely emptied privies and ash-pits which were singled out for their overcrowding and unsanitary conditions in 1850 in Robert Rawlinson's Report to the Board of Health. Furthermore, even good houses were subject to subsidence as the surface collapsed into deserted mine-workings. An observer in 1850

saw in Hanley and Shelton many crushed and deserted dwellings; in some cases contiguous houses leaning away from each other, and in others smashed down lintels and riven walls. I was told that in more instances than one, these movements of the earth had been productive of most afflicting consequences to honest and industrious workmen, who had invested their hard earned savings in small building speculations, and whose property was thus virtually destroyed.[84]

Despite the pockets of poor housing, unsanitary conditions, and danger of subsidence, there was a larger and better quality supply of housing in the Potteries in the mid-nineteenth century than in other industrial areas including the town of Preston, where there was a 'severe housing shortage' in 1851. In 1861 there were more 'uninhabited houses' and 'housing building' listed in the published census for the Potteries than for Preston in 1851. There were no inhabited cellars and few back-to-back houses in the Potteries. Most of the housing in 1861 was less than sixty years old (though Etruria was an exception) and it had been built on new streets laid out on largely open ground. Unlike Preston—an important market town and port before the cotton trade came to dominate the town—the Potteries had a relatively small legacy of sub-standard cottages laid out in courts and squares and scarcely any middle-class houses taken over as tenements by poorer workers.

Rents for a typical house were 2*s.* to 3*s.* a week, or about 10 per cent of the weekly wages of a journeyman potter in full work. Houses were

[83] *Morn. Chron.* 24 Jan. 1850, 4.   [84] *Morn. Chron.* 28 Jan. 1850, 5.

usually built in small groups by builders, employers or building societies, sometimes made up of the employees of one employer. Contemporaries commented on the prevalence of house ownership among working men.[85] This may have been true before the 1836 strike by the potters, when it was claimed that many were forced to sell their houses, but they had little chance of recovering them before 1850, and detailed property plans in 1858 and 1864 prepared in connection with planned railway extensions do not support this contention. The property-owning pattern was one in which the typical house-owner possessed a few adjoining properties and sometimes himself lived in one. Thus, it was a pattern of small-scale property ownership, but it does not support the argument that most potters owned their own houses.[86]

Most of the houses were in two-storey terraces built on a standard four-room cottage plan.[87] The front door opened straight into the living room, with a kitchen behind it, a pantry beside or under the staircase, and two rooms upstairs. The back door usually opened on to an individual yard with an ash-pit and a privy.

The Reporter for the *Morning Chronicle* described the interior of the best and worst working-class houses in the district. The three examples of the best houses happened to be in Etruria, although 'in Stoke, Hanley, Shelton and Burslem there are many streets inhabited by the working population, in which the houses are just as well built and as well furnished'. He describes the interior of one of the better houses as follows:

The lower apartments were paved with bricks, the upper were floored with boarding. The living room, I could see, was generally used for cooking, the kitchen being appropriated to the purposes of a scullery. There was a capital range, containing boilers, ovens and apparatus for roasting, all as clean as hard brushes and black lead could make them. I may mention also that in the case of a great number of these cottages the doorstep was brightly black leaded. In almost every house in the village a handsome eight day clock ticked in a corner and one side of the living room was occupied by a sofa, perhaps not very elegantly shaped, but ample, and covered with glazed calico. In the kitchen was a good store of pots, pans and tea and dinner ware; and behind the house was a garden about twenty yards by six or seven . . . [in another house] a carpet was spread over the brick floor, a roaring fire danced and flickered upon the perfectly

---

[85] *Morn. Chron.* 28 Jan. 1850, 5; PP 1857, sess. 2, xi, 752, 762, 779, 783; one witness estimated that one-quarter of the working men in the Potteries owned their own homes.

[86] Townley, 'Urban Administration', 44.

[87] For the 'typical' plans of workers' terraced housing in the Potteries, see *VCH*, viii, 114–15.

polished range and fire-irons; there was a clock and a large and handsome chest of drawers in the room, a central table, and several smaller ones, a sofa and a comfortable easy chair. . . . Upon the several ledges and ridges of the old-fashioned chimney piece were set a profusion of little china ware ornaments—dogs, vases and shepherdesses tending their flocks beneath very green crockery trees. There was also a bookcase, very fairly stocked and newspapers and cheap serial publications lay in the broad window sill. . . . In the next house I visited there were two rooms on each floor. . . . Here, also, the floor was at least partially carpeted, and a horse covered with good white crisp linen was airing before the fire. Among a number of portraits and engravings hanging upon the walls was a very fair copy, executed in oil of David's picture (I think it is) of Napoleon crossing the Alps. The brass candlesticks which were ranged upon cupboard and shelf were as bright as a Dutch housewife could wish them; and at the end of the garden was a small greenhouse. There gardens were one and all provided with proper private accommodations. The fences were formed of old 'saggars'; and a fair quantity of kitchen vegetables were, as I was informed, produced by each patch of land.[88]

The reporter also described examples of the worst class of housing in Hanley and Shelton.

The older houses are sometimes built on all sides of a small airless square, with a narrow passage leading to the street. Occasionally the common ash-pits and conveniences are erected in this delectable quadrangle. More generally, each house has its backyard—these places being too often, however, in a filthy state of dirt and neglect—frequently piled up with broken saggars, articles which the people seem wonderfully prone to collect and treasure. . . . Even in the poorest class of dwellings it was curious to observe how the fashion in furniture prevailing in the district was perceptible; wretched imitations of sofas—all rickety boards and torn and dirty calico—were often drawn near the fire. In more than one instance these served as day beds, and probably night beds too, for sick children. . . .[89]

Common to the interior of all classes of houses in the Potteries, however, were china ornaments, though they were not always used as decoration.

Little chinaware ornaments are, as may be conceived, profusely scattered through the cottages in the pottery districts. A curious use to which I observed small busts of the Queen and Prince Albert put, was placing them under the legs of sofas, like caryatides, so as to raise the article of furniture from a damp brick paved floor.[90]

---

[88] *Morn. Chron.* 28 Jan. 1850, 5.
[89] Ibid.   [90] *Morn. Chron.* 24 Jan. 1850, 5.

TABLE 1.5   *Crude Death-Rates (per 1,000 persons): Stoke-upon-Trent and Wolstanton Registration Districts and England and Wales 1841, 1861, 1871, 1881* (5-year averages centring on these dates)

	Stoke and Wolstanton	England and Wales
1841	26.1	21.8
1861	25.7	21.9
1871	25.7	22.0
1881	23.5	19.9

Finally, as in other industrial districts, pictures on the walls were common in the interiors of houses in the Potteries, though their quality and subject differed.

> In the houses of the worst class . . . the inhabitants of which are obviously at once slatternly and poor—the seldom failing pictorial decoration upon the walls is derived, with significant frequency, from the illustrations of some penny highwayman novel. In more comfortable dwellings, although occupied, perhaps, by individuals of the same nominal rank in the social scale, you may find a stiff family portrait or two—probably a crown or half-crown's worth—from some vagrant artist; or perchance there are engravings of some Chartist or Radical leader belonging to the political school of the 'pater familias'. But enter the dirty untidy dwelling, where the earth is unswept, the bed unmade, and everything betokens want and squalor—and almost to a certainty you find, stuck by pins or wafers to the wall, a coarse woodcut showing Claude du Val with his face masked, prancing in a laced coat beneath a gallows, or Dick Turpin, on Black Bess, with a cocked pistol in either hand, clearing the turnpike-gate, on his famous ride to York.[91]

4. Disease and Death

Mortality rates in the Potteries were high throughout the period 1840–80 compared with those of England and Wales as a whole (Table 1.5), and they were subject to large fluctuations (Figs. 1.7 and 1.8). Despite the comparatively small size of its individual towns, relatively high employment and wages, as well as relatively good housing, the Potteries generally had a mortality rate not significantly different from that in the largest cities in the country. In 1841 the average annual death-rate for

[91] Ibid.

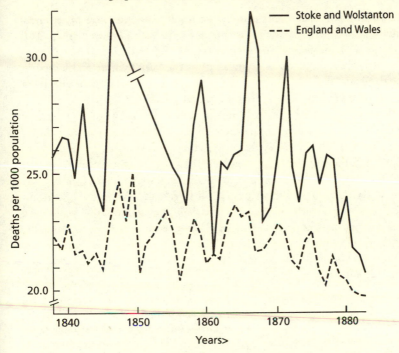

FIG. 1.7   Crude Death-Rate for Stoke-upon-Trent and Wolstanton Registration
Districts, England and Wales: 1838–1883

* data not available for 1847–54.
Sources: Annual Reports of the Registrar General; *Abst. of Brit. Hist. Stats.*, 361.

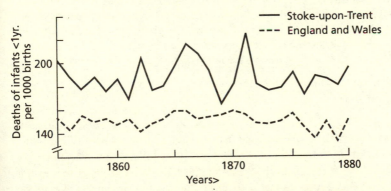

FIG. 1.8.   Infant Mortality in Stoke-upon-Trent Registration District, England and
Wales: 1855–1880

the Stoke–upon–Trent registration district was exceeded by only twenty-eight of the 324 registration districts in England and Wales.[92] In 1863 an individual living in the Stoke–upon–Trent registration district had a 25 per cent greater chance of dying during the year than an individual in England and Wales as a whole, and a 33 per cent greater chance of dying during the year than those living in rural districts.[93]

Both the conditions of work in the pottery industry and the sanitary conditions in the towns contributed to the high mortality rates. Within the Potteries, those (especially men) employed in pottery manufacture had a significantly higher death-rate than non-potters throughout the period. Potters were subject to a special investigation in 1860 by the Medical Officer to the Privy Council, Dr Greenhow. But in 1880 the death rates for potters (males) in age-groups 25–45 years and 45–65 years were still so high that the doyen of the mid-nineteenth century vital statistics, Dr Farr, described the industry as 'one of the unhealthiest trades in the country'. The mortality of male potters (in these age-groups) was exceeded only by

the figures for costermongers, Cornish miners and inn and hotel servants. This excessive mortality is in the greatest part due to phthisis and diseases of the respiratory organs . . . mortality under these two headings is almost three times as great in this industry as among average males. There is only one occupation . . . viz mining in Cornwall, in which the mortality from these two causes is higher, and scarcely any other which comes near to this. The mortality from diseases of the circulatory system is also extremely high, almost the highest in the tables; the inhalation of the dust induces emphysema and chronic bronchitis, or 'potters' asthma' and this in turn gives rise to heart disease. The various processes of the manufacture differ very greatly as regards their unhealthiness. . . . Taking, however, the aggregate industry, the two main conditions that produce this terrible mortality are the inhalation of air charged with fine irritating dust, and exposure to great vicissitudes of temperature. The mortality ascribed to alcoholism and to liver disease seems to imply a certain but not very great amount of intemperance.[94]

One of the physicians to the North Staffordshire Infirmary reported that in 1863

the mean age of death of male potters in Stoke parish, of twenty years and upwards, was 46 and one half, and that of males, not potters, was 52. The mean age at death of males of all classes, aged twenty and upwards, in all England, is fifty-six, and in the city of London fifty-two. Therefore the value of life among

[92]   Townley, 'Urban Administration', 103.
[93]   Calculated from J. T. Arlidge, 'On the Mortality of the Parish of Stoke-upon-Trent' (Hanley, 1864), 3.
[94]   PP 1884–5, xvii, 408.

male potters is nine and one half years less than that of males in the general population of the country.[95]

Furthermore, he calculated that in 1863 in the parish of Stoke-upon-Trent '83 in every 100 male potters die before completing their 60th year, and that only 17 in 100 live beyond that period; whereas, 66 only in every 100 males, not potters, die before attaining the 60th year, and 35 or more than twice 17, survive beyond that age'.[96]

Not only were the mortality rates of males, particularly potters, relatively high but also they were higher than females especially in the middle years (25–64 years). Life-tables for the Potteries (see the Appendix to this chapter) indicate that male mortality rates increased sharply and more rapidly than female mortality rates between 25 and 64 years, so that the difference between male and female mortality rates increased. The gender difference in mortality is reflected in higher male mortality rates from pulmonary disease.[97] In addition, higher proportions of male potters than either non-potters or female potters who were out-patients at the North Staffordshire Infirmary suffered from bronchitis.. These figures suggest that there was a relationship between the gender differences in mortality and morbidity and the gender division of labour in the potworks in which men tended to work in potting departments where they were exposed to large amounts of dust while women tended to work over a shorter period of the life cycle and in the decorating departments where their exposure to dust was limited.[98] These differences have implications for family employment patterns and sources of assistance which will be explored in later chapters.

It would be a mistake, however, to attribute the high overall rate of mortality in the Potteries solely to working conditions in the pottery industry. In two adjacent working-class areas in Hanley, for example, there was a 100 per cent discrepancy in mortality figures in 1841. The area with the greater density of population had an annual death-rate of 30 per 1,000, while the death-rate in the other was 15 per 1,000.[99]

Moreover, large numbers of children died before they could have begun work in the potbanks at about age 10. Infant mortality was especially high, with that of males exceeding that of males in York by 24 per cent as well as that in England and Wales as a whole by 28 per cent (see Table 1.6).

Minor stomach disorders killed many infants. Periodic epidemics

---

[95] Arlidge, 'Mortality', 19.   [96] Ibid. 18.   [97] Ibid. 9, 20, 22–3.
[98] J. T. Arlidge, *On the Diseases Prevalent Among Potters* (London, 1872), 3–7.
[99] Townley, 'Urban Administration', 93.

TABLE 1.6 *Age-Specific Mortality Rates (per 1,000): Stoke-upon-Trent and Wolstanton Registration Districts, York, and England and Wales, 1838–1844*

Age	Stoke and Wolstanton[a]		York[b]		England and Wales	
	males	females	males	females	males	females
<1	285	195	214	163	205	154
1–4	38	40	33	36	37	36
5–9	10	9	12	10	9	9
10–14	7	7	5	5	5	6
15–24	9	12	8	7	8	8
25–34	9	12	11	11	10	10
35–44	15	16	14	12	13	12
45–54	24	21	20	15	18	16
55–64	48	34	32	27	31	28
65–74	90	71	70	60	66	59
75–84	167	163	157	128	144	132
85–94	272	305	277	308	297	276

[a] Figures for Stoke-upon-Trent and Wolstanton Registration Districts from PP 1849 xxi, 64.
[b] Figures for York and for England and Wales from Armstrong, *Stability and Change*, 127

occurred, including cholera in 1848–9, and typhus and typhoid were endemic. Scarlet fever, measles, whooping cough, smallpox, and tuberculosis were other fatal diseases. In addition, there were numerous fatal accidents such as children's burns, as well as the diseases of the lungs and respiratory system particularly prevalent in the Potteries.

The life-tables for the Potteries (see the Appendix to this chapter) indicate that expectation of life at birth for males in 1838–44 was 35 years, compared with 40 years for England and Wales as a whole; for females life-expectancy was 37 years in the Potteries and 42 years in England and Wales as a whole. Furthermore, the figures for the Potteries did not change greatly in the twenty years up to 1858–64.[100]

5. Migration

The rapid increase in the population of the parliamentary borough of Stoke-upon-Trent has already been mentioned. This growth was due

[100] The life-tables are presented in the Appendix to this chapter.

TABLE 1.7   *Birthplaces of the non-institutionalized[a] resident populations:*
Potteries Sample 1861, Preston 1851 (%)

Birthplace	Potteries		Preston[b]	
	Total Population	In-migrants[c]	Total Population	In-migrants[b]
In Potteries or Preston	63	—	48	—
1–29 miles	19	54	35	70
30 miles and over	13	37	8	16
Ireland	3	9	7	14
Not traceable	2	—	2	—
All (%)	100	100	100	100
N	6,707	2,473	6,741	3,345

[a] Visitors are also excluded.
[b] Figures for Preston from Anderson, *Family Structure*, 37.
[c] Excluding not traceable.

both to a high birth-rate and to in-migration, but in contrast to almost all large towns, including the cotton towns of Lancashire, net natural increase rather than net in-migration played a comparatively large role in the Potteries. Between 1841 and 1851 approximately 45 per cent of the increase in population was accounted for by net in-migration, in contrast to York where in-migration accounted for roughly 68 per cent of the increase in population.[101] Moreover, in the next decade the proportion of increase in population in the parliamentary borough ascribed to net in-migration fell to 22 per cent. In other words, a comparatively large proportion of the population in the Potteries was born locally and did not migrate. This contrast potentially had significance for family relationships. Yet, at the same time there was also some migration into the Potteries, and its characteristics repay examination.[102] In this section, therefore, I present evidence of the pattern of birthplaces of the residents of the Potteries, and for those who did migrate into the area, evidence of where they came from, at what ages they migrated, and their occupations.

The birthplaces of the residents of the Potteries are grouped by distance in Table 1.7, which shows that 63 per cent of the population of

[101] Calculated following the method used by A. Armstrong, *Stability and Change in an English County Town: A Social Study of York 1801–1851* (Cambridge, 1974), 87.
[102] There was also migration out of the Potteries. See F. Thistlethwaite, 'The Atlantic Migration of the Pottery Industry', *Econ. Hist. Rev.* 11 (1958), 264–78.

TABLE 1.8 *Proportion of the Population living in the Potteries and Preston who had been born there, by Age and Sex: Potteries Sample 1861, Preston 1851ª (%; N = 100% in brackets)*

| | Potteries | | Preston | |
Age	Male	Female	Male	Female
0–4	89 (509)	91 (533)	86 (418)	85 (452)
5–9	83 (409)	81 (404)	73 (389)	79 (359)
10–14	72 (357)	75 (379)	66 (392)	66 (349)
15–19	72 (319)	66 (328)	54 (390)	52 (418)
20–24	59 (318)	68 (300)	39 (316)	40 (398)
25–34	52 (520)	54 (532)	30 (473)	33 (546)
35–44	47 (426)	52 (399)	25 (379)	32 (411)
45–54	48 (272)	49 (270)	25 (230)	25 (319)
55–64	36 (130)	51 (144)	14 (156)	13 (160)
65+	36 (70)	39 (73)	23 (93)	20 (101)

ª Figures for Preston from Anderson, *Family Structure*, 39.

the parliamentary borough of Stoke-upon-Trent were born within its boundary. Taking the adults (all persons 20 years and over) alone, 52 per cent of the Potteries adult residents were born in the Potteries in contrast with 30 per cent of the adults in Preston who were born in Preston. Compared with Preston, there were more locally born, fewer short-distance migrants, and more long-distance migrants in the Potteries.[103] The relatively small amount of migration into the Potteries compared with Preston can also be seen when the proportions of each age-group born in the Potteries and Preston are compared in Table 1.8, and the sex-ratios are compared in Table 1.9.

[103] A priori this difference in locally born and short-distance migrants might be an artefact of the differences in area of the parliamentary boroughs, for the parliamentary borough of Stoke-upon-Trent included three times the area of the parliamentary and municipal borough of Preston (13.3 sq. miles vs. 4.4 sq. miles), PP 1859, sess. 1, xxiii, 122–3. I would argue, however, that the difference in migration patterns is not a statistical artefact of the difference in areas. In both cases the boundaries tightly encircle the built-up areas [PP 1867–8, xx, 267, 317], and neither included villages that might be the source of short-distance migrants. Moreover, as will be discussed below, there was relatively little movement among the towns within the Potteries. Indeed, a priori one might expect the Potteries to have more short-distance migrants because of the large concentration of population adjacent in the borough of Newcastle-under-Lyme.

TABLE 1.9   *Sex-Ratios (males : females):*
Potteries Sample 1861, Preston 1851

Age	Potteries	Preston
0–19	98	101
20–34	103	86
35–54	104	82
55+	90	95
Overall	99	92

The proportion born in the Potteries remained high through all age-groups, while in Preston the number of girls aged 15–19 and 20–24 exceed the numbers aged 10–14 by 12 per cent and 11 per cent respectively. Also, for the Potteries the overall number of males and females was nearly equal with slightly more males in the age-groups 20–54 years, while in Preston there were more females overall and particularly in the age-groups between 20 and 54 years.

Of those residents who migrated to the Potteries, a substantial number came from rural areas of Staffordshire and neighbouring counties within 30 miles of the Potteries. Beyond 30 miles significant sources of migrants to the Potteries included Birmingham and the Black Country to the south, Lancashire and Yorkshire to the north, Wales (particularly Flintshire and Denbighshire) to the west, and Ireland.

Predictably, the migrants did not distribute themselves evenly throughout the Potteries. Etruria, for example, had relatively few migrants, while the number in central Burslem was relatively large.[104] The Irish, in particular, tended to cluster together. There were only three Irish-born residents in Etruria in 1861, while 8 per cent of the population of central Burslem in 1851 and 1861 were born in Ireland. Although the proportion of Irish-born in the Potteries population was lower than the 7 per cent in Preston, one observer discovered in 1892 that

perhaps the most compact and numerous body of Irish, not merely in Staffordshire, but in the whole of the Midlands, are to be found in . . . the Potteries . . . our

[104] For further discussion of the birthplaces of Etruria residents see below, Ch. 4, sect. 2, and M. W. Dupree, 'Family Structure in the Staffordshire Potteries 1840–1880', D.Phil. thesis (Oxford, 1981), 241–3. For central Burslem, see: D. G. Stuart (ed.), *The Population of Central Burslem 1851 and 1861*, Department of Adult Education, University of Keele Local History Occasional Paper no. 2 (1973).

people here marry more among themselves and are more homogeneous than elsewhere in the Midlands: in fact they are more like you find them in the Lancashire towns.[105]

The migrants from Wales, too, tended to retain a separate identity. Many were colliers and ironstone miners and they were united around their chapels with the common bond of language. In Hanley, for example, 300 Welsh attended the opening of the Welsh Chapel in the 1850s.[106]

The pattern of birthplaces of residents of Etruria also indicate that local patterns of migration existed within the Potteries. Migrants to Etruria were not drawn equally from all Potteries towns. There were very few in-migrants to Etruria from the extreme ends of the Potteries. Only 0.5 per cent came from Tunstall, 0.1 per cent from Fenton, and 0.2 per cent from Longton. At the same time 9 per cent of the population was born in Hanley, 7 per cent in Stoke, 4 per cent in Burslem, and 2 per cent in Newcastle. The difference was not a direct function of increasing distance from Etruria. Higher proportions of the Etruria population were born in places 5–10 miles from Etruria (4 per cent), 10–20 miles from Etruria (5 per cent), Birmingham and the Black Country (4 per cent), industrial towns in Lancashire, Yorkshire, and the Midlands (5 per cent), and Scotland (1 per cent). Hanley showed a similar pattern of comparatively little movement among the towns. Almost 90 per cent of the Hanley residents in 1851 who were born in the Potteries were born in Hanley itself, and the only discernible emigration was from Stoke.[107]

These figures relate to the birthplaces of the whole population of the Potteries or Etruria taken as a group. But within the Potteries different groups had different patterns of birthplaces. Although the overall level of migration into the Potteries was lower, those who migrated into the Potteries were the same groups that migrated into Preston—the young and married couples. In both areas changes in the proportions of locally born inhabitants occur in the age-span 10–34 years, indicating concentration of migration into younger age-groups. The in-migration of married couples to the Potteries is suggested by the 13 per cent of those couples whose eldest surviving, co-residing child was under five years and born outside the Potteries.

The most striking differences in the birthplaces of residents of the Potteries are among pottery-workers, ironworkers, and miners (see Table 1.10): 84 per cent of the pottery-workers were born in the Potteries,

[105] J. Denvir, *The Irish in Britain* (London, 1892), 426.

[106] Some implications of this clustering for families and the provision of social welfare will be discussed in Ch. 7, sect. 2, 'Churches, Chapels, and Sunday Schools'.

[107] Townley, 'Urban Administration', 30.

TABLE 1.10   *Birthplaces of Potters, Ironworkers, and Miners:*
Potteries Sample 1861 (%)

Birthplace	Potters	Ironworkers	Miners
Potteries	84	30	32
Within 10 miles	6	9	14
Elsewhere	10	61	54
N	1,461	137	238

while only 30 per cent of the ironworkers and 32 per cent of the miners were born in the area. In the relatively small village of Etruria 60 per cent of the pottery-workers had been born in the same village and 86 per cent were born within the Potteries, while only 10 per cent of the ironworkers residing in Etruria were born in the Potteries.

Thus, pottery-workers tended to be born locally, while ironworkers for the expanding and newly established ironworks in the area tended to be drawn from other iron-making centres in the country, particularly the Black Country, and not from the local Potteries population. This difference in migration patterns between potters and ironworkers is the logical and expected result of the contrast between a large, long-established local industry and a small newly established, but rapidly expanding industry that drew its labour-force from the iron industry's own regional equivalents of the Potteries. However, coal-mining was a long-established occupation in the Potteries; it was complementary to the pottery industry and they expanded together. So, it is surprising, given the high proportion of locally born pottery-workers, to find that such a small proportion of coal-miners were born in the Potteries. In addition, there were mines outside the Potteries to account for the short-distance migration; and miners from Wales, in particular, contributed to the numbers of long-distance migrants. In his evidence to the Select Committee on the rating of mines the manager of Lord Granville's collieries and ironstone mines observed that 'there has been a considerable immigration of miners into the district in consequence of the opening out of the mines'.[108]

Thus, the different birthplace patterns among potters, ironworkers, and colliers reflect both the existence of networks of other areas of mining and ironworking in the country with channels of communication and circulation of workers among them, and the lack of other large

[108] PP 1857, sess. 2, xi, 751.

centres of pottery manufacture in Britain.[109] The percentages, however, do hide some in-migration of pottery workers from other centres of pottery manufacture in Britain. There were pottery workers born in Bristol, Derby, Glasgow, Worcester, Hull, and London, as well as a sprinkling of designers from France. Presumably there was also some circulation of local pottery workers to these other centres, but the option to leave the Potteries and continue to practise their craft could not have been open to many.

6. Population Turnover

Having looked at migration from the point of view of those persons born elsewhere who moved into the Potteries, it is also possible to examine migration from the perspective of those who moved out of or remained in a small area within the Potteries. The small area in this case is the village and enumeration district of Etruria. Although it is not possible to find out how many moved house but remained within the village, because house numbers were not given in Etruria in 1841, 1851, or 1861, such movement probably caused little disruption of family or community solidarity. Moreover, the lack of house numbers does not impair an examination of population turnover and persistence within the enumeration district.[110]

Regardless of the method used to indicate population turnover and persistence—whether tracing male household heads, or individuals, or all household heads forward from the 1851 census[111]—there were high rates of persistence in Etruria compared with other northern towns or cities in the mid-nineteenth century.

---

[109] R. Dennis, *English Industrial Cities of the Nineteenth Century* (Cambridge, 1984), 33 points out that long-distance migration was associated with skilled workers moving to locations where 'their skill was in demand or where they reckoned that they had better employment prospects'.

[110] Dennis, *English Industrial Cities*, 251, 264, 267–8. In ch. 8 he provides a useful and comprehensive discussion of 'mobility, persistence and community' in light of existing literature and his own study of Huddersfield.

[111] Tracing individuals forward in this way means that those not present in the later census were either dead, had moved out of the enumeration district, or were absent due to an error. See R. Dennis, 'Intercensal Mobility in a Victorian City', *Trans. Instit. Brit. Geog.* NS 2 (1977), 352–3; C. Pooley, 'Residential Mobility in the Victorian City', *Trans, Instit. Brit. Geog.* NS 4 (1979), 260; R. Dennis, 'Community and Interaction in a Victorian City: Huddersfield 1850–1880', Ph.D. thesis (Cambridge, 1975); D. H. Parkerson, 'How Mobile were Nineteenth-Century Americans?', *Historical Methods*, 15 (1982), 99–109; D. W. Galenson and D. S. Levy, 'A Note on Biases in the Measurement of Geographic Persistence Rates', *Historical Methods*, 19 (1986), 171–9.

One direct comparison can be made with Huddersfield, where only 35 per cent of the male household heads in a sample from the 1851 census enumerators' books were present in the same enumeration district in 1861.[112] By contrast in Etruria 49 per cent of the male household heads present in 1851 were also present in 1861 (of those not present, at least 18 per cent had died during the decade). A similar difference emerges if the male household heads are traced in the other direction, from 1861 to 1851 (thereby eliminating the effect of mortality but adding the problem of the comparability of the area, e.g. additional houses were built in Etruria between 1851 and 1861). In Etruria, where the population increased by 21 per cent during the decade, 54 per cent of the household heads present in 1861 had been present in 1851. In Huddersfield, where the population only increased by 14 per cent, just 37 per cent of the male household heads in 1861 had been present in the same enumeration district in 1851.

Turning from male household heads to individuals, the same pattern of relative persistence emerges: 53 per cent of all males in Etruria who were aged 10 and over in 1861 (and therefore alive in 1851) had been living in the village in 1851; while in Preston 40 per cent of the males in one enumeration district were found in the same house or within 200 yards of the same house they had occupied ten years earlier.[113]

The high rate of persistence in Etruria is further emphasized when it is compared with the rate in Liverpool. A higher proportion of all household heads present in 1851 in Etruria remained within the tiny area of that enumeration district in 1861 (51 per cent) than could be traced in the entire city of Liverpool (48 per cent) between 1851 and 1861.[114]

It might be argued that these comparisons are of little interest because Etruria may not be typical of the Potteries. It is possible that a higher proportion of persons and households stayed in Etruria than in other working-class residential areas in the Potteries because of the proximity of large employers (the Wedgwood potworks and Lord Granville's Shelton Bar Iron Works and coal-mines), who offered regular employment and wages. But there were other large employers, such as Mintons, with a core of long-serving employees. Also, areas may have had high persistence rates without large employers, as large employers had no necessary effect on persistence. For example, persistence in Etruria was higher than in a 'planned community' such as Saltaire, but it was not out of line with some areas of speculative housing around other Yorkshire mills.[115]

---

[112] Dennis, 'Intercensal Mobility', 352–3; id., *English Industrial Cities*, 256–7.
[113] Anderson, *Family Structure*, 260–2.
[114] Pooley, 'Residential Mobility', 260–2.
[115] Dennis, *English Industrial Cities*, 267–8.

Nevertheless, even if Etruria were atypically stable, the persistence rates in Etruria would still give an indication of the upper limit in the range of experience of areas in the Potteries and of the extent of stability despite the flux of movement emphasized in descriptions of other nineteenth-century towns and cities. Moreover, the relatively high persistence rates in Etruria may at most only slightly exaggerate the more general picture, as recent research stresses differences among cities and subgroups within cities and suggests that successful industrial towns had higher rates in comparison with large cities such as Leeds, seaports, and older less successful industrial towns. Furthermore, difficulties with record-linkage indicate that even the highly transient picture of nineteenth-century American cities needs to be revised.[116]

To sum up, the Potteries emerge as an area dependent on a narrow range of industries offering expanding, though fluctuating, employment, and dominated by the pottery industry. Wages were relatively high but subject to considerable variation, leaving the standard of living of many families in a precarious position during crises. There was in-migration among ironworkers, miners, and the Irish in particular, but the relative lack of in-migration and high persistence among potters shaped the overall picture. Housing of comparatively good quality was available at generally low rents. But alongside this image of relative prosperity were high rates of respiratory disease especially for men, and a high and fluctuating mortality rate, reinforced by poor sanitation and some of the working conditions in the pottery industry. Together these form key features of the background for patterns of co-residence, family employment, and sources of assistance.

Appendix: 'Abridged' Life-Tables for the Potteries

The following life-tables for males and females in the Potteries at two different dates were calculated following the method described in G. W. Barclay, *Techniques of Population Analysis* (New York, 1958), 107–11, 286–9. The tables are based on age-specific death-rates which were derived from the number of deaths of males and females in each age-group found in the Registrar General's Annual Reports for the Stoke-upon-Trent and Wolstanton registration districts in 1838–44 and for the Stoke-upon-Trent registration district in 1858–64, and from the age-structures in the 1841 and 1861 published censuses.

[116] Ibid. 258; Parkerson, 'How Mobile?', 99, 107; D. P. Davenport, 'Duration of Residence in the 1855 Census of New York State', *Historical Methods*, 18 (1985), 5–12; Galenson and Levy, 'Note on Biases', 177.

TABLE 1.A1 'Abridged' Life-Table: Stoke-upon-Trent and Wolstanton Registration Districts 1838-1844—Males

Years	(1) $_nM_x$	(2) $_nq_x$	(3) $_np_x$	(4) $_nd_x$	(5) l_x	(6) $_nL_x$	(7) T_x	(8) e_x	(9) e_x
<1	—	.21078	.78922	21,078	100,000	85,245	3,491,491	34.9	39.9
1-4	.038	.14213	.85787	11,217	78,922	292,872	3,406,246	43.2	46.7
5-9	.010	.04878	.95122	3,303	67,705	330,300	3,113,374	46.0	49.7
10-14	.007	.03440	.96562	2,215	64,402	316,429	2,783,074	43.2	47.1
15-24	.009	.08612	.91388	5,356	62,187	595,111	2,466,645	39.7	43.2
25-34	.009	.08612	.91388	4,495	56,831	499,444	1,871,534	32.9	36.1
35-44	.015	.13954	.86047	7,303	52,336	486,867	1,372,090	26.2	29.4
45-54	.024	.21429	.78571	9,650	45,033	402,083	885,223	19.7	22.8
55-64	.048	.38800	.61290	13,697	35,383	285,354	483,140	13.7	16.5
65-74	.090	.62069	.37931	13,460	21,686	149,556	197,786	9.1	10.8
75+	.188	1.00	0	8,826	8,826	48,230	48,230	5.5	6.5

(1) $_nM_x$ = age-specific death-rate for the Stoke-upon-Trent and Wolstanton registration districts 1838-44 from the Registrar General's Annual Report, except for 75+ years:

$$\text{average no. of deaths of males age 75+ per year} \over \text{no. of males age 75+ from the 1841 census}$$

(2) $_nq_x$ = probability of dying between age x and age $x + n$

$_1q_0$ = $\dfrac{\text{average no. of deaths of males} < 1 \text{ yr. per year}}{\text{average no. of males born per year}}$

$_nM_x$ converted to $_nq_x$: $_nq_x = \dfrac{2n\,_nM_x}{2 + n\,_nM_x}$ (Barclay, 287).

TABLE 1.A1 *Notes continued*

(3) $_np_x$ = probability of surviving between age x and age $x + n$.

$_np_x = 1 - _nq_x$.

(4) $_nd_x$ = number of deaths between age x and age $x + n$.

$_nd_x = l_x * _nq_x$.

(5) l_x = survivors at exact age x.

$l_{x+n} = l_x - _nd_x$ or $l_{x+n} = l_x * _np_x$.

(6) $_nL_x$ = years lived between age x and age $x + n$

$_1L_0 = .31_0 + .71_1$

$$_nL_x = \frac{_nd_x}{_nM_x}$$

$$L_{75} = \frac{l_{75}}{M_{75}}.$$

(7) T_x = total years lived after exact age x.

$T_x = T_{x+n} + _nL_x$.

(8) e_x = expectation of life. Average number of years lived after exact age x.

$$e_x = \frac{T_x}{l_x}.$$

(9) e_x = English Life-Table 1838–44 (PP 1884–5, xvii, 373–4).

TABLE 1.A2 '*Abridged*' *Life-Table: Stoke-upon-Trent and Wolstanton Registration Districts 1838–1844—Females*

Years	(1) $_nM_x$	(2) $_nq_x$	(3) $_np_x$	(4) $_nd_x$	(5) l_x	(6) $_nL_x$	(7) T_x	(8) e_x	(9) e_x
<1	—	.168	.83200	16,800	100,000	88,240	3,668,744	36.7	41.9
1–4	.040	.14815	.85185	12,326	83,200	308,152	3,580,504	43.0	47.3
5–9	.009	.04401	.95599	3,119	70,874	346,556	3,272,352	46.2	50.3
10–14	.007	.03440	.96560	2,331	67,755	333,000	2,925,796	43.2	47.7
15–24	.012	.11328	.88672	7,411	65,424	617,583	2,592,796	39.6	43.9
25–34	.012	.11328	.88672	6,572	58,013	547,667	1,975,213	34.1	37.0
35–44	.016	.14815	.85185	7,621	51,441	476,313	1,427,546	27.8	30.6
45–54	.021	.19005	.80995	8,328	43,820	396,571	951,233	21.7	24.1
55–64	.034	.29060	.70940	10,314	35,492	303,353	554,662	15.6	17.4
65–74	.071	.52399	.47601	13,193	25,178	185,817	251,309	10.0	11.5
75+	.183	1.00	0	11,985	11,985	65,492	65,492	5.5	6.9

Note: For interpretation of variables see Table 1.A1.

TABLE 1.A3 *'Abridged' Life–Table: Stoke–upon–Trent Registration District 1858–1864—Males*

Years	(1) $_nM_x$	(2) $_na_x$	(3) $_np_x$	(4) $_nd_x$	(5) l_x	(6) $_nL_x$	(7) T_x	(8) e_x
<1	—	.201	.799	20,100	100,000	85,930	3,413,999	34.1
1–4	.050	.18181	.81818	14,527	79,900	290,540	3,328,069	41.7
5–9	.009	.04401	.95599	2,877	65,373	319,667	3,037,529	46.5
10–14	.006	.02956	.97044	1,847	62,496	307,833	2,717,862	43.5
15–24	.008	.07692	.92308	4,665	60,649	583,125	2,410,029	39.7
25–34	.010	.09524	.90476	5,332	55,984	533,200	1,826,904	32.6
35–44	.016	.14815	.85185	7,504	50,652	469,000	1,293,704	25.5
45–54	.028	.24561	.75439	10,598	43,148	378,500	824,704	19.1
55–64	.045	.36735	.63265	11,957	32,550	265,711	446,204	13.7
65–74	.091	.62543	.37457	12,880	20,593	141,538	180,493	8.8
75+	.198	1.00	0	7,713	7,713	38,955	38,955	5.1

Note: For interpretation of variables see Table 1.A1.

TABLE 1.A4 *'Abridged' Life-Table: Stoke-upon-Trent Registration District 1858–1864—Females*

Years	(1) $_nM_x$	(2) $_nq_x$	(3) $_np_x$	(4) $_nd_x$	(5) l_x	(6) $_nL_x$	(7) T_x	(8) e_x
<1	—	.165	.835	16,500	100,000	88,450	3,784,027	37.8
1–4	.049	.17851	.82149	14,852	83,500	303,102	3,695,577	44.3
5–9	.009	.04401	.9559	3,021	68,648	335,667	3,392,475	49.4
10–14	.005	.02469	.97531	1,620	65,627	324,000	3,056,808	46.6
15–24	.008	.07692	.92308	4,923	64,007	615,375	2,732,808	42.7
25–34	.011	.10427	.89573	6,161	59,084	560,090	2,117,433	35.8
35–44	.012	.11321	.88679	5,991	52,923	499,250	1,557,343	29.4
45–54	.016	.14815	.85185	6,953	46,932	434,563	1,058,093	22.6
55–64	.033	.28326	.71674	11,325	39,979	343,182	623,530	15.6
65–74	.075	.54545	.45455	15,629	28,654	208,387	280,348	9.8
75+	.181	1.00	0	13,025	13,025	71,961	71,961	5.5

Note: For interpretation of variables see Table 1.A1.

2

Households and Families

GIVEN the potentially disruptive processes of industrialization and urbanization, what were the patterns of co-residence in the Potteries in 1861, i.e. who lived with whom? Did individuals related by blood or marriage live together? Furthermore, what patterns of relationships existed within nuclear families—between husbands and wives and parents and children, particularly with regard to marriage and family size?

1. Residence Patterns

Although it is important not to exaggerate their significance, patterns of co-residence are relatively easy to measure with census enumerators' books; hence, an examination of census enumerators' books provide a good starting-point for comparison of the patterns of family relationships in the Potteries with other areas, particularly another industrial area such as Preston.

The sample of the census enumerators' books for the Potteries contained 1,373 households, or co-residing groups as Anderson prefers to call them, and 6,707 individuals. By definition, a co-residing group includes all the names listed in an enumerators' book from one entry 'head' in the column headed 'relation to head of family' to the last name preceding the next entry of 'head'. The head is the 'occupier defined in the census as either the resident owner or the person who pays the rent whether for the whole house or for a part of one. The census enumerators' books also indicate separate houses (there were 1,322 in the Potteries sample); so it is possible to distinguish all people living in one house.

The residence patterns that emerge from the enumerators' books reveal that in the Potteries, as in Preston, there were some alternatives to the family as a residential group. But in both areas over 90 per cent of the residents lived in the same household or co-residing group as at least one other person related to them by blood or by marriage; 91 per cent of the 6,707 residents in the Potteries sample lived in the same co-residing group as at least one other person related to them (see Table 2.1). Of the

TABLE 2.1 *Number of People Living with at Least One other Person Related to them by Blood or by Marriage: Potteries Sample 1861*

Those related to at least one other person in the household		6,100
Those not related to at least one other person in the household		607
Servants (unmarried, widowed, or married but spouse absent)	(170)	
Lodgers (unmarried, widowed, or married but without children or spouse absent)	(362)	
Head of household alone (or with unrelated person only)	(75)	
TOTAL		6,707

non-related 9 per cent, seventy-five persons (1 per cent) headed a household and lived either alone or with persons not related to them. The rest of the 9 per cent lived either as lodgers, servants, live-in employees, or apprentices and were not shown in the enumerators' books as related to other members of the household. Some of these may have had siblings living with them in lodgings, and a few lodgers were probably related to the household head though not recorded as such. Therefore the total number of people living with relatives of one kind or another was probably closer to 93 per cent of the population. This is similar to the 95 per cent Anderson found in Preston. Thus, like Preston, the Potteries can be characterized as predominantly a familistic community but one in which some alternatives to residing with family or kin did exist.

From the analysis of the enumerators' books, however, a difference emerges between the Potteries and Preston, with fewer persons per house in the Potteries than in Preston. At least part of the difference is undoubtedly explained by the better housing conditions in the Potteries which were described in Chapter 1. In the Potteries there was an average of five persons per house while there was an average of six persons per house in Preston in 1851.[1] This contrast did not manifest itself in

---

[1] The Potteries average of 5.2 persons per house, while greater than the average of 4.5 persons per house in Etruria, was similar to the average in England and Wales as a whole (5.4) and less than the 6.1 in Preston.

differences either in the size of nuclear families or in the number of
servants (3 per cent of the sample in both the Potteries and Preston).
Instead, there was a difference in the extent to which nuclear families
shared a house with people outside the immediate nuclear family of the
head regardless of whether the others were kin, lodgers, or another co-
residing group. Thus, it appears that these were the flexible categories in
industrial towns with different housing conditions, and I want to turn
first to an examination of these three categories of household members
outside the immediate nuclear family.

Kin

The overall extent of the co-residence of kin outside the nuclear family
and some of the detailed patterns of the co-residence of kin in the
Potteries in the mid–nineteenth century differ from those in other areas.
The differences reflect, at least in part, local variations in the supply of
housing, the prevalence of poverty, the rate of mortality, and the frequency of migration. Although there is not enough evidence from studies
of other urban communities in Britain in the nineteenth century to 'provide a basis for a systematic typology adequate to explain how and why
their kinship patterns differed', it is clear that

the degree of local kinship [depended] on the stability or instability of the
population, which in its turn depended and depends on such factors as the state
of the local economy, the extent of change in the physical environment, and the
availability (and accessibility) of housing.[2]

Turning first to the overall extent of sharing with kin, the information
in Table 2.2 suggests that a smaller proportion of co-residing groups in
the Potteries than in Preston contained related persons other than members of the current nuclear family (i.e. grandparents, uncles, aunts, cousins, nieces, and nephews). 18 per cent of the households in the Potteries
included kin, compared with 23 per cent of the households in Preston in
1851. The proportion of households with kin in the Potteries was also
lower than the 21 per cent in Oldham in 1851 and 22 per cent in York
in 1851; yet, it was about the same as the proportion in Northampton
and South Shields in 1851, and it was greater than the 15 per cent found
in the average of selected sub-districts presented in the 1861 published

[2] P. Willmott, 'Kinship and Urban Communities: Past and Present', *The Ninth H. J.
Dyos Memorial Lecture*, Victorian Studies Centre, University of Leicester (Leicester, 1987),
12, 14–15.

TABLE 2.2   *Structure of the Families of Household Heads: Potteries
Sample 1861, Preston 1851*

	Potteries		Preston[a]
	N	%	%
Head alone (or only with unrelated persons)	75	5	4
Nuclear families			
Childless married couples	176	12	10
Married couples or widowed persons with unmarried children only	924	65	63
Stem families (two or more lineally related ever-married persons and their nuclear families, if any)	110	8	10
Composite families			
Unmarried siblings only	18	1	1
Other kin	129	9	12
TOTAL	1,432	100	100
Additional nuclear families within composite families	11		
Additional nuclear families within stem families	56		
Unmarried person with child	12		
	79		

[a] Figures for Preston from Anderson, *Family Structure*, 44.

census.[3] Furthermore, the proportion of households in the Potteries containing kin was significantly greater than the 9 per cent in England and Wales in 1966 and 10 per cent in Bethnal Green in 1955—proportions which are considered indications of strongly kin-oriented communities.[4] Thus, despite the relatively low proportion of households containing kin compared with Preston, it is apparent that kinship relations of some kind were being maintained in the Potteries in 1861.

[3] For Oldham, Northampton, and South Shields see J. Foster, *Class Struggle and the Industrial Revolution: Early Industrial Capitalism in Three English Towns* (London, 1974), 99; for York see W. A. Armstrong, *Stability and Change in an English County Town: A Social Study of York 1801–1851* (Cambridge, 1974), 185; PP 1863, liii, pt. 1, p. 114.

[4] M. Anderson, *Family Structure in 19th Century Lancashire* (Cambridge, 1971), 44.

The explanation of the differences among nineteenth-century towns in the proportions of households which contained kin outside the nuclear family is an open question. As mentioned above, however, the contrasts are probably partly related to local differences in housing, poverty, mortality, and migration.[5] The difference between the Potteries and Preston offers an illustration. On one hand, the relatively high proportion of locally born inhabitants in the Potteries compared with Preston suggests that individuals in the Potteries would be more likely to have kin in the area with which to reside; hence, one should expect a higher incidence of co-residence of kin in the Potteries than in Preston. On the other hand, one of the functions of co-residence with kin appears to be to assist the adjustment of migrants to a new community.[6] Therefore, with relatively few migrants in the Potteries, this need is relatively less and co-residence of kin could be expected to be less frequent in the Potteries than in Preston. The relatively large supply of housing and greater affluence in the Potteries would also lead one to expect there to be relatively less need for co-residence with kin as a source of assistance, and hence a smaller proportion of households containing kin in the Potteries than in Preston.

Although the Potteries and Preston differed in the overall proportions of co-residing groups which included kin, they were similar with regard to the relationships of the kin who co-resided. In both areas a relatively high proportion of co-residing groups contained parents and married children compared with some other nineteenth-century towns. The 8 per cent of households in the Potteries which can be characterized as 'stem' families, containing 'two or more lineally related ever-married persons',[7] was slightly less than the 10 per cent of households in Preston and in Oldham in 1851, but it was a larger proportion than the 5 per cent of households in Northampton and 4 per cent of households in South Shields in 1851.[8] These differences have been interpreted in different ways, but I shall postpone discussion of them until Chapter 8.

Despite the relatively high proportion of households containing

---

[5] For the Potteries see Ch. 1 above.

[6] Anderson, *Family Structure*, 153; L. Lees, *Exiles of Erin: Irish Migrants in Victorian London* (Manchester, 1979), 18.

[7] These include: the head's mother or mother-in-law, father or father-in-law, or the head's married son or daughter and their spouses if living.

[8] For Preston see Anderson, *Family Structure*, 44; figures for Oldham, Northampton, and South Shields quoted in M. Anderson, 'Family, Household and the Industrial Revolution', in M. Anderson (ed.), *Sociology of the Family* (Harmondsworth, 1971), 83 from J. Foster, 'Capitalism and Class Consciousness in Earlier 19th Century Oldham', Ph.D. thesis (Cambridge, 1967).

'stem' families in the Potteries and Preston compared with some other nineteenth-century towns, the figures in Table 2.2 suggest that less than half (44 per cent) of the households which included kin contained 'stem' families, while more than half of the households which included kin contained 'other' kin of the head (i.e. aunts, uncles, siblings, nieces, nephews, or cousins). The proportion of households containing 'stem' families is low compared with the 55 per cent of families with kin in England and Wales in 1966 and the 65 per cent of those in Swansea in 1960.[9] Moreover, in both the Potteries and Preston it was relatively unusual for 'stem' families to contain two married couples of two succeeding generations; more common was the co-residence of a married couple and a widowed parent.[10] The interpretation of the difference is again an open question, but it may reflect at least in part differences between mid-nineteenth- and mid-twentieth-century mortality rates.

A picture of the relationship of the co-residing 'other kin' emerges when the co-residence of kin is considered from a different perspective in Table 2.3. This table gives a full list of the relationships to the head of the household of all the kin present in these households. In the Potteries, as in Preston, the most notable feature of the table is the high percentage of nieces, nephews, and grandchildren without parents found in the households. These 'parentless children' make up a large proportion (26 per cent in the Potteries and 28 per cent in Preston) of all co-residing kin, compared with 5 per cent in England and Wales in 1966 and Swansea in 1960.[11] In addition, in the table for the Potteries there are various 'step' relationships[12] indicated, which, like the relatively high proportion of 'parentless children', suggest relatively high mortality among young parents, as well as the occurrence of re-marriage. Discussion of the functional importance of the patterns of co-residence with kin in the Potteries appears below in Chapter 8.

Lodgers

Another category of household members outside the immediate nuclear family was lodgers. Lodging in the Potteries as in other nineteenth-

---

[9] Anderson, *Family Structure*, 44.

[10] e.g. in the Potteries of 34 married or widowed persons over age 65 who lived with married or widowed children, only two were married and lived with married children; for Preston, see Anderson, *Family Structure*, 44–5.

[11] Anderson, *Family Structure*, 45.

[12] As well as 'step' there were three other terms used in the enumerators' books for fostering including 'adopted', 'orphan', and 'nurse child'.

TABLE 2.3   *Relationship of Co-residing Kin to Household Head: Potteries Sample 1861, Preston 1851*

Relationship of kin to household head	Marital status of kin						Preston[a]
	Unmarried	Married	Widowed	Married but spouse absent	N	% of kin N = 450	% of kin
Father, or father-in-law	—	2	13	1	16	4	3
Mother, or mother-in-law	—	3	30	2	35	8	6
Married son, or son-in-law		42	3	0	45	10	11
Married daughter, or daughter-in-law	—	43	2	8	53	12	12
Grandchild, with parent	61				61	14	14
Grandchild, no parent	47				47	10 ⎤13	13
Grandchild, no parent but unmar. dau.	12				12	3 ⎦	
Sibling, or sib.-in-law	68	8	7	4	87	19	19
Niece or nephew, with parent	11				11	2	4
Niece or nephew, no parent	51	4			55	13	15
Great-niece or nephew	6				6	1	4
Aunt	1	0	2	0	3	1	—
Uncle	0	0	0	0	0	1	—
Cousin	6	0	0	1	7	2	1
Second cousin	1	0	0	0	1	—	—

Relative, but rel'shp n.k.	6	0	1	0	7	2	—
Step-father	—	1	0	0	1	—	—
Married step-son, or son-in-law	—	1	—	—	1	—	—
Married step-dau., or dau.-in-law	—	1	—	0	1	—	—
Step-grandchild	1	0	0	—	1	—	—
TOTAL (N)	272	104	59	16	(450)		

ª Figures for Preston from Anderson, *Family Structure*, 45.

century cities[13] was a housing arrangement suited to migrants and to individuals and families in particular phases of the life cycle—unmarried men and women between 20 and 29 years of age in the years before marriage, young married couples, and widowed persons.[14] But, while lodgers existed in the Potteries in 1861, there were relatively few. The enumerators classified 436 persons or 6 per cent of the individuals in the Potteries sample as lodgers or boarders; there were twice as many (12 per cent) in Preston in 1851. Moreover, in the Potteries the demand for lodgings differed. Male lodgers outnumbered females by two to one, and nearly three-quarters of the lodgers were unmarried, while in Preston there were roughly equal numbers of male and female lodgers, and only half were unmarried.[15] The differences probably reflect the higher proportion of migrants in the Preston population and the relative housing shortage in Preston.[16]

The supply of lodgings in the Potteries ranged from large lodging houses to private households where lodgers were taken in. Mr X describes a large cheap lodging house in Hanley during the period, called a 'crib' or 'paddincan' by his fellow lodgers. He secured a whole bed for himself there 'at the not very exorbitant sum of four pence for the night'. Alternatively he could have had half a bed for three pence. Regular lodgers paid eighteen pence a week with 'the seventh night in'. There were at least twenty persons staying that night, including 'men of various ages, females who all seemed to belong to a draggled type of womanhood, precocious juveniles in tatters and babies.' The men included

a tall and still youthful man who had evidently been a soldier; his eye still has fire, and his voice a deep diapason of command, as he tells how he spent some of his best days abroad in the Crimea and India and was turned off when he came home with only 6*d.* a day for two years, at the expiry of which period he 'took to the road', and had become as he stated rather scornfully 'a downright needy' or to use a more polite phrase a 'regular beggar'. His vis à vis on the opposite and close by the fire is a very old grey-haired person who sits silent with a short pipe between his teeth, and looks as if he was living in some far period of the past or was holding converse with the dead among whom he must soon be numbered. Yonder is a cripple who has had beer at many a public-house since he went forth

---

[13] L. Davidoff, 'The Separation of Home and Work? Landladies and Lodgers in 19th and 20th century England', in S. Burman (ed.), *Fit Work for Women* (London, 1979); T. Hareven and J. Modell, 'Urbanisation and the Malleable Household: An Examination of Boarding and Lodging in American Families', *Journal of Marriage and the Family*, 35 (1973), 467–79; Anderson, *Family Structure*, 46–8; Armstrong, *Stability and Change*, 180–4.

[14] See below for detailed discussion of the residence patterns of these groups.

[15] Anderson, *Family Structure*, 46–7.   [16] See above Ch. 1, sects. 3 and 5.

in the morning and who is counting out the coppers which he had collected. . . .
Two or three 'shallow coves' or fellows who appeal to public benevolence by
going forth half naked in the coldest and wildest weather are having their supper,
not a bad one either. . . . Gazing at them with a wolfish glare, his head between
his hands, leans a powerful 'navvy' in a white slop and with the inevitable red
neck kerchief tied à la mode. He states he has come to look for a job on the new
loopline.

A 'female attendant or deputy' showed him to his bed.

I was told to take off my boots before I ascended, and was led up a narrow
stairway to a large, low, square apartment, where there were no less than six beds
for 'single men', each intended to hold a couple and one smaller couch for any
person who might prefer, as I did, companionless singularity. . . . The beds were,
however, . . . tolerably clean, though but lightly covered. . . . There were two
coarse linen sheets, no blanket and a single rug, not of the very thickest texture
either.[17]

Although enumerators had difficulty in drawing the line between a
lodging house and a private household where lodgers taken in were the
sole support,[18] it is clear that such large lodging houses were in the
minority. The more respectable sections of the working class seem to
have lodged with a family or widow, as individuals or as one of a small
group. Of all households containing lodgers, 57 per cent had one lodger,
27 per cent had two, 11 per cent had three or four, and 5 per cent had
more than four. One household contained nine and another ten lodgers,
but only 4 per cent of all lodgers lived in a house with more than six
other lodgers. The Potteries fall between Colchester, where 70 per cent
of the households with lodgers had only one lodger, and Preston, where
41 per cent of the households with lodgers had only one lodger, and 21
per cent of all lodgers lived in a house with more than six other lodgers.[19]

While lodgers tended to be young and unmarried, landlords and landladies tended to be married or widowed middle-aged people, though
there was a tendency for those taking in lodgers to be younger in the
Potteries than in Colchester (see Table 2.4).

As in other nineteenth-century cities, the taking in of lodgers was a
way of providing a livelihood for widows or other women left without
support.[20] It was a way for women to support dependants at a time when
women's wages were often below subsistence even for themselves alone.
Nearly one-quarter of the households headed by women in the Potteries

---

[17] *SS* 28 Jan. 1871, 6.   [18] Davidoff, 'Separation', 85–6.
[19] Anderson, *Family Structure*, 47.   [20] Davidoff, 'Separation', 83.

TABLE 2.4   *Households with Lodgers: Potteries Sample 1861,*
Colchester 1851

Age of household head	Potteries 1861 Households (%)		Colchester 1851[a] Households (%)	
	All	with lodgers	All	with lodgers
30 years or less	22	19	16	16
31–50 years	56	55	61	38
51 years or more	22	26	23	46
N	1,368	242		

[a] Figures for Colchester from Davidoff, 'Separation', 83.

TABLE 2.5.   *Income of Families with Lodgers—Married Couples*
Heading Households Containing Lodgers: Potteries Sample 1861 (%)

Family wage-expenditure (*s./d.* below and above 0)	Households with information available	
	with lodgers	without lodgers
−15/− to −4/−	5.4	3.6
−3/11 to 3/11	17.6	12.4
4/− to 11/11	34.5	29.5
12/− to 19/11	25.0	29.5
20/− and above	17.6	25.2
N	148	703

contained lodgers—a higher proportion than those headed by either married couples or other men.

But, taking in lodgers also was important to married women living with their husbands. Married couples headed 74 per cent of the households which contained lodgers in the Potteries. Here the taking in of lodgers tended to supplement the family income rather than provide the sole support. Disproportionate percentages of households headed by married couples where family income left them near the poverty-line took in lodgers to supplement their wages (see Table 2.5).

Furthermore, married couples at each life-cycle stage took in lodgers to roughly the same extent, increasing in life-cycle stage 6, when couples

TABLE 2.6 *Percentage of Households in Each Life-Cycle Stage with Lodgers: Potteries Sample 1861*

Life-cycle stage	No. in life-cycle stage	% of households with lodgers
1	125	18
2	73	14
3	413	17
4	135	14
5	238	15
6	87	23
7	15	27

in middle age took in lodgers to provide income and fill up beds when grown children had left home and husbands' ability to earn high wages declined (see Table 2.6). For married women taking in lodgers was a way of supplementing family income without having to leave the home. For women it was 'a kind of subsistence employment—a way of life as much as making a living'.[21] In the Potteries only 11 per cent of the wives in households containing lodgers had another occupation as well, compared with 17 per cent of all married women.

Although 20 per cent of the households headed by unmarried men or widowers contained lodgers, this exaggerated the proportion of men who took in lodgers as a way of making a living or of supplementing the family income. In only one case was there no woman present in the household as a housekeeper or a daughter. Also, this is an over-estimate because in six cases those counted as lodgers were children of servants. The relationship of lodger implied above would not exist in these cases, although the experience for the children may have been similar. In two cases those listed as lodgers were children of 'housekeepers' so that the household appears to be headed by a man who was unmarried in name only. The household of Alphonse Parton, 21 Foley Road, Longton is an example.

Name	*Relation to Head*	*Marital Status*
Alphonse Parton	Head	Unmarried
Mary Wilkinson	Housekeeper	Unmarried
Levi Wilkinson	Son	Unmarried

[21] Ibid. 67.

Henry Wilkinson	Son	Unmarried
Edward Wilkinson	Son	Unmarried
Martha Wilkinson	Daughter	Unmarried
Emma Wilkinson	Daughter	Unmarried
Thomas Wilkinson	Son	Unmarried

Shared Houses

Sharing a house with another co-residing group may be seen as an alternative to sharing with kin or living in lodgings. In Preston 23 per cent of the households shared a house with one or more than one other household,[22] while in the Potteries only 8 per cent of the co-residing groups shared a house with another co-residing group.

Married Couples

These are aggregate figures, but a similar picture of relatively little sharing in the Potteries emerges if one looks at the same picture from the perspective of a specific group—married couples. There were a number of possible patterns of residence for married couples. They might head a household of their own; or they might live in someone else's household—a kinsman's or a landlord letting them lodgings. The extent to which married couples in the Potteries in 1861 chose these different options at different periods of the life cycle is shown in Table 2.7: 89 per cent of the married couples in the Potteries headed their own households and were the sole occupiers, compared with 72 per cent in Preston. Figures for the whole group can be misleading, yet even the proportion of married couples in life-cycle stage 1 with no children in the Potteries (76 per cent) is far greater than the 44 per cent of married couples in life-cycle stage 1 in Preston, again indicating more sharing in Preston. The difference in residence patterns must be at least partially explained by the larger supply of better-quality housing in the Potteries compared with the 'severe housing shortage' in Preston described in Chapter 1.[23]

This extended discussion of the tendency of nuclear families and married couples in the Potteries to share a house with people outside the nuclear family whether kin, lodgers, or another co-residing group, less frequently than in Preston, is important for giving perspective to the residence

[22] Anderson, *Family Structure*, 48.
[23] Further discussion of the implications of this table appears below in Ch. 8, Sect. 2. 'Young Married Couples'.

TABLE 2.7 *Married Couples: Residence Pattern by Life-Cycle Stage, Potteries Sample 1861, Preston 1851* (%)

| | | | Life-Cycle Stage | | | | |
	1	2	3	4	5	6	All
Heads own household							
Occupies house							
Potteries	76	67	91	94	98	95	89
Preston	44	56	76	85	82	73	72
Shares house							
Potteries	4	11	4	4	1	2	4
Preston	13	20	14	13	16	23	15
Does not head household							
Live as lodgers							
Potteries	9	6	2	2	0	1	3
Preston	28	14	5	1	1	4	8
Live as kin							
Potteries	12	16	3	0	0	3	4
Preston	15	10	4	0	0	1	5
All married couples (N)							
Potteries	157	94	435	138	240	109	1,173
Preston	159	59	388	122	234	106	1,068

Source: Figures for Preston from Anderson, *Family Structure*, 49.

patterns. An examination of residence patterns in the Potteries in 1861, however, would not be complete without both a brief description of the other non-family members who appeared in various households and a description of the residence patterns of two specific groups—young unmarried men and women and widowed persons.

Servants, Apprentices, Employees Living In, and Visitors

These categories are sometimes amalgamated. Anderson, for example, places apprentices in the same category as servants because of similarity of age and marital status, and he suggests that employees who live in, i.e. shop assistants or trade servants, might be grouped with lodgers on the

TABLE 2.8a   *Household Status of Individuals who were Neither Members of the Immediate Nuclear Family nor Kin: Potteries Sample 1861* (%)

Household status	% of all individuals	N
Lodger	6.4	436
Servant	2.5	171
Visitor	0.9	64
Employee living-in	0.5	35
Apprentice	0	12
N		6,771

TABLE 2.8b   *Proportions of All Co-residing Groups with Lodgers, Servants, Apprentices, Live-in Employees, and Visitors, Categorized by Marital Status of Head: Potteries Sample 1861*

	% of All Households with					
Head	Lodger	Servant	Apprentice	Live-in employee	Visitor	All hshlds. (N = 100%)
Married male	16	8	1	1	3	1,089
Other men	20	24	1	3	4	96
Women	24	6	1	2	3	182
All	18	9	1	1	3	1,367

grounds of similar age, marital status, and subordinate position.[24] Davidoff, on the other hand, sees all of these groups, as well as lodgers and kin outside the nuclear family, in the context of the provision of personal female service, and she emphasizes the ambiguities of definition which resulted from the Registrar General's decision that the basic unit in the census should be the family, whatever actual living arrangements may have been.[25] Here I merely want to set out the proportion of individuals in each category (Table 2.8a), and the proportions of households containing such individuals (Table 2.8b).

[24] M. Anderson, 'Standard Tabulation Procedures for the Census Enumerators' Books 1851–1891', in E. A. Wrigley (ed.), *Nineteenth Century Society: Essays in the Use of Quantitative Methods for the Study of Social Data* (Cambridge, 1972),144; id., *Family Structure*, 46.
[25] Davidoff, 'Separation', 76–7.

TABLE 2.9 *Distribution of Servants among the Six Towns, Potteries Sample 1861*

Town	Servants (N)	% of pop.
Tunstall	11	1
Burslem	29	2
Hanley and Shelton	67	3
Stoke	32	5
Fenton	7	1
Longton	25	2

The 171 servants in the Potteries sample (94 per cent were female) made up nearly 3 per cent of the Potteries sample population, and they were found in 8 per cent of the households headed by married couples. Three-quarters of the servants were under 25 years old, and 92 per cent were unmarried. One household had six servants, another four servants, and the rest of the households with servants had three or less. Servants tended to be distributed roughly evenly among the six towns (see Table 2.9).

Only twelve boys, or less than 1 per cent of the sample population, lived in households as 'apprentices' (i.e. they were listed as such in the column 'relation to head of household' in the enumerators' books). They ranged in age from 12 to 18 years, and they were found in less than 1 per cent of the co-residing groups (see Table 2.8*b*). There were three apprentice tailors, two apprentice shoemakers, two apprentice chemists, one apprentice harness-maker, one apprentice baker, and one apprentice ironmonger. In several cases there was probably little difference between 'apprentice' and an 'assistant who lived in'.

There were thirty-five trade assistants (i.e. listed as 'assistant' or 'employee' in the column headed 'relationship to household head'). Twenty-seven of these were men and eight were women. They lived in sixteen, or approximately 1 per cent, of the co-residing groups. Ranging in age from 15 to 59 years, they included an agricultural labourer, a barge assistant, a barmaid, and a clothier's assistant. The distinction between 'assistant' and 'servant', as well as 'apprentice' appears to be ambiguous.

On census night, 3 per cent of all households had at least one visitor and 64 or nearly 1 per cent of the sample population were listed as visitors. Visitors ranged from those who were staying one night to those who stayed longer as part of their employment, looking for employment, or possibly providing assistance. Betty Hawkings, a 63-year-old widow, for example, was a visitor in a Hanley household with no parents but five children, the eldest of whom was 14.

Young, Unmarried Men and Women

Young, unmarried men and women, like married couples, could follow one of several patterns of residence. They might live with parents, with kin, in lodgings, or live in as servants. The extent to which age and migration influenced the pattern chosen is illustrated in Table 2.10.

Most young persons, especially those under 20 years of age, lived with one or both of their parents as part of a nuclear family. Of those not living with parents, a large proportion probably had no parents in the Potteries with whom they could live. Some may have been orphans, the parents of others may have left the Potteries, and many were in-migrants who had left their parents behind in the villages or towns of their birth or last residence.

As Anderson found in Preston, migrants to the Potteries were less likely to live with parents than those born in the Potteries. Of the in-migrants not living with parents, those living with kin may have lived in the Potteries most of their lives, having come with parents or siblings many years earlier, or they may have migrated recently and been taken in by kin, given a home, and helped to find a job. The rest of the migrants went into lodgings and, particularly girls, into service.

Only 5 per cent of the 15–19 age-group and 20 per cent of the 20–4 age-group lived in lodgings, and migrants were more than twice as likely to live in lodgings as those in each age-group born in the Potteries. Thus, while the option of living in lodgings did exist, it is probable that many of those born in the Potteries and not living with parents had no parents in the Potteries with whom they could live. From the age-specific mortality rates in the life-tables for the Stoke and Wolstanton registration districts 1838–44 (Chapter 1, Appendix), it is possible to estimate that 8 per cent of the 15–19 age-group and 16 per cent of the 20–4 age-group in 1861 had neither parent alive.[26] This suggests that only 6 per cent of the boys aged 15–19 and 18 per cent of the boys aged 20–4 who were born in the Potteries had parents alive but were not living with them.

---

[26] This calculation assumes that the mean age of their parents when these children were born was 33, that the children lived 17 and 22 years respectively, and that the probabilities of mortality were independent for each parent. These estimates are slightly lower than the 10 per cent and 19 per cent which Anderson estimates for Preston, but the figures are subject to a margin of error. Anderson, *Family Structure*, 54, 206.

TABLE 2.10 *Residence Patterns of Unmarried Persons Aged 10–34, Categorized by Age and Migrancy: Potteries Sample 1861*

	All young persons	Living with parents		Young persons not living with parents						All	
				in ldgs	with kin	in svce.	visitor	apprentice or employee living in	institution		
	N	N	%	N	N	N	N	N	N	N	%
Males											
10–14 yrs.											
Potteries	264	234	87	6	21	0	0	1	2	30	13
Within 10mi.	27	21	78	3	1	1	0	1	0	6	22
Elsewhere	76	62	82	6	5	0	2	2	1	14	18
15–19 yrs.											
Potteries	228	195	86	8	19	2	1	3	1	33	14
Within 10mi.	20	15	75	0	3	1	0	1	0	5	25
Elsewhere	67	40	60	13	6	1	1	7	0	27	40
20–4 yrs.											
Potteries	127	84	66	20	21	0	0	2	0	43	34
Within 10mi.	13	8	62	1	0	0	2	4	0	5	38
Elsewhere	77	18	23	38	8	3	5	10	0	59	77
25–34 yrs.											
Potteries	69	40	58	16	11	1	0	1	0	29	42
Within 10mi.	10	4	40	5	0	0	0	0	1	6	60
Elsewhere	44	11	25	23	4	1	2	5	0	33	75

TABLE 2.10 *continued*

	All young persons	Living with parents		Young persons not living with parents							
								apprentice or employee living in	institution	All	
				in ldgs	with kin	in svce.	visitor				
	N	N	%	N	N	N	N	N	N	N	%
Females											
10–14 yrs.											
Potteries	285	238	84	7	18	18	0	0	4	47	16
Within 10mi.	31	22	71	0	2	7	0	0	0	9	29
Elsewhere	64	54	84	1	4	4	1	1	0	10	16
15–19 yrs.											
Potteries	204	156	77	6	20	19	3	0	3	48	23
Within 10mi.	34	17	50	1	1	14	1	0	1	17	50
Elsewhere	72	40	56	3	6	19	1	1	3	32	44
20–4 yrs.											
Potteries	105	76	72	11	8	10	1	0	0	29	28
Within 10mi.	13	2	15	0	2	8	1	1	0	11	85
Elsewhere	36	14	39	2	1	18	1	1	0	22	61
25–34 yrs.											
Potteries	53	38	72	3	8	4	2	0	0	15	28
Within 10mi.	12	3	25	2	1	5	2	1	0	9	75
Elsewhere	24	16	59	0	1	10	1	0	0	11	41

Furthermore, of those born in the Potteries not living with parents, 58 per cent of the boys aged 15–19 and 42 per cent of the girls in that age-group lived with kin. This again suggests that a large proportion of those who had kin but not parents in the area lived with kin, and in practice lodging was not taken up as an alternative to living with parents or kin.

There was, however, a difference between boys and girls in the extent to which they lived with parents as they grew older. Approximately equal proportions of boys and girls aged 10–14 lived with parents regardless of whether or not the boys and girls were born in the Potteries. In the 15–19 age-group, however, boys, particularly those born 'elsewhere', tended to live in lodgings, while girls, born within 10 miles or 'elsewhere', tended to go into residential domestic service.[27] Of those born in the Potteries, slightly more girls than boys lived away from parents. Again domestic service accounts for the differential. Thus, in this age-group, girls were less likely to co-reside with parents than boys. However, the pattern is reversed in the age-groups above twenty years, and girls were more likely than boys to live with parents, apart from boys born within 10 miles who were more likely than girls to live with parents, again presumably because girls born within 10 miles tended to go into domestic service.

These figures have been used to indicate the age when children 'left home'.[28] More children seem to have resided with parents longer in the Potteries and Preston in the mid-nineteenth century than in pre-industrial England.[29] In the Potteries and in Preston half or more of the age-group 20–4 lived with parents.[30] Furthermore, in the mid-nineteenth century a smaller proportion of boys in rural areas in the 15–19 age-group (56 per cent) lived with their parents than they did in the Potteries or in Preston (79 per cent). The implications of this difference have been the focus of a controversy between Michael Katz and Michael Anderson.[31] Katz suggests that the larger proportion of boys living with parents in Preston means that family ties and commitments were somehow stronger in the city than in the country. Anderson rightly replies that it is a mistake to infer attitudes from structural description, for 'the frequency

[27] This pattern in the Potteries follows the general pattern described by Davidoff, 'Separation', 78–9.
[28] R. Wall, 'The Age at Leaving Home', *J. of Fam. Hist.* 3 (1978), 192.
[29] Ibid. 193.   [30] Cf. Ibid. 190, Table 2.
[31] M. Katz, 'Review Essay: Family Structure in 19th Century Lancashire' *J. of Soc. Hist.* 7 (1973–4), 88–92; M. Anderson, 'Review Essay: The People of Hamilton, Canada West, Family and Class in a Mid-19th Century City', *J. of Fam. Hist.* 2 (1977), 139–49.

with which teenage boys leave home has no necessary relationship at all to the attitudes that they hold towards their family relationships'.[32]

In general, then, apart from migrant boys and girls who were domestic servants, there was a tendency for young, unmarried persons to reside with parents or kin, at least until marriage, and occasionally after marriage, as we saw earlier in this section when considering the residence patterns of married couples.

Widowed Persons

The residence patterns of widowed persons in the Potteries, as well as in Preston, indicate that kin were important to those who may have been in need. In the Potteries 20 per cent of widowed persons lived with kin, with the kin as head of the household; and 22 per cent of widowed persons headed their own household and took in kin. Thus, 42 per cent of all widowed persons lived with kin (other than unmarried children), compared with 39 per cent in Preston.[33] As a result, although there was less sharing with kin outside the nuclear family in the Potteries than in Preston, there was more sharing between widowed persons and kin. Furthermore, kin were important particularly for older widowed persons. Of those aged 65 and over, 78 per cent had one or more kin in the same household, and 22 per cent had no known related person living in the same household. These patterns indicate the importance of kin in the Potteries, and as I shall argue below in Chapter 8, they also suggest that while dependence or mutual assistance probably characterized the relationship of some widowed persons with kin, in other cases the widowed person provided assistance.

Conclusion

Residence within a nuclear family, whether the family of 'orientation' or of 'procreation', was the normal pattern for the Potteries taken as a whole. As we saw in the first section of this chapter, this pattern was even more marked in the Potteries than in Preston, for overall there was less sharing with persons outside the nuclear family in the Potteries than in Preston. This difference was related to the differences in housing, migration, and mortality described in Chapter 1. If this synchronic picture of co-residence in the Potteries is turned into a diachronic view, it implies, however, that children resided with parents until marriage and with their spouse or an unmarried child until death. Although this may

---

[32] Anderson, 'Review Essay', 147.   [33] Anderson, *Family Structure*, 55.

have been the pattern for many, the proportion of people in the population as a whole in 1861 who did occupy some non-nuclear family residential status suggests that an even higher proportion occupied a family
position outside an immediate nuclear family at some time in their lives
whether due to the mortality of parents, spouse, or children, migration,
dependence, mutual assistance, or deliberate rejection. These explanations and implications of the co-residence patterns will be discussed in
more detail below in Chapter 8.

2. Relationships Within Nuclear Families

The preceding section suggests that, although a significant proportion
of individuals in the Potteries resided outside a nuclear family at some
time during their lives, residence within a nuclear family was the most
common pattern for most of the population most of the time. Thus,
aspects of relationships within nuclear families—between husbands and
wives and parents and children, particularly marriage and births—require
examination.

Marriage

Nuptiality. Taking the population of the Potteries as a whole one-third
was unmarried in 1861. But such an aggregate figure disguises the fact
that it was a young population with a very high possibility that an
individual ultimately would marry. Nuptiality—the proportion of surviving children who married—was as high or higher in the Potteries than
in England and Wales as a whole.

Women in the Potteries were more likely to marry in due course than
women in either England and Wales as a whole or women in a town such
as York with a high ratio of females to males (see Table 2.11). Only 6 per
cent of women aged 45–54 in the Potteries were still unmarried, compared with 12 per cent of women in England and Wales in the same age-
group, and 16 per cent in York.[34] The proportion of men in the Potteries
who never married was slightly higher than that of women, but it
hovered around the national average of approximately 10 per cent.[35]

---

[34] Figures for both women and men in the Potteries are calculated from: Potteries
sample 1861; Stoke-upon-Trent registration district 1861 and Wolstanton registration district 1861 in the 1861 Census PP 1863, liii, pt. 2, pp. 178, 195. Figures for Eng. and Wales
are calculated from PP 1863, liii, pt. 1, pp. 285–6, 278–9. Figures for York are calculated
from Armstrong, *Stability and Change*, 162.

[35] There was some variation within the area in this figure: in the Stoke-upon-Trent
registration district it was 8 per cent, while in Wolstanton it was 12.5; the figure for the
Potteries sample as a whole was 12 per cent, compared with 10.5 per cent for England and
Wales overall.

TABLE 2.11 *Percentage of Each Age-Group Ever-Married: Potteries Sample 1861, England and Wales 1861, Preston 1851, York 1851*

Age-group	Potteries m	Potteries f	Eng. & Wales m	Eng. & Wales f	Preston m	Preston f	York m	York f
15–19	1	6	.5	3	2	3	.3	3
20–4	32	48	23	34	30	29	21	31
25–34	76	82	69	70	73	64	67	69
35–44	89	91	86	84	88	84	83	80
45–54	88	94	90	88	94	90	87	84
55–64	95	94	91	89	95	92	88	84

Sources: see n. 34; figures for Preston from Anderson, *Family Structure*, 133.

The proportion of men and women between the ages of 45 and 54 who are unmarried reflect the proportions ultimately marrying, but it is in the proportions who were unmarried in the age-group 25–34 that the largest differences in marriage proportions between different areas of the country occur.[36] The proportions in this age-group reflect both differences in the proportions ultimately marrying and differences in the age at first marriage. In the Potteries (Table 2.11) higher proportions of both men and women in this age-group were married than in England and Wales as a whole, the county town of York, or even the cotton town of Preston.[37]

Age at First Marriage. The proportions of men and women married at different ages not only reflects the proportion ultimately marrying and variations in marriage patterns in different areas of the country, but also they give an indication of the age at first marriage.[38] The 'singulate mean age of marriage' developed by Hajnal is an estimate of the mean age of marriage of single persons based on proportions unmarried at different ages.[39] This figure is inaccurate to the extent to which the married and unmarried have different age-specific mortality or migration rates, but it is the best indicator available for the age of first marriage in the Potteries

[36] M. Anderson, 'Marriage Patterns in Victorian Britain: An Analysis based on Registration District Data for England and Wales 1861', *J. of Fam. Hist.* 1 (1976), 58.

[37] Anderson, 'Marriage Patterns', 76 demonstrates that the sex-ratio of the population, particularly at extreme values, was an important constraint on marriage chances. This seems to be the case with these three differences.

[38] See Anderson, 'Marriage Patterns', 57 for a thorough discussion of the advantages and disadvantages of proportion-based indicators.

[39] J. Hajnal, 'Age at Marriage and Proportions Marrying', *Pop. Studies* 7 (1953), esp. 129–30.

as well as for England and Wales as a whole. The precise ages of the bride and groom were often not recorded in the parochial marriage registers; instead, 'of full age' appears frequently in the 'age' column of the registers, unless the bride or groom were minors.[40]

Although the youngest married males in the Potteries sample were 19 years old, the singulate mean age of marriage for men was approximately 25 years of age. It was, however, considerably less than that for men in England and Wales as a whole (27 years old). The youngest married female in the Potteries was 16 years old, but the next youngest was aged 18. The singulate mean age of marriage for women in the Potteries was roughly 24 years of age. Again, it was lower than that of women in England and Wales as a whole (26 years old) by about the same amount as that of men in the Potteries in relation to men in England and Wales.

Thus, the mean age of marriage for both men and women in the Potteries was two years below the mean age of marriage for men and women in England and Wales as a whole. This is what one would expect given that it was customary to set up a household of one's own on marriage and the housing supply made it possible, and that men could earn full wages by the age of 21 in the major occupations in the Potteries.[41] But, as for the nation as a whole, the mean age for women was one year less than that for men.

Although on average the mean age of marriage for women was one year less than that of men, only 13 per cent of the married couples in the Potteries census sample fit this average picture of a one-year age-gap between husband and wife. The age-difference was five years or less between 78 per cent of the husbands and wives. An example of 'rough music' or 'charivari' in Hanley in 1878 indicates that this conformity in the relative ages of husbands and wives was not a statistical artefact but was subject to informal but explicit community limits.[42]

[40] Anderson, 'Marriage Patterns', 58 n. 11. In the Potteries e.g. SCRO. D/3229/6. Etruria, St Matthew, Marriage Register 1849–69, does not give precise ages; SCRO. D3463/1/19, Tunstall, Christchurch, Marriage Register 1857–65 and SCRO. D3277/1/2/3, Longton, St James, Marriage Register 1858–67 give precise ages.

[41] Anderson, 'Marriage Patterns', 64, 71 finds that for men 'a clear relationship existed between living in areas dominated by "traditional" industrial occupations such as textiles, coal-mining . . . and one's statistical chances of marriage and of an early marriage age'. He also finds a relationship between a high incidence of domestic service and low marriage rates for women. Housing supply is described above in Ch. 1. Nearly three-quarters of married couples without children headed their own household, suggesting that the ability to set up an independent household was a pre-requisite for marriage.

[42] E. P. Thompson, 'Rough Music: Le Charivari Anglais', *Annales E.S.C.* (*Economies, Societes, Civilisations*) 27 (1972), 285–312, esp. 299.

The occasion was the wedding of a Hanley grocer named William Lomas, aged 68, and a widower with grown children, to Ellen Milne, a girl of 18 who lived with her parents in Shelton. Her parents apparently approved of the match, though his children probably did not. The social difference between them was not enough to cause such a reaction; instead it was the age-difference and the 'enormous proportions' of the groom that were subject to disapproval. The public objection was strong enough for a large crowd to gather during the working week and for disapproval to be expressed in part by dressing up a donkey in funeral attire, perhaps to suggest death in life for the bride and the mixing of rites of passage. The newspaper account is particularly vivid.

The event has been looked forward to with great interest for some weeks, or probably months past, the wedding day [a Tuesday] having been fixed and delayed several times. At an early hour this morning, however, the near approach of the happy circumstance was proclaimed in the neighbourhood in which the bride and bridegroom lived by the driver of a donkey cart, who, with his donkey specially dressed with boughs of trees, and black and white papers, and himself wearing a long hatband, perambulated the principal streets in Shelton. This unusual scene in the streets, of course, was the means of collecting together some thousands of persons in the neighbourhood of Norfolk Street who kept up a continual ironical shout till the wedding party left the bride's father's about ten o'clock. The party, in a four-wheeler, arrived at Bethesda Chapel exactly at half-past ten, where crowds of the roughest and noisiest persons conceivable had assembled, the vehicle containing the party being followed by the irrepressible donkey cart. Their arrival at the chapel was the signal for a general uproar of vulgar jest, shouts, hisses, and a number of missiles were thrown at the old gentleman and the young girl as they alighted, doing considerable damage to their wearing apparel. Some of the missiles caught the carriage windows and completely smashed them. By this time Inspectors Vickers and Wall had arrived on the scene with a force of six or eight officers, who did all they could to keep back the mob from the chapel, but their efforts were futile, and the building was soon filled [it seated 2,500] with perhaps the most riotous and disorderly assembly that ever congregated in a place of worship. At twenty minutes to eleven the bride, accompanied by her father and mother and a young lady named Bamford of Wolstanton, attended by the bridegroom, emerged from the vestry, being received with a deafening noise of jarring sounds from those assembled in the body of the sacred building, and also the galleries, both being by this time completely filled. The marriage service was commenced, the . . . circuit minister officiating, but so great was the uproar that not a single word read by the minister, not a single response by the bride or bridegroom could be heard, even by those who stood next to the party themselves. When the gentleman was asked to put the ring on his young bride, he placed the indispensable article on the third finger of the right hand, which action called from the facetious multitude howls, groans, hisses, ironical cheers, and laughter, amidst the waving of hand-kerchiefs and caps. [The minister] attempted to appease the half-infuriated and half-humorous people, but to no purpose. The bridegroom had his mistake pointed out to him, and he rectified his mistake by placing the ring on the proper finger of the left hand, saying as he did so, with a somewhat chagrined coun-tenance, 'I thought this would be a quiet place to get married at, but if I had to do it a thousand times again I'd . . .', the last words of the sentence being lost in the hubbub that prevailed. When leaving the communion rail, the party got separated, the bride seeking a quick shelter in the vestry, whilst the bridegroom was so crushed and jostled about that he could scarcely keep on his feet; indeed the old gentleman had the greatest difficulty to reach the vestry, being assisted in doing so by the bride's father, who dealt out one or two blows at the vestry door. The bridegroom, on reaching the interior, fell on a chair more than a little exhausted. The vestry was assailed, and one of the windows broken by the mob. The offices of registration having been performed, the party attempted to leave the chapel, and with the assistance of the officers, managed to reach the carriage with no further injury than the ladies' dresses being torn. Eight officers escorted the happy pair home, four being on either side of the vehicle, and the irrepress-ible donkey, in funeral attire, brought up the rear at a short distance.[43]

Despite further harassment in Stone on their honeymoon night and on their return to Stoke the next day, business in the groom's shop was 'unusually brisk' and the bride was behind the counter 'looking remark-able cool'.

Despite the age-difference and the 'rough music', this marriage was typical in that all marriages had to take place between 8 and 12 a.m.[44] May, however, was a somewhat unusual time of the year for marriage in the Potteries in the mid-nineteenth century. Higher proportions of marriages occurred in the last two quarters of the year. Examination of marriage registers suggests that holidays were the most popular time for marriages within the working classes. The major holidays—the Wakes Weeks in August and Christmas, and especially Christmas Day—fell in the second half of the year, but Easter Day also had a disproportionately large number of marriages.[45] The seasonality of marriage in the Potteries between 1855 and 1864 shows a different pattern than that in the agricul-tural areas of North Staffordshire around Leek, Cheadle, and Uttoxeter,

---

[43] *SS* 11 May 1878, 8.

[44] Unless by special licence or Quaker or Jewish weddings, PP 1867–8, xxxii, 7–8. Report of the Royal Commission on the Marriage Laws. In the marriage registers there is evidence of five marriages on one day between 8 a.m. and noon.

[45] Marriage Registers from the Potteries cited above.

where the smallest proportion of marriages were in the third quarter of the year.

The wedding of William Lomas and Ellen Milne was also unusual in that it took place in a New Connexion Methodist Church and not according to the rites of the Established Church. Nearly twice as many people are recorded as attending Nonconformist, especially Methodist, chapels as attended Anglican services in the Potteries on Census Sunday 1851. But in 1862, 89 per cent of the marriages in the Stoke-upon-Trent registration district took place according to the rites of the Established Church, with only 5 per cent occurring in registered places of worship such as the Bethesda Chapel, 5 per cent in Catholic Churches, and 1 per cent in the Superintendent Registrar's Office. The proportion of marriages in the Established Church was somewhat lower in the Wolstanton registration district, but it was still higher than the proportion of marriages in England and Wales as a whole.[46] Thus, the Potteries was an urban area where Nonconformity was strong but civil marriage was not. This was due in part to the prevalence of both Wesleyan Methodists, who tended to advise marriage in the Established Church, and Primitive Methodists who did not marry in chapels.[47] (There is no evidence about New Connexion Methodists; it is possible that they had the same policy as the Wesleyans except where their churches were registered, for example Bethesda in Hanley where the Lomas–Milne wedding took place.) The Potteries is an urban area similar to Lincolnshire, both of which provide a contrast in experience to the areas of high Nonconformity and high civil registration, such as Wales and Cornwall, that formed the subject of a recent controversy.[48]

Horizons of Marriage. The extent of occupational endogamy in the Potteries is discussed below in Chapter 3. In terms of geographical endogamy, analysis both of the Anglican marriage registers for several parishes within the Potteries between 1860 and 1862 and of the sample of the census enumerators' books for the Potteries in 1861 suggest that the

[46] PP 1864, xvii, 73; Registrar General's Twenty-Fifth Annual Report, 1862.

[47] The Revd William Robinson, President of the Primitive Methodist Conference wrote that 'the Christian body to which I . . . belong do not perform the ceremony of marriage among themselves. The ministers of the society leave the members to go to the Established Church and other Churches': PP 1867–8, xxxii, 58.

[48] O. Anderson, 'The Incidence of Civil Marriage in Victorian England and Wales', *Past and Present*, 69 (1975), 50–87; R. Floud, P. Thane, and O. Anderson, 'Debate: The Incidence of Civil Marriage in Victorian England and Wales', *Past and Present*, 84 (1979), 146–62.

geographical horizons of marriage were limited. Most marriage partners came from the same town within the Potteries and frequently even from the same street within the town.

On the marriage registers the bride and groom specified her and his 'residence at the time of marriage'. Although there are ambiguities associated with this information,[49] it does give an indication of the geographical horizons of marriage in the mid-nineteenth century.[50] Within the Potteries, for example, St John's Parish covered a substantial part of Burslem including much of the central area of the town, and it might be expected to be one of the more cosmopolitan parishes in the Potteries.[51] Yet, between 1860 and 1862 there were 203 marriages, and in 91 per cent of these marriages both the groom and the bride resided in Burslem at the time of the marriage. Of the remaining 9 per cent, in 2.5 per cent or five of the marriages one partner came from Tunstall. There were no marriages involving a partner from any of the other four Potteries towns; however, in 3 per cent or six marriages one of the partners resided in a town or village close to the six towns, i.e. Wolstanton, Milton, Kidsgrove, Audley, Talke, Chesterton. In three marriages a partner came from a Cheshire village or town within twenty miles of Burslem, i.e. Whitchurch, Bosley, Church Eaton. In only 2 per cent or four marriages did a partner come from beyond twenty miles; there were two grooms from Liverpool, a bride from Colchester, and a bride from Penrith.

The figures above refer to all marriages between 1860 and 1862 within the parish, but, as with other areas, there is evidence that in this parish,

[49] D. E. C. Eversley, 'Exploitation of Anglican Parish Registers by Aggregative Analysis', in E. A. Wrigley (ed.), *An Introduction to English Historical Demography* (London, 1966), 64 argues that the Settlement Laws encouraged grooms to name the parish of marriage as the place of residence, thereby exaggerating the extent of endogamy. This argument is discussed and refuted by P. J. Perry, 'Working-Class Isolation and Mobility in Rural Dorset 1837–1936: A Study of Marriage Distances', *Trans. Instit. Brit. Geog.* 46 (1969), 123–24. Perry suggests that the 'registers are sufficiently (but not perfectly) reliable as a record of residence'. R. Dennis, 'Distance and Social Interaction in a Victorian City' *J. of Hist. Geog.* 3 (1977), 240–1.

[50] In addition to Perry, 'Isolation and Mobility' and Dennis, 'Social Interaction' others who have used marriage registers to examine the geographical origins of marriage partners in 19th-cent. England include: R. F. Peel, 'Local Intermarriage and the Stability of Rural Population in the English Midlands', *Geography*, 27 (1942), 22–30; B. Maltby, 'Easingwold Marriage Horizons', *Local Pop. Studies* 2 (1969), 36–9; and B. Maltby, 'Parish Registers and the Problem of Mobility', *Local Pop. Studies* 6 (1971), 32–43.

[51] The Marriage Registers of the Parish of St John the Baptist, Burslem for the years 1860–2 were in the custody of Revd P. L. C. Smith, the incumbent, when I used them. The Registers are now deposited in the Staffordshire County Record Office.

the higher and wealthier the social group, the broader the geographical horizons of marriage.[52] Marriage by 'common licence' cost £4 4s. compared with a few shillings or no fee for marriage by banns.[53] Thus, marriage by licence can be taken as an indication of relative wealth. There were fourteen marriages by licence out of the 203 marriages in St John's Parish.[54] Both the bride and groom resided in Burslem in less than half of the marriages by licence, compared with 91 per cent of all marriages. Thus, the overall figures for St John's parish underestimate the narrowness of the geographical horizons of marriage for most people.

Not only was there endogamy within towns within the Potteries, but in Wellington Parish in Hanley, the marriage registers include the name of the street rather than merely the town of residence.[55] In this parish between 1860 and 1862 in 36 per cent of the marriages both the bride and groom lived in the same street. If those with partners residing on neighbouring streets were included, the proportion of marriages between brides and grooms residing very near to each other would be even higher.[56]

The endogamy in Burslem is greater than that which Perry found in a study of twenty-seven Dorset parishes.[57] Between 1857 and 1866 81 per cent of the marriages in these parishes were 'intra-parochial'. Moreover, these figures exclude those most likely to marry a partner from outside of the parish, e.g. farmers and servants. This should maximize the extent of intermarriage. The extent of endogamy is also greater in Burslem than

[52] Perry, 'Isolation and Mobility', 124–5; Dennis, 'Social Interaction', 238, 245–50 concerns intra-urban marriage partners only, but his analysis takes into account not only the distance, but also residential segregation, because he matches marriage-register information with census enumerators' books. This type of analysis is not attempted here. L. Stone, *Family Sex and Marriage in England 1500–1800* (London, 1977), 62.

[53] PP 1867–8, xxxii, 7 includes a description of this method. The fee cited is £4 8s. 6d. including the fees on solemnization, and is that of the Diocese of Rochester. The fees vary, but that of £4 4s. in the Diocese of Lichfield in 1863 (without fees on solemnization) is similar. I am grateful to the Archivist of the Lichfield Joint Record Office for this information.

[54] The occupations of the grooms, fathers of grooms, and fathers of the brides married by licence were not exclusively, but tended to be, of relatively high social status. The occupations included: mine agent, coal master, farmer, collector, merchant, commission agent, bookseller, chemist, inspector of Inland Revenue, wine merchant, gentleman, overlooker, surgeon, Wesleyan minister, engineer, miller, butcher, foreman, publican, artist, hosier, potter.

[55] The marriage registers for Wellington Parish 1860–2 are in the parish church (St Luke's) in the custody of the incumbent, Revd M. F. West.

[56] These figures correspond roughly to those which Dennis found in Huddersfield, although the figures are not strictly comparable. He found that in 1861 32.2 per cent of marriage partners from within Huddersfield resided less than .5 km. from each other at the time of marriage: Dennis, 'Social Interaction', 243.

[57] Perry, 'Isolation and Mobility', 124–5.

TABLE 2.12a *Of All Husbands Born in and Residing in Various Towns, Percentage whose Wife was Born in the Same Town*

Husband born and residing in:	% with wife born in same town
Tunstall	67.6
Burslem	68.3
Hanley	78.4
Hanley and Shelton	69.3

Source: Potteries Sample 1861.

in four Northampton parishes in the middle of the nineteenth century.[58] These, however, were rural parishes with relatively small populations. There is evidence that endogamy increases with the size of the population of the area, and this probably explains, at least partially, the relatively high proportion in Burslem which had a population of 22,327 in 1861.[59] In the absence of information for towns of comparable size in the 1860s, it is not possible to know whether Burslem is unusual,[60] but further indication of the extent of endogamy comes from another source— the census enumerators' books.

From the marriage registers it is not possible to ascertain how long an individual resided in the place indicated at the time of marriage—it may have been anything from since birth to a few weeks. The enumerators' books, however, give an indication of the limitations on the geographical horizons of marriage from this perspective. They give the place of birth of the husband and wife, although they do not indicate subsequent moves. Over two-thirds of the husbands born in and residing in various Potteries towns in 1861 were married to a woman born in the same town (see Table 2.12a). The proportion of wives born in and residing in various Potteries towns in 1861 who were married to men born in the same town was only slightly lower than that of husbands (Table 2.12b). There are no comparable figures for mid-nineteenth-century English towns; however, the proportions in the Potteries towns for both men and women are over twice as high as the 28 per cent of men born in places

---

[58] Peel, 'Local Intermarriage', 27.

[59] Perry, 'Isolation and Mobility', 126, 128, 132; D. A. Coleman, 'The Geography of Marriage in Britain 1920–1960', *Annals of Human Biology*, 4 (1977), 110–15; PP 1862, 1, 440.

[60] Dennis, 'Social Interaction' does not give comparable figures for Huddersfield in the mid-19th cent.

TABLE 2.12*b* *Of All Wives Born in and Residing in Various Towns,*
Percentage whose Husband was Born in the Same Town

Wife born in and residing in:	% with husband born in same town
Tunstall	65.7
Burslem	68.3
Hanley	64.5
Hanley and Shelton	61.7

Source: Potteries Sample 1861.

with 10,000–50,000 people, i.e. similar to the population of the Potteries towns who marry women from the same town, and the 29 per cent of women born in such towns who marry men from the same town in England and Wales in 1960.[61]

Duration of Marriage, Remarriage, and Hybrid Families. During the mid-nineteenth century it was common for death to disrupt relationships between husbands and wives, and parents and children. I shall argue later that it was death far more than factory work which disrupted families in the Potteries in the mid-nineteenth century. The duration of marriage was short, remarriage was frequent, and 'hybrid' families were common.

As might be expected given the relatively high age-specific mortality rates in the Potteries, the duration of marriage was comparatively short. In the late 1850s and early 1860s it was likely that roughly 30 per cent of the marriages in the Stoke-upon-Trent registration district would be broken up by the death of one of the partners in the first fifteen years of marriage, compared with 22 per cent of the marriages in England and Wales as a whole. Moreover, the median duration of first marriages in the Stoke-upon-Trent registration district in this period was slightly less than twenty-five years, compared with approximately twenty-eight years in England and Wales.[62]

---

[61] Dennis, 'Social Interaction', 115.

[62] The method of calculation was adapted from H. S. Shryock and J. S. Siegel, *Methods and Materials of Demography* (Washington DC, 1973), ii, 573–4. The male and female singulate mean ages of marriage (see above, Ch. 2, Sect. 2, 'Age at First Marriage') were used as the ages of marriage in England and Wales for husbands (27.1 years) and wives (26.2 years) and in the Potteries for husbands (25 years) and wives (24 years). In the calculation for England and Wales the age-specific death-rates for men and women 1858–64 from *Abst. of Brit. Hist. Stats.* 38, 40 were used. The age-specific death-rates for men

One of the implications of these figures is that relatively few husbands and wives would have time together after their children left home; relatively few parents survived to experience the 'empty nest'. If the probability that a couple would survive twenty-five years of marriage was less than 50 per cent, then the probability that a couple would have a life together after their children left home was even lower.

In addition, these mortality figures suggest that remarriage was frequent. In the Stoke-upon-Trent registration district between 1858 and 1864 an average of 18 per cent of all marriages was a remarriage for the bride or groom. Although the rate is less than the 22 per cent of marriages in four registration districts in central Glasgow in 1855, it is about the same as that for England and Wales as a whole (18 per cent).[63] Remarriage was more common for widowers than for widows, but the difference in the Potteries was considerably less than that in other areas. In the Stoke-upon-Trent registration district 56 per cent of those remarrying were widowers and 44 per cent were widows, compared with 65 per cent widowers and 35 per cent widows in Glasgow in 1855, and 61 per cent widowers and 39 per cent widows in England and Wales in 1861. Moreover, in the Potteries the tendency for widowers to marry spinsters and widows to marry widowers was less marked than in Glasgow. 57 per cent of the widowers in the Stoke-upon-Trent registration district married spinsters, compared with 65 per cent of the widowers in Glasgow in 1855, and 46 per cent of the widows married bachelors in the Potteries compared with 35 per cent of the widows in Glasgow in 1855.[64]

If it were probable that death would disrupt the relationship between husband and wife within the first fifteen years of marriage in the Potteries

and women in the Potteries used in the calculation came from the 'abridged' life-tables for the Stoke-upon-Trent registration district 1858–1864 (see Tables 1.A3 and 1.A4), which were derived from the number of deaths by age-groups 1858–64 in the Registrar General's Annual Reports (PP 1860, xxix, 704–5 for 1858; PP 1861, xviii, 166–7 for 1859; PP 1862, xvii, 158–9 for 1860; PP 1863, xiv, 158–9 for 1861; PP 1864, xvii, 166–7 for 1862; PP 1865, xiv, 166–7 for 1863; PP 1866, xix, 186–7 for 1864), and from the age-structure of males and females in the 1861 census (PP 1863, liii, pt. 2, 178).

[63] The remarriage rates in mid-19th-cent. Britain in general seem to be lower than those in the 17th cent., when they were 33 per cent in Manchester in 1650, or in the mid-20th-cent. United States, where they were again about 33 per cent, see Stone, *Family*, 56; PP 1863 xiv, 50–1 for the remarriage rate for England and Wales in 1861.

[64] The remarriage rates for the Stoke-upon-Trent registration district are calculated from the figures in the Annual Report of the Registrar General 1858–64: for Glasgow see M. Drake, 'The Remarriage Market in Mid-19th Century Britain', a paper presented to the International Colloquium on Historical Demography, Kristiansand, Norway, 7–9 September 1979, ESRC Cambridge Group Library C/650.3.

in the mid-nineteenth century, then death was also likely to disrupt the relationship of parents and children. The life-tables suggest that a quarter of all children in the Potteries would lose one parent and 6 per cent would lose both parents before they were 15. The relatively high proportion of 'parentless' children residing in households in the Potteries was noted earlier in this chapter. Furthermore, the relatively short duration of marriage implies that a considerable proportion of brides and grooms would not have both parents living at the time of their first marriage.[65] Marriage registers do not usually include such information, but for one year the marriage register of one parish in the Potteries indicated whether or not the father of the bride or groom was dead. In Sneyd parish adjacent to Burslem in 1860 the fathers of 21 per cent of the brides and grooms marrying for the first time were dead (28 per cent of the grooms and 15 per cent of the brides).[66] The number of marriages is small (35 marriages providing 70 possible fathers), and unfortunately the ages of the brides and grooms are not given if they are over 21. Yet, most of the grooms and living fathers of grooms and brides were colliers or potters, and the figures are not widely different from those expected from a crude calculation using mortality rates for the Stoke-upon-Trent registration district.[67] Thus, these figures may give some indication of the pattern for the Potteries more generally.

Other marriage registers give an indication not only of the extent to which the fathers of brides and grooms had died, but also the extent to which their mothers had remarried. Where the surname of the grooms and spinster brides do not match the surname of their fathers, it suggests that their mothers remarried and the child either adopted the surname of the step-father and listed the name of the natural father in the register or the child kept the surname of the natural father and listed the name of the step-father in the register. In the marriage register of Christ Church, Cobridge, a parish located between Burslem and Hanley, between 1860

[65] If the mean age of first marriage in the Potteries was 24 years for women and 25 years for men and the median duration of marriage was 25 years, then a couple would have roughly a 50 per cent chance of both living to see the marriage of their eldest child. Strictly speaking, these figures refer to 1858–64 and thus the same figures are being applied to two different cohorts, but the changes in mortality rates between 1840 and 1880 are not large enough to change this rough picture.

[66] The Marriage Register for Sneyd Parish 1860 is in Holy Trinity Church, Sneyd in the custody of the incumbent, Revd M. G. Johnson.

[67] Taking the age-specific death-rates for men in the registration district of Stoke-upon-Trent, it is probable that roughly 27 per cent of the men who married at the mean age of marriage (i.e. 25 years) would not survive twenty years of marriage and hence would not live to see their eldest child married.

and 1862, 7 per cent of the 246 grooms and spinster brides had a different surname than their fathers.[68] John Barker, for example, a 23-year-old crate-maker listed his father as Samuel Machin; while John Doncaster, an engraver, was the father of Jane Nixon, a 25-year-old bride.

The results of remarriage are also evident. There were a significant number of 'hybrid' families or co-residing groups containing a 'step' father or 'step' child. Over 2 per cent of the co-residing groups in the sample of the census enumerators' books for the Potteries contained a step-father or step-child. In Burslem, for example, Thomas Chapman, a carter aged 33, resided with his wife Sarah aged 31, his step-son John Brooks aged 7, his step-daughter Ellen Brooks aged 4, and his own son Thomas Chapman aged nine months. In this case a widow had remarried. If, however, a widower with children remarried a spinster or a widow without children, the family could not be detected as a 'hybrid' family in the enumerators' books unless the widower had died and his wife became the 'head'. An example again comes from Burslem where Ann Bloor, a widow aged 49 resided with her three children, Thirza Bloor aged 17, George Bloor aged 11, and Edward Bloor aged 10, and her step-son Thomas Bloor aged 18. Thus, it is likely that considerably more than 2 per cent of the co-residing groups were 'hybrid' families.

Other Aspects of Relationships between Husbands and Wives. There is very little evidence concerning other aspects of relationships between husbands and wives in the Potteries. Elizabeth Bott's study of how husbands and wives in mid-twentieth-century Britain performed their conjugal roles suggests that living within close-knit networks of kin and neighbours, husbands and wives tended to have 'segregated' roles; in other words, spouses carried out as many tasks as possible separately and independently of each other, with a strict division of labour in the household; in particular, they spent little leisure time together.[69] Young and Willmott turn this characterization into a description of changes over time; it becomes the stage 2 which they use to describe the working-class wage-earning families of the nineteenth century.[70] There is evidence of both patterns in the mid-nineteenth-century Potteries. John Finney's autobiography leaves this impression of leisure time spent with workmates

---

[68] The marriage registers for Cobridge Parish 1860–2 are in Christ Church, Cobridge in the custody of the incumbent, Revd C. R. Goodley.

[69] E. Bott, *Family and Social Network* (New York, 1971; 1st pub. 1957). A similar picture, though different reasons, emerges from a study of a Yorkshire mining village in the 1950s, N. Dennis, F. Henriques, and C. Slaughter, *Coal is Our Life: An Analysis of Yorkshire Mining Community* (1st edn., London, 1956; 2nd edn., London, 1969), esp. 180–6.

[70] M. Young and P. Willmott, *The Symmetrical Family* (Harmondsworth, 1973), 27–32.

and neighbours.[71] Another piece of evidence, however, suggests that husbands and wives did spend leisure time together and thus the segregation of roles between husbands and wives in the mid-nineteenth-century Potteries was not as extreme as the Bott and Willmott and Young models would suggest, even in an area with a high proportion of locally born and hence close-knit networks of kin, workmates, and neighbours. The following account of a case brought before the Potteries stipendiary magistrate, Mr Rose, in April 1851 suggests that it was not unusual for a husband and wife to spend leisure time together in a pub even where there was the possibility of danger.

John Lightfoot and John Bennett were brought before Mr Rose on Tuesday, charged with an assault on a married woman named Rosanna Eardley.... The assault occurred at the Old Crown Inn, Burslem, on the 22nd of March and appeared to have originated through ill-feeling entertained towards the complainant's husband (who works at Messrs. Mayers from whose employ the defendants have been dismissed) because he had declined to become a member of the Potters' Union. All parties being at the Old Crown, the complainant's husband was assailed by the term 'knobstick', being applied to him by the defendants, and she herself by receiving a severe blow on the lip from Lightfoot whom the other defendant Bennett pushed upon her. Mr Rose after severely commenting on their conduct in assaulting a woman because her husband had exercised the right to dispose of his own labour, fined Lightfoot £2 and Bennett £1 and costs to be paid in fourteen days.[72]

Births

Fertility and Completed Family Size. Various measures of fertility for the Potteries and for England and Wales in 1861 appear in Table 2.13. The crude birth-rate (births per 1,000 persons) and the general fertility rate (births per 1,000 women aged 15–44) were higher in the Potteries than in England and Wales. Although the difference narrows due to the lower age of marriage and higher nuptiality in the Potteries,[73] both the marital fertility rate (births per 1,000 married women aged 15–44) and the legitimate fertility rate (legitimate births per 1,000 married women aged 15–44) were slightly higher in the Potteries than in England and Wales as a whole. The influence of high proportions married in the Potteries is also reflected in Coale's indices. Coale's index of overall fertility (I_f) in the Potteries is higher than that for England and Wales, while the index of marital fertility (I_g) hovers around the level of that for England and

---

[71] See below Ch. 4, Sect. 3.   [72] *Staffs. Advert.* 5 Apr. 1851, 5.
[73] See above, Ch. 2, Sect. 2, 'Age at First Marriage'.

TABLE 2.13 *Measures of Fertility: England and Wales, Stoke-upon-Trent Registration District, Wolstanton Registration District 1861*

	Crude Birth-Rate	Fertility Rate			I_f	I_g	I_m
		General	Marital	Legitimate			
Eng. and Wales[a]	34.6	147.4	300.1	281.1	.359	.670	.502
Stoke Reg. Dist.[b]	40.9	174.0	303.2	283.3	.411	.646	.594
Wols. Reg. Dist.	45.2	200.8	322.9	298.5	.475	.683	.644
Stoke and Wols. Reg. Dists.	42.7	185.3	311.9	290.0	.439	.662	.616

[a] Figures from *Abst. of Brit. Hist. Stats.* 12, 16, 29; for Coale's indices (I_f, I_g, I_m), Coale and Watkins, *Decline of Fertility*, 88.

[b] Figures for the number of births from PP 1863, xiv, 83, Annual Report of the Registrar General 1861; for the denominators, population, and women aged 15–44, PP 1863, liii, pt. 2, 178, 1861 Census; for married women aged 15–44, 195; for the five-year age-groups of females aged 15–49 necessary for Coale's indices, the published census's ten-year groups were adapted using the proportions in the five-year groups in the sample of the 1861 census enumerators' books for the Potteries and the method of calculation followed Woods, *Population Analysis*, 118–20.

TABLE 2.14   *Child–Woman Ratios: England and Wales, Stoke–upon–Trent Registration District, Wolstanton Registration District 1861*

	No. of married women aged 15–44 yrs	No. of children less than 5 yrs	Child–woman ratio[a]
England and Wales[b]	2,318,258	2,700,700	1165.0
Stoke Reg. Dist.[c]	9,612	10,468	1089.1
Wols. Reg. Dist.	7,601	8,502	1118.5
Stoke and Wols. Reg. Dists.	17,213	18,970	1102.1

[a] Col. 2 divided by col. 1.
[b] *Abst. of Brit. Hist. Stats.* 12, 16.
[c] PP 1863, liii, pt. 2, 178–95.

Wales (it is lower for the Stoke-upon-Trent registration district and the combined registration districts and slightly higher for the Wolstanton and Burslem registration district alone), and the index of the proportion married (I_m) is considerably higher than that for England and Wales.

On average, then, women in the Potteries had slightly more children than women in England and Wales, yet at the same time more children were likely to die before their fifth birthday in the Potteries. Approximately 32 per cent of the children born in the Potteries died before their fifth birthday, compared with 26 per cent of children born in England and Wales.[74]

'Child–woman' ratios (the number of children enumerated in a census in the age-group 0–4 years per 1,000 married women aged 15–44) provides a measure of 'effective' fertility which takes into account infant and child mortality,[75] and Table 2.14 indicates that the child–woman ratios were lower in the Potteries than in England and Wales. Calculation of completed family size adjusted for the mortality of children aged 0–4 years and women aged 15–44 years suggests that a child born in the

[74] The 'abridged' local life-table for the Stoke-upon-Trent registration district 1858–1864, above, Tables 1.A3 and 1A4; English life-table based on mortality 1838–54, PP 1884–5, xvii, 373.
[75] Shryock and Siegel, *Methods and Materials*, ii, 500–4; T. Hareven and M. Vinovskis, 'Marital Fertility, Ethnicity and Occupation in Urban Families: An Analysis of South Boston and the South End in 1880', *J. of Soc. Hist.* 8 (1975), esp. 69–76; R. Woods, *Population Analysis in Geography* (London and New York, 1979), 111.

Potteries could expect to have five brothers and sisters,[76] two of whom would die before they reached the age of five and one of whom would be likely to die before the age of 25.[77]

Illegitimacy. The social pressures confronting women who had illegitimate children in the mid-nineteenth-century Potteries can be glimpsed through the newspaper reports of three cases in the Coroner's Court. In these cases the illegitimate child, and occasionally the mother, did not survive.

In September 1842 Elizabeth Hurst, aged 21, died after drinking 'gin and steel filings' and steel filings and savin tea in an attempt to induce an abortion and 'thus secretly, by the murder of the infant with which she was pregnant, to hide her shame from the world, she being a single woman'.[78] She had been living as a domestic servant in Longton up until two months before her death, when she moved back home to Stoke to live with her parents (her father was a sawyer) and unmarried sister. The father of the child was apparently Samuel Smith, a watchmaker, with whom 'she kept company' beginning at Christmas. She thought that Smith would marry her, but it appears that he would not and instead gave her the potions to induce an abortion. Although her family suspected that she was 'in the family way', she repeatedly denied it; nor did she admit to taking anything to procure an abortion until a few hours

---

[76] The completed marital fertility ratio for the Potteries was calculated using 'own-children' following Hareven and Vinovskis, 'Marital Fertility', 76. Children under five in the census enumerators' books were linked to their mothers in order to derive age-specific child–woman ratios. The five-year age-specific ratios for married women aged 20–44 were added together to indicate the average number of children a woman aged 20 could have expected to have if the current age-specific fertility ratios were to have continued for the next twenty-five years of her life. This assumes that all children were with their mothers on census night. Also, however, it neglects the influence of mortality amongst children aged 0–4 and women aged 20–44. R. Woods and C. W. Smith ('The Decline of Marital Fertility in the Late Nineteenth Century: The Case of England and Wales', *Pop. Studies* 37, (1983), 219) point out that 'as a result they do not reflect the total number of births that is likely to have occurred or the number of women who could have had them. It is therefore necessary to devise methods of estimating inflation factors for 0–4-year-olds' and women in the age-groups 15–19 to 40–4. The procedure used here involved an adaptation of the methods of adjustment outlined in Shryock and Siegel, *Methods and Materials*, ii, 502–5, 534, and Woods and Smith, 'Decline of Marital Fertility', 219–22. The 'abridged' local life-table for the Stoke-upon-Trent registration district 1858–1864 (Tables 1.A3 and 1.A4) provided the source of survival rates to adjust age-specific ratios of children under 5 to women by restoring deaths among children and women. The calculation gives an estimate of 6.0 for completed marital fertility.

[77] Taken from the 'abridged' local life-table for the Stoke-upon-Trent registration district 1858–1864, Tables 1.A3 and 1.A4.

[78] *N. Staffs. Merc.* 10 Sept. 1841.

before she died. Yet, despite her unwillingness to admit her predicament to her family, her mother testified that 'it seemed to prey very much upon her mind for she sighed and groaned so much in the night that they could scarce any of them sleep; she would also sit in solitude and weep for half an hour together; but she would not tell anything, keeping it all to herself'.

Unlike Elizabeth Hurst, Fanny Lowndes aged 22, a gold-grinder in a Longton pottery, did not die, but she did have to face trial for the 'willful murder of her infant'.[79] Also, unlike Elizabeth Hurst, who confronted the father of the child and whose family suspected her condition, no one would have known that Fanny Lowndes even had been 'in the family way' except for unusual circumstances which led to the discovery of the body of the baby in the bottom of a privy. The baby boy, 'a seven months child well-developed for that age', had not been attended at all. The cord was not severed, and there were no marks of violence on it; the baby had lived only a few minutes after birth, if at all. For about eight months Fanny Lowndes had been 'keeping company' with James Boughey, and about two weeks before the birth she moved into lodgings with a widow in Fenton in a neighbourhood where she was a stranger, although she had a mother living in Longton. On the evening of the birth she testified that

On Sunday about half-past five, I took a little rum in my tea, and was taken with a pain in my stomach. I was alone in the house where I lodge by myself. I had occasion to go to the privy. While there, I was taken unwell, and was delivered of a child while I was on the petty seat. I never told any one, I being among strangers. I returned into the house and sat down in a chair near the window. James Boughey came about half an hour after, some time about six. He asked me if I was going out. I said, 'Yes, I should like to go to my mother's for my boots. We called at a public house, and had a pint of warm ale and a pint of cold. We left and went to my mother's, in Wood Street, Longton. I got my boots, and returned back to my lodgings. I never told anyone I was in the family way'.[80]

The next morning she went to work at 6 a.m. Thus, Fanny Lowndes wanted to hide her pregnancy not only from her mother and others generally, but also from the probable father, James Boughey. Unlike Elizabeth Hurst, she did not seem to feel that pregnancy should lead to marriage, but in both cases it was part of the process of 'keeping company'.

Both Elizabeth Hurst and Fanny Lowndes knew they were pregnant

[79] *SS* 20 Jan. 1866, 8; 27 Jan. 1866, 6.   [80] *SS* 27 Jan. 1866, 6.

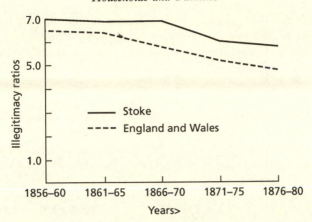

FIG. 2.1 Illegitimacy Ratios for Stoke-upon-Trent Registration District and England and Wales: 1856–1880

Note: Illegitimacy ratios are calculated as illegitimate births divided by the total number of births; the figures are five-year averages.

and attempted to hide it. Mary Ann Culverhouse did not know that she was 'in the family way' and nor did her mother.[81] Mary Ann, aged 25, had been in service in Manchester but had recently returned home near Tunstall saying the doctor told her she 'was in a decline and that she must go to her native air'. Her father, a forge labourer, and her mother believed her. One morning several weeks afterwards Mary Ann suddenly cried out to her mother that she 'felt full of pain'. Soon thereafter she gave birth to 'an illegitimate daughter and the circumstance affected [her mother so greatly] that she died in a few minutes afterwards'. The baby was born dead or died within minutes of birth and Mary Ann died several days later. Thus, the shock of her daughter delivering an illegitimate child was apparently sufficient to cause the death of Mrs Culverhouse.

Although the children in these cases died before or at the time of birth, over 7 per cent of the births in the Stoke-upon-Trent registration district between 1856 and 1860 were recorded as illegitimate (see Fig. 2.1). The proportion dropped somewhat by 1880. It was in the middle rank of towns in 1857—lower than that in Norwich (10.5 per cent), the town with the highest proportion in 1857, about the same as Newcastle-on-Tyne (7.2 per cent) and Manchester (6.7 per cent), and higher than Portsmouth (4.3 per cent), Sunderland (3.9 per cent), and Northampton

[81] *SS* 5 Mar. 1870, 7.

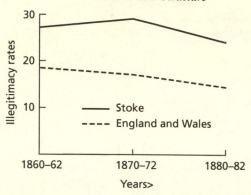

Fɪɢ. 2.2   Illegitimacy Rates for Stoke-upon-Trent Registration District and England
and Wales: 1860–1880

Note: Illegitimacy rates are calculated as the number of illegitimate births per thousand
unmarried women aged 15–44, following Shryock and Siegel, *Methods and Materials*,
478.

(4.0 per cent), the towns with the lowest proportions in 1857.[82] Although
it was in the middle of the ratios for nineteenth-century towns, the
illegitimacy ratio in the Stoke-upon-Trent registration district was above
the ratio for England and Wales as a whole (Fig. 2.1) which was 6.5 per
cent between 1856 and 1860. The other measure of illegitimate fertility,
the illegitimate fertility rate (illegitimate births per 1,000 single women
and widows aged 15–44) was 27.2 between 1860 and 1862 (see Fig. 2.2).
Again this measure was lower than the 55.5 in the registration district
with the highest rate between 1860 and 1862 (Knighton, Radnor),[83] but
considerably higher than the rate in England and Wales (18.6) shown in
Fig. 2.2.

    Despite Laslett's warning that it is dangerous to compare measures of
illegitimacy between different areas at one time rather than trends over
time in one area, it is interesting that a comparison of the Potteries with
England and Wales does reveal the relationships between illegitimacy,
fertility, and marriage age that Laslett finds in trends of these measures.[84] Laslett and colleagues observe an inverse relationship between the

    [82] T. H. Hollingsworth, 'Illegitimate Births and Marriage Rates in Great Britain 1841–
1911', a paper presented at the International Colloquium on Historical Demography,
Kristiansand, Norway, 7–9 Sept. 1979. ESRC Cambridge Group Library C/651.2.
    [83] Ibid. 7.
    [84] P. Laslett, 'Introduction', in P. Laslett, K. Oosterveen, and R. M. Smith (eds.),
Bastardy and its Comparative History (London, 1980), 10, 22.

illegitimacy ratio and age at marriage. In other words, when the illegitimacy ratio is relatively low the age of marriage is relatively high both for England and Wales and for the counties. Furthermore, there is a direct relationship between illegitimate fertility and marital fertility. In other words, when the age of marriage is relatively high illegitimacy is relatively low; when the age of marriage is relatively low, illegitimacy is relatively high. Furthermore fertility and illegitimate fertility seem to follow the same pattern—when one is high the other is high and vice versa. When one falls the other falls; when one rises, the other rises (with illegitimacy usually leading the way, for example in the second half of the nineteenth century). Wrigley and Schofield suggest that

> Rules of social conduct which have sufficient strength to prevent the young from marrying until the later twenties and that keep a significant minority unmarried for life, are also likely to be effective in preventing less permanent unions. Conversely, where marriage is early and almost universal, sanctions against intercourse outside marriage may be weak.[85]

Thus, variations in illegitimacy should be understood in terms of variations in courtship and marriage practices.[86] In the Potteries the relatively high illegitimacy measures compared with England and Wales, corresponds with relatively low age of marriage and high proportion of ever-married persons. Also, it corresponds with relatively high fertility, i.e. marriage was relatively early and frequent and marital fertility was relatively high.

As might be expected, there were variations within the Potteries in illegitimacy measures (see Fig. 2.3). Longton had the highest, Burslem, Stoke, Tunstall, and Fenton were grouped in the middle, and Hanley and Shelton had the lowest illegitimacy ratios, and the differentials were maintained overall from 1855 until 1880. The relationships between age of marriage and illegitimacy and fertility and illegitimacy, however, do not appear to hold for the towns. Longton had the highest illegitimacy ratio, but also the highest instead of the lowest age of marriage; and fertility in the town was half-way between the other towns.

What happened to the illegitimate children in the Potteries? The marriage register for Christ Church, Tunstall for 1860–2 in place of the occupation of the father of a bride or groom indicates if the bride or groom were illegitimate: 5.2 per cent of the brides and grooms (11

---

[85] E. A. Wrigley and R. S. Schofield, *The Population History of England 1541–1871: A Reconstruction* (London, 1981), 266.

[86] Laslett, *Bastardy*, 53.

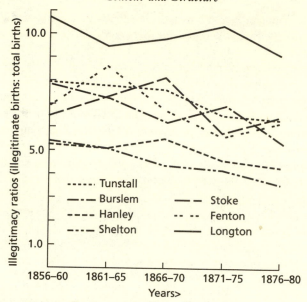

F ɪ ɢ. 2.3   Illegitimacy Ratios for the Potteries Towns (Registration Sub-Districts):
1856–1880

Note: Illegitimacy ratios are calculated as illegitimate births divided by the total number
of births, following Shryock and Siegel, *Methods and Materials*, 478; the figures are
five-year averages.

grooms and 10 brides) were illegitimate.[87] The illegitimacy ratio was 9.6
per cent in the Stoke and Wolstanton registration districts in 1845[88]
about the time these brides and grooms marrying between 1860 and 1862
were born. Thus, assuming no migration and the mortality rates from
the local life-table, about 60 per cent of the illegitimate children born
would survive to marriage age so that nearly all of the illegitimate children were marrying. The grooms who were illegitimate were in a variety
of occupations, and they married brides whose fathers were in a variety
of occupations. None of the brides who were illegitimate married potters,
but otherwise they married grooms in a variety of occupations. In two of
the marriages a groom who was illegitimate married a bride who was
illegitimate. The prime example is the marriage of William Wilshaw, a

[87] Marriage Register of Christ Church, Tunstall 1860–2, SCRO. D3463/1/19 [1857–
65].
[88] PP 1847–8, xxv, 65.

bachelor of Tunstall aged 27, and Elizabeth Welsby, a spinster aged 32 also of Tunstall. His occupation was 'police officer'.

3. Conclusion

The tendency for relatively high proportions of individuals to reside in a nuclear family, whether as parent or child, described in the first section of the chapter, is reflected in the second. A relatively high proportion of the Potteries population married eventually. On average the age of marriage for men and women was two years younger than in the country as a whole. There is evidence of community sanctions against exceeding the normal limits with regard to the age difference between brides and grooms. Marriage horizons were geographically limited, often to the same neighbourhood. And, most marriages took place according to rites of the Church of England. The birth-rate was relatively high. In addition, the illegitimacy ratio was comparatively high, but there is some evidence that a large proportion of illegitimate children ultimately married. At the same time, the death-rate meant that the duration of marriage was relatively short and the probability of infant and child death was high.

PART II

Employment and Families

3

Work and Family Patterns

IN 1862 F. D. Longe, the Assistant Commissioner who investigated the Potteries for the Royal Commission on Children's Employment, commented that 'pottery manufacture offers employment of some kind or other to persons of every age and sex'.[1] The sample of the 1861 census for the Potteries generally confirms Longe's comment (Table 3.1). Men and boys made up two-thirds, and women and girls one-third, of the labour-force; the youngest pottery-worker in the sample was 6 years old and the oldest was over 80 years old.[2] Within this broad range, who worked in the pottery industry? What were the individual and household characteristics of the pottery labour-force? What patterns of family employment and intermarriage, of fertility and marriage age, and of family incomes were associated with those who worked in pottery manufacture? In short, what effect did the availability of paid employment outside the household for women and children have on the social, demographic, and economic structure of family life in the Potteries? Exploration of this question at the same time provides evidence of how separate the pottery workforce was from the other occupational groups in the Potteries, of the extent to which certain patterns of household and family relationships varied among the different occupational groups in the area, and of the 'flexibility' and complexity of family decision-making even in an area dominated by one industry.

1. The Process of Pottery Manufacture

Although the pottery labour-force included both sexes and a wide range of ages, men, women, and children were unevenly distributed among the different parts of the highly subdivided production process in a pottery manufactory. Wide variations in hiring methods, wages, mechanization, and effects on health also characterized the many branches and occupations involved in pottery manufacture.

---

[1] PP 1863, xviii, 97.
[2] He may have retired but still described himself as a potter.

TABLE 3.1   *Age- and Sex-Structure of the Pottery Labour-Force:*
Potteries Sample 1861

Age	Males			Females			Total		
	n	%	Cum%	n	%	Cum%	n	%	Cum%
5–9	20	2	2	5	1	1	25	2	2
10–14	146	16	18	112	20	21	258	17	19
15–19	147	16	34	138	25	46	285	19	38
20–4	126	14	48	99	18	64	225	15	53
25–9	91	10	58	45	10	74	145	10	63
30–4	97	10	68	36	7	81	133	9	72
35–9	84	9	77	33	6	87	117	8	80
40–4	71	8	85	33	6	93	104	7	87
45–9	59	6	91	14	3	96	73	5	92
50–4	34	4	95	12	2	98	46	3	95
55–9	25	3	98	7	1	99	32	2	97
60–4	14	2	100	7	1	100	21	1	98
65–9	10	1	101	3	1	101	13	1	99
70–9	4	0	101	0	0	101	4	0	99
80+	1	0	101	0	0	101	1	0	99
TOTAL	929			553			1,482		

Notes:
63 per cent of the pottery labour-force is male and 37 per cent female.
The fact that the cumulative percentages are not equal to 100 is due to rounding errors.

In the 1860s there were two major departments within a pottery manufactory: the potting department, which was made up of the various branches in which clay was prepared and ware formed; and the finishing department, which included the branches in which the decorating, sorting, and packing of the ware took place.[3]

The production process began with the preparation of the clay by the mixing of the various ingredients, straining it to remove impurities, and further mixing to give it an even consistency. The 'slip-makers' employed

---

[3] The following description of the process of pottery manufacture in the early 1860s is based on: PP 1863, xviii, 98–102; and F. W. Botham, 'Working-Class Living Standards in North Staffordshire 1750–1914', Ph.D. thesis (London, 1982). There is an especially useful table setting out the number and sex of workers in the various departments of pottery manufacture in the Report by the Inspector of Factories, Robert Baker in PP 1865, xx, 55–6. For changes in the process of pottery manufacture during the century see below, Ch. 6.

in this branch were men, assisted by boys aged 14 or 15. The work was heavy and dusty but vitally important as the proper preparation of the clay was essential for ware to emerge from the ovens after firing without breakage; the piece-work wages of most of those employed in the subsequent stages of production depended on this, and they often complained that breakages were due to the uneven consistency of the clay rather than their work.

In the branches in the potting department where ware was formed, boys and women worked as assistants to male throwers, turners, 'handlers' (who formed and affixed handles), and 'flat-pressers' (who formed plates and were the largest single group of male potters accounting for 22 per cent in the early 1860s). The second largest group of male potters (14 per cent in the early 1860s) were 'hollow-ware pressers' making cups, bowls, and jugs. They did not employ assistants but they included large numbers of apprentices who began at the age of 14. Men also worked as mould-makers making the moulds for flat and hollow-ware pressers.

After the objects were formed the ware was usually fired once before passing to the decorating department. The 'saggar-makers', who made the rough clay containers in which ware was placed during firing were men, as were the 'placers', who loaded the saggars into the kiln, and the ovenmen and firemen, who fired the kiln and judged the temperature and length of firing.

The majority of girls and women in the pottery labour-force worked in the various branches of the finishing department. A few young women worked as 'scourers', a dangerous job due to the dust, smoothing the rough surfaces of the fired ware prior to decoration. Most girls and young women, apprenticed at the age of 11 or 12, worked as paintresses, painting earthenware in a room with ten to thirty other girls and young women under the supervision of an older woman. Men were primarily employed as 'dippers', dipping ware in liquid lead glaze. Both men and women worked as 'gilders' in manufactories where ware was decorated with gold, though women only worked as 'burnishers' to bring out the brightness of the gilt. Men and women worked together in the printing shops, where men worked as 'printers' printing designs on to tissue paper, and then young girls working as 'paper-cutters' cut them out, and women rubbed or 'transferred' them on to the ware. In the course of the decorating processes ware might be fired as many as seven or eight times. At the conclusion of decoration the ware went to the warehouse, where men and boys worked together with women and girls sorting and packing it.

Thus, in general women and girls worked together with men and boys in the throwing and turning branches and in the printworks and ware-house. Women and boys were interchangeable as assistants in the throwing and turning branches, for example,

the thrower generally required the assistance of two women or girls, one to turn his wheel and the other to 'take off' the ware when formed. . . . Apprentice throwers employ girls of 14 years and upwards as their assistants. These women and girls are hired by the employer. The throwers form the highest and best paid branch of the potters; but are now few, compared with the other branches.

These workmen [turners] are employed in finishing the round ware after it has been shaped by the thrower. A woman or girl is generally employed to work the treddle and assist them in their work. In some cases boys are employed instead of the women.[4]

Otherwise the sexes tended to be employed in different tasks and different places in the manufactory; specific tasks were graded by age and sex. Men, for example, were slip-makers, throwers, turners, flat-pressers, hollow-ware pressers, and dippers; while women were transferers, paintresses, burnishers, and scourers.

There were several patterns of hiring arrangements. Employers hired men directly in the potting department, including slip-makers, throwers, turners, hollow-ware pressers, flatware pressers, and the women assistants in the potting department, as well as paintresses and warehouse girls and boys and errand boys. There was also sub-contracting in some branches of both the potting and decorating departments. For example, plate-makers, cup-and-saucer makers, and handlers employed boys in particular to sweep out shops and stoves and light fires, as well as to wedge clay, run moulds, and turn wheels. Dippers also hired boys to carry ware, and in the printing shops paper-cutters were hired by women who in turn were hired by printers.

One consequence of the sexual division of labour within a potworks was that it left little scope for a nuclear family to remain together as a work group. It was possible, however, for members of the same family to work at different tasks within the same factory or industry.

2. Family Employment Patterns

Family employment patterns are the result of employers' demand for labour combined with family decisions as to which members supply

4 PP 1863, xviii, 98.

labour inside and outside the home. A full explanation of the patterns would require an exploration of employers' demand for labour which this book cannot attempt. Suffice it to say that various economic and social factors produced a strong, continuous, and increasing demand for women's labour in the pottery industry.[5] In this context it is possible to explore the individual and family characteristics of those employed in the pottery labour-force in comparison with the characteristics of those not employed in order to give some indication of the effect of the 'option' of women's and children's employment on family decisions about labour-force participation. The comparison can also cast light on the relative autonomy of the family and economy.

'Occupation' is commonly used as a category of analysis in history and the social sciences. Its use assumes that members of different occupational groups exhibit distinctive social behaviour with regard to, among other things, certain aspects of family life, such as marriage, fertility, co-residence, family employment, and mortality. In other studies miners and ironworkers have been singled out for their exceptional behaviour.[6] Due to the nature of the work and its isolated geographical location these occupational groups are associated with strong, homogeneous, 'industrially based occupational cultures',[7] characterized by families headed by a single male wage-earner, little paid employment of women and children outside the home, high fertility, and a high degree of role segregation between husbands and wives. The fact that the pottery industry offered employment to children and women provides a test[8] of the extent to which the Potteries population was socially segregated by occupation. Given the emphasis in some of the literature relating to textile-workers on the evidence that the women employed in the mills were the wives and daughters of textile-workers,[9] together with the low labour-force

[5] M. W. Dupree, 'Family Structure in the Staffordshire Potteries 1840–1880', D.Phil. thesis (Oxford, 1981), 45–50, 281–4, 334–40, 344–8.

[6] M. R. Haines, *Fertility and Occupation: Population Patterns in Industrialization* (London, 1979); L. Tilly, 'Demographic Change in Two French Industrial Cities, Anzin and Roubaix, 1872–1906', in J. Sundin and E. Soderlund (eds.), *Time, Space and Man: Essays in Microdemography* (Stockholm, 1979); S. Szreter, 'The Decline of Marital Fertility in England and Wales *c*. 1870–1914', Ph.D. thesis (Cambridge, 1984).

[7] J. Foster, *Class Struggle in the Industrial Revolution: Early Industrial Capitalism in Three English Towns* (London, 1974), 125.

[8] Other tests are the extent of occupational mobility both intragenerational and intergenerational and occupational intermarriage based on analysis of information from local marriage registers: see below, this ch., sect. 2; also, Dupree, 'Family Structure', 180–8.

[9] See e.g. C. Nardinelli, 'Child Labour and the Factory Acts', *J. Econ. Hist.* 40 (1980), 739–55; N. J. Smelser, *Social Change in the Industrial Revolution: An Application of Theory*

participation of wives and daughters of miners and ironworkers and their social homogeneity, one might expect that it was the wives and children of pottery-workers who worked in the potteries. In addition, industrially based occupational cultures existed in the Potteries. In the early 1860s there were separate unions within the major industries in the Potteries; different occupational groups contained different proportions of migrants; and contemporaries perceived occupational groups as separate.

Yet, what were the employment links between parents and children and husbands and wives at one time? What were the career patterns of boys and the employment links between sons and fathers? What were the employment links between brides and grooms? What were the career patterns of girls and how flexible was the employment of wives and mothers in terms of both interactions between different industrially based occupational groups within the area and in terms of working or not working in factory employment outside the home?

Employment Links at One Time between Parents and Children and Husbands and Wives

Children between the ages of 6 and 14 years (inclusive) made up nearly 20 per cent of the pottery labour-force. Whose children worked in the Potteries? F. D. Longe, the Assistant Commissioner who investigated the area for the Royal Commission on Children's Employment in 1862, suggested that the children employed in the potworks were not the children of healthy, 'respectable' working potters. Instead, they tended to be the children of widows, colliers, and fathers who were 'incapable of working or of drunken habits'.[10] It is not possible to discover whether fathers were incapable of working[11] or were of 'drunken habits' from the enumerators' books, but it is possible to estimate the extent to which the

---

to the Lancashire Cotton Industry 1770–1840 (London, 1959); P. Joyce, *Work, Society and Politics: The Culture of the Factory in Later Victorian England* (Brighton, 1980), 117; A. V. John, 'Introduction', in A. V. John (ed.), *Unequal Opportunities: Women's Employment in England 1800–1918* (Oxford, 1986), 25; for the pottery industry in a later period, see R. Whipp, 'Women and the Social Organization of Work in the Staffordshire Pottery Industry 1900–1930', *Midland History*, 12 (1987), 103–21.

[10] PP 1863, xviii, 99.

[11] Only six, or less than 1 per cent, of the children aged 8 to 12 in the sample had fathers who were listed as either 'not employed' or 'retired'. However, it is possible that those 'incapable of working' may have recorded their most recent occupation.

children aged 8 to 12[12] who were employed in the pottery industry were the children of potters or of widows and colliers.

The relationship between the employment of children and the father's presence and occupation is set out in Table 3.2. A relatively high proportion (23 per cent) of the children who worked in the pottery industry lived with their mothers only, compared with 13 per cent of all children aged 8 to 12 years. Moreover, it is evident that over one-third of the children aged 8 to 12 without fathers living in the household worked in the pottery industry. These relatively high proportions of children of widows confirm Longe's suggestion that widows' children tended to work in the potworks. Nevertheless, this should not obscure the fact that over three-quarters of the children who worked in the industry lived with both parents.

As might be expected given the high proportion of potters in the population, a large percentage (40 per cent) of the children employed in the potworks were the children of potters. Yet, there is a significant relationship between fathers employed in mining and children's employment in pottery, as well as between fathers employed in pottery and children's employment in pottery. Moreover, surprisingly only 23 per cent of the children aged 8 to 12 years whose fathers were potters were employed in the pottery industry, compared with 33 per cent or one-third of the children of miners. Thus, again coinciding with Longe's observation regarding the employment of colliers' children, a child of a miner was more likely to be employed in the pottery industry than was a child of a potter. Therefore, in general, it should not be assumed (as has been done for cotton-workers)[13] that the young children of pottery-workers also worked in the pottery industry.

Whose daughters and wives were working in the industry? In 1861

[12] Contemporaries considered 'children' as an undifferentiated category with regard to their employment. The Royal Commissions on the Employment of Children in 1842 and 1862 investigated the employment of both boys and girls, and factory and education legislation applied equally to boys and girls. Although, there were well-established differences between the jobs of boys and the jobs of girls within the factory and their age at starting work, the differences were not great enough to jeopardize discussion of them together as 'children'. In 1861 children made up nearly 20 per cent of the pottery labour-force. The Children's Employment Commission divided children into those aged 12 years and below, and those 13 to 18; the line between 12 and 13 corresponded roughly to the age when boys began apprenticeships. Furthermore, the age-group specified in the Factory legislation restricting the employment of children was 8 to 12 years. Hence, the analysis of children here uses the age-category 8 to 12 years (inclusive).

[13] See Nardinelli, 'Child Labour', 739–55.

TABLE 3.2　The Employment of Children and the Presence and
Occupation of Fathers: Potteries 1861[a] (%)

Father's Occupation	Children's Occupation				
	Pottery	Other	Scholar	Not Empl.	All
No Father	**[23]**	[16]	[9]	[14]	[13]
	35	9	36	21	100 (101)
Potter	**[40]**	[18]	**[36]**	**[30]**	**[34]**
	23	4	56	17	100 (262)
Miner	**[16]**	[9]	[7]	[13]	[10]
	33	7	36	25	100 (77)
Ironworker	[4]	[5]	[7]	[10]	[7]
	12	6	56	27	100 (52)
Labourer	[7]	[9]	*[5]*	**[12]**	[7]
	18	9	*40*	33	100 (55)
Other[b]	*[11]*	**[43]**	[36]	*[21]*	[29]
	8	11	68	*14*	100 (222)
All %	100	100	100	100	100
(N)	(154)	(56)	(412)	(147)	(769)
	20	7	54	19	100 (769)

[ ] = column %
( ) = n
bold = the relationship between the categories is positive and significant at .05 level (Haberman's adjusted residual)
italics = the relationship between the categories is negative and significant at .05 level (Haberman's adjusted residual)
[a] based on a file of the children aged 8–12 years in the 1861 census sample of the Potteries
[b] 'Other' is a residual category which contains shopkeepers, tradesmen, professional men, etc.

(Table 3.3), as expected given the high proportion of potters in the population, the largest proportion (37 per cent) of unmarried women in the pottery labour-force who resided with their parents were the daughters of potters. But, although the absolute numbers are small, a slightly higher proportion of the unmarried daughters of miners (71 per cent) were employed in the pottery industry than daughters of potters (69 per cent); furthermore, 55 per cent or over half of the daughters of labourers worked in the potworks. There is a significant relationship between

TABLE 3.3   *The Employment of Unmarried Daughters (age 15 and over), and the Presence of Parents and Occupation of Fathers: Potteries 1861[a] (%)*

Parent's Presence/ Father's Occup:	Daughters' Occupation			
	Pottery	Other	Not Empl.	All
Mother only	[25] 62	[17] 22	[17] 17	[21] 100 (79)
Father only	[8] 50	[3] 9	[17] 41	[9] 100 (32)
Both parents, Father's occup:				
Potter	[37] **69**	*[19]* *18*	*[18]* *14*	[28] 100 (103)
Miner	[8] **71**	[4] 19	[3] 10	[6] 100 (21)
Ironworker	[2] 33	[3] 25	[6] 42	[3] 100 (12)
Labourer	[6] 55	[6] 30	[4] 15	[5] 100 (20)
Other[b]	*[14]* 28	[47] **45**	[36] 28	[27] 100 (101)
All %	100	100	100	100
(N)	(194)	(96)	(78)	(368)
	53	26	21	100 (368)

[ ] = column %
( ) = n
bold = the relationship between the categories is positive and significant at .05 level (Haberman's adjusted residual)
italics = the relationship between the categories is negative and significant at .05 level (Haberman's adjusted residual)
[a] from the Potteries census sample 1861
[b] 'Other' is a residual category which contains shopkeepers, tradesmen, professional men, etc.

TABLE 3.4   *The Employment of Wives and Occupation of Husbands: Potteries 1861*[a] (%)

Husband's Occup.	Wife's Occupation			
	Pottery	Other	Not Empl.	All
Potter	**[64]**	[37]	*[34]*	[38]	
	21	5	74	100	(443)
Miner	[14]	[10]	[13]	[13]	
	13	4	83	100	(151)
Ironworker	[4]	[10]	[7]	[7]	
	6	8	86	100	(79)
Labourer	[6]	[5]	[10]	[9]	
	8	3	89	100	(108)
Other[b]	*[13]*	[40]	[35]	[33]	
	5	7	89	100	(381)
All %	100	100	100	100	
(N)	(144)	(63)	(955)	(1162)	
	12	5	82	100	(1162)

[ ] = column %
( ) = n
bold = the relationship between the categories is positive and significant at .05 level (Haberman's adjusted residual)
italics = the relationship between the categories is negative and significant at .05 level (Haberman's adjusted residual)
[a] based on a file of the married couples in the 1861 census sample of the Potteries
[b] 'Other' is a residual category which contains shopkeepers, tradesmen, professional men, etc.

fathers' employment in mining and daughters' employment in pottery, as well as between fathers' employment in pottery and daughters' employment in pottery. Thus, an unmarried daughter of a miner who resided with her parents was as likely to work in the pottery industry as the daughter of a potter.

The relationship between the employment of married women and the occupations of their husbands in 1861 appears in Table 3.4. Although 64 per cent of married women in the pottery workforce were the wives of potters, only 21 per cent of the wives of potters were employed in the industry, not much higher than the 13 per cent of the wives of miners who worked in the potteries.

Thus, the evidence for wives in combination with the evidence for children and unmarried daughters, indicates that it is dangerous to assume that the wives and daughters of potters were necessarily employed in the industry. These patterns also indicate that miners, who in other areas seem to be a homogeneous occupational group, displayed a considerable amount of interaction with other occupations in the Potteries. Moreover, the patterns are a further reminder of the flexibility of the roles of wives and mothers as they respond to opportunities they did not have in single-industry communities. This flexibility and its limitations also becomes apparent in the career patterns of men and women in the pottery labour-force.

Career patterns of boys and men: occupational links between sons and fathers

Boys tended to begin work at a slightly earlier age than girls. Although there was one boy aged 6 and two aged 7 recorded as employed, it was exceptional for boys to start before the age of 9 and girls before the age of 11. Charles Shaw, in his autobiography *When I Was a Child*, describes beginning work in a pottery at 'a little over seven years of age'.[14] But in 1861 the proportion of boys who were employed was only significant above the age of 9. This corresponds with the Children's Employment Commissioner's finding that nine years was the average age for beginning work for fifty-eight boys employed by flat-pressers in the industry in 1862.[15] Boys began apprenticeships in the industry at the age of 13 or 14. It is at this stage that the sons of potters tended to enter the industry. This is also the stage at which some miners' sons and others who had worked in the potworks as children shifted to work in the mines. And it was the age at which boys started work in the ironworks. A journeyman potter could eventually earn more than a miner and many of the ironworkers, but he was older when he reached his maximum earnings. 'Lads' between 13 and 18 years of age who were employed in collieries or ironworks in North Staffordshire earned twice as much as those employed in the potteries.[16] The pattern of employment of men in the major occupational groups in the Potteries over the life cycle is set out in Fig. 3.1. It shows the proportion of men in each age-group employed in pottery manufacture, mining, ironworks, and as labourers in the Potteries, and for comparison the proportion of men in each age-group employed in cotton factories in Preston. The evidence in Fig. 3.1 reveals

[14] C. Shaw, *When I Was a Child* (1st pub., London, 1903; repr., Firle, Sussex, 1977), 11.
[15] PP 1863, xviii, 99.
[16] Dupree, 'Family Structure', 45, 47, 130–1, and above, Ch. 1.

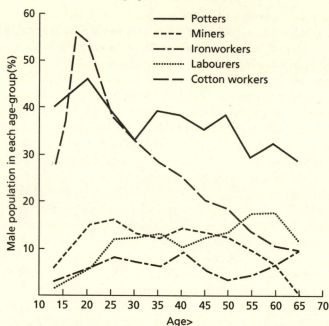

FIG. 3.1 Percentage Distribution by Occupation of Men in Different Age-groups in the Potteries in 1861 (for Potters, Miners, Ironworkers, and Labourers) and in Preston in 1851 (for Cotton-Workers)

Note: Figures for the Potteries from the Potteries Sample 1861; figures for Preston from Anderson, *Family Structure*, 27.

that the proportion of men aged 20 to 25 years and above in the pottery industry fell slightly, which reflects the migration into the area by miners, labourers, and especially ironworkers, while potters were overwhelmingly locally born. There was, however, little movement of men out of the pottery industry after the age of 30, in sharp contrast to the movement of men out of cotton and into labouring and trading after this age in Preston.[17]

Not only did boys and men in the major occupational groups tend to remain in them after beginning their apprenticeships at age 13 or 14 so

[17] M. Anderson, *Family Structure in 19th Century Lancashire* (Cambridge, 1971), 25–9. Some pottery-workers probably moved into lower-paying jobs within the industry as they grew older. This was the case e.g. with John Finney, who was listed in the enumerator's book in 1851 as a 'fireman' and in 1861 as a 'potter labourer': Dupree, 'Family Structure', 49; also see above, pp. 58–60.

that intragenerational occupational mobility between industries was limited, but also there was little intergenerational change. Ultimately sons tended to follow their father's into pottery, mining, labouring, or ironworking. Unlike the differing occupations of fathers and co-resident sons aged 10 and above among textile-workers in nineteenth-century Bruges,[18] in the Potteries co-resident sons aged 10 and above tended to follow their fathers' occupations (see Table 3.5). There is a significant positive association between the occupations or fathers and sons in all occupational groups. In addition sons of fathers who were not employed tended to be either labourers or not employed. Furthermore, there are a number of significant negative associations between fathers and sons in different occupations. The sons of miners, those employed in other occupations and those not employed tended not to be employed in pottery manufacture; nor were the sons of potters or those in other occupations employed in the mines; nor were sons of potters employed as labourers; and finally, sons of potters, miners, and labourers tended not to be employed in 'other' occupations.

The tendency of sons to follow their fathers' occupations from adolescence continued later in the life cycle. Evidence from the occupations of grooms and their fathers in the marriage registers suggests patterns similar to those of co-resident sons from the census enumerators' books (see Table 3.6).[19] Among all occupational groups there is a tendency for sons to follow fathers in the same occupation. Yet, potters and labourers displayed similar patterns, while miners differed somewhat. Of those grooms who were potters 64 per cent had fathers who were potters; and grooms who were labourers were nearly as likely (62 per cent) to have fathers who were labourers. However, only about half of the grooms who were miners were also the sons of miners, so that miners seem to be somewhat less occupationally segregated than potters or labourers.

Table 3.7 attempts to take account of the differences in the proportions of the various occupational groups among the population of grooms and fathers. The actual number of fathers and sons is compared with the expected number of sons who would have fathers in various occupations

[18] R. Wall, 'Employment Patterns and Family Structures: The Case of Early Nineteenth Century Bruges' (unpublished paper), 19.

[19] The marriage registers have an advantage over the census in that they are not restricted to sons residing in the same household as fathers, nor to sons with fathers who were alive; however, the fathers in the marriage registers might not have resided in the Potteries, thus limiting the extent to which they indicate links or separation among occupational groups within the Potteries. A comparison of the two methods for potters reveals roughly the same pattern: see Dupree, 'Family Structure', 184.

TABLE 3.5   *The Employment of Fathers and Sons Aged Ten and Above: Potteries 1861[a]* (%)

Father's Occupation	Son's Occupation						
	Potter	Ironworker	Miner	Labourer	Other	Not Employed	All
Potter	[57] **69**	[27] 4	[12] 3	[4] 1	[20] 16	[40] 8	[36] 100 (208)
Ironworker	[3] 31	[27] **31**	[0] 0	[4] 4	[4] 27	[5] 8	[5] 100 (26)
Miner	[8] *31*	[10] 5	[61] **48**	[0] 0	[5] *12*	[8] 5	[11] 100 (65)
Labourer	[9] 38	[3] 2	[14] 12	[59] **26**	[6] *18*	[8] 5	[11] 100 (65)
Other[b]	[22] 27	[33] 5	[14] *3*	[22] 3	[65] **55**	[33] 6	[36] 100 (204)
Not employed	[0] *0*	[0] 0	[0] 0	[11] 43	[1] 14	[8] **43**	[1] 100 (7)
All %	100 44	100 5	100 9	100 5	100 31	100 7	100
(N)	(249)	(30)	(51)	(27)	(174)	(40)	(571)

[ ] = column %
( ) = n
numbers in **bold** = the relationship between the categories is positive and significant at .05 level (Haberman's adjusted residual)
numbers in *italic* = the relationship between the categories is negative and significant at .05 level (Haberman's adjusted residual)
[a] based on a file of the married couples and their co-residing children, lodgers and kin in the 1861 census sample of the Potteries
[b] 'Other' is a residual category which contains shopkeepers, tradesmen, professional men, etc.

TABLE 3.6 *Inter-Generational Occupational Change 1860–1862: Potteries Marriage Registers*

Occupation of Groom	% whose fathers were:							
	Potters	Miners/colliers	Labourers	Ironworkers	Shoemakers	Other	NK	(N)
Potter	64	4	6	1	6	17	3	(201)
Miner/collier	6	49	18	1	3	21	3	(140)
Labourer	4	4	62	0	8	23	0	(52)
Ironworker	3	11	13	21	5	42	5	(38)
Shoemaker	11	11	22	0	11	44	0	(9)
Other	8	2	8	0	2	79	2	(205)
TOTAL								(645)

TABLE 3.7　*Sons and Fathers: Index of Association*

| | | Fathers were | | | | |
| | | | | | | |
Groom	Potters	Miners/ colliers	Labourers	Ironworkers	Shoemakers	Other
Potters	262	29	39	50	150	44
Miners/colliers	26	360	126	35	71	51
Labourers	16	28	431	0	194	141
Ironworkers	11	74	92	1,358	129	78
Shoemakers	65	111	222	0	276	155
Other	32	14	59	0	36	198

Note: 100 = unity (ie. actual number equals the expected number)
Source: Potteries marriage registers 1860–2.

if such selection were random. Again potters, miners, and labourers tended to be in the same occupation as their fathers to a far greater extent than expected.[20] Far fewer potters had fathers who were miners or labourers than expected (Table 3.7). This relative isolation of potters from miners and labourers is seen more clearly in Fig. 3.2, which portrays these links among occupational groups from Table 3.7 in a different way. The links can be seen from the point of view either of the fathers or of the sons. From the viewpoint of the sons, to a greater extent than expected, potters had fathers who were potters or shoemakers; miners had fathers who were miners or labourers; labourers had fathers who were labourers, shoemakers, or from 'other' occupations; and shoemakers had fathers who were shoemakers, labourers, miners, or in other occupations. From the point of view of the fathers, to a greater extent than expected, potters had sons who were potters; miners had sons who were miners or shoemakers; labourers had sons who were labourers, shoemakers, or miners; shoemakers had sons who were shoemakers, potters, or labourers; and fathers in 'other' occupations had sons in 'other' occupations or who were labourers.

If fathers and sons in each occupational group are taken together and ranked in terms of the number of links they have with fathers or sons in

[20] One perhaps surprising minor result is that potters tended to have fathers who were shoemakers to a much greater extent than expected even though the percentage of potters with shoemaker-fathers was relatively small (6 per cent). Moreover, the percentage of potters with miners or labourers as fathers is similar to that of shoemakers (Table 3.6).

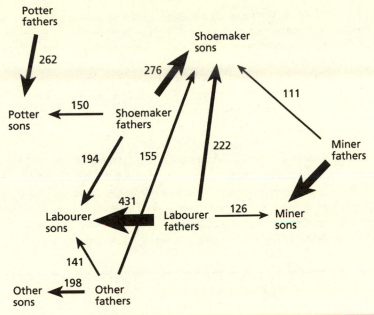

F IG. 3.2 Intergenerational Occupational Links between Fathers and Sons:
Potteries Marriage Registers 1860–1862

Note: This figure is based on the index of association presented in Table 3.7, excluding
ironworkers.

T ABLE 3.8 *Links Among Occupational Groups: Marriage
Register Data, Potteries 1860–1862*

Occupational group	No. of Links with other groups
Potters	1
Miners	2
'Other'	2
Labourers	4
Shoemakers	5

other groups (i.e. over 100 per cent; in other words the actual number is
greater than the expected if the distribution were random), then the
order gives a very crude measure of the degree of occupational segregation. Potters were the most segregated; shoemakers the least (see Table
3.8).

This ranking, however, is somewhat misleading in that it obscures the asymmetry of some of the changes in occupations between fathers and sons. Sons who were miners, for example, were relatively likely to have a father who was a labourer, but sons who were labourers were not likely to have fathers who were miners. In other words, there was movement between generations from labourer to miner, but rarely from miner to labourer. Similarly there was some movement from shoemaking to pottery, but rarely from pottery to shoemaking. Labourers and shoemakers, however, seemed to move in either direction.

Thus, there was some occupational change between fathers and sons, and particularly significant were the sons of labourers who became miners. However, in general, sons tended to follow the same occupation as their fathers.[21] Miners, however, were more likely than other groups to mix with another occupation. They were relatively likely to have fathers who were labourers and, as we shall see below, to intermarry with daughters of potters.

The tendency of co-resident sons and grooms to follow in the same industry as fathers in the Potteries was associated with the relative wages, the size of firms, and the hiring system. If adult miners earned less than potters in general, then there would be a financial necessity for the sons of miners to work in the potteries as children and then take advantage of the higher wages for adolescents in the mines. At the same time the potters, who earned relatively more, could better afford to have their sons wait to begin work as apprentices who then worked for less as adolescents but looked forward to better long-term earnings.[22]

The size of firms also played a role in accounting for the tendency of adolescent sons in the Potteries to follow the same occupation as their fathers. This pattern in the Potteries is in contrast to the patterns in Colyton and Bruges in the nineteenth century, where farmers, craftsmen, and artisans diversified employment between fathers and sons in order to minimize the risks of unemployment for entire families during downturns of a particular trade, a pattern of diversified family employment which has been associated with the concept of the 'adaptive family

---

[21] This was true to an even greater extent than they married brides from the same background, see below, Tables 3.9 and 3.11.

[22] For an analysis of the extent to which family standards of living were dependent on the earnings of the head or on the employment of family members in the major occupational groups in the Potteries see Dupree, 'The Community Perspective in Family History: The Potteries during the Nineteenth Century', in A. L. Beier, D. N. Cannadine and J. Rosenheim (eds.) *The First Modern Society: Essays in English History in Honour of Lawrence Stone* (Cambridge, 1989), 567–72 and sect. 4, 'Family Standards of Living', below.

economy'.[23] How can the different patterns be explained? The trades in Colyton and Bruges, whether rural or urban, were carried out in small units which it can be assumed would be equally affected by a downturn in trade so that differences in the security of employment were associated with different industries. In contrast, in the Potteries' labour market there were differences in the security of jobs between the firms within industries and even within individual firms. Men in the Potteries worked in industries characterized by relatively large units which were affected by declines in trade in a variety of ways. Moreover, within firms there could be differences in the effect of downturns on individual employees.

In the 1860s, as we saw in Chapter 1, there were eight iron manufacturers in the North Staffordshire area including one, Earl Granville, in the centre of the parliamentary borough who employed 1,500 ironworkers and miners. Miners were employed in the approximately 200 coal and ironstone mines in the area, each of which employed substantial numbers. Potters worked in potworks employing from thirty to forty up to 600 or more people, the average being about 200.

Pottery firms were characterized not only by a wide range in the number of employees, but also by a great variety in types of products and in wages, which mediated changes in trade. In the early 1860s the smaller firms producing china especially for the American market were clustered in Longton, the town at the southern end of the Potteries, and they were particularly hard hit by the reduced trade with the United States due to the Civil War. The larger firms produced higher-quality ware and offered higher wages and stable long-term employment to a portion of their labour-forces.

Representative of the larger firms was Josiah Wedgwood and Sons which will be explored in more detail below in Chapter 4. Although not the largest nor most innovative firm in the 1860s, it can serve as an example, employing 500 in 1842 and 780 in 1886. Wedgwoods had a core of highly skilled, long-serving employees, many of whom benefited from company houses in Etruria, the village adjacent to the potworks. Yet, a substantial proportion of Wedgwood workers lived outside Etruria and

---

[23] R. Wall, 'Work, Welfare and Family: An Illustration of the Adaptive Family Economy', in L. Bonfield, R. Smith, and K. Wrightson (eds.) *The World We Have Gained : Histories of Population and Social Structure, Essays Presented to Peter Laslett* (Oxford, 1986), 294; Wall, 'Employment Patterns', 19. For further discussion see M. Dupree, 'Social and Economic Aspects of the Family Life-Cycle: Individuals, Households and the Labour Market in the Staffordshire Potteries During the Mid-Nineteenth Century', in R. Wall and O. Saito eds. *Social and Economic Aspects of the Family Life Cycle: Europe and Japan, Traditional and Modern* (forthcoming, Cambridge University Press).

formed the less secure periphery of the firm's labour-force. They were more likely to be out of work if there were a downturn, like the skilled workmen employed by the large firm of J. Ridgways who lost their jobs temporarily and received outdoor relief under the Poor Law.[24] Thus, rather than diversifying the employment of fathers and sons in different industries for security in case of a failure of a particular trade, for many security in the Potteries meant becoming part of the stable core of a workforce such as Wedgwood's.

Yet, to explain why the different members of families in the Potteries did not go around the area looking for the industry or the firm with the highest wages and minimum risk, it is necessary to look at the hiring system. Individuals in the Potteries did not operate in a perfect market for labour. Labour recruitment in nineteenth-century industrial areas was highly dependent on family influence. At Wedgwoods, as in other pottery firms, the hiring of skilled potters who shaped and fired the ware and of women who painted and decorated ware was by the employer directly, but there is ample evidence that employers used family ties. Family ties were important for recruitment both to employers and to workers. For example, in 1851 John Finney, aged 13, the son of a fireman at Wedgwoods, applied for an apprenticeship at Wedgwoods, and he had no doubt that he would be accepted. Moreover, when an employer failed, Poor Law records show several members of the same family applying for relief.[25] Furthermore, the skilled workmen in some branches of the trade hired their own assistants. At any one time only a few would even have had children of their own of the right age for an assistant. If so, they might hire them; otherwise they might hire the children of relatives or the relatives of fellow workmen or neighbours.

Families at most times and in most places provide members with knowledge and influence. In nineteenth-century industrial areas such as the Potteries this knowledge and influence was more likely to be effective if exercised directly to influence particular firms. In contrast, by the later twentieth century it is indirect influence through the encouragement of the acquisition of educational qualifications which is more likely to be effective in helping family members to obtain a job. Thus, it is not surprising that school beyond the most elementary education was not prized among any of the occupational groups in the mid-nineteenth-century Potteries. Less than 10 per cent of the co-resident sons aged 10

---

[24] Dupree, 'Family Structure', 365–6.
[25] See for example: PRO MH12/11465 and 11466.

TABLE 3.9   *Percentage of Sons of Fathers in Various Occupations who Marry Daughters of Fathers in Various Occupations* (%)

Daughter of	Son of				
	Potter	Miner/collier	Labourer	Ironworker	Other
Potter	48	31	22	7	23
Miner/collier	13	28	14	27	12
Labourer	4	11	33	27	7
Ironworker	0	2	1	13	1
Other	35	28	29	27	58
Total sons (N)	166	97	90	15	277

Source: Potteries marriage registers 1860–2.

and above of fathers employed in any occupation were still in school (Table 3.5 above).

Intermarriage

With sons tending to follow fathers into the same industry, it might be expected that they also married daughters of men in the same industrial occupational group.[26] Yet, with unmarried daughters of miners working in the potworks, was there intermarriage between miners' daughters and potters' sons? The analysis of marriage registers from the Potteries for 1860–2 presented in Tables 3.9 and 3.10 suggests that the sons of potters tended to marry daughters of potters and vice versa and that the sons of labourers tended to marry daughters of labourers and vice versa. For example, 48 per cent of the sons of potters married daughters of potters and 41 per cent of the daughters of potters married sons of potters; 33 per cent of the sons of labourers married daughters of labourers and 44 per cent of the daughters of labourers married sons of labourers. But, a larger proportion of the sons of miners married daughters of potters (31 per cent) than daughters of miners (28 per cent); and a relatively high proportion of the daughters of miners (23 per cent) married sons of

[26] A somewhat similar use of marriage register material has been made by others such as Foster, *Class Struggle*, 125–7, 260–9; G. Crossick, *An Artisan Elite in Victorian Society* (London, 1978), 121–7, 130–3; R. Q. Gray, *The Labour Aristocracy in Victorian Edinburgh* (Oxford, 1976), 111 n. 2, 111–14, 119–20; see the Methodological Appendix for a description of the method of analysis used here.

TABLE 3.10 *Percentage of Daughters of Fathers in Various Occupations who Marry Sons of Fathers in Various Occupations* (%)

Son of	Daughter of				
	Potter	Miner/collier	Labourer	Ironworker	Other
Potter	41	23	9	0	21
Miner/collier	15	28	16	29	10
Labourer	10	13	44	14	9
Ironworker	1	4	6	29	2
Other	33	33	26	29	58
Total daughters (N)	195	98	69	7	276

Source: Potteries marriage registers 1860–2.

potters compared with the proportion of daughters of miners (28 per cent) who married sons of miners.

Tables 3.9 and 3.10, however, simply present percentages of fathers of brides and grooms with various occupations. While these do give a picture of the relative proportions of those of different occupational backgrounds who married each other, they do not take account of the fact that a far higher proportion of brides (30 per cent) and grooms (26 per cent) were the sons and daughters of potters than of the other occupational groups (e.g. 15 per cent of the brides and 15 per cent of the grooms had fathers who were miners). Table 3.11 attempts to take account of these differences. It presents the percentages by which the observed marriages differ from the expected number of marriages, given the different proportion of marriage partners from various occupational backgrounds and assuming the selection of marriage partners was random.[27] This analysis suggests that without exception those with the same occupational background tended to marry one another. Here, contrary to the indications in Tables 3.9 and 3.10, the sons and daughters of miners had a slightly greater tendency to marry each other than the sons and daughters of potters, with the actual number exceeding the expected by 86 per cent compared with 59 per cent for potters' children. Moreover, while Table 3.9 indicates that the sons of miners were relatively unlikely to marry the daughters of labourers (11 per cent), Table 3.11 suggests

[27] See the Methodological Appendix for the method of calculation.

TABLE 3.11 *Likelihood of Intermarriage among Sons and Daughters*
with Fathers in Various Occupations

| | Father of the Bride | | | | |
Father of the Groom	Potter	Miner/collier	Labourer	Ironworker	Other
Potter	159	88	33	0	80
Miner/collier	103	186	103	103[a]	65
Labourer	74	96	302	55[a]	67
Ironworker	52[a]	413[a]	564[a]	1,550[a]	144[a]
Other	77	77	59	36	135

Notes:
Total marriages = 645
Index of Association = actual as percentage of the expected number of marriages given the relative sizes of the groups in the marrying population; when the actual equals the expected, the score is 100
[a] Expected cell frequency below 5

Source: Potteries marriage registers 1860–2.

that given the relative sizes of these groups in the marrying population, the sons of miners were as likely to marry daughters of labourers as daughters of potters.

In conclusion, the evidence is slim, but if the results of both of the methods of calculation are taken together, we may conclude that those with the same occupational background were most likely to marry one another. Nevertheless, this should not be exaggerated. Within each of the occupational groups more than half of the sons married brides from a different occupational background. The sons of miners, in particular, tended to marry brides from different occupational backgrounds (especially daughters of potters) to a greater extent than either the sons of potters or the sons of labourers.

How Flexible were the Career Patterns of Girls and Women?

Very few girls worked in a pottery before the age of 10 or 11 years. Yet, nearly 75 per cent of the female pottery-workers were under 30 years of age, compared with 58 per cent of the male pottery-workers. The relatively young age-structure of the female labour-force and the fact that only 14 per cent of all married women worked in the pottery industry indicate that women tended to work in the industry for a limited period before marriage but then left the workforce thereafter.

Some women, however, did work in the industry after marriage. As in textile areas, married women in the pottery labour-force were more likely to have no children, and no children under 10 years of age, compared with wives not employed in the pottery industry. Also as in the textile industries, a few women may have worked continuously after marriage, while others, particularly widows and women whose husbands were absent on census night, stopped and restarted work as necessary.[28]

In the cotton-textile industry, married women with children tended to stop work as soon as children were able to start so that there was a 'trade-off' and 'children substituted for their mothers as family wage earners'.[29] In contrast, this pattern does not characterize the potteries. If it did, there would be few children employed in the potteries whose mothers were also employed there. Instead, there was little difference between the proportion of children aged 8–12 working in the potteries who had mothers who also worked in the potteries and the proportion whose mothers were not working. Indeed, the proportion of children working in the potteries whose mothers also worked in the potteries was slightly higher. In these families children's earnings increased family incomes rather than substituted for mother's employment. For example, 12-year-old William Bardin, who worked in the biscuit warehouse at the Copeland and Garratt pottery in Stoke, told the Children's Employment Commissioner: 'I got a mother, she is a potter, 6 brothers and sisters, 3 are potters'.[30] This difference between the Potteries and cotton-textile areas emphasizes the flexibility of women's roles.

Other evidence of the flexibility of women's participation in paid work outside the home comes from a comparison of women's employment patterns in the Potteries in 1861 and 1881. During this period the extension of factory legislation to the pottery industry (which will be explored in Chapters 5 and 6), together with the Education Act of 1870, restricted the employment of children in the industry. Alongside the reduction in the number of children, the most striking difference in the pottery labour-force between 1861 and 1881 was the increase in the proportion of women, from 37 per cent to 44 per cent. The women coming into the

---

[28] E. Garrett, 'The Trials of Labour: Motherhood versus Employment in a Nineteenth-Century Textile Centre', *Continuity and Change*, 5 (1990), esp. 146–9; Anderson, *Family Structure*, 71; Dupree, 'Family Structure', 158.

[29] J. Scott and L. Tilly, *Women, Work and Family* (London, 1978), 133–4, 195.

[30] Dupree, 'Family Structure', 136–9; PP 1843, xiv, 249.

labour-force included unmarried women as well as some of the few previously unemployed mothers of the children whose employment was restricted. Furthermore, the proportion of unmarried daughters aged 15 and over of potters who lived with their parents and who worked in the potworks increased from 69 per cent in 1861 to 76 per cent in 1881, and the proportion of wives of potters who were employed in the potteries increased from 21 per cent in 1861 to 32 per cent in 1881.[31] In addition, the gender division of labour began to alter as gradual changes in the production process led to women's employment in the potting department as flat-pressers rather than assistants for the first time.[32]

Thus, interaction between occupational groups in the Potteries was limited with regard to intergenerational occupational change between fathers and adolescent sons and to intermarriage. Nevertheless, there is considerable evidence that work in pottery manufactories was associated with interaction between different occupational groups in the employment patterns of parents and children aged 8 to 12, unmarried daughters, and wives and mothers. Even the wives of potters, who are characterized as working in the potteries in the late nineteenth and twentieth centuries[33] displayed flexibility in whether or not they worked outside the home, with a relatively small proportion doing so in 1861 and a substantial increase by 1881.

3. Fertility and Ages of Marriage

The flexibility of the roles of wives and mothers as they responded to needs and opportunities in a particular locality also becomes apparent in another, and surprising, way in the relationship between women's factory work and certain aspects of the demographic behaviour of occupational groups.

Studies of occupational differences in fertility associate high female labour-force participation in factory occupations with relatively low and declining fertility.[34] The relatively high fertility of coal-mining areas in

---

[31] For 1861 see above Tables 3.3 and 3.4; for 1881 see below Table 6.3 based on the 1-in-24 sample of the census enumerators' books from the Potteries in 1881.

[32] See below, Ch. 6, esp. 261, 268.

[33] R. Whipp, *Patterns of Labour: Work and Social Change in the Pottery Industry* (London, 1990), 65–6, 73–5, 84.

[34] Haines, *Fertility and Occupation*; Tilly, 'Demographic Change'; Szreter, 'The Decline of Marital Fertility'; N. F. R. Crafts, 'A Cross-Sectional Study of Legitimate Fertility in England and Wales, 1911', *Research in Economic History*, 9 (1984), 89–107; R. Woods, 'Approaches to the Fertility Transition in Victorian England', *Pop. Studies* 41 (1987),

England, France, and the United States and the relatively low fertility in cotton-textile areas in England and France have been associated with the low levels of married women's employment outside the home in coal-mining areas and the high levels of industrial employment of married women in textile areas. The Potteries provides a very different kind of area in which to examine these links. The mix of industries in the district allows comparisons of changes in patterns of family employment, in estimates of marital fertility, and marriage ages to be made among different occupational groups in the same area. Do miners' wives continue to have relatively high fertility even in an area where there was an opportunity for female employment? Do potters' wives, like the wives of textile-workers, have relatively low fertility?

Given that the levels of women's employment outside the home in the Potteries are similar to those in textile areas and that the proportion of women in the pottery labour-force rose between 1861 and 1881, one would expect fertility and marriage patterns in the Potteries to be similar to those in textile areas which led the fertility decline among industrial workers, and where the average age of marriage for women was rising.

What makes the Potteries a critically important area for study is that it does not fit these expectations. The 1911 Fertility Census shows that the potters who married in 1881–5 were among the groups with the highest fertility. They reached the levels of men in the predominantly male or 'machismo' coal and iron industries.[35]

Moreover, within the Potteries a comparison of estimates of marital fertility based on child–woman ratios in 1861 suggests that differences among the occupational groups within the area were small.[36] In an area where there were opportunities for the paid employment of women and children outside the household, there were similarities in the fertility patterns among separate occupational groups, including miners and iron-workers who are usually noted for their exceptional behaviour.

Thus, it is possible that there was a 'community effect' which over-rode the occupational differentials. This is plausible given the evidence

298–307; N. F. R. Crafts, 'Duration of Marriage, Fertility and Women's Employment Opportunities in England and Wales in 1911', *Pop. Studies* 43 (1989), 331–5; W. Seccombe, 'Starting to Stop: Working-Class Fertility Decline in Britain', *Past and Present*, 126 (1990), 152; Garrett, 'Trials of Labour', esp. 121–5, 137–49.

[35] Dupree, 'Family Structure', 117–19; Szreter, 'The Decline of Marital Fertility', esp. 270, 326–7.

[36] Dupree, 'Family Structure', 196–8.

of intermixing of occupations in family employment patterns, marriage patterns, and in intergenerational and intragenerational occupational mobility.[37] What is surprising is that the 'community effect' is not that of low fertility which one would expect given the nature of the industry that dominated the area.

Marriage ages as well as fertility do not appear to fit expectations. The proportions ever-married for both men and women in the Potteries suggest that marriage ages were far lower than those in a textile town such as Preston (where only 29 per cent of women aged 20–4 were married compared with 48 per cent in the Potteries). Moreover, despite the increasing proportion of women in the pottery labour-force between 1861 and 1881, the age of marriage changed little.[38] In short, the pottery-workers do not follow the textile pattern. Their experience is contrary to the generalizations associating the relatively high and increasing employment of women in industry with declining fertility and increasing age of marriage.

How women were able to cope with high labour-force participation and high fertility is not clear, but it is plausible to suggest that the solution lay in child-care arrangements. Given that pottery employers provided little in the way of child-care facilities, it is possible that child-care arrangements developed as part of a 'community culture' rather than a single, separate 'industrially based occupational culture'. Burslem's municipal day nursery closed after a short period in the 1870s due to the reluctance of working mothers to patronize it,[39] but a detailed study of women pottery-workers with children under 15 years of age in the census enumerators' books for two enumeration districts in Shelton in 1871 found a recognizable alternative adult care-giver (a relative or lodger) in about half the households, and siblings of about ten years of age who might have provided care for younger children in several others.[40] The mistress of the Hanley and Shelton Girls' National School complained in 1842 that the absence of girls 'is to be attributed to their mothers who

[37] See above, this chapter, pp. 152–169. In addition, Eilidh Garrett's careful study of fertility and married men's and women's employment in Keighley suggests the importance of looking at both the husband's and the wife's employment patterns and the complexities of their relationship to fertility in a textile town in the second half of the nineteenth century: Garrett, 'The Trials of Labour', 137–49.

[38] For 1861 see above, 122; for 1881 see PP 1883, lxxx, 236, and my sample of the 1881 enumerators' books from the Potteries.

[39] *SS* 21 Dec. 1872, 5; 4 Apr. 1874, 5; 17 Apr. 1875, 5.

[40] R. Hall, *Women in the Labour Force: A Case-Study of the Potteries in the Nineteenth Century*, Dept. of Geography and Earth Science, Queen Mary College, London, occ. paper no. 27 (London, 1986), 43.

keep them at home to do their household work and nursing'.[41] In addition, there is evidence of the provision of childcare outside the household. The minister of a chapel in Hanley commented in 1842 on the 'numerous cases in this township of little infants being left to the care of old women, who have the care of their own household, besides attending to the little charges'.[42] Also, because of the relatively high proportion of the population in the Potteries that was locally born, there was a greater likelihood that working women had relatives in nearby households who might provide child-care and could follow the pattern identified in Lancashire cotton towns, where a coroner testified in 1871 that children are 'taken care of either by a person in the house or by some neighbour, and my impression is that it is usually done by some neighbour' who might also be a relative.[43] Finally, there is also evidence from the early twentieth century that the cost in the Potteries was 70 per cent lower than the cost of child-care in Lancashire towns and 78 per cent lower than the cost in England and Scotland generally.[44] Hence, although evidence about child-care in the Potteries is scattered, it suggests that the supply of child-care may have been greater and cost less than in Lancashire. Moreover, the provision of child-care in the neighbourhood as well as in the household means that it is important in considering the flexibility of women's roles to look outside as well as inside both the nuclear family unit used in neoclassical economists' analyses of labour-force participation and fertility and the co-resident household unit used in some demographic and family history.[45]

In order to examine the ways in which the 'option' of women's and children's employment affected the economic structure of families, however, it is necessary to turn back to the nuclear family unit and occupation as a category and to examine standards of living.

4. Family Standards of Living

Among other things, patterns of family employment and fertility such as those emerging above have implications for standards of living, which in

[41] PP 1843, xiv, 273.

[42] Ibid.; also quoted in M. Hewitt, *Wives and Mothers in Victorian Industry* (London, 1958), 132.

[43] PP 1871, vii, 99; Hewitt, *Wives and Mothers*, 128–33.

[44] PP 1904, xxxii, paras. 9025–31 and App. V, 128; quoted in Hewitt, *Wives and Mothers*, 132 and Hall, *Women in the Labour Force*, 43–4.

[45] M. Anderson, *Approaches to the History of the Western Family 1500–1914* (London, 1980), 17–38, 65–6, 75–84.

turn help to explain the patterns. It is possible to put the information about labour-force participation and family composition together with estimates of incomes and compare the standards of living of families of married men in major occupational groups in the Potteries. In his study of the labour-force of a paper-making firm and a weaving firm in south-east Scotland in the mid-nineteenth century, John Holley points out that two fairly clear and in some ways opposite models of the determination of family standard of living emerge from the literature.[46] The first model is that of the 'symmetrical' family in which the family standard of living was governed by the 'pre-industrial' pattern of multiple earners within the family; the second model is that of the 'asymmetrical' family characterized by the 'industrial' pattern of the adult male head as the sole bread-winner. Young and Willmott among others[47] see these models as two stages in development, and they argue that there has been a change from the 'symmetrical' to the 'asymmetrical' form over the past 150 years. Holley, focusing his study on the effects of technological change, expected to find this change; instead of the asymmetrical replacing the symmetrical, however, he found that both patterns of family income determination appeared at the same time. Family standard of living was correlated with the head's income for high-paid workers, but with the demographic and labour-force-participation characteristics of households headed by labourers. Thus to resolve these issues for the Potteries it is necessary, first, to determine the extent to which the family standard of living of married men within the various occupational groups was determined by the head's income, and second, to compare the family standard of living and its determination among the different occupational groups.

The least-squares regression of the head's income against family standard of living (shown in Table 3.12) shows a moderate to strong correlation (.78) between head's income and family standard of living for iron-workers and a moderate correlation (.53) for those in 'other' occupations. For potters, miners, and labourers there was relatively little association. Thus, there is evidence of asymmetry for ironworkers.

---

[46] J. Holley, 'The Re-division of Labour: Two Firms in 19th Century South-east Scotland', Ph.D. thesis (Edinburgh, 1978); 'The Two Family Economies of Industrialism: Factory Workers in Industrial Scotland' *J. of Fam. Hist.* 6 (1981), 57–69.

[47] M. Young and P. Willmott, *The Symmetrical Family* (Harmondsworth, 1973); see e.g. D. Levine, 'Industrialization and the Proletarian Family in England', *Past and Present*, 107 (1985), 168–203 and *Reproducing Families: The Political Economy of English Population History* (Cambridge, 1987), esp. 172–80; W. Seccombe, *Weathering the Storm: Working-Class Families from the Industrial Revolution to the Fertility Decline* (London, and New York, 1993), 21, 111–24.

TABLE 3.12 *Determinants of Family Standard of Living for Families Headed by Married Men in Various Occupations: Potteries 1861*

Occupation of head	Determinants of family standard of living (coefficients of correlation)			
	Head's income r	Excess of earners over dependants[a] r	N	(missing values)
Ironworker	.78	.24	65	(10)
Other	.53	.40	185	(200)
Potter	.31	.39	400	(28)
Miner	.19	.28	149	(2)
Labourer	.22	.69	100	(11)
All	.49	.40	912	(261)

Note:
'Family Standard of Living' = the estimated income minus the minimum standard of family expenditure for each nuclear family. The aggregate income was calculated for each nuclear family headed by a married couple where the income of all family members could be estimated from the figures for the earnings of the different occupations (assuming a full week's work). Information was sufficient for incomes to be calculated for 78 per cent of the families headed by married couples in the Potteries sample. Income from lodgers was ignored and it was assumed that co-residing children gave all their income to the family. The minimum standard of family expenditure was based on Rowntree's scale of primary poverty expenditure as used by Anderson (*Family Structure*, 201) but adjusted for lower rents in the Potteries. See the Methodological Appendix at the end of the book for further information regarding the procedure used to calculate family standards of living.
[a] 'Excess of Earners Over Dependants' = the number of earners minus the number of dependants in each nuclear family headed by a married couple where the income of all family members could be estimated. Earners and dependants were weighted in terms of the 'adult equivalent needs' used by Foster (*Class Struggle*, 256).

The extent to which the standard of living was determined by the head's income or the labour-force participation of family members can be operationalized as a variable measuring the excess of earners over dependants in terms of needs. This variable with an r of .69 explains the variation in living standard of families headed by labourers better than did the income of the head. Thus, the family composition, i.e. the number of people of working age and the extent of their labour-force participation, was far more important for the standard of living of labourer-headed families than was the income level of the head.

Comparisons of the average standard of living among various occupational groups (shown in Table 3.13) reveals patterns which follow from

TABLE 3.13 *Mean Values of each of the Three Variables Used in Table 3.12 for Married Men in Various Occupations who Headed Households: Potteries 1861*

Occupation of head	Head's income (s. per week)	Family standard of living (s. above or below poverty-line)	Excess of earners over dependants (adult males = 100)
Ironworkers	31	16	137
Potters	27	16	164
Other	26	15	164
Miners	24	13	159
Labourers	15	5	147

Note:
For explanation of methods of calculating variables see notes to Table 3.12.

these correlations. Families headed by potters and ironworkers had similar average standards of living (approximately 16/- per week above the poverty-line) even though the average pay of a household head who was an ironworker was higher (over 31/- per week versus 27/- for potters). In other words, living standards did not decline directly with the differences in the wages of heads. Families headed by potters had a higher rate of labour-force participation and fewer dependants than those of ironworkers. Nor was high labour-force participation directly related to low earnings by the head: potters, miners, and others had higher excesses of earners over dependants and higher head's incomes than did labourers.

The contrast among the living standards of the various occupational groups can be seen more starkly when the pattern of the standard of living over the life cycle is considered (see Fig. 3.3). The pattern for each of the occupations is the same, but the level of labourers is consistently below the rest. However, the relatively low standard of living of labourers was alleviated to some extent by the taking in of lodgers, which is not included in the previous figures.

To sum up, occupational groups embodying each of the two contrasting principles which determine family standards of living co-existed within the Potteries. For ironworkers, family standard of living was related to the income level of the head; for labourers it was related to the excess of earners over dependants within the household. Among the potters and miners, however, family standard of living was not correlated strongly with either the income of the head or the excess of earners over dependants.

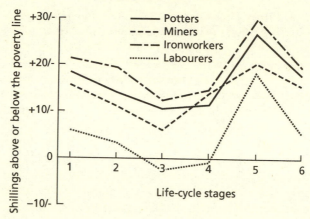

FIG. 3.3   Standard of Living by Life-Cycle Stage for Various Occupations of
Husbands: Nuclear Families headed by Married Couples in the Potteries Sample 1861

Moreover, the average standard of living of various occupational groups
could be the same but for different reasons. Ironworkers and potters, for
example, had similar mean family standards of living, yet ironworkers
had relatively high income for the head, while potters had a relatively
high excess of earners over dependants. Furthermore, all other occupational groups displayed a similar pattern of standard of living over the
life cycle, but that of labourers was considerably lower.

Thus, the availability of employment for women and children in the
Potteries provided increased scope for families to mediate between the
wage-structure and the age-structure on the one hand, and the standard
of living on the other.[48] Furthermore, at the community level the availability of employment for women and children decreased the inequality
in the distribution of income, providing an economic basis for a 'community culture'.

5. Conclusion

The social, demographic, and economic effects of the availability of
employment for women and children in the major industry of the
area are reflected in the particular combination of patterns of family

---

[48] E. A. Wrigley, 'Population History in the 1980s', *J. of Int. Hist.* 12 (1981), 207–8,
225–6; J. Humphries and J. Rubery, 'The Reconstitution of the Supply Side of the Labour
Market: The Relative Autonomy of Social Reproduction', *Cambridge Journal of Economics*,
8 (1984), 331–46.

employment, intermarriage, fertility, marriage ages, and family incomes in the Potteries. These patterns reveal both interaction and separation, differences and similarities among industrially based occupational groups. Nearly all are contrary to what might have been expected based on the experience of the areas. They emphasize not only the importance of the careful description of the links between families and employment over the life cycle, but also the need to link this to particular communities at particular times and to make comparisons. Thus, they highlight the flexibility, complexity, and 'relative autonomy' of family decision-making, even in an area dominated by one industry.

Members of families in the Potteries, including those of miners usually characterized as isolated and homogeneous, exhibited a variety of arrangements for family employment involving the intermixing of different industrially based occupational groups. Rather than the employment of the wives and children of pottery workers in the potworks, as might be expected in the early 1860s, relatively few wives and children aged 8–12 of potters worked. Miners' children aged 8–12 were more likely to work in the potworks than those of potters, and the older, unmarried daughters of miners were just as likely as those of potters to work in the potteries. Yet, families in the Potteries did not entirely diversify their patterns of family employment among industrially based occupational groups as recent studies suggest occurred in Colyton and Bruges and associate generally with the concept of the 'adaptive family economy'. From the ages of 13 or 14 sons tended to follow fathers into the same industry in the Potteries. Family influence with employers was an important feature of the system of labour recruitment. This was in contrast both to a system in which a head hired his own nuclear family members and to the pattern common in the later twentieth century of helping family members get a job by indirect family influence through encouraging the acquisition of educational qualifications. Although occupational endogamy tended to characterize marriage patterns, large proportions of the sons and daughters of miners married those of potters. Moreover, the flexibility of the roles of women, as wives, mothers, and daughters is clearly apparent in the growing proportions of wives and daughters of potters employed in the potworks by 1881, and in the co-existence in the Potteries of the employment of women in the pottery industry with relatively high marital fertility and low marriage ages, contrary to the association in cotton textile districts between the employment of women, low marital fertility, and high ages at marriage.

Finally, in the Potteries there was variety among the industrially based occupational groups in the patterns of family income determination, with that of ironworkers determined by the head's income, that of labourers strongly related to the labour-force participation of family members, and that of potters and miners in between. Yet, albeit by different methods, each of the groups, apart from the labourers, reached a similar level of family income. This created an economic basis for a 'community culture' which reinforced the social and demographic basis evident in the inter-industrial mixing and similarities which emerged in the patterns of family employment, fertility, and to a lesser extent intermarriage. The sources of assistance such as neighbours, the Poor Law, friendly societies, churches, voluntary hospitals, and civic authorities available to individuals to meet various crises in their lives were also part of such a 'community culture'.[49] The more these sources of assistance are investigated, as they will be in Chapters 7 and 8, the more important it becomes that the analysis of family structure itself is linked closely to the community as well as occupational context.

[49] Anderson, *Family Structure*, 136–9; Dupree, 'Family Structure', 349–417.

4

Firm, Family, and Community:
Wedgwoods and Etruria

T HE 'relative autonomy' and flexibility of the relationships between family ties and work and the importance of a 'community perspective' are apparent in the patterns of co-residence, family employment, marriage, fertility, and standard of living of the main occupational groups of the parliamentary borough of Stoke-upon-Trent as a whole. Are these themes also apparent from the perspective of neighbourhoods and the experience of an individual in the Potteries? To what extent did the wide-ranging paternalism of individual factory employers, emphasized in some accounts of mid-nineteenth-century textile areas, also exist in the Potteries? In such accounts the employment of family members played a key role in linking employer influence and employer–worker reciprocity both inside and outside the factory.[1] Comparison between Patrick Joyce's picture of wide-ranging employer influence in mid-nineteenth-century Lancashire cotton towns and the relationship between Wedgwoods and the adjacent village of Etruria in the Potteries in the same period offers an approach to such questions.

One might expect Etruria between 1840 and 1880 to be a factory-dominated neighbourhood exhibiting the characteristics which Joyce emphasizes in his portrayal of Lancashire factory towns. The differences which emerge reflect the 'relative autonomy' of managerial and household strategies and point to the importance of a 'community perspective' encompassing both factory and family.

In his study of Lancashire towns Patrick Joyce stresses the influence of large factories on the factory neighbourhood and the relationship of paternalism and deference between masters and workers and between the factory and the adjacent neighbourhood. Of central importance are the

[1] P. Joyce, *Work, Society and Politics: The Culture of the Factory in Later Victorian England* (Brighton, 1980); J. Lown, *Women and Industrialization: Gender at Work in Nineteenth-Century England* (Cambridge and Oxford, 1990).

links between the family of workers inside and outside the factory; these were reinforced by the rituals surrounding the master's family.

According to Joyce's argument, after 1850 in Lancashire 'the coming of social stability and the acceptance of power relations' corresponded with the development of deference and employer paternalism in the factory towns. Joyce defines deference as 'the social relationship that converts power relationships into moral ones, and ensures the stability of a hierarchy threatened by the less efficient, potentially unstable, coercive relationship'. It depends on the ability of the masters to manage the opposing tensions of differentiation from, and identification with, the men. He emphasizes the dominance that the employers exerted 'over the ordinary business of people's lives inside and outside the factory'. He stresses that this did not involve a single stratum in the form of a labour aristocracy but 'the whole of the workforce'. Skilled workmen who hired their own assistants were themselves subject to the authority of foremen and managers. Moreover, employer influence occurred 'at the level of everyday life' in terms of the family and neighbourhood community as well as the workplace. In particular, Joyce stresses the importance of the influence of the employer and the factory over the immediate neighbourhood. The neighbourhood surrounding a factory was not a working-class enclave; instead, it was permeated by the influence of the factory and the employer. The hierarchy of authority in the factory was repeated within the neighbourhood, and the factory was not merely a seat of production, but also a centre of social life. The family played an important linking role between the factory and the neighbourhood. Directly, it did so through the employment of all family members within the factory and the repetition of the same authority relationships inside the factory and inside the family. Indirectly, the 'mythology of the employer family' had the effect of binding the employer and the workforce together and was expressed in the rituals associated with rites of passage in the employer's family which made up a considerable amount of the factory-centred social life and which 'extended the symbolic boundary from the factory to the neighbourhood'.[2]

1. Etruria

Unlike Saltaire, built in the early 1850s for 2,000 people with almost complete paternalism,[3] in 1861 the village of Etruria was already ninety

---

[2] Joyce, *Work, Society and Politics*, esp. 92–3, 111, 181.

[3] For a definitive account of Titus Salt and Saltaire, see J. Reynolds, *The Great Paternalist: Titus Salt and the Growth of Nineteenth-Century Bradford* (London, 1983).

years old, and, with a population of 966, it had considerably fewer inhabitants. Moreover, from the outset the adjacent pottery firm of Josiah Wedgwood and Sons was not the all-encompassing employer of the Titus Salt variety. Yet, the common origin and continuing relationship throughout the nineteenth century of the village and firm make them an especially appropriate test of the applicability to the Potteries of Joyce's model of employer influence and employer–worker reciprocity outside and inside the factory. If any firm and neighbourhood in the Potteries exhibited the characteristics of the 'piecemeal paternalism' Joyce emphasizes in his Lancashire towns, it would be Wedgwoods and Etruria. At the same time, the village and firm were representative of medium to large firms in the Potteries more generally in terms of size, organization, and proximity to housing, mines, and ironworks.

The Village

The village of Etruria was situated in the valley between Hanley and Newcastle-under-Lyme (Map 4.1). The village lined the Hanley-to-Newcastle toll road near the point where the road crossed the Trent and Mersey Canal, and by 1861 it also included several shorter side streets (Map 4.1). Adjacent to the village were the potworks of the firm of Josiah Wedgwood and Sons, the ironworks of Earl Granville's Shelton Coal and Bar Iron Company, the North Staffordshire Infirmary, fields, and a grove of trees known as Etruria Grove with 'blackberries and wild raspberries and beautiful wild flowers'.[4] Although in 1861 the village of Etruria was part of a number of larger administrative areas[5] and it lacked an administrative boundary other than that of a census enumeration district,[6] there are three reasons for treating the village as a unit.

First, the village owed its origin and name to Josiah Wedgwood, and by the mid-nineteenth century the people who lived there and the community itself were still closely tied to the Wedgwood factory. In 1766 Josiah Wedgwood bought 350 acres known as the Ridgehouse Estate between Hanley, Burslem, and Newcastle where he built a factory and a

---

[4] J. Finney, *Sixty Years' Recollections of an Etruscan* (Stoke-upon-Trent, 1903), 2.

[5] These included: the parliamentary borough of Stoke-upon-Trent; the municipal borough of Hanley; the township of Shelton; the parish of Stoke-upon-Trent; the ecclesiastical district of Etruria; the poor law union and the superintendent registrar's district of Stoke-upon-Trent.

[6] PRO H. O. RG9/1934–7. The census enumerator's district included: Etruria, Etruria Hall, Etruria Wharf, Etruria Tollgate, Fold Street, Chapel Street, and Salem Street. The enumerator listed only the name of the street, place, or name of the house; there were no street numbers listed. It is this unit that the subsequent analysis of the enumerator's book for 1861 uses.

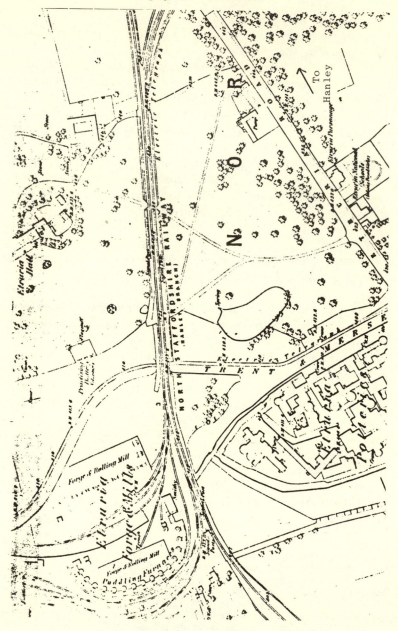

MAP 4.1   Etruria, 1865
Source: OS Hanley (1865), scale 25″ to 1 mile, HBRL.

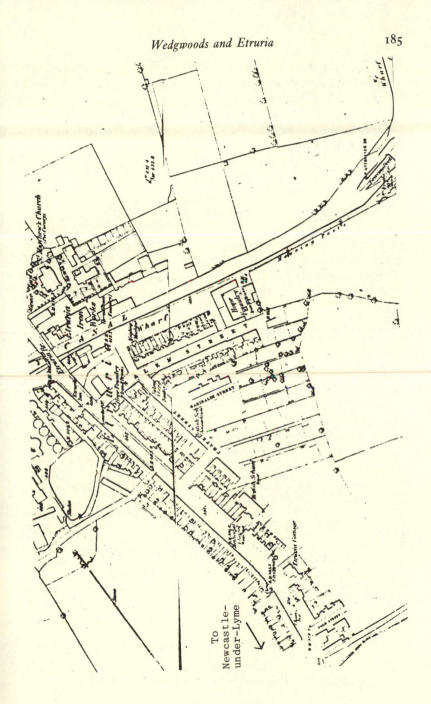

village for his employees.[7] In 1844 the Wedgwood family owned 'more than 100 houses and shops, comprising the whole of the Village of Etruria', plus Etruria Hall, the Ridge House farm, and the Etruria Potworks.[8] They were all put up for auction in 1844, but even in 1862 the Wedgwoods still possessed the potworks, and 127 of the 203, or over 60 per cent of the houses in Etruria.[9]

Second, in 1861 the village was still separated geographically from surrounding towns and groups of houses by trees, fields, and the Shelton Bar Iron Works.[10]

Finally, the people who lived in Etruria saw themselves as living in a separate village. In 1861 Etruria had an Artillery Volunteer Company, a fire brigade, the Etruria British School, the Etruria Wesleyan Chapel, and an Anglican church.[11] When George V and Queen Mary visited the Wedgwood works in 1913, Queen Mary asked an old workman if he were a native of the Potteries. He replied, 'No, Madam, I am an Etruscan'.[12]

The Firm

Although in the 1860s Josiah Wedgwood and Sons was smaller than firms such as Mintons or Davenports, each of which employed over 1,000 workers,[13] Wedgwoods was still a relatively large employer in an industry with an average of less than 200 employees per firm.[14] Moreover, the number of employees increased during the period, growing from approximately 500 in 1841[15] to 723 in 1883.[16] This section briefly describes the firm in terms of its masters, products, marketing, profits, division of labour, and wage negotiations.

---

[7] A. Finer and G. Savage (eds.), *Selected Letters of Josiah Wedgwood* (London, 1965), 42, 84.

[8] 'Particulars of the Estate of the late Josiah Wedgwood, Esq. to be sold at Auction . . . 1844', HBRL. For possible reasons why the estate was put up for sale, see R. Reilly, *Wedgwood*, ii (London, 1989), 61; S. Gater, 'A House of Long-Standing: A Study of Josiah Wedgwood and Sons in the Second half of the Nineteenth Century', MA in Victorian Studies diss. (Keele, 1986), 11–13.

[9] 'Municipal Borough of Hanley: Rate Book May 8, 1862', HBRL.

[10] 'Ordnance Survey Map of Hanley, scale 1 : 500, surveyed 1865', HBRL.

[11] Finney, *Recollections*, 19, 21. Also, W. White, *White's Staffordshire Directory* (1851), 220, 231–3 refers to Etruria as a separate place.

[12] E. J. D. Warrillow, *History of Etruria 1760–1951* (Hanley, 1954), introduction (page not numbered).

[13] R. M. Hower, 'The Wedgwoods—Ten Generations of Potters', *J. of Econ. Business Hist.* 4 (1932), 676–7.

[14] PP 1863, xviii, 43.   [15] Ibid. 676.

[16] WMSS. 29219–46: List of Hands on Works compiled by Cecil Wedgwood, March 1883.

In 1868 Godfrey Wedgwood, one of the partners in the firm, pointed out that the pottery masters came from two different backgrounds.

The men who get on here as masters are either those who begin as working potters and from their intimate knowledge of the practical part of potting are able to make savings in business that others cannot, or are the sons of manufacturers who come to the business early and inherit the advantages their fathers have made for them.[17]

Godfrey Wedgwood and the other Wedgwoods who headed the firm between 1840 and 1880 fall solidly into his second category of masters. They were the sons of manufacturers; they came to the business early; and they inherited the advantages their fathers had made for them. In 1840 Josiah Wedgwood and Sons was a partnership between Josiah Wedgwood II and two of his sons, Josiah III and Francis, known as Frank. Both of the sons had spent three or four years 'learning the business' before becoming partners: Josiah III in 1823 at the age of 28 and Frank in 1827 at the age of 27. In November 1841 Josiah II withdrew from the business, and several months later he was followed by Josiah III. Thus, Frank, whom his mother described as 'right-minded, steady and just what an English merchant ought to be, exact to punctilio in all his dealing, active and industrious', became the sole head of the firm.[18]

In order to release some of the money which he had tied up in the firm, Frank Wedgwood formed a partnership with John Boyle in 1843, and after Boyle's death with Robert Brown. The partnership with Brown lasted from 1846 until Brown died in 1859. Immediately after Brown's death Frank took on as a partner his eldest son, Godfrey, who had been working at what one of his cousins called 'that nasty potshop' since 1851 when he was eighteen.[19] In the course of the 1860s Frank Wedgwood brought his other two sons into the partnership: Clement Francis in April 1863 and Laurence in November 1868; and in November 1870 Frank retired, leaving his three sons equal partners in the firm. In order to secure the succession, the sons drew up an agreement in 1873 allowing each partner to introduce 'as a clerk and pupil' one son who, after

[17] WMSS. 15A/1: G. W. Godfrey Wedgwood (hereafter) to Rhoda Cattley, 6 July 1868.

[18] H. Wedgwood and B. Wedgwood, *The Wedgwood Circle 1730–1897* (London, 1980), 183, 197, 238; Hower, 'Ten Generations', 673–4; E. Darwin, *A Generation of Family Letters*, i (Cambridge, 1904), 294.

[19] Frank Wedgwood attended Cambridge, but he did not send any of his sons to University.

reaching twenty-one years of age and being a pupil for at least three years, might succeed his father as partner.[20]

In the mid-nineteenth-century Potteries the Wedgwoods were not unusual in keeping ownership and even management within the family. The careful grooming of successors rather than sale was the common way to transfer ownership, particularly for large manufacturers.[21] Godfrey Wedgwood remarked in 1871 that 'the sale of works of this size is so rare in the Potteries that it is difficult to hear anything about the [basis] on which they have been valued or the competence of the valuers'.[22]

Throughout the period 1840–80 J. Wedgwood and Sons devoted the majority of its production to transfer-printed dinnerware.[23] Yet, somewhat ironically for the firm whose founder was a pioneer in the development of the factory system with its sub-division of labour and standardized product,[24] Wedgwoods produced a larger proportion of ornamental ware and small lots than other firms in the Potteries in the mid–nineteenth century. Writing to another manufacturer in 1868 Godfrey Wedgwood remarked that 'our business is a peculiar one from the quantity of old shapes we make and the number of small lots we have to make'.[25]

Yet, despite the continuing production of ornamental ware, there was not much change in design and style between the early nineteenth century and 1860. Josiah Wedgwood II was not an innovator with regard to the introduction of new products, indeed he discontinued some products such as bone china, dip jasper, and jasperware with a solid tinted body, subsequently losing the recipe for dip jasper.[26] The author of one of his

---

[20] Hower, 'Ten Generations', 674–5; B. and H. Wedgwood, *Wedgwood Circle*, 243, 256, 265, 297, 304; Reilly, *Wedgwood*, ii, 61, 63–4, 67–8, 84; M. Batkin, *Wedgwood Ceramics 1846–1959: A New Appraisal* (London, 1982), 9, 14.

[21] Minton followed this pattern, see E. Aslin and P. Atterbury, *Minton 1798–1910: Exhibition, Victoria and Albert Museum, August–October 1976* (London, 1976), 7–8. Davenport also followed the pattern, but succeeding generations did not take as active a part in the management as at Wedgwoods or Mintons, see T. A. Lockett, *Davenport Pottery and Porcelain 1794–1887* (Newton Abbot, 1972), 20–6.

[22] WMSS. 15A/1: G. W. Godfrey Wedgwood (hereafter) to Josiah Wedgwood III, 26 June 1871.

[23] B. and H. Wedgwood, *Wedgwood Circle*, 263. For photographs and a discussion of the firm's products during the 19th cent., see Batkin, *Wedgwood Ceramics* and Reilly, *Wedgwood*, ii.

[24] N. McKendrick, 'Josiah Wedgwood and Factory Discipline', *Hist. J.* 6 (1961), 31–3.

[25] WMSS. 15A/1: G. W. to John Ridgway, 17 Sept. 1868.

[26] B. and H. Wedgwood, *Wedgwood Circle*, 165–6, 263, 290; Hower, 'Ten Generations', 675; W. Mankowitz, *Wedgwood* (London, 1966; 1st pub. 1953), 133–8. Jasper is a dense, white, vitrified stoneware body of nearly the same properties as porcelain. When formed thin it is translucent, and has a fine unglazed surface. When coloured throughout, the body is called solid jasper; when the white body is dipped in a solution of coloured jasper, it is called jasper dip.

obituaries commented that 'As a manufacturer, Mr Wedgwood seemed content to inherit the celebrity which attached to his name. He rarely appeared as a competitor with contemporaries in the fields of enterprise'.[27] Nor did Frank Wedgwood have much interest in design or in changing fashion. He, too, chose to capitalize on Josiah I's success, 'reproducing urns, vases, ewers, inkwells and figures that had sold well in the past and eliminating those items that had not found a substantial market'.[28] For the Great Exhibition at the Crystal Palace in 1851 the firm revived production of dip jasperware which Josiah II discontinued forty years previously, and after the Exhibition it became a staple part of the company's production of decorative items.[29] But, the products in the Wedgwood display in 1851 might have been exactly the same if the Exhibition had taken place seventy-five years earlier.[30] Also, judging by the number of feet of exhibition space purchased in the Crystal Palace, Minton and Ridgway were by far the leading firms.[31]

In the late 1850s, however, there was some change and expansion in the range of Wedgwood products, as the company re-established its reputation as a leading producer of art wares. Emile Lessore, a celebrated French artist who had been working at Mintons, became dissatisfied and sought out Wedgwood in 1859, and he worked for them until his death in 1876, when he was followed by Thomas Allen among others. Lessore painted landscapes and figures on Wedgwood plaques, bowls, vases, teaware, and dessert services, and these were an instant success. By the early 1870s the firm established a department in the potworks for the decoration of printed and hand-painted dishes, plaques, vases, bottles, and tiles.[32] Furthermore, in 1857 Tito Clemente Ristori was 'engaged to make Majolica Ware and porcelain for Josiah Wedgwood and Sons'.[33] The majolica, too, was a success. It differed from that of other manufacturers such as Minton and Doulton because 'most of the majolica items which Wedgwood made were . . . from eighteenth and early nineteenth century moulds—thus shapes that had previously been made in Cane, Jasper or Basalt now made their appearance in brilliant colours with a shiny opaque glaze'.[34] Thus, neither of these changes required new moulds, bodies, or a major reorganization of production.

[27] *N. Staffs. Merc.* 15 July 1843.   [28] B. and H. Wedgwood, *Wedgwood Circle*, 252.
[29] Batkin, *Wedgwood Ceramics*, 27.
[30] Hower, 'Ten Generations', 675; B. and H. Wedgwood, *Wedgwood Circle*, 265–6, 270.
[31] *Staffs. Advert.* 'Exhibitors in the Pottery District', 29 Mar. 1851.
[32] Batkin, *Wedgwood Ceramics*, 60.
[33] WMSS. 29232–46. The General Hiring Book, 22 Dec. 1857.
[34] B. and H. Wedgwood, *Wedgwood Circle*, 265, 290, 297; Hower, 'Ten Generations', 675.

In addition to the arrival of Lessore in 1859, Godfrey Wedgwood became a partner in the firm. He took more interest in the design and in extending the range of products. In particular, he improved the quality of the jasper, by making dip and solid jasper with a tinted body, and he expanded the parian range.[35] Also, in 1878, the firm restarted production of bone china, and in 1875 it reintroduced tiles and plaques into its range, opening a new tile department in 1882 in competition with Minton and Doulton.

Thus, despite the conservatism in design of Josiah II and Frank Wedgwood, the firm did expand its range of products in the 1860s and 1870s. Moreover, throughout the period it continued to produce a relatively large proportion of ornamental items 'in small lots'.

During the period 1840 to 1880 the firm sold its ware to retailers at home and abroad, rather than directly to the general public. However, the firm did directly promote the products by displaying Wedgwood ware at international exhibitions, including the Great Exhibition of 1851 and international exhibitions in London in 1862 and 1871, Paris in 1855, 1867, and 1878, Vienna in 1873, and Sydney in 1879. In addition, in 1875 the firm opened showrooms in London to display samples and facilitate sales to retailers.[36] Furthermore, the firm used travellers to ascertain the requirements of a particular market and made efforts to produce products for specific markets. In Britain it manufactured electrical ceramics for the Electric Telegraph Company and the North Western Railway in the 1850s and the Post Office in the 1870s. It sent travellers twice a year into the home market divided into two sections—the northern journey consisting of Leeds, York, Edinburgh, Glasgow, and Ireland, and the southern journey including the area south and east of Southampton, Oxford, Cambridge, and Lyme. For the American market the firm supplied 'a fancy and a plumber's ware', in other words, decorative, luxury, and from the 1870s commemorative goods on the one hand, and useful or functional goods such as closet pans, urinals, and plug wash-basins (often decorated with lavish floral decorations or an American flag) on the other. The firm also concentrated efforts on expanding exports to the Russian market in the 1870s, sending a traveller

---

[35] Batkin, *Wedgwood Ceramics*, 14, 18. Parian (called Carrara by Wedgwoods because of its resemblance to the marble from Carrara in Northern Italy) was a new clay body developed in the 1840s from a mixture of two-thirds felspar and one-third china clay. It was particularly appropriate for statuary busts and figures as it was highly translucent with a fine texture and was usually left unglazed.

[36] Hower, 'Ten Generations', 678.

there once a year from 1874 as part of the 'foreign journey' to Holland, Belgium and Northern Germany, and Italy twice a year.[37]

Despite the conservatism prior to the late 1850s in the range of products, the company made profits. In the sixteen years between 1844 and 1859, profits ranged from a low of £2,400 in 1859 to a high of £14,500 in 1851 with an average of £8,155 or 22 per cent of the estimated value of the firm in 1859.[38] Over the period between 1847 and 1883 the net annual results ranged from a loss of £211 in 1870 to a profit of £13,614 in 1882, with an average annual profit of £6,830 (between 12 per cent and 15 per cent of the average net worth).[39]

Although there were periodic rearrangements in the duties of managers,[40] alterations in the fabric of the factory in the 1870s,[41] and 'improvements' associated with the introduction of china manufacture in 1878,[42] the factory continued to be organized on the principles established by Josiah I—the separation of different processes and the division of labour. The works were divided into two sections—the ornamental works (OW) and the useful works (UW)—each with its own kilns and its own set of hands. In order to introduce china manufacture, Clement Wedgwood simply added a new section without having to undertake a major reorganization of the existing sections. In 1883 in china, there was a slip-maker and there were plate-makers, throwers, turners, a mould-maker, dippers, biscuit ovenmen, paintresses, printers and transferers, gloss ovenmen, and warehouse-men and -women, as well as china overseers. All of these were distinguished from those in the OW and the UW. Furthermore, the majority of workers continued to be skilled regardless of section. Out of 723 men, women, and young persons working at Wedgwoods in 1883, there were only four 'Odd boys' and five 'Odd men', and this extremely low proportion of the workforce without a specific skill was similar to that nearly 100 years earlier.[43] Moreover, apart from the apprentices who moved among different branches,[44] the majority of workers specialized in one particular branch alone with nearly

---

[37] Gater, 'A House of Long-Standing', 57–8, 66–7; Reilly, *Wedgwood*, ii, 76–81.

[38] For profits 1844–59, see WMSS. 42–28598. The value of the business on Robert Brown's death in 1859 was £37,064: see Hower, 'Ten Generations', 678.

[39] Hower, 'Ten Generations', 678.

[40] WMSS. 15A/1: G. W. to Enoch Mountford, 26 Dec. 1868; WMSS. 15A/1: Clement Wedgwood to George Hulme, 21 June 1872.

[41] The wages of bricklayers and joiners working at Wedgwoods were separated into those for 'alterations' and those for 'usual work', see WMSS. 29218–46: List of Workers and Wages Nov. 1872–Feb. 1873 Compared with those from Nov. 1875–Feb. 1876.

[42] B. and H. Wedgwood, *Wedgwood Circle*, 312.

[43] McKendrick, 'Factory Discipline', 33.   [44] See below, p. 210.

constant employment in it.[45] In addition to those in the three sections mentioned above, distinct occupations in 1883 included artists, brick-layers, burnishers, carters, casters, cup-and-saucer makers, engine and millmen, engravers, gilders, handlers, joiners, modellers, marl-grinders, packers, enamel paintresses, tile paintresses, majolica paintresses, pin-makers, polishers, saggar-makers, sliphousemen, and sorters as well as two persons employed in the showroom and nine administrative posts in the counting-house.

Wages in the Wedgwood factory were comparable with those in other firms. Despite wide variation in the products, competition for sales, and differences in religion and politics, Wedgwoods co-operated with other manufacturers, particularly Mintons, in questions concerning wages. In 1867, for example, workmen at Mintons apparently based a request for higher wages on the grounds that Wedgwood was paying a higher rate for similar pieces of ware. In response to a letter from the head of Mintons concerning the issue, Godfrey Wedgwood remarked 'we must be on our guard against the men raising prices on us by unfair quotations of this sort, and I shall always be glad to compare prices with you whenever we are quoted as being above you'.[46] Even when the Wedgwoods had little direct interest in the immediate issue, they supported co-operation with other employers over an issue of principle regarding wages. In 1872 Godfrey Wedgwood, for example, wrote saying

I enclose a donation of £10 (we have 10 earthenware ovens bisket and glost) as a donation toward the fund for indemnifying the sufferers by the Burslem Lock-out. We do not consider the question one which touches us, but give this donation because we do not like to stand aloof from any attempt at combination amongst the masters against the men on a matter of principle to regulate our dealings with them.[47]

The co-operation also extended beyond the Potteries. In 1868 Godfrey Wedgwood attempted to hire throwers from Glasgow when his own earthenware throwers wanted a rise in the day wage; but he came to 'terms with the earthenware throwers' before it was necessary to go ahead.[48]

---

[45] A typical agreement between Wedgwoods and their workmen stated that the employer 'was at liberty to stint us in anyway' but if he did so he 'must give us our discharge if applied for before we are put on full work again', see WMSS. 29230–46, 21 Oct. 1842.

[46] WMSS. 15A/1: G. W. to C. M. Campbell, 24 Mar. 1867.

[47] WMSS. 15A/1: G. W. to M. F. Blakiston, 8 Feb. 1872.

[48] WMSS. 15A/1: G. W. to Mr Wardlaw, Messrs. Cochranes Works, Glasgow. 4 Sept. 1868; 14 Sept. 1868.

2. Paternalism and Deference?

On the basis of the foregoing description of the village and firm, one would expect Etruria to be a factory-dominated neighbourhood exhibiting the relationships of deference and paternalism which Patrick Joyce emphasizes in his portrayal of Lancashire factory towns—but was it?

Similarities

During the period 1840 to 1880 the Wedgwoods' relationship to their workforce, the village of Etruria, and public life in the Potteries more generally fits Joyce's description in three ways. First, J. Wedgwood and Sons exhibited two necessary conditions for, and indications of, the existence of a deferential relationship. As we saw above, the firm maintained wages and employment throughout the period. In addition, the Wedgwoods refrained from using obvious coercion over their workforce, although they occasionally sought the intervention of the law in order to discipline workmen. During a dispute with some of his plate-makers in 1872, Godfrey Wedgwood turned to his solicitor explaining that

we have some platemakers who have given in their notice to leave. Since doing which although they have kept proper hours, they have not done half the amount of work that they can and usually do. We wish to know whether the magistrate could convict them of 'neglect of work' on these grounds or whether absence from the manufactory is necessary. The platemakers owe issues varying from 40/- to 80/- being sums overdrawn on account. We presume that our work book showing the necessary accounts and the biscuit warehouse evidence . . . would be sufficient evidence in the County Court to prove the debt.[49]

Yet, confirming Joyce's view, Godfrey Wedgwood also felt it important to be seen to refrain from coercion, despite the need to maintain discipline. In 1868 the lodgeman at the potworks was 'subject to ill-treatment' by two men. One of the men, named Copeland, worked at Wedgwoods, while the other did not. Godfrey Wedgwood wanted to punish them and he turned to his solicitor for advice. Godfrey explained that he wanted to avoid taking a weak case before the magistrates, because a verdict of not guilty or a light penalty would 'show men like these how far they might go in insulting a fellow workman without risk of punishment'. However, if the solicitor was not sure of the case against Copeland, Godfrey wrote that 'I should like to frighten him at any rate if possible'. He wanted 'to give publicity to the matter and let it be known that we shall protect our

---

[49] WMSS. 15A/1: G. W. to R. Stevenson, 24 Feb. 1872.

servants'. At the same time, Godfrey saw the importance of the employer appearing to refrain from coercion when he suggested that if there were a strong case against the two men, he would 'magnanimously let them off when it comes before the Court'.[50]

Second, within the potworks the Wedgwoods who headed the firm between 1840 and 1880 inherited and continued the structure of authority and dependence and the methods of factory discipline which Josiah I had established.[51] The bell, the clocking-in system, the detailed written instructions for each occupation and for each object, and especially the hierarchy of authority relying on an overlooker or foreman in each section, rather than one overall manager, persisted. Francis Wedgwood and subsequently his sons made final decisions and had ultimate responsibility, but they divided and delegated responsibility to a variety of overseers. The overseers of the OW and UW in turn delegated some responsibility, such as that of hiring and paying assistants to workmen in some branches, including throwing and flat-pressing.

Despite incomplete company records, it is possible to illustrate the hierarchy of authority through examples from the hiring agreements of several individuals during the period. Richard Griffiths, for example, did the hiring, allocations, and overseeing of work in the warehouse in the late 1830s and 1840s. In 1840 the warehousemen agreed

> to serve Richard Griffiths in Messrs. J. Wedgwood and Sons warehouse from Martinmas 1840 to Martinmas 1841 at the daily wages set against our signatures here under; to make ourselves generally useful in any warehouse work. The said Richard Griffiths to be at liberty to change our work or any part of it when ever any vacancy or other circumstance makes it expedient. [52]

William Adams was foreman of the OW for over forty years ending in 1866. A complete list of those working in the OW in 1864 reveals that it was a microcosm of the potting department and ovens of a potworks, lacking only a warehouse and decorating department.[53] As foreman of the OW, William Adams was in charge of thirty-seven persons, including:

---

[50] WMSS. 15A/1: G. W. to R. Stevenson, 25 June 1868; 26 June 1868; 27 June 1868. G. W. to Mr Boulton, 26 June 1868. In the end Copeland promised 'to behave better in future', and he 'offered £1 towards the Widows Fund at Etruria'.

[51] McKendrick, 'Factory Discipline', 38–46.

[52] WMSS. 29228–46: Hiring Book 1814–42.

[53] WMSS. 29187–46: OW Complete List, Oct. 1864. The final products, however, were somewhat unusual in that they did not require painting, printing, or dipping.

2 slip-makers
1 thrower and his assistants
4 turners and their lathe-treaders
4 ornament-makers and their assistants
4 pressers and a mould-runner
1 handler
2 biscuit firemen, a placer, and a coaler
1 scourer
1 gloss fireman and two placers

The two slip-makers, the scourer, the firemen, the placers, and the lathe-treaders were paid by time rather than by the piece, and it was one of William Adams's duties to keep a timebook recording time worked and payments each week. It is particularly interesting that the lathe-treaders were paid directly by the firm rather than by the turners. The lathe-treaders were children, and this suggests that not all children were directly under the authority of an individual workman. The mould-runner and the four ornamenters' assistants, however, were also children, and they as well as the two women who assisted the thrower were paid by, and under the direct authority of, the individual workmen, rather than the firm. The list, therefore, reveals that there were a variety of patterns with regard to the relationship of skilled men and assistants: the slip-makers and the handler did not have assistants; the firemen and turners had authority over the placers and lathe-treaders respectively, but this was not reinforced by direct payment; and the thrower and ornamenter both paid and had authority over their assistants. The important point, however, is that they all worked as a unit under the authority of William Adams.

Not all foremen were exclusively managers. Daniel Steele, for example, worked as a turner as well as foreman of the UW in 1842. Moreover, managers' duties included not only overseeing workmen, but also the materials. In 1856 John Greatbatch agreed to

. . . overlook all the potters at the White Bank and the ovenmen and in particular see to the prentices . . . see the trial bits of stone out of the Biscuit ovens and stop all short fired ware from going into the biscuit house . . . make out the miller's account weekly. . . try all the clay that comes up according to the directions in the blending book and see that all materials are such and in such order as they should be.[54]

[54] WMSS. 29232–46: General Hiring Book, 203.

When John Greatbatch left in 1867, the management of the UW was divided between George Hulme who became 'foreman of the throwers, handlers and turners' and Thomas Griffiths who agreed to 'manage UW potters, flatpressers and settle their books'.

There were also overseers in the decorative branches. In 1847 Enoch Mountford, for example, agreed 'to serve J. Wedgwood and Sons as foreman of the enamel and gilding department of their business for one year at 36/– per week'. There is no evidence of an overseer of the printers; however, in 1872 one of the nine printers, Rhodes, earned slightly more than the others suggesting that there was a hierarchy within the branch among the printers as well as between the printers and the transferers and paper-cutters who worked for them. In 1872 there were only four individuals listed as overlookers. This list may not be complete or the company may have had vacancies, but even if there were seven in 1872 as there were in 1875, this suggests that there was some subdivision of authority at the level of the workshop, such as that among the printers.

Thus, coinciding with Joyce's view of textile factories, there was extensive differentiation among occupations within the potworks, and this relatively large number of distinct branches reveals no identifiable 'labour aristocracy'. In some branches the skilled workmen hired and paid as well as supervised their own assistants, but even these were subject to the authority of an overlooker.

The third way in which the Wedgwoods and Etruria appears to coincide with Joyce's model of Lancashire factory towns is in the continuity of employment of individuals and family groups, often across generations, in the potworks; and this continuity carried over to the village of Etruria. There is no doubt that some individuals worked for Wedgwoods for a long period. In 1843, of the 105 workpeople whose agreements indicated the number of years employed with the firm, four had worked for the firm for forty years or more, nine had worked between thirty and thirty-nine years, nine had between twenty and twenty-nine years' service, and ten had been with the firm for between ten and nineteen years.[55] A casual glance at the names of workpeople on lists and hiring agreements during the period reveal surnames such as Lovatt, Griffiths, Greatbatch, Morgan, Till, and Adams, appearing and reappearing: several members of the same extended family, sometimes across generations, worked for the firm. Some quantification of the extent of family employment comes from the 105 workpeople who signed agreements in

---

[55] WMSS. 29234–46: Workpeople's Agreements 1843.

1843. Over 50 per cent still either worked for the firm in 1883 or some-one with the same surname worked for the firm. Although some with the same surname in 1883 might not have been related to those in 1843, this tendency toward an overestimate is balanced by those in 1843 who had only daughters (whose husband and children could not be counted) or who had no children (and thus no children who could have been em-ployed in the potworks).

Although the continuity of employment is striking and the Wedgwoods publicized it, it should not be over-emphasized. As we saw above, in 1868 Godfrey Wedgwood was willing to bring in throwers from Scotland, and again in 1872 he wrote to the same Glasgow firm asking for help in finding a 'manager over our throwers and turners branch', saying that 'we should be glad to get one of your countrymen. . . . The fact is we should be glad to know of any potter managers that would be inclined to move south from your part of the country as now that we have a place vacant we would make changes if it was for the sake of catching a really good manager.[56] Also, we shall see below that neither of the two sons of a man who worked for Wedgwoods for over fifty years repeated his experience.

Nevertheless, the continuity of employment of individuals and family groups carried over into the village of Etruria: 60 per cent of the indi-viduals listed as pottery-workers in the village in 1861 were born in Etruria; and of the sons of potters living in Etruria that were employed, 85 per cent also worked in the pottery industry. Moreover, a simple analysis of the heads of households in Etruria in 1861 reveals that 113 out of 203 (56 per cent) had the same surname as at least one other house-hold head in the village. There were seven heads with the last name of 'Adams', five 'Tills'; seven cases of three household heads with the same surname; and thirty-one cases in which two heads shared the same sur-name. Although some with the same surname may not have been related, that number must be counterbalanced by married daughters still living in the village who cannot be identified and counted. Direct evidence of the link between continuity of employment with Wedgwoods and resi-dence in Etruria comes from an account of a dinner in 1859 presided over by Frank Wedgwood in honour of nine of the company's longest-serving workmen. The 'average time of servitude', to quote the inscrip-tion on their photograph, was fifty-four-and-a-half years, and all nine lived in Etruria.[57] If one looks at the age-structure of the potters living in

[56] WMSS. 15A/1: G. W. to Mr Wardlaw, 7 June 1872.
[57] L. Jewitt, *Life of Josiah Wedgwood* (London, 1865), 395–6; Finney, *Recollections*, 19–20.

TABLE 4.1   *The Age- and Sex-Structure of Pottery-Workers: Etruria*
1861

Age	male			female			all		
	N	%	cum%	N	%	cum %	N	%	cum %
5–9	0	—	—	2	1	—	2	1	—
10–14	22	13	13	9	11	—	31	12	13
15–19	32	18	31	22	27	39	54	21	34
20–4	26	15	46	17	21	60	43	17	50
25–9	24	14	60	12	15	74	36	14	64
30–4	13	7	67	5	6	80	18	7	71
35–9	19	11	78	5	6	86	24	9	80
40–4	11	6	84	6	7	94	17	7	87
45–9	7	4	88	2	2	96	9	3	90
50–4	1	1	89	1	1	97	2	1	91
55–9	5	3	92	1	1	98	6	2	94
60–4	5	3	94	1	1	99	6	2	96
65–9	8	5	99	0	—	99	8	3	99
70–80	2	1	100	0	—	99	2	1	100
TOTAL	175	100	100	83	100	99[a]	258	100	100

Source: Etruria Census Enumerator's Book, 1861

[a] This figure does not equal 100 due to rounding error.

Etruria (shown in Table 4.1), there were ten males between 65 and 80 years old. One of these was Emile Lessore, the French artist working at Wedgwoods, and the remaining nine were those honoured at the dinner two years before. Thus, at least all of the longest-serving Wedgwood employees lived in Etruria.

Furthermore, coinciding with Joyce's description of textile factories, the Wedgwood workforce celebrated events in the employer's family. An event such as the coming of age of Godfrey Wedgwood in 1854, was celebrated by the workpeople as well as the gentry.

In the year 1854 also occurred Godfrey Wedgwood's 21st birthday. He was presented with an address from the workmen of the Wedgwood factory. . . . There was a factory holiday with a picnic for all workmen and their families. The following evening the Frank Wedgwoods gave a ball in Godfrey's honour, to which all the gentry from miles around came.[58]

[58] B. and H. Wedgwood, *Wedgwood Circle*, 257.

Outside the factory the Wedgwoods owned a considerable proportion of the houses.[59] I have not been able to locate any direct statements by the Wedgwoods of their housing policy. If, however, the 'gross estimated rental' in the ratebook covering Etruria for 1862 is assumed to be a close approximation to the actual rent paid, then the average of a little over 1/ – per week is substantially less than the rents of 3/– per week paid by working men elsewhere in the potteries in the 1850s.[60] Occasionally, too, a house appears as part of the hiring agreement between Wedgwoods and a foreman. When they hired William Carr in 1867, for example, he became the 'tenant of the house lately occupied by John Greatbatch'. His remuneration included one-half rent for the house, one-half rates, gas, and coals. Later in the year the house became rent free.[61]

Patrick Joyce argues that in Lancashire employer influence was expressed through the factory itself rather than through housing; though, where employers did own houses this undoubtedly reinforced their influence, allowing further scope for paternalism.[62] In Etruria there is evidence that widows continued to live in their houses after the death of their husbands. Although the number was small, a higher proportion of women over the age of 15 were widows in Etruria than in England and Wales in four of the six age-groups above age 45, with a particularly marked difference in the age-groups between 45 and 55.[63]

Deliberately or not, the Wedgwoods seem to have provided a form of widows' relief by allowing widows to remain in their houses, in combination with opportunities for the employment of themselves or their children in the potworks. In 1861 there were seven widows living in Etruria who had been living in the village in 1851 and married to potters. In nearly all cases either the widow or her children were employed in pottery manufacture in 1861. Ann Till, for example, the widow of Joseph Till who was a presser in 1851, still lived in a house owned by the Wedgwoods in 1861 with five of her children ranging in age from 11 to

---

[59] See above, p. 186.

[60] HBRL, 'Rate Book Borough of Hanley 1862'. The difference is in 'gross estimated rental' and not in rent actually paid; the relation between the two is not clear. See also: PRO. MH12/13013; MH12/21433; MH12/48014: 'Able-bodied Men in Receipt of Outdoor Relief under the Labour Test Order, 1855'.

[61] WMSS 29232–46: The General Hiring Book, 27 Mar. 1867; 2 Dec. 1867.

[62] Joyce, *Work, Society and Politics*, 121–3.

[63] In Etruria 21 per cent of women aged 45–9 and 47 per cent of women aged 50–4 were widowed compared with 13 per cent and 19 per cent of women in these age-groups in England and Wales: see M. Dupree, 'Family Structure in the Staffordshire Potteries 1840–1880'; D. Phil. thesis (Oxford, 1981), 233.

TABLE 4.2   *Place of Residence of the Wedgwood Workpeople: 1843*

Place of residence	No. of workers	%
Etruria	49	47
Shelton	13	13
Newcastle	12	12
Wolstanton	8	8
Stoke	7	7
Hanley	7	7
Burslem	3	3
Fenton	1	<1
Tunstall	1	<1
Other	3	3
TOTAL	104	100

Source: WMSS. 29234–46: Workpeople's Agreements, 1843.

23, all of whom were employed as potters or paintresses in 1861. Moreover, her son Thomas and his family lived in a house either next door or across the street.

Differences

Despite the similarities there are a number of important ways in which the relationship between J. Wedgwood and Sons and Etruria differed from the model which Patrick Joyce constructs on the basis of Lancashire factory towns. First, the patterns of employment and relationships of authority within the factory were not transferred directly to family and social relationships outside the factory. Although Etruria was the only possible 'factory village' for Wedgwood employees, only a relatively small proportion of the Wedgwood workforce lived in Etruria, thereby limiting the extent to which those in the factory were linked with the village surrounding it. In 1843 less than half of the workpeople who signed agreements[64] lived in the village (Table 4.2); by 1883 the proportion had dropped to 25 per cent (Table 4.3).[65]

---

[64] Although the agreements cover a wide range of occupations, they do not include ovenmen, painters, and paintresses among others. The 104 agreements cover about one-fifth of the workforce.

[65] This continued to be the case until the 1930s when the firm moved from Etruria to Barlaston. Then some lived nearby in Shelton but 'two-thirds came from scattered parts of the Potteries': S. Gater and D. Vincent, *The Factory in a Garden: Wedgwood from Etruria to Barlaston—the Transitional Years* (Keele, Staffordshire, 1988), 43.

TABLE 4.3 *Place of Residence of Wedgwood 'Hands': 1883*

Place of residence	No. of workers	%
Etruria	172	25
Shelton	3	<1
Newcastle	214	31
Wolstanton	25	4
Stoke	25	4
Hanley	128	18
Other	29	4
n.k.	104	15
TOTAL	700	101

Source: WMSS. 29219–46: List of Hands on Works compiled by Cecil Wedgwood, March 1883.

Those employed at Wedgwoods who lived in Etruria did not comprise the entire workforce, nor did they include all those who were relatively highly paid.[66] Nevertheless, those in the Wedgwood workforce who lived in Etruria tended to be the stable core of the workforce. As we saw above, they were likely to have long service with the firm over successive generations. Furthermore, the patterns of co-residence, and married women's and children's employment suggest that they were relatively well-off. Yet, even within these families there was autonomy regarding labour recruitment, which in turn limited the family basis of authority within the workplace on which Joyce puts such strong emphasis.

There was little sharing of houses or 'huddling' by co-residing groups. Thus, 91 per cent of the co-residing groups had a house to themselves. This average of just over one (1.04) co-residing group per house is slightly less than the 1.2 average for England and Wales in 1861. Moreover, the average of 4.5 persons per house in Etruria was low compared with the parliamentary borough of Stoke-upon-Trent (5.2), England and Wales (5.4), and Michael Anderson's Preston (6.1).[67] In addition, most people who were not solitary lodgers or servants lived with their current nuclear family only and not in households which included other kin (see Table 4.4).

The general pattern was of one nuclear family per household, and only

[66] WMSS. 29236–46: Warehouse Timebook, 1843.
[67] See Dupree, 'Family Structure', 81.

TABLE 4.4   *Structure of the Families of Household Heads: Etruria 1861*

Type of family	No.	%
Head alone (or with unrelated persons only)	2	1
Nuclear families		
Childless married couples	38	18
Married couples or widowed persons with unmarried children only	137	64
Stem families (two or more lineally related ever-married persons and their nuclear families, if any)	18	9
Composite families		
Unmarried siblings only	3	1
Other kin	15	7
TOTAL	213	100

Note: Additional nuclear families: within composite families (3); within Stem families (9); others i.e. servants and lodgers (5).

Source: Census Enumerator's Book, Etruria 1861.

17 per cent of the co-residing groups contained related persons (i.e. grandparents, uncles, aunts, cousins, nieces, and nephews) other than members of the current nuclear family of the head. This is about the same as the proportion in the parliamentary borough and less than the 23 per cent in Preston in 1851. Like the pattern in the parliamentary borough and Preston, most of the kin who co-resided in Etruria were parentless children. And in Etruria there were relatively few lodgers (3 per cent of the population) and they were present in only 9 per cent of the co-residing groups—again far fewer than the 23 per cent of Preston households and similar to the parliamentary borough as a whole.[68]

In addition, relatively few married women were employed. Nearly one-third of the individuals living in Etruria and employed in pottery manufacture were women and girls; but, of these only 14 per cent were married women. Moreover, of all unmarried women living in Etruria 88 per cent were employed, while only 18 per cent of all married women were employed, with those employed in pottery accounting for a total of 12 per cent of married women in the village. Of the wives who did work in Etruria, a substantial proportion (29 per cent) were in life-cycle stage

[68] A higher proportion of households headed by widows (18 per cent) took in lodgers in Etruria, but this again was less than the proportion in Preston (33 per cent).

one and had no children who would have suffered from lack of attention. Furthermore, only 10 per cent of children under 10 years of age in Etruria had mothers listed as employed in the census enumerator's book—with a total of 9 per cent employed outside the home. In one case where the mother worked in the pottery industry, the house contained an otherwise unemployed grandmother, probably available as a guardian. In two other cases where the mother was a pottery-worker, there was some other unemployed person in the house (i.e. kin or lodger) who might have been available. That leaves only five cases where there was no co-residing unemployed person who might watch children while the mother worked. These may have been cared for by a relative living elsewhere in the village or they might attend the village school.

If, as historians argue, the main reason why mothers left their homes and families and went out to work was that their families sorely needed the extra money to raise a standard of living which the low wages of the husband would otherwise have forced below the poverty-line,[69] then the low proportion of working wives and mothers in a village such as Etruria, dominated by an industry with a relatively high female participation rate, indicates that either the wages of the husbands were high enough or that an alternative answer to poverty was chosen. The low percentage of shared houses eliminates one alternative answer to poverty. Although it is possible that the relatively few married women in Etruria employed in pottery manufacture was the result of a deliberate policy by the company rather than the choice of the workpeople, it still means that those living in Etruria did not choose these alternative sources of family income, suggesting that the earnings of those family members in employment were sufficient.

In addition to the low proportion of married women employed, there was a relatively low proportion of children employed in Etruria. In the age-group 9 to 14, 23 per cent of the children in Etruria were employed, compared with 31 per cent in central Burslem, one of the Potteries towns. In Burslem children as young as 7 and 8 were recorded as employed in the pottery industry, while in Etruria no boys under 9 and no girls under 11 were employed. Furthermore, only 9 per cent of the pottery workforce in Etruria was made up of children, while 19 per cent of Burslem's pottery workforce was composed of children.

The relatively low proportions of married women and children living

[69] M. Hewitt, *Wives and Mothers in Victorian Industry* (London, 1958), 189–95; E. Roberts, *Women's Work 1840–1880* (Basingstoke and London, 1988), 15–16.

in Etruria who were employed in the pottery industry suggest that the link between the factory and the village was not as close as Joyce suggests when he writes that 'it was the family in work that made the connection of factory and community such an intimate one'.[70] In other words, there was autonomy within the nuclear family; the factory did not carry over into the family as completely as Joyce implies. Despite the workmen with fifty or more years of service who were honoured in 1859, the length of employment should not be exaggerated, for the age-structure of those employed in the pottery industry and living in Etruria (Table 4.1) indicates that over half of those employed in pottery manufacture in Etruria were under 25 years old; nearly two-thirds were under 30 years of age; and 90 per cent were under 50 years old. This last figure points up the fact that the nine workmen singled out for their long service were exceptions and quite atypical of the pottery labour-force as a whole at a given time. Moreover, even the sons of long-serving employees did not necessarily work in the pottery industry or if apprenticed to Wedgwoods remain with the firm.[71] In addition, the skilled workmen in some branches of the trade hired their own assistants. But, at any one time only a few would even have had children of their own of the right age for an assistant. If so, they might hire them or the children of relatives. But, they were also likely to go further afield and hire those with weaker ties such as relatives or acquaintances of other workmen or neighbours. Furthermore, while family and kinship ties were undoubtedly important in getting a job even among the skilled potters and the women decorators and paintresses who were hired directly by Wedgwoods, the Wedgwoods did go outside their workforce in the case of the throwers from Scotland cited above.[72]

Not only was the authority structure of the factory and the family not repeated directly in the factory, but also the factory hierarchy was not transferred completely to the village. Although an overlooker such as Henry Brownsword or John Greatbatch occupied a house in Etruria rent-free from the company which was valued at £10, and was enough for him to be one of the parliamentary electors in the village in 1862, William Adams the OW overlooker lived in a house valued at £4 1s. that does not seem to have been differentiated from the houses of other workers.

Second, despite the influence of the Wedgwoods and the factory within

[70] Joyce, *Work, Society and Politics*, 117.   [71] Finney, *Recollections*.
[72] See above, pp. 192, 197.

the village and area, there was autonomy within the family and community outside the factory. The influence of the Wedgwoods outside the factory in terms of assistance for those in need, and particularly in terms of politics, religion, and even social life was limited both by the Wedgwood's policies and by the initiative of the workpeople. While Wedgwoods assisted widows with housing and there was a Widow's Fund at the factory, the co-residence of kin, particularly 'parentless children' and the extent to which kin lived within the village suggest that family and kin provided a source of assistance, independent of the factory, for short-term and long-term child-care, as well as illness and other needs both minor and major for many people within Etruria.

In 1868 Godfrey Wedgwood provided a clear statement of the Wedgwoods' policy with regard to exerting influence over their workmen in parliamentary elections. Writing to the Liberal candidate for the parliamentary borough of Stoke-upon-Trent, he said

I shall be glad to support you at the forthcoming election, but hope you will not put down that promise at more than it is worth. It is only a promise of my personal vote. It has been always a matter of honour with us not to influence our workmen, and however much I wish you success, I cannot break through the rule.[73]

In the end the 1868 election in the Stoke-upon-Trent parliamentary borough was not contested, and as a result it is not possible to tell how the workmen in Etruria would have voted. Nevertheless, the poll-books for 1859–62 indicate that the Wedgwoods' Liberal allegiance did not influence all of their workmen living in the village who were able to vote. John Greatbatch, a foreman, voted for the Liberal candidates; while Henry Brownsword, a modeller and later a foreman, voted for the Tory candidates in both 1859 and 1862. Moreover, neither the Wedgwoods nor the other large employer, Col. Roden (who was resident in the village), exerted influence over others in the village to vote Liberal. Jesse Shirley, a bone merchant, and George Kirk, an ironfounder, for example, both voted for the Tory candidate in 1859 and in the 1862 bye-election.[74]

Josiah Wedgwood I did not build a church or make any provision for religious worship in Etruria. Nor did his successors, Josiah II and Frank, intervene. In 1819, in response to a petition from workmen, the Wedgwoods

[73] WMSS. 15A/1: G.W. to Lt. Col. Roden, 18 July 1868.
[74] Stoke-upon-Trent parliamentary borough, poll-books 1859 and 1862, William Salt Library, Stafford.

provided land in the village, and the workmen built a Wesleyan Chapel. In 1847 the Church of England established a chapelry in Etruria without any initiative on the part of the Wedgwoods.[75] Thus, if similar religious observance between employer and workpeople was 'a measure of dependence of the operative',[76] then the Wedgwood operatives were not dependent. Instead, they exhibited considerable autonomy and independence. Similarly, in other voluntary organizations that provided a focus for social life in Etruria, the factory and the employer were not necessarily 'the central elements in forging the neighbourhood bond'. Frank Wedgwood established a reading-room with newspapers for the use of workers, which he offered to support until it became self-supporting, but the Etruria Volunteer Corps, for example, was initiated by the workmen, and they sought employer patronage only later.[77]

And third, Etruria in 1861 was not a homogeneous village of pottery-workers. The period 1840–80 was a significant period of transition for Etruria. The model village of Josiah I was changing within as the adjacent Shelton Coal and Bar Ironworks expanded after the first furnaces were completed in 1842. The ironworks bought Etruria Hall in 1844 and the managing partner of the ironworks replaced the Wedgwoods as the resident employer by moving into Etruria Hall. He lived there until his wife died, and by 1864 the Hall had become the headquarters building for the ironworks. The Company built some houses in Cobridge for its workers, but a number of ironworkers also moved into Etruria. Between 1851 and 1861 Etruria grew from 154 houses and 767 people to 203 houses and 966 people. The census attributed a similar overall increase in the size of the township of Shelton of which Etruria was a part, to 'the steady progress of the china, earthenware and iron trades and the development of the collieries of the district and the extension of building operations'.[78] In 1862 ironworkers comprised 10 per cent of the employed population in Etruria (see Table 4.5). In this way the village reflected the occupational variety of the Potteries as a whole.

Ironworkers formed a distinct group in the village because of their origin as well as their occupation. Only 17 per cent of the ironworkers living in Etruria in 1861 were born in Etruria and nearly 75 per cent came from outside the Potteries, compared with 60 per cent of the pottery-workers who were born in Etruria and the nearly 86 per cent born within the Potteries.[79] Not only did the ironworkers encroach upon

---

[75] Finney, *Recollections*, 5.　　　[76] Joyce, *Work, Society and Politics*, 176.
[77] Reilly, *Wedgwood*, ii, 70; Finney, *Recollections*, 21–2.
[78] PP 1862, lxvi, pt. 2, 301.　　　[79] Dupree, 'Family Structure', 241–3.

TABLE 4.5 *Occupational Groups: Etruria 1861, Central Burslem 1861*

Occupational group	% of employed population	
	Etruria	Central Burslem
Agricultural	1.0	0.3
Shopkeepers	3.3	12.0
Non-factory crafts	6.0	13.0
Manufacturers and merchants	1.0	0.0
Pottery	56.0	39.0
Ironworkers	10.0	0.3
Professional	2.2	1.3
Clerical	3.0	1.0
Servants	7.0	10.0
Private Income	0.2	0.8
Semi-skilled	0.0	8.0
Miners	0.0	5.0
Labourers	9.0	8.0
Supervisory	0.4	0.0
Employed but n.k.	1.0	0.0
N	460	1,513

Sources: Census Enumerator's Book, Etruria 1861; D. G. Stuart (ed.), *The Population of Central Burslem 1851 and 1861*, Department of Adult Education University of Keele Local History Occasional Paper no. 2 (Keele, 1973), 30, Table 10.

the relative homogeneity of the village, but the smoke from the iron-works assaulted the village from above, and the ironworks' associated coal-mines literally began to undermine the village during this period. The smoke and smell of calcinating ore drove the North Staffordshire Infirmary to a new location; the trees in Etruria Grove withered and died; and the first evidence of the subsidence of the Wedgwood potworks appeared.

However much the village changed within during the period, the iron-workers were similar to the potters in some respects. Both groups were relatively well-off with a low proportion of married women and children employed and little sharing of houses. Together, they made Etruria a bastion of the 'respectable' working class. Furthermore, even in the period of Josiah I the village was not self-sufficient. The employment structure reveals that there were few individuals in retailing occupations living in the village in 1861. Although there were ovens for baking bread, for most retail items the villagers depended on the market and shops in Hanley. Arnold Bennett could never have drawn his portraits of lower-middle-class society of *Clayhanger* and *The Old Wives' Tale* from Etruria alone.

Conclusion

Although Wedgwoods and Etruria exhibited some of the characteristics of the piecemeal paternalism Patrick Joyce emphasizes in his description of Lancashire towns, this should not be overemphasized. Etruria was as close as a factory and area within the Potteries came to Joyce's view of factory and neighbourhood in Lancashire. Yet, its increasing mixture of industries and occupational diversity was typical of the Potteries as an urban area and of industrial Britain more generally. In 1840 the paternalism of Josiah I was still recognizable, with the Frank Wedgwoods living in the Hall and the village still geographically and physically similar to the model village of the 1770s. By 1880 the Wedgwoods had long since moved from the Hall, to be replaced by the ironworks, and the village had become absorbed into the area geographically as the ironworks expanded and transformed its appearance.

A relatively small proportion of the Wedgwood workforce lived in Etruria in the mid-nineteenth century. Even within the village the transfer of the authority structure and influence of the factory through family employment patterns was by no means as complete as Joyce and others[80] who focus on the family work group have argued. Although labour recruitment was highly dependent on family influence, in Etruria, as in Michael Anderson's Preston, the family work-group was a minority pattern. It left room for a considerable degree of autonomy within families and the wider village community. In Etruria this 'relative autonomy'

---

[80] N. J. Smelser, *Social Change in the Industrial Revolution: An Application of Theory to the Lancashire Cotton Industry 1770–1840* (London, 1959) suggests that employers in the cotton industry used family-based work groups to utilize family authority for supervision within the factory until technical innovations in weaving in the 1820s and 1830s broke up the family work-group within the factory. M. Anderson, *Family Structure in Nineteenth Century Lancashire* (Cambridge, 1971) and 'Sociological History and the Working-Class Family: Smelser Revisited', *Social History*, 3 (1976), 317–44 argues (in contrast to Smelser and like the evidence for the Potteries here) that the pattern of family work-groups was not the predominant pattern in the industry, though the pattern continued at least into the 1850s. For an argument for the overwhelming predominance of the family work-group within the production process in the pottery industry between 1890 and 1920 see R. Whipp, *Patterns of Labour: Work and Social Change in the Pottery Industry* (London, 1990), 65–6, 73–5, 84.

included the low labour-force participation of married women and younger
children and even some choice of jobs for adolescent boys and older men.
It also meant that employers such as Wedgwoods had to rely more on
relationships within the workplace for authority and on co-operation
with other employers than Joyce's model suggests. This is not to advocate a return to a view of the firm or family isolated from its surroundings.
On the contrary, it suggests the need for a 'community perspective'
which is wider than a single factory and its immediate neighbourhood.[81]

3. John Finney

The 'relative autonomy' of managerial and household strategies which
point to the importance of a 'community perspective' encompassing both
factory and family are also apparent from evidence of the experience of
a potter born in Etruria. In 1902, inspired by the death of Queen Victoria
and the coronation of Edward VII, John Finney composed his autobiography *Sixty Years' Recollections of an Etruscan*. He was well-suited to
his task. He was only sixty-four when he wrote, and his memory appears
to be accurate where incidents can be corroborated in other sources.
Moreover, in recounting his own experiences, he mentions a large number
of other people, so that the autobiography provides evidence of the
behaviour and attitudes of a wider group, and it gives a sense of the
preoccupations peculiar to a particular time, place, and society.

John Finney's father, born in Longton, was a fireman at Wedgwoods
who had worked for the firm since he was aged 12 and was one of the
nine workmen with over fifty years' service honoured by the firm in
1859. Finney's mother, also not a native of Etruria, was listed as a
laundress in the 1851 enumerator's book. Until he left home on marriage
in 1862 aged 24, John Finney lived with his parents and younger brother,
Joseph, in the same house in Etruria where he was born. His childhood
progression from school to work seems to have been typical for a child
growing up in Etruria in the 1840s. He began school aged 4 or 5 at the
only day-school in the village. Subsequently, he and some of his contemporaries moved to a school in Shelton, while others went to one in
Newcastle. When aged 11 or 12 he and his contemporaries left school
and began work. Some, including Finney, worked for Wedgwoods, but

---

[81] See M. Dupree, 'The Community Perspective in Family History: The Potteries during the Nineteenth Century', in A. L. Beier, D. N. Cannadine, and J. Rosenheim (eds.),
The First Modern Society: Essays in English History in Honour of Lawrence Stone (Cambridge, 1989), 549–73.

others went to different places such as Kirk's Foundry in Etruria. When he began at Wedgwoods he worked for a skilled workman in the potting department, and then was an assistant to a lathe-turner making jasperware, named Henry Foster, who 'had no children of his own and seemed to think nobody else ought to have any—for long'.[82] Thus, even though his father worked in the firm, the young Finney did not work with him in a family work-group.

In 1851, at the age of 13, John Finney began a new phase of his life when he was apprenticed to hollow-ware pressing at Wedgwoods. He worked with four different potters, as apprentices were shifted from one shop to another. Some of his contemporaries did not complete the seven years apprenticeship 'preferring soldiering', nor did Finney finish. He quarrelled with a warehouseman and as a result his indentures were cancelled. For two years he worked for a firm in Burslem 'until one of the American panics came'. He then went back to Wedgwoods where he remained until 1867, when he moved to another firm at Cauldon Place to make sanitary ware.

Neither the change to apprentice, the interlude in Burslem, nor the move to Cauldon Place altered the importance of activities outside the hours of work or the source of his associates. They remained primarily his fellow apprentices and subsequently his workmates. One significant effect of moving from 'lad' to apprentice, however, was that he and his fellow apprentices had more time at their disposal. This gave them 'better opportunities of seeing cricket', and later they became football enthusiasts. On holidays they would go on outings which involved walking long distances.[83] Furthermore, they also took an interest in the wider world; the Crimean War in particular made a deep impression.

Wedgwoods structured the activities of Finney and his friends negatively through the time of work, but also positively by promoting activities outside of the normal tasks and working hours at the factory. These included the journey of nearly all of the workmen from Wedgwoods to the Great Exhibition during Wakes Week 1851, when the firm paid for the hotel rooms and attempted to promote saving by matching the funds saved by individuals for the excursion. The Wedgwoods also promoted the Etruria Fire Brigade, giving two suppers a year and half a guinea a year to each fireman. The suppers featured songs and much home-brewed ale.

The Volunteer Movement had the central place in John Finney's

---

[82] Finney, *Recollections*, 3.   [83] Ibid. 13–14, 17–18, 20.

recollections. Although the initial meeting was held at the Wedgwood works, it was not promoted by the Wedgwoods, but by men under the influence of the example of other areas in the Potteries and their belief that 'there were young men enough in the village to form a corps of their own'. However, they did approach Frank Wedgwood first to ask if he would be the Captain of the corps. Refusing because of his age, he suggested instead that they ask the managing partner of the Shelton Bar Ironworks, who had recently moved into Etruria Hall. He accepted with enthusiasm, and some of the members of the corps worked at the ironworks, thus marking an integration of potters and ironworkers in Etruria. Nevertheless, the hierarchy of the corps tended to mirror the hierarchy of the workplace, whether pottery or ironworkers. The two major employers in the village were sought out to serve as Captain, and foremen at the pottery were sergeants.

In 1861 Finney married the daughter of a boatman, and it was apparently a compatible marriage.[84] On his marriage he moved to Stoke, to the same street as his wife's parents, and he subsequently raised a family. Yet, marriage and change of residence seem to have made relatively little difference to the nature of his activities outside work or to his companions. He continued to work for Wedgwoods, and he remained in the Volunteer Corps.

He writes, for example, that on the morning after the Volunteers participated in the ceremony surrounding the laying of the foundation stone for the North Staffordshire Infirmary

a party of us had arranged to go to Trentham, but we happened to meet about a dozen of Jones' ovenmen coming off the works, all with clean slops, aprons, and light Tommy hats on; and they looked a game lot. They were off to John Norbury's who kept the 'Greyhound' at the bottom of Hill Street, so we decided to go with them, knowing there would be more fun there than at Trentham for us: our wives went on without us.[85]

Furthermore, when he went to live among new neighbours on marriage, he made friends with them, taking up gardening and becoming a regular at a local pub where twenty or more would meet on a Saturday and Monday night to discuss politics and 'other matters concerning working men'. Even then, the neighbourhood turned out not to be completely new, as soon his 'old friend John Keele got married, and came to live nearby'.[86] Similarly, when he moved from Wedgwoods to Cauldon Place in 1867, there was relatively little change in the work, workmates, or

[84] Ibid. 5.   [85] Ibid. 28.   [86] Ibid. 26.

activities outside work. It was not new work; he had done it before at Wedgwoods.[87] Moreover, he 'was not a stranger to the men there, for some of them had been at Wedgwood's'.[88] And finally, although he eventually retired from the Volunteer Corps in 1869, outings with workmates continued.

A number of conclusions about the relation of work, family and community life in Etruria emerge from Finney's account. First, the period appears to have been relatively prosperous. Finney refers to the 'American panics' as an expected part of life in the pottery industry which did not last long. Moreover, although he was dismissed from Wedgwoods, he had little difficulty finding employment. Second, Finney and his contemporaries commonly thought of others in terms of their occupation. After he began work the Etruscans in his account soon dissolved into potters, foundrymen, boatmen, and navvies. Occupational identity was important, but the occupational divisions were far from castes. John Finney's brother, for example, became a joiner rather than a potter like his father and brother; and John Finney married the daughter of a boatman.[89]

Third, within the occupational groups it was fellow workmates and not a single employer who provided continuity for an individual. The extent of the flow of potters from Wedgwoods to Cauldon Works is particularly striking. Nevertheless, after Finney moved he worked next to the same man for over thirty years. Furthermore, while some of the activities and groups which Finney describes were factory-centred or actively promoted by the employer, most were not. The workplace emerges primarily as a source of companions and shared experiences which became the basis for association outside the workplace. Outside the workplace they carried on a wide variety of activities in which employers were not involved directly, including sports, gardening, walking, and especially singing and music. Finney comments on the choirs in which he sang at the Wesleyan Chapel and later the Church of England Chapel. Moreover, musical ability was a basis for respect. In short, Finney and his friends created a lively and varied existence outside working hours.

Finally, regarding the 'Etruscan' in the title, rivalries between fire brigades and pride in the Volunteer Corps suggest that a strong sense of belonging to a unit existed for those who lived in Etruria in the mid-nineteenth century and that it was recognized by others. Nevertheless, close ties with Hanley are also evident. It is there that the newspapers

---

[87] Ibid. 13.   [88] Ibid. 30.   [89] Ibid. 7, 31. See above, p. 211.

were read; the hustings were erected on Nomination Day; the circus came; theatres and other places of entertainment were located; and there was a market where all did their shopping. Moreover, as a matter of course children from Etruria went to Shelton or Newcastle for schooling beyond the most elementary.

John Finney's experience, like the evidence earlier in the chapter, suggests that the Wedgwoods' relationship to their workforce and the village of Etruria between 1840 to 1880 fits Joyce's description in several ways. The extensive differentiation among occupations within the potworks and the relatively large number of distinct branches reveal no identifiable 'labour aristocracy'. The hierarchy of authority relied on an overlooker or foreman in each section, rather than one overall manager. Francis Wedgwood and subsequently his sons made final decisions and had ultimate responsibility, but they divided and delegated responsibility to a variety of overseers. The overseers in turn delegated some responsibility, such as that of hiring and paying assistants, to workmen in some branches, including throwing and flat-pressing, as John Finney's experience as a lad reveals.

John Finney's autobiography also reveals the continuity of employment of individuals and family groups, often across generations, in the potworks; and this continuity carried over to the village of Etruria. There is no doubt that some individuals, such as John Finney's father, worked for Wedgwoods for a long period, and the continuity of employment of individuals and members of families carried over into the village of Etruria.

Despite the similarities, Finney's experience reinforces suggestions made earlier in the chapter that there were a number of important ways in which the relationship between J. Wedgwood and Sons and Etruria differed from the model which Joyce constructs on the basis of Lancashire factory towns.

The patterns of employment and relationships of authority within the factory were not transferred directly to family and social relationships outside the factory. There was autonomy within the nuclear family: the factory did not carry over into the family as completely as Joyce suggests. Even the sons of a long-serving Wedgwood employee such as John Finney's father did not necessarily work in the pottery industry or if apprenticed to Wedgwoods remain with the firm.[90]

Despite the influence of the Wedgwoods and the factory within the

[90] Finney, *Recollections.*

village and area, there was autonomy within the family and community outside the factory. The factory and the employer were not necessarily 'the central elements in forging the neighbourhood bond'. The Etruria Volunteer Corps of which John Finney was a member, for example, was initiated by the workmen, and they sought employer patronage only later.[91] Moreover, members of the Volunteer Corps were drawn from the ironworks as well as the pottery, thereby diluting the influence of a single factory and employer.

[91] Finney, *Recollections*, 21–2.

5

Families, Employers, and the Origins of the Factory Acts Extension

ALTHOUGH there were limits to the paternalism of individual employers such as Wedgwoods in the Potteries, employers acting together took paternalistic initiatives regarding protective legislation. Relationships among employers[1] were significant in bringing about legislation which created a new context for family and work relationships in the area. At the same time the nature of the 'relative autonomy' of managerial and household strategies in individual pottery firms were important in helping to account for the minimal worker participation in the movement for factory legislation in the Potteries.

The events leading up to the extension of the Factory Acts to the pottery industry in 1864 and its effects in the Potteries followed a different pattern from that in the textile areas and from general interpretations of the extension of protective legislation in Britain.[2] The role of manufacturers, the focus of controversy, and particularly the role of pottery-workers and their family relationships, as well as the consequences of the Act for the industry and employment patterns, were specific to this region and repay examination in some detail.

1. The Movement for State Intervention in the Pottery Industry

Before 1861 there was little interest in, and no direct action or agitation for, government regulation of employment in the pottery industry. Pottery manufacturers had testified before select committees concerning the question of state intervention for the regulation of the employment of children, young persons, and women in pottery manufacture,[3] and the

---

[1] A. C. Howe, *The Cotton Masters 1830–1860* (Oxford, 1984).

[2] Ibid.; P. Joyce, *Work, Society and Politics: The Culture of the Factory in Later Victorian England* (Brighton, 1980), xx; J. Lown, *Women and Industrialization: Gender at Work in Nineteenth-Century England* (Cambridge and Oxford, 1990), 95–9, 214.

[3] PP 1816, iii, 294–307; PP 1834, xx, 303–25.

Potteries had been subject to two Parliamentary inquiries about the effect of employment in the manufacture of pottery on those employed in it.[4] But opposition or indifference characterized attitudes toward legislative regulation of labour in the industry.

Testifying before a select committee in 1816 on behalf of the pottery manufacturers, Josiah Wedgwood II opposed the inclusion of the industry in Sir Robert Peel's Bill. He argued that the manufacture of pottery differed from textiles in two ways. First, the size and structure of pottery manufactories meant that the operatives were distributed in scattered workshops of only two storeys rather than concentrated in one large unit as in textile 'factories'. And second, the small scale on which water- or steam-powered machinery was used in pottery manufactories was very different from the large-scale use in textile factories.[5]

In 1840–1 a sub-commissioner from the Shaftsbury-initiated Royal Commission of Inquiry into Children's Employment investigated the pottery manufactories of North Staffordshire, and his report is included in the Commission's Report of 1842. In the Potteries there was no comment in the local newspaper on either the sub-commissioner's investigation or the Commission's Report when it was published on 30 January 1843. Nor was the Potteries an exception in its lack of reaction to the Report.[6]

At the same time the Potteries did not lack the capacity to respond to national issues. Sir James Graham's 'Amended' Factory Education Bill, for example, provoked massive meetings and petitions in the predominantly Nonconformist Potteries. In May 1843 meetings were held in different parts of the Potteries 'to pass resolutions and agree on the form of petitions against the "amended" Bill'. An estimated 1,200 people attended one meeting presided over by Francis Wedgwood, and they heard speakers condemn the Bill as one intended 'to educate children in the principles of the Church of England'.[7] In June the Potteries sent a petition opposing Graham's Bill.[8]

The only evidence that there was interest in the Ten Hours Bill in the Potteries is a leading article in the *Potters' Examiner* of 20 April 1844 devoted to Lord Ashley's speech on the Bill. The editor, William Evans, wrote,

---

[4] PP 1843, xv, 213–333; PP 1857–8, xxiii, 386–8; PP 1861, xvi, 440–51.
[5] J. Thomas, *The Rise of the Staffordshire Potteries* (Bath, 1971), 10–11.
[6] M. W. Thomas, *The Early Factory Legislation* (London, 1948), 210.
[7] *Staffs. Merc.* 20 May 1843.   [8] Ibid. 10 June 1843.

His Lordship's facts apply principally to the cotton districts, but the same startling statements would apply equally as true to the pottery districts also. Nay! it is a matter of doubt or not whether the lives of potters are not shorter in the aggregate than those cited by Lord Ashley relative to the cotton districts. It had become a matter of curiosity to see an aged potter, who is in the daily practice of working in the clay. How requisite then, is it for every operative potter to seriously reflect on the poisonous nature of his employment, and ask himself is there no escape?[9]

According to Evans, however, escape for potters lay in emigration, and he and the Potters' Union invested their resources and energy in the Potters' Emigration Society which purchased land in Pottersville, Wisconsin before it collapsed.[10] Finally, there is evidence that a 'Short Time Committee' existed in the Potteries in 1850, but apparently it had little support.[11]

Thus, for pottery manufacture, the 'principal facts' linking the conditions of employment in the industry to pernicious effects on the health and education of the persons employed in it had been in the public domain since 1842, but there was little suggestion that these 'facts' required legislative intervention until 1861 and 1862. The experience of the pottery industry appears to support the generalization articulated from Dicey to Perkin that in the 1860s there was

a major change in the attitude of the State to the free market and . . . toward the entrepreneur—from the assumption that the market could be safely left to the hidden hand of self-interest and competition, save in very exceptional cases where the bargainers were particularly vulnerable to exploitation, to the assumption that, although the market should still be free, the strong could not be expected not to exploit the weak unless the State laid down some very firm rules of conduct for all bargainers.[12]

In addition, the extension of factory legislation to pottery manufacture lends some support to the view that the 'inspectors are the dynamic of accelerating bureaucratic involvement in legislation',[13] or in other words, 'the role of zealots and experts as agents of legislative change'.[14] The Factory Inspectors' Reports on the operation of the Factory Acts in the cotton and woollen districts were used widely in arguments to justify

---

[9] Quoted in Thomas, *Staffordshire Potteries*, 208–11.
[10] See below, Ch. 7, pp. 301–2.   [11] *SS* Dec. 1863.
[12] H. Perkin, *The Origins of Modern English Society 1780–1880* (London, 1969), 439.
[13] B. Harrison, 'State Intervention and Moral Reform in Nineteenth Century England', in P. Hollis (ed.), *Pressure From Without in Early Victorian England* (London, 1974), 307.
[14] R. Macleod, 'Statesmen Undisguised', *Amer. Hist. Rev.* 78 (1973), 1399–1400.

similar intervention in the Potteries. Moreover, an HM Inspector (though of Schools, not of Factories) played an active role in initiating discussion of the question in the Potteries.[15] Yet, it was a group of leading pottery manufacturers who played a critical role. It was 'perhaps the first instance in which the agitation for the security and advantage of the working people against excessive hours and labour had been initiated by the masters themselves.'[16]

Activity in the Staffordshire Potteries on the issue of government intervention in pottery manufacture followed Shaftsbury's motion in Parliament in August 1861 for a 'fresh inquiry to be made into the conditions of employment of children and young persons in trades and manufactures not already regulated by law'.[17] In December 1861 at a meeting of manufacturers presided over by C. B. Adderley, Conservative MP for North Staffordshire, the Revd H. R. Sandford, HM Assistant Inspector of Schools, presented evidence of the 'defective state of education in the district . . . and means by which this evil might be remedied'.[18] As a result of the meeting twenty-six of the 'principal manufacturers of the district' agreed on and transmitted a 'Memorial' to the Home Secretary, Sir George Grey, 'expressing an opinion in favour of some restriction on the employment of children'.[19]

The Memorialists presented various facts with reference to the health and education of children in the Potteries and argued that their employment at 'a very early age' was the cause of certain 'moral and physical evils'. It was the origin of 'a vast amount of ignorance'; and the employment of children 'at so tender an age' stunted their growth, and caused in many cases a tendency to consumption, distortion of the spine, and other complaints. Yet, much as they deplored these evils, they felt it would not be possible to prevent them by any scheme of agreement among the manufacturers, since only a portion of the employers could be brought to consent to such an agreement. The Memorialists expressed the belief that 'some legislative enactment is wanted to prevent children from being employed at so early an age, and to secure to them at any rate a minimum of education'; and they urged that the Legislature appoint a commission to inquire into the subject and 'consult as to the best means of remedying the evils complained of'.[20]

---

[15] See below, pp. 220, 238.   [16] *Hansard*, 3rd ser., 1864, clxxv, 1711.
[17] B. L. Hutchins and A. Harrison, *A History of Factory Legislation* (Westminster, 1903), 150.
[18] PP 1863, xviii, 122–3.   [19] *SS* 15 Feb. 1862; PP 1863, xviii, 122–3.
[20] PP 1863, xviii, 418; *Hansard*, 3rd ser., 1864, clxxv, 1710–11.

The Memorial did not specify the nature of the restriction on the employment of children. Sandford argued at the meeting in favour of 'Parliament extending to the children in the Potteries the same law which already regulates the employment of children in mills and in bleaching and dying works; I mean the short-time regulations of the Factory Act'.[21] But also, at the meeting, 'a proposal was made that no children should be allowed to work till they are ten years of age; that after that a certificate that the child could read and write should be required as a condition of his being employed until he had reached his twelfth year'.[22] In essence, these were the educational provisions of the Mines Regulation Act. This division between those in favour of the extension of the Factory Acts and those in favour of applying the provisions of the Mines Regulation Act continued through 1864 and the passage of the Factory Acts Extension Act. The pattern of the future discussion of the question was already firmly fixed at this early meeting.

In February 1862 the newly appointed Royal Commission on Children's Employment gave the Memorial top priority and arranged for immediate investigation of the pottery industry.[23] The inquiry of the Assistant Commissioner, Mr Longe, generated meetings in the Potteries to discuss the question until the publication of the First Report of the Children's Employment Commission in June 1863. During this period, the promoters of the rival modes of legislation vied with each other for the support of manufacturers and for the ear of the Assistant Commissioner. Furthermore, the discussion of the case for state regulation of the employment of children in pottery manufacture was widened, first to include foremen or overlookers; and eventually, over a year after the manufacturers' first meeting, working potters joined the discussion.

In June 1862 manufacturers supporting the Mines Act provisions prohibiting the employment of children under 10 held at least one 'unofficial' meeting and then passed a resolution through the Chamber of Commerce. Frederic Bishop, a manufacturer, reported to the Assistant Commissioner that

at an unofficial meeting of about 10 or 12 manufacturers at my house on 4th June last, the majority were of opinion that the employment of children in the manufactories under 10 years of age might be prohibited, and the hours of work of children between 10 and 13 might be restricted. . . . All manufacturers whom I have heard speaking on the subject hitherto have been of opinion that the half-time system would not be practicable at the manufactories.[24]

[21] Ibid.   [22] Ibid.   [23] PP 1863, xviii, 97.   [24] PP 1863, xviii, 117.

Later in the month a meeting of the Chamber of Commerce passed the following resolution supporting the position of Bishop and his colleagues 'Resolved, that in the opinion of this meeting it would be practicable and desirable to prohibit by law the employment in the manufactories of children under 10 years of age, and to restrict the hours of employment of children under 13 years of age to 10 and one half hours per day'.[25] At the same time the outspoken advocate of the extension of the Factory Acts to the Potteries, the Revd H. R. Sandford, HM Assistant Inspector of Schools, was busy promoting his case in the same circles, speaking at a meeting of the Chamber of Commerce and publishing his argument in pamphlet form.[26]

In late October the discussion came out from behind the closed doors of the manufacturers' houses and Chamber of Commerce rooms, and shifted to a semi-public meeting in Hanley Town Hall with newspaper coverage of the proceedings. Later in the week there was a similar meeting in Fenton. The attendance widened to include foremen as well as 'others practically acquainted with the working of children in the Potteries'.[27] The mayor presided, the Assistant Commissioner and the omnipresent Revd Sandford were also present. The purpose of the meeting was to consider 'the propriety of seeking legislative interference towards the education of children working in the Potteries'.[28] Sandford presented his case for legislative intervention and then for the educational provisions of the Factory Acts, though he also mentioned that the Mines Act provisions, which prohibited the employment of children under 10, were an alternative. Speaking for the manufacturers, John Dimmock summed up their previous discussions. He

spoke of the anxiety of the manufacturers on the subject. They had held many meetings and they had come to the conclusion that the half-time system ought to be adopted or that children under 10 years of age ought not to be employed. The feeling was very strong that the time had arrived for legislation on the subject. A little intercourse, and a few meetings like that would enable them to get to the root of the evil and come to some definite resolution on the subject.[29]

In short, the meetings publicized the position the manufacturers had reached long ago that legislation was desirable, and they provided a forum for promoters of the different legislative remedies to put their arguments before the Assistant Commissioner. In addition, with the

---

[25] Ibid.   [26] *SS* 1 Nov. 1862.   [27] Ibid.
[28] Ibid.   [29] Ibid.

movement thus legitimized, the *Sentinel*, persuaded by Sandford, declared itself in favour of the extension of the Factory Acts.[30]

The emergence of the manufacturers' movement into the public arena culminated with a meeting in late December 1862. The *Sentinel* hailed a new era in 'the progress of the education movement in this district', for 'we now know in an authoritative and public manner the position of the manufacturers in regard to the question'.[31] This position was the same as that expressed in the Memorial agreed to one year previously,

> that something must be done to improve the condition of the children employed in the Potteries, is, then admitted on all hands: how best to improve their condition remains only to be solved. . . . The question is, not whether the present system shall be continued, but what better system shall be adopted.[32]

Furthermore, with the exception of Lord Harrowby, the chairman, and C. B. Adderley, MP for North Staffordshire, the attendance was limited to the same groups—manufacturers and foremen—as the previous meetings. At the end of the meeting, however, it was agreed that the time had come to extend the discussion one step further. 'It was thought desirable that public meetings should be held early in the new year to give the operative potters and others an opportunity of expressing their views.'[33] The theme of this December meeting was unanimity among manufacturers. The *Sentinel* summed it up by saying, 'perhaps there never was an alteration contemplated in any system of labour in which the employers of that labour so heartily and spontaneously acquiesced in the change'.[34] The 'spontaneous acquiescence' of some employers, if it ever existed, did not last long. Always present in the background was disagreement about which legislative remedy to adopt.

The shift of emphasis was apparent at the public meeting of manufacturers and workpeople in Longton called in response to the motion at the December meeting in Stoke. Manufacturers questioned whether the state of education and health was as bad as portrayed. Some manufacturers criticized Sandford for using figures only from Church of England schools and ignoring Dissenting and privately supported schools; another manufacturer pointed to Sunday Schools, declaring that they were adequate and eliminated the need for state intervention at all. Others questioned the testimony of local medical men. Regional and civic chauvinism is visible in arguments against the Factory Acts: the Potteries were different from Lancashire; the shortage of boys due to the half-time system

---

[30] Ibid.   [31] *SS* 27 Dec. 1862.   [32] Ibid.
[33] Ibid.   [34] Ibid.

would force Longton manufacturers to employ girls to do boys' work, and enter into the same deplorable practice as the manufacturers at the other end of the Potteries in Tunstall. In any case the Factory Acts would not solve the problems. Opposition to the Factory Acts even slid over into doubts about the desirability of any legislation at all. Mr Aynsley, a prominent Longton china manufacturer, had been present at the December meeting in Stoke, and he stated

that in inquiries amongst his work people he had certainly found the opinions he had expressed at Stoke corroborated as regards the impracticability of the half-time system. But on thinking the matter over he saw other obstacles as insurmountable as far as legislative interference was concerned.[35]

Finally, Mr Knight, another manufacturer, reminded the meeting that no matter what they thought, the question of legislative intervention was out of their hands. It now depended on the report of the Children's Employment Commissioners, and they should discuss the legislative alternatives.[36]

In June the First Report of the Children's Employment Commission appeared, recommending, among other items, the extension of the educational clauses of the Factory Acts to pottery manufacture. In July 1863 the *Sentinel* published a detailed summary of the Report, and in August they published an article by Edwin Chadwick on the section referring to the Potteries.[37] Local reaction to the Report, however, did not emerge in the press until October. When it came, it was critical. It pointed to exaggerated statements in the Report and opposed the recommended extension of the Factory Acts. At first, the opposition to the educational provisions of the Factory Acts led to opposition to any legislation and even a proposal for the voluntary agreement of the manufacturers on a measure similar to the educational provisions of the Mines Regulation Act. Eventually reconciled to the inevitability of some legislation, the opposition settled on support for the provisions of the Mines Act.

Reaction to the Report came first from a group not previously involved in the discussion—the Anglican Clergy. The question of education and employment was 'discussed at considerable length at the quarterly rural diaconical meeting'. The Rector of Stoke, the Revd Lovelace T. Stamer, was chairman. Like the Longton manufacturers in January, the clergy favoured no legislation rather than the half-time system of the Factory Acts. But they went further, saying that 'the manufacturers and employers of the trade should themselves decide upon a course which

---

[35] *SS* 10 Jan. 1863.   [36] Ibid.   [37] Ibid.

would enable the children to have the advantage and education before they went out to work, without the interference of Government'.[38] A partial explanation of the late addition of the clergy to the discussion and evidence of a close tie between the Rector of Stoke and the leading pottery manufacturers emerged the same week in the report of a meeting of the Council of the Potteries Chamber of Commerce. The meeting 'discussed the Commissioners Report and the contemplated mode of action', and in the first item of the proceeding 'the conclusions come to at the meeting of the clergy were endorsed, and the Rev. L. T. Stamer was thanked for having brought the question before the clergy as he had done'.[39] The Chamber probably included most of the Memorialists and certainly the chairman of the meeting, Francis Wedgwood, signed the Memorial, yet the Chamber 'unanimously condemned any legislation at the present time, and was especially opposed to the application of the Factory Act'.[40] The meeting concluded with the formation of a committee 'to collect statistics for the purpose of contradicting' the 'exaggerated' and 'incorrect' statements in the Report of Mr Longe.

The manufacturers' change of opinion did not go unnoticed. One correspondent to the *Sentinel* expressed surprise at the course which the discussion upon the subject was taking in the Potteries.

Before the Government inquiry 26 manufacturers signed a memorial to the Home Secretary that some legislative enactment was wanted. Have the circumstances of this district undergone some sudden and miraculous change since 1862? . . . I think we have a right to call upon the 26 manufacturers who signed the memorial to the Home Secretary, immediately to come forward, as their declared statements, principles and wishes are assailed and treated almost with scorn.[41]

By December opinion in the Chamber of Commerce had shifted again to acceptance of the inevitability of legislative intervention. The published Report of the Committee argued against the Factory Acts and in favour of the Mines Act.[42] Soon after, a response to the Chamber of Commerce report which countered the Chamber's arguments and advocated the Factory Acts appeared anonymously in the *Sentinel*. Those who favoured the Mines Act still tried to mobilize a strong, unified opposition to counter the Children's Employment Commission which backed extension of the Factory Acts. Speakers at public meetings, however, continued to express opinions in favour of no legislation at all, or they brought up alternatives other than either the Factory Acts or Mines Acts and dependent

---

[38] *SS* 10 Oct. 1863.　　[39] Ibid.　　[40] Ibid.
[41] *SS* 17 Oct. 1863.　　[42] *SS* 12 Dec. 1863.

on alternative diagnoses of the evils, such as drink or the employment of mothers.[43] A final attempt to reach a unanimous position came at a public meeting in Hanley in January 1864.[44] The meeting was 'convened pursuant to a numerously signed requisition', and H. R. Grenfell, the Liberal MP for the Stoke-upon-Trent parliamentary borough, 'several of the principal manufacturers of the locality', and a cotton manufacturer from Rochdale were on the platform. A motion in favour of the prohibition of employment of children under 10, essentially the provisions of the Mines Act, was withdrawn when it became clear that there was sufficient support for the Factory Act for the meeting to be unable to reach a unanimous decision. Instead, a motion was carried 'that a committee be appointed to watch and assist the Government in legislating for the improvement of the condition of children employed in the potteries'. The promoter of this motion argued that

although the manufacturers had taken up the Mines in preference to the Factory Act, he thought they might take a medium course; and he thought that unless they agreed upon some practical and feasible scheme government would force upon them some scheme of their own, and their present feeling was that the Factory Act which was so repugnant to the manufacturers should be applied. His only object was to move such an amendment as would postpone discussion on details, and enable the district if it was possible, to arrive at a unanimous decision.[45]

Grenfell reported that

the Home Secretary had, as yet, come to no decision as to what measure he would bring into the House of Commons, but every bit of information he could obtain persuaded him more and more that, of the two Acts, the Factory Act was by far the better of the two—(applause)—and he said, unless his constituents could provide him with some information which was calculated to refute that which he had before him, then he thought it more than probable that it would be considered the duty of the Government to bring in a measure for the application of the Factory Act to this district . . . if they still adhered to the resolution they had arrived at that they thought the Mines Act the better of the two, and could not show that, they must be prepared to see the Government bring in a measure something like the Factory Act.[46]

The committee, notable for having only one workman among its members, did not succeed in arriving at a unanimous decision in time. It was still meeting in March, when the Government brought forward the Factory Acts Extension Bill for its first reading. The committee finally

---

[43] *SS* 26 Dec. 1863; 23 Jan. 1864. [44] *SS* 23 Jan. 1864.
[45] Ibid. [46] Ibid.

reported at a meeting in April where 'the attendance was not very large'.[47] A resolution passed in favour of the Mines Act and against the Factory Acts, but it had no effect. Nor did petitions against the Factory Acts, drawn up in the early months of 1864 and signed by flat-pressers, the workmen whose assistants would be affected by the proposed Bill, have any effect. Unanimous over objectives, yet divided over means, opposition in the Potteries to the recommendations of the Children's Employment Commissioners succumbed to the 'indecision and consequent delay' which 'have hitherto characterized the councils of our committees and public meetings'.[48]

The Factory Acts Extension Bill 'embodied all the recommendations of the Commissioners in its clauses'.[49] The Bill received its first reading without debate on 17 March 1864. The motion for the second reading, however, was agreed to only after a long debate. H. A. Bruce, for the Government, moved the second reading and argued the case for government intervention and the application of the Factory Acts, giving emphasis to the pottery manufacturers' Memorial. In response, the MPs for North Staffordshire and for the parliamentary borough of Stoke-upon-Trent argued that the Bill should be referred to a select committee. All pointed out the opposition of the manufacturers to the Factory Acts and their preference for the educational clauses of the Mines Regulation Act. Three of the MPs, two Conservatives and one Liberal, favoured the Mines Act while the fourth, C. B. Adderley, favoured the half-time system, but he too would consent to a select committee. Sir George Grey, however, suggested that the Bill 'should be read a second time without opposition and that the only point in dispute, the question as regards the half-time should be settled in a Committee of the whole House' rather than a select committee; for, the 'probable effect of referring the Bill to a special committee would be to postpone legislation upon the subject for another year'.[50] The House adopted this procedure. Discussion which was irrelevant to pottery manufacture dominated the committee stage, and the Bill passed through the House without further debate. It went through the House of Lords with only a brief debate and received Royal assent on 25 July 1864.[51]

[47] *SS* 2 Apr. 1864.   [48] Ibid.
[49] *Hansard*, 3rd ser., 1864, clxxv, 1709.   [50] Ibid. 1708–26.
[51] Ibid. 27 and 28 Vict., c.48 'Factory Acts Extension Act, 1864'. The purpose of the Act was 'to provide for the effectual cleansing and ventilation of the Factories in which are carried on the Manufactures and employments specified in the first schedule hereto, and for the Regulation of the Labour of the Children, Young Persons and Women employed therein.' The Act extended the provisions then in force of five Acts hitherto applying only to textile manufacture to six other manufactures and employments. The overwhelming

2. Points of View

The events associated with the extension of factory legislation to the potteries are relevant to many themes. For example, they provide an opportunity to examine both the social and moral aspects of a movement for state intervention together.[52] The extension of factory legislation to pottery manufacture was, to use the terminology of the Victorians themselves, a 'social' reform which in the minds of most supporters in the Potteries was directed at moral purposes and which some contemporaries also saw as a rival to other types of reform, both social, such as public health, and moral, such as temperance.[53]

To take another example, interpretations of the extension of factory legislation give the impression that after 'the passionate controversies of 1844'[54] the extension was inevitable, that 'the precedent was created and

majority of the persons affected by this Act were employed in 'the Manufacture of Earthenware'; and the great majority of these were employed in the Staffordshire Potteries. The 'Factory Acts' consisted of the provisions then in force of the following five Acts:

> 4 Wm. IV c.103: An Act to Regulate the Labour of Children and Young Persons in the Mills and Factories of the UK;
> 7 Vict., c.15: An Act to Amend the Law Relating to Labour in Factories;
> 14 Vict., c.54: Subject as above;
> 17 Vict., c.104: An Act Further to Regulate the Employment of Children in Factories;
> 20 Vict., c.38: An Act for the Further Amendment of the Laws Relating to Labour in Factories.

In addition, the Factory Acts Extension Act, 1864 widened the definition of 'factory' to include 'any place in which persons work for hire', in the six specified trades. According to the historians of factory legislation, Hutchins and Harrison, it was the first that included a home industry (fustian). It was also 'the first time that the Factory Acts had been applied to trades in which the motive power was not steam, water or machinery'. Thus, for earthenware manufacture the Act's definition of 'factory' included 'any place in which persons work for hire in making or assisting in making, finishing or assisting in finishing earthenware of any description'. Also, 'masters were empowered to make special rules for the observance of cleanliness and ventilation, and to attach a penalty not exceeding £1 for the breach thereof, the rules so made to be subject to the approval of H.M. Secretary of State. By another section children, young persons and women were forbidden to take their meals in any room in which certain specified processes were carried on'. The extension of the Factory Acts to earthenware manufacture was also qualified by the provision that they be implemented in successive stages: Hutchins and Harrison, *Factory Legislation*.

[52] Harrison, 'State Intervention', 289.

[53] For a detailed account of contemporaries' views of the 'physical' and 'moral' 'evils' and their arguments for and against state intervention, see M. Dupree, 'Family Structure in the Staffordshire Potteries 1840–1880', D.Phil. thesis (Oxford, 1981), 293–312.

[54] Hutchins and Harrison, *Factory Legislation*, 252. For surveys of the more general debate regarding the growth of government in the 19th cent. see e.g. V. Cromwell, 'Interpretations of Nineteenth Century Administration: An Analysis', *Vict. Studies* 9 (1966), 245–55; G. Sutherland, 'Recent Trends in Administrative History', *Vict. Studies* 13 (1970), 408–11; R. Macleod, 'Statesmen Undisguised', 1386–1405.

the rest was pure routine'.[55] There was less need for child labour, the experience in textiles disproved the fears of economic disaster, and Shaftsbury's former adversaries, Graham and Roebuck, now supported him.[56]

Viewed from Parliament, the extension of factory legislation to pottery manufacture does look inevitable. A resolution requesting the formation of a Royal Commission to inquire into 'the employment of Children and Young Persons in Trades and Manufactures not already regulated by Law' passed the House of Lords unanimously in February 1862. The 'Factory Acts Extension Bill', based on the recommendations of the First Report of this Royal Commission, passed through both Houses of Parliament between March and July 1864 without a division.[57]

From the viewpoint of interested manufacturers, workmen, medical men, and clergy in the Staffordshire Potteries, however, the extension of the Factory Acts to pottery manufacture was more complex and less inevitable. Initially there appeared to be a local consensus that state intervention was necessary. The local discussions did not raise explicitly issues of 'general principle' about state intervention and seemed to concentrate on the 'details' of means rather than ends.[58] Also, many clauses in the Factory Acts were not controversial (except for some concern about the cost and the extent of the manufacturers' liability), including such matters as the power of inspectors, the posting of abstracts and notices, registration of persons under 18 employed in the factory, acquisition of surgical certificates for persons under 16 employed, the hours of employment of young persons and women, meal-times, holidays, lime-washing factory rooms, proceedings before Justices, penalties or appeals, and specific recommendations relating to potteries for ventilation and reduced temperature in the potting and finishing departments, regular hours and meal-times, and for special regulations for particularly dangerous departments such as dipping and scouring.[59]

Yet, there was significant controversy centring on which legislative remedy was preferable for combating the 'moral' evil of the lack of education among children in the Potteries. Just as nineteenth-century contemporaries' perceptions of similarities and differences among cities

---

[55] Macleod, 'Statesmen Undisguised', 1402

[56] G. F. A. Best, *Mid-Victorian Britain 1851–1875* (rev. edn., St Albans, 1973), 135; an extreme version of this view appears in Hutchins and Harrison, *Factory Legislation*, 252.

[57] *Hansard*, 3rd ser., 1864, clxxv, 1709.

[58] *SS* 27 Dec. 1862; Best, *Mid-Victorian Britain*, 135. See also Dupree, 'Family Structure', 312–13.

[59] PP 1863, xviii, 433–5.

had implications for the nature of the legislation adopted,[60] contemporaries' perceptions of the similarities and differences among industries affected their support of one legislative remedy over another. Moreover, the question of whether the educational clauses of the Factory Acts or the educational clauses of the Mines Regulation Act should be applied to pottery manufacture might appear 'more one of detail than of principle',[61] but it served in part as a cover for opposition to state intervention, and it was strong enough to persist and continue after 1864 and the passage of the Factory Acts Extension Act.

Two themes stand out that are particularly relevant to manufacturers, workpeople, and family relationships. The first is the role and attitudes of manufacturers and other élite groups in the Potteries, together with the relationship between this local opinion and the formulation and progress of the legislation through Parliament. And the second is the minimal participation of working people in the local discussions.

Pottery Manufacturers

Although there was disagreement from the outset over the nature of the legislative remedy and their opinions subsequently changed, the manufacturers who signed the Memorial to the Home Secretary were the key group in the Potteries initiating and supporting state intervention. 'So anxious were they that their trade should not be carried on to the moral or physical injury of those employed, that they were the first body of manufacturers who had themselves sought to inflict this restrictive legislation on their trade.'[62] The Memorialists mention that the employment of children at an early age was 'injurious to their health', but their primary concern was that employment at an early age was detrimental to education. In the early stages the *Sentinel* sometimes referred to the movement as an 'educational movement', and it is plausible to see it as part of 'the final of three phases in the conquest of literacy'.[63] Moreover, three of the Memorialists' five points support the argument that 'some legislative enactment is wanted to prevent children from being employed at so early an age, and to secure to them at any rate a minimum of education'.[64] The special focus of their concern was that the early age at which children began to work in pottery manufactories led to a lack of

---

[60] R. Dennis, *English Industrial Cities of the Nineteenth Century* (Cambridge, 1984), 24.
[61] *SS* 27 Dec. 1862.   [62] *Hansard*, 3rd ser., 1864, clxxv, 1724.
[63] L. Stone, 'Literacy and Education in England 1640–1900', *Past and Present*, 42 (1969), 93.
[64] PP 1863, xviii, 418.

attendance at day-school and basic illiteracy in the district.[65] Yet, there were also other circumstances that encouraged the manufacturers to support the Memorial.

The twenty-six manufacturers who signed the Memorial were believed to represent 'nearly the whole of the principal pottery works in Staffordshire'.[66] According to the local newspaper, the Memorial 'displayed the signatures of most of the leading manufacturers of the district'.[67] It is difficult to check these statements because the membership of the total group of 'principal' and 'leading manufacturers' is impossible to specify precisely; nor is it possible to determine how many of the Memorialists fall into the 'leading' group, or how many 'leading' manufacturers are absent from the list of Memorialists. It is clear, however, that the names of at least five 'principal' or 'leading' firms by any definition were not represented among those who signed the Memorial.[68] Therefore, the Memorialists probably included a majority, but certainly not all, of the leading firms. It is possible that manufacturers connected with these five firms attended the meeting but refused to sign the Memorial.[69] Even if they are added to the Memorialists, however, and allowance is made for some additional non-signers, the manufacturers at the meeting probably represented not more than 25 per cent of the total number of firms manufacturing pottery in the district.[70] Therefore, the

[65] For a detailed examination of their case, see Dupree, 'Family Structure', esp. 301–9.
[66] PP 1863, xviii, viii.   [67] *SS* 15 Feb. 1862.
[68] The five firms include: W. T. Copeland, Stoke (he was an MP for the parliamentary borough of Stoke-upon-Trent); Messrs. Livesey, Powell & Co., Hanley; T. C. Brown-Westhead, Moore & Co., Hanley (they took over John Ridgway's manufactory after his death in 1859); Messrs. Aynesley & Co., Longton; Messrs. Davenport & Co., Longport. For Spode–Copeland, see among others, A. Hayden, *Spode and His Successors* (London, 1925); for Brown-Westhead, Moore and Co., see G. A. Godden, *Ridgway Porcelain* (London, 1972); for Davenport, see T. A. Lockett, *Davenport Pottery and Porcelain 1794–1887* (Newton Abbot, 1972).
[69] The owners of four of the five firms emerged as outspoken opponents of the application of the Factory Acts and supporters of the Mines Regulation Act. Therefore, it is possible that they attended the meeting but felt that the Memorial was too closely associated with support for the Factory Acts and refused to sign.
[70] The 26 Memorialists represented 14 per cent of the 180 manufactories estimated in the Report of the Children's Employment Commissioners. Adding to the 26 Memorialists the five leading firms which were not represented among the Memorialists brings the total to 31 firms or 17 per cent of the 180 manufactories. This, however, underestimates the proportion of firms represented at the meeting, because some firms had more than one manufactory. Therefore, 25 per cent seems a reasonable estimate. The conversion into firms is based on: (1) the knowledge that each signature on the Memorial represented one firm; (2) the assumption that the Children's Employment Commissioners' reference to 180 manufactories referred to the total number of manufactories; and (3) an allowance for the firms that have more than one manufactory which would tend to be the 'leading' firms.

Memorialists and the participants in the initial discussion appear to have comprised a small, albeit powerful, sub-group of the total body of pottery manufacturers in North Staffordshire.

The movement for state intervention can be seen as a movement of the 'good', usually large, manufacturers to impose minimum standards on the 'bad', usually smaller, manufacturers. 'The Factory Act was in reality, a protection of the good manufacturer against the bad.'[71] Though representing a disproportionate share of the trade, the 'leading manufacturers' who signed the Memorial[72] at most amounted to only a quarter of the approximately 150 pottery manufacturers who, it was well-known, presided over manufactories with wide differences in size, products, conditions, and hours. Moreover, much of the initial discussion took place in the Chamber of Commerce, which had a membership of at most forty firms.[73] In addition, the Memorialists' view that it would be impossible to reach voluntary agreement among manufacturers indicates contemporary awareness of such a division among manufacturers.

Furthermore, the state of the pottery trade in 1861 suggests that it was in the interest of the larger manufacturers to support restriction of child labour, and this provides a partial explanation for the manufacturers' Memorial. In December 1861 when the Memorialists met, the pottery trade was feeling the effects of the American Civil War on the American market. Before 1861 America had provided about 45 per cent of the market for pottery exports, so it is not surprising that exports for the year 1861 were 26 per cent below those of 1860 (see Fig. 5.1 and Table 5.1). Exports to the United States had fallen to one-third of their previous level. Neither other existing markets nor new markets were able to compensate for the decrease in exports to the United States. The new treaty with France, which was to lower duties on Staffordshire pottery on 1 October 1861, was not expected to provide much relief for the stagnation due to the 'foolish and fratricidal war across the Atlantic'.[74]

Since no one knew how long the American market would be depressed, firms previously involved in the American trade attempted to enter other markets, with the effect of increasing the competition and lowering prices.[75] The situation in the pottery trade at the end of 1861 fits a case described by Sir John Hicks in *The Theory of Wages*:

[71] *Hansard*, 3rd ser., 1864, clxxv, 1725.
[72] See above, p. 229.   [73] *SS* 6 Jan. 1866.
[74] *SS* 28 Sept. 1861.   [75] *SS* 22 Sept. 1860.

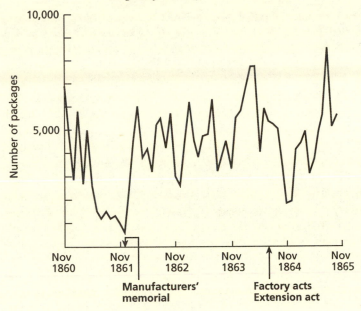

F IG. 5.1   Exports of Earthenware and Porcelain to the United States,
November 1860–October 1865.

Note: Figures are based on the number of packages sent each month from Liverpool to
five US ports: New York, Boston, Philadelphia, New Orleans, and Baltimore.
Source: *SS*, 18 Nov. 1865.

the more the extent and duration of a fluctuation in trade can be foreseen, the
more are its effects on wages a matter of policy. Seasonal fluctuations can be very
clearly foreseen, but there are other kinds where some foresight is possible,
though it is much less definite and reliable. In these cases the element of conscious policy will be less important; more play is given to 'natural' economic
forces.

An example can be taken from those little temporary slumps to which many
industries (but particularly export industries) are subject, as the result of harvest
variations or political disturbances. Suppose an industry finds one of its markets
closed by a revolution. The firms particularly specialised to that market will find
themselves faced with two alternatives (once the possibility of making for stock
has been exhausted)—either they must close down, or they must cut prices and
try and force their way into the markets of other firms. This second alternative
will take time, and if the disturbance is expected to be brief, it will not be
worthwhile. . . .

Now the prosperous firms, although not directly suffering from the disturbance, will be in a position to take advantage of it by lowering wages. But it does
not necessarily follow that they will do so. For the moment they could get

TABLE 5.1 *The Share of the Year's Total Exports (declared value) of British Earthenware and China to All Countries 1859–62* (%)

Destination	1859	1860	1861	1862
Hanse Towns	—	3	5	4
France	—	1	2	4
USA	46	45	20	27
Brazil	4	4	8	6
British N. America	5	6	8	6
British India	6	5	8	7
Australia	6	5	8	10
Other Countries	33	31	41	36
TOTAL (£)	1,313,801	1,450,641	1,070,530	1,217,532
Annual % change		+10	−26	+14

Source: calculated from Figures in *SS* 25 July 1863, Annual Report of the Chamber of Commerce.

sufficient labour at a lower rate of wages; but only for the moment. Once trade recovered they would have to raise wages again. Employers in these firms are therefore confronted with a choice: either reduce wages and snatch this temporary advantage, but with the compensating disadvantage of worsened relations and a possible exodus of good workmen, determined to seek better remuneration and security even though they know circumstances to be unfavourable. Or on the other hand maintain wages, sacrifice a temporary profit, but avoid these more lasting dangers. The decision between these courses will depend in large measure on the expected duration of the depression. The longer it is likely to last, the more advantageous reduction becomes.

The transition between this case and the next is gradual . . . if they maintain wages they must either maintain prices and so lose trade or cut prices and so incur direct losses. . . .

The wage policy of entrepreneurs in a period of depression is very largely a question of circulating capital . . . if wages are maintained there is an obvious incentive to reduce the number of men employed.[76]

With increased competition and lower prices in the pottery trade there were incentives to cut the costs of production. Wages accounted for an estimated 40 per cent of these costs,[77] the largest single factor, so there was incentive to reduce wages in particular. One way to do this was to

[76] J. Hicks, *The Theory of Wages* (London, 1932), 51–3.
[77] *SS* 22 Sept. 1860.

substitute child for adult labour. Evidence that this occurred in the Potteries comes from complaints about the use of a larger than average number of children as assistants in some firms.[78] Therefore, as long as the depression in the American market and the uncertainty about its duration continued, it would be in the interest of larger manufacturers to counter the practice of using child labour. Also, it was to their advantage to reduce the hours of children, young persons, and women. These measures would enable them to cut costs while at the same time minimizing the chance of the 'worsened relations and possible exodus of good workmen' that Hicks describes. Hence, there was support for the Memorial.

The common interests of 'leading' pottery manufacturers overcame civic, religious, and political differences. The movement was able to override strong civic pride within the Potteries and unify 'principal' manufacturers from all of the Potteries towns. The Memorialists, for example, included representatives from all of the towns except Fenton. The manufacturers supporting legislative intervention also cut across religious divisions: Francis Wedgwood was a Unitarian; Colin Minton Campbell of Mintons was an Anglican; and E. J. Ridgway was a member of the family that was the pillar of the Methodist New Connection in the Potteries. Differences in political parties were also submerged: Wedgwood and Ridgway were Liberals, while Campbell was a Conservative and fifteen years later became Conservative MP for North Staffordshire.

Thus, before the publication of the Children's Employment Commissioners' Report, there was unity among the 'principal' manufacturers that legislative intervention in the employment of children was desirable, but there was less unity over the question of which mode of legislation should be applied. There were a few manufacturers who spoke out at public meetings and whose statements can be construed as favouring the extension of the Factory Acts. E. J. Ridgway, for example, stated that if 'the half–time system were adopted, it would be a great benefit to the potteries'.[79] More manufacturers took the view that the half-time system was not unworkable, although either measure would cause inconvenience, and that the decision could be left to those who drew up the Act. Francis Wedgwood fell into this category.

His opinion was that the labour of children in potworks ought to be regulated by law, but whether in the way of not employing them before 10 years of age, closing the manufactories at 6 p.m. or the half–time system, he left to those who had to draw up the act. Either would be a benefit to the children; neither would

[78] *SS* 10 Jan. 1863.   [79] PP 1863, xviii, 42.

be impracticable, nor would any master have any right to complain. As either would cause a good deal of trouble at the outset he would say, take the one that was best for the children.[80]

In the end this ambivalence worked in favour of the extension of the Factory Acts. In the debate over the second reading of the Bill in the House of Commons, Grenfell alleged that there was unanimous feeling in the district in favour of the application of the clauses of the Mines Regulation Act rather than the Factory Acts, and he hoped the Bill would be referred to a select committee. But, he was able to conclude,

at the same time . . . he felt convinced that the manufacturers of the Pottery district were desirous of obtaining the best measure for the workmen, and that whichever measure of these two was selected by Parliament, in the wisdom of which they had the fullest confidence . . . they would receive it with the full intention to do their utmost to make it conducive to the health, morals and education of this important district.[81]

After the publication of the Children's Employment Commissioners' Report, opinion changed and the 'leading manufacturers' were unified in opposition to the application of the Factory Acts. The unanimous resolution of the Council of the Potteries Chamber of Commerce against the Commissioners' Report and its recommendation of the application of the Factory Acts and the report of the Committee of the Chamber of Commerce signified the opposition of the leading manufacturers and their support first for voluntary action only and then reluctantly for the Mines Act. Why had their attitude changed?

A Longton manufacturer attributed the shift of opinion to the lack of foresight of the manufacturers who signed the Memorial. He commented on the Children's Employment Commissioners' Report that

many people had been taken by surprise. Manufacturers, he believed, put their names to the memorial without fully considering the purport of it, and when they came to see what it really was they were astounded that they should even have signed it. . . . Some of the men who were then making the most stir about it were parties who had put their names to the memorial calling on the Government to interfere.[82]

Also, it is possible to argue that a change in the state of trade offers a partial explanation of the shift in attitude. In spite of the Civil War, trade with the United States had revived by mid-1863 (Fig. 5.1, above), and

---

[80] *SS* 27 Dec. 1862. [81] *Hansard*, 3rd ser., 1864, clxxv, 1723.
[82] *SS* 28 Nov. 1863.

the total value of all exports had regained its pre-war peak. When the Children's Employment Commissioners' Report was published, the Annual Report of the Chamber of Commerce in July 1863 observed that

> though the trade is still very injuriously affected by the continuance of the American war, it is gratifying to find that of the diminution in the general exports in 1861, and which continued without improvement during the first six months of 1862, nearly one half was recovered in the last six months of 1862, and that the exports for the first five months of 1863 show a still more favourable progress.[83]

Although all manufacturers seemed to be opposed to the application of the Factory Acts, there were differences in the strength of the opposition in the different towns. Longton, for example, was 'leading the avant-garde in the counter movement in connection with this important question of child labour in the Potteries'.[84] Longton manufacturers were especially outspoken in opposition to the Factory Acts at district meetings and town meetings on the issue before and particularly after the publication of the Report of the Children's Employment Commission. Longton was singled out for its lack of schools and bad conditions in some of the testimony, so that wounded civic pride exacerbated their opposition.[85] Furthermore, Longton manufacturers had more to lose, because a higher proportion (33 per cent) of the children aged 8–12 in Longton were employed in pottery manufacture than in the other towns (Table 5.2).

Although Fenton and particularly Burslem also had relatively high proportions of children aged 8–12 employed in pottery, Tunstall, Hanley, and Stoke had relatively low proportions of children employed in pottery manufacture. Thus, to some extent the position of the manufacturers in the various towns with regard to the Factory Act extension reflected the proportions of children aged 8–12 they employed.

Others in the Local Élite and Outsiders

Other groups also played an active role in the local discussion of the extension of legislation to pottery manufacture. Local medical men played an important role. Their testimony, linking high mortality and poor health to employment in pottery manufacture, was particularly important in the case for state intervention. The Memorialists, Sandford, and the Children's Employment Commissioners relied on the testimony of

[83] *SS* 25 July 1863.   [84] *SS* 13 Feb. 1864.
[85] *SS* 10 Jan. 1863; 10 Oct. 1863; 23 Nov. 1863.

TABLE 5.2   *Percentage of Children aged 8–12 Employed in Pottery Manufacture in Various Potteries Towns (%)*

Town	Not employed			Employed in Pottery			Employed Elsewhere			N		
	m	f	both	m	f	both	m	f	both	m	f	both
Tunstall	58	83	69	19	13	16	23	5	15	52	40	92
Burslem	57	76	68	37	22	28	6	2	4	71	92	163
Hanley and Shelton	80	83	81	14	9	12	6	8	7	132	120	252
Stoke	80	88	86	10	6	7	10	6	7	31	50	81
Fenton	52	83	67	36	13	25	12	4	8	25	24	49
Longton	53	67	60	38	29	33	9	4	7	66	72	138

Source: Potteries Sample 1861.

local physicians and physicians at the North Staffordshire Infirmary.[86] Although most medical men did not actively promote legislative intervention, one North Staffordshire Infirmary physician, Dr J. T. Arlidge, spoke out in favour of restricting children's employment at an early meeting, and a local surgeon, Benjamin Boothroyd, was Mayor of Hanley and presided over the semi-public meeting of manufacturers and foremen in late October 1862, early in the movement.[87] Later, however, when the emphasis of the discussion shifted from the need for state intervention to active opposition to the extension of the Factory Acts, Dr Arlidge's testimony in the Children's Employment Commission Report was severely criticized as exaggerated. Critics took exception particularly to his observation that

the potters as a class, both men and women, but more especially the former, represent a degenerated population, both physically and morally. They are as a rule stunted in growth, ill-shaped, and frequently ill-formed in the chest; they become prematurely old, and are certainly short lived; they are phlegmatic and bloodless, and exhibit their debility of constitution by obstinate attacks of dyspepsia, and disorder of the liver and kidneys, and by rheumatism. But of all diseases they are especially prone to chest disease, to pneumonia, phthisis,

[86] Dr Boothroyd's testimony at public meetings regarding the unhealthiness of potters appeared in *SS* 1 Nov. 1862, 23 Jan. 1864; for Dr Arlidge's testimony to the Children's Employment Commission, see PP 1863, xviii, 120.
[87] *SS* 1 Nov. 1862; 27 Dec. 1862.

bronchitis, and asthma. One form would appear peculiar to them and is known as potter's asthma or potter's consumption.[88]

The criticism became a weapon, for a short time the only weapon, against the recommendations of the Children's Employment Commission. Arlidge complained that

it is unfair to single me out and make the agitation against the propositions of the Commissioner hinge so much on my statements when those of other medical men in the district all point more or less distinctly to the same general conclusions. And it is illiberal and un-English to initiate a persecution against an individual for the honest expression of his opinion. . . . Your agitation against the proposed measures of the Commissioners may be highly proper, but I strongly object to the manner in which you have chosen to introduce it, by selecting the statements of a single individual as its fulcrum.[89]

In the House of Commons debate over the Bill, Grenfell used a letter from Arlidge qualifying his testimony to support the suggestion that the Bill be referred to a select committee, and Grenfell added

Arlidge's statement was so astounding that almost everyone connected with the district took notice of it, and having himself been present at several meetings in the district, called for the purpose of discussing the Government measure, and hearing so much of Dr Arlidge's statement, he thought there must be some mistake in it.[90]

If the doctors supported the Factory Act approach, one prominent clergyman was on the other side. The Rector of Stoke, Sir Lovelace Stamer, played an important role in legitimizing and supporting the manufacturers' opposition to the Factory Acts, which suggests close ties within the lay and clerical élite of the district which surmounted religious differences between the Rector and the predominantly Nonconformist manufacturers.[91]

Persons from outside the Potteries also played a role within the Potteries in supporting both the movement for state intervention and the extension of the Factory Acts. The controversy over which legislative measure to apply can be seen as one in which outsiders tended to promote the extension of the Factory Acts against the opposition of a majority in the district. In the debate over the Factory Acts Extension Bill in the House of Commons Grenfell remarked that

---

[88] PP 1863, xviii, 106.   [89] *SS* 8 Oct. 1863.
[90] *Hansard*, 3rd ser., 1864, clxxv, 1722.   [91] See above, p. 233.

he had heard no reason as yet why the first three clauses of the Mines Regulation Act should not be applied instead of the half-time clauses of the Factory Act. It was the unanimous feeling of the manufacturers and workmen that such should be attempted. The whole of the clergy were in favour of it, and indeed, he might say that the Rector of Stoke only a few days ago assured him [Mr Grenfell] that he considered it better for the health and more conducive to the education of the district.[92]

Mr Livesley, a Hanley manufacturer, complained 'that the chief advocates of the Factory Acts were gentlemen who were unacquainted with the pottery trade and were therefore unable to judge its peculiarities'.[93]

The government inspector, the Revd Sandford, HM Assistant Inspector of Schools, was another outsider who played an active role in initiating the movement for state intervention and promoting the case for the extension of the Factory Acts in the Potteries. Sandford 'had something to do with bringing the evil under the notice of the manufacturers of the district'.[94] When he brought the case for state intervention before the manufacturers in December 1861, he had the weight of the factory inspectors' reports and experience in Lancashire behind him. Soon he came to be the major spokesman in favour of the Factory Acts in the Potteries, and he came to be identified with them to such an extent that the controversy over which was the best legislative measure seemed to be a 'contest between the school Inspector and the manufacturers'.[95] Later, Sandford provoked one manufacturer to complain that 'he did not think of saying anything at that early stage of the meeting, but as Mr Sandford had given them a tolerable strong dose, and as he figured so prominently in the report, he should like to ask him a few plain questions'.[96]

Lord Harrowby, who was also an outsider, chaired a meeting in the Potteries and used his social position and association with Shaftesbury and the factory movement twenty years before to encourage government intervention and to favour the Factory Acts. Another outsider was Mr Longe, the Assistant Commissioner, whose report was crucial to the cases for both state intervention and extension of the Factory Acts, as well as the focus for the Potteries opposition to the Act. Finally, in an attempt to counter the opposition to the Factory Acts in the Potteries, another outsider, Mr Ashworth, a manufacturer from Rochdale, attended public meetings 'to explain the half-time system as in operation in the cotton districts'.[97]

---

[92] *Hansard*, 3rd ser., 1864, clxxv, 1723.   [93] *Birm. Daily News* 11 Apr. 1864.
[94] *SS* 23 Jan. 1864.   [95] *SS* 27 Dec. 1862.   [96] *SS* 23 Jan. 1864.   [97] Ibid.

The local MPs tried to bridge the distance between London and the Potteries. One local MP played an important part in initiating the movement within the Potteries for state intervention, and another was a leader of the local opposition to the Factory Acts. At the time of the debate over the Bill, the four local MPs were divided between the Factory Acts and the Mines Regulation Act, but the division was not along party lines. C. B. Adderley, Conservative MP for North Staffordshire, chaired the meeting that produced the manufacturers' Memorial, and he probably provided up-to-date information on the implications of Shaftesbury's motion for a Royal Commission on Children's Employment. Adderley attended the meeting of manufacturers and foremen, presided over by Lord Harrowby, and he gave his support to both legislative intervention and the extension of the Factory Acts. W. T. Copeland, a pottery manufacturer, Conservative MP for the parliamentary borough of Stoke-upon-Trent and former Lord Mayor of London, actively supported the local opposition to the Commissioners' Report. He maintained 'that the blue book had cast a stigma upon the Staffordshire manufacturers which they could ill bear',[98] and he severely criticized the testimony of Dr Arlidge.[99] At the time of the debate in the House of Commons over the Factory Acts Extension Bill, Adderley favoured the half-time system, while the other three, including two Conservatives (Copeland and Viscount Ingestre) and one Liberal (H. R. Grenfell) supported the clauses of the Mines Regulation Act.[100]

The divergence of local and central interests is striking. Opinion in the Potteries, Whitehall, and Westminster converged at the time when the manufacturers sent their Memorial to the Home Secretary requesting legislative enactment and inquiry. But, once the Memorial had triggered the Royal Commission, the emergence of a deep division in local opinion meant that it could not hinder the progress through Parliament of the Factory Acts Extension Act. Not even the united opinion of the four local MPs could carry the suggestion that a select committee consider the Bill.

Pottery Workers and Families

The 'trickle down' pattern of the discussion of the issue within the Potteries helped to preclude either active support for, or opposition to, state intervention on the part of small manufacturers and workmen. The

---

[98] *Hansard*, 3rd ser., 1864, clxxv, 1724.   [99] *SS* 8 Oct. 1863.
[100] *Hansard*, 3rd ser., 1864, clxxv, 1720–6.

movement for legislation began with private meetings of manufacturers and the Chamber of Commerce; then the manufacturers and foremen held semi-private meetings bringing in an outsider, Lord Harrowby, as chairman; and only then did they bring in workmen and hold public meetings. The pattern also indicates the strength of the control of the local élite of large pottery manufacturers, allied in this case with the Rector of Stoke.

Yet, for a question which contemporaries recognized 'was important to them as a district, manufacturers and workmen, to parents and children',[101] the minimal participation by working people either as employees or parents in the discussions is unexpected. Moreover, in light of the active participation of working people thirty years earlier in the factory movement in the cotton districts, the lack of participation, or even apparent interest, among working potters is somewhat surprising. Working people played no direct role in the initiation of the movement for factory legislation in the Potteries, nor did they participate in the discussion until over a year after it began.[102] Further evidence of workmen's lack of interest in the movement comes from a letter in the *Sentinel* pointing out that working men did not even protest when there was only one of them nominated to a committee at a public meeting.

Permit me to ask Mr Blakiston why he proposed more masters and bailiffs on the committee than workmen on Wednesday evening at the child labour meeting? Why not have equal numbers of workmen with masters and bailiffs? Is it because he wanted the masters to be able to carry anything that they proposed, and thus thwart the objects the workingmen might bring forth? The committee that was reappointed only has one workman on it. . . . Is it fair and just to the working classes? I certainly should have objected to it at the meeting, but waited for the workmen to bring it forward themselves.[103]

There are a number of reasons for the inactivity of working potters in the movement for factory legislation in the Potteries. First, opinion among the working potters was divided (when they finally participated in discussions of the issue). Some opposed legislation, expressing strong suspicions of the state. Mr Martin, a working potter in Burslem, for example, 'thought that if the question were left to the employers and employed, they could decide the question much better than any commissioners from London could (Great applause.)'.[104] Others supported legislative intervention and the Factory Acts in particular.[105]

---

[101] *SS* 23 Jan. 1864. [102] See above, pp. 220–1, 228.
[103] *SS* 23 Jan. 1864. [104] Ibid. [105] *SS* 10 Jan. 1863.

Second, the exact form of state intervention was unclear, and whatever form it took, it would affect so many aspects—the condition of the workrooms, hours of work, schooling—that there was no single focus for support or opposition. Third, the educational clauses came closest to providing a single focus, but even if their effect was assumed to be a reduced supply and increased wages for assistants, this would not equally affect all manufactories. The subdivided structure of pottery manufactories and the complexity of the organization of work meant that some branches used child labour for assistants and others did not. Workers in different branches were affected differently. Although flat-pressers were the largest single group of adult workmen affected, there were only about 1,000 of them in a total labour-force of approximately 27,000.[106] Even if interests were clearer, the pottery-workers would have had difficulties in organizing a movement. Within a manufactory, workshops were relatively small and physically separated from each other.[107] Furthermore, trade-union organization in the early 1860s was almost non-existent, surviving only in a few craft unions.[108]

If the structure of work was complex, the structure of families differed as well.[109] Thus, even if its effects in the workplace had been clear-cut, the Act would not have a uniform effect on family incomes. This would depend on such factors as: the occupation of parents, i.e. if either of them worked in a pottery manufactory and if so, whether in a branch requiring child assistants, or in the case of wives, if they worked as assistants; the life-cycle stage of the family, i.e. how many children were of an age to work; and lastly on such imponderables as the relative value a family placed on education, income, and work. The families with most to lose were those with a father employed in a branch, such as flat-pressing, in which he required assistants and employed one or more of his own children aged 8–12 years, but none of his other family members were employed in pottery. But, as we saw above in Chapter 3, only 23 per cent of all the children (aged 8–12) of potters, regardless of their branch, worked in pottery manufactories. Thus, potters did not protest on the grounds of loss of family income to a large extent because a relatively small proportion of their children were employed in potworks in 1861. Instead, the parents of children aged 8–12 working in the Potteries were a heterogeneous group unlikely to organize to express an

---

[106] PP 1865, xx, 54–5, 66.   [107] PP 1863, xviii, 98.

[108] W. H. Warburton, *The History of Trade Union Organization in the North Staffordshire Potteries* (London, 1931), 137–9, 168–71.

[109] See above, pp. 152–7.

opinion. The number of families losing out altogether was further diminished by those with older children or women whose wages were likely to rise following the restriction of child labour. As a result there may have been a transfer of income within households away from male potters in branches requiring assistants and away from children towards young persons and women, but without jeopardizing overall household income and discouraging protest based on loss of family income.

3. Conclusion

The movement for protective legislation and its effects in the Potteries in the 1860s followed a different pattern from the earlier movement in the textile areas. The initiative for the extension of the Factory Acts to the pottery industry in the 1860s came from local manufacturers, influenced by the government's school inspector for the area. Their initiative, unlike the movement in textile areas, was not the result of technological change and a corresponding decline in the extent of child labour. In the textile regions there was a continuous decline in the proportion of children in the cotton industry's labour-force from the late eighteenth century, when it was almost entirely pauper apprentices. This long-run decline of labour was due both to a reduction in the demand for the labour of children as a result of technical changes and to a reduction in the supply of children available to work because rising real incomes meant that families no longer needed the income from the labour of young children.[110] In the Potteries, however, there was no overall decline in child labour before the extension of the Factory Acts. In fact, from 1851 to 1861 the proportion of the pottery labour-force made up of children rose from 15 per cent to 17 per cent (see Table 5.3), suggesting a fundamentally different pattern from that of the cotton industry.

Moreover, there were no major technical changes in pottery manufacture in the period before the extension of the Factory Acts which would have reduced the demand for child labour.[111] Steam power continued to be restricted to use primarily in preparatory processes and it replaced child labour for turning potters' wheels only in large manufactories.

---

[110] C. Nardinelli, 'Child Labour and the Factory Acts', *J. of Econ. Hist.* 40 (1980), 750; id., *Child Labour and the Industrial Revolution* (Bloomington and Indianapolis, Ind., 1990), esp. 61–2, 115.

[111] See above, Ch. 1. Also, F. Celoria, 'Ceramic Machinery of the 19th Century in the Potteries and other Parts of Britain', *Staffs. Arch.* 2 (1973), 32; R. Samuel, 'Workshop of the World: Steam Power and Hand Technology in Mid-Victorian Britain', *History Workshop*, 3 (1977), 54.

TABLE 5.3   *Children Aged 5–14 as a Proportion of the Pottery Labour-Force: England and Wales 1851–1881*

	Children employed in pottery			Pottery labour-force	Children as % of the pottery labour force
	Boys	Girls	Total	Total	
1851	3,572	2,040	5,612	34,300	15
1861	4,230	2,349	6,579	38,072	17
1871	3,176	2,349	5,525	45,122	12
1881	2,404	1,883	4,287	46,596	9

Source: Published Census 1851–81.

Although in one of the quotations above there is mention of the pugmill, which reduced the amount of wedging required of a boy in order to prepare the clay for use by a thrower or presser, manufacturers in the Potteries neither developed nor used it widely until after the extension of the Factory Acts.[112] If anything, the Factory Acts encouraged, rather than resulted from, changes in the process of production. Also, any child labour saved by the pugmill was counterbalanced by the tendency in some manufactories to hire large numbers of assistants and few journeymen rather than a large number of journeymen each with only a few assistants.

Nevertheless, there is evidence to suggest that the overall increase in the proportion of children in the pottery labour-force before 1861 may have masked a decrease in demand for children on the part of workmen in large manufactories, while small employers increased the proportion of children. But there is no evidence to suggest that small employers would inevitably follow the pattern of large employers and reduce the number of children hired. Particularly in the highly competitive branches of the industry producing large quantities of low-priced earthenware, it was in the interests of the small employers to keep wage costs as low as possible, and the employment of children was a feasible way to do this. Viewed in this way, the extension of the Factory Acts becomes the result of a struggle which the small employers lost.

Furthermore, the supply of child labour in the Potteries was not decreasing because of rising real incomes among potters before the

[112] Celoria, 'Ceramic Machinery', 32.

extension of the Factory Acts. First, between the 1830s and 1860s there were large fluctuations in trade and no substantial increase in real wages for potters, though after the early 1860s and the end of the Civil War in the United States in 1865, work was more constant. Second, and even more important, the contention that rising real incomes for cotton textile-workers affected the supply of child labour assumes that the children employed were the children of cotton textile-workers who were experiencing a rise in real incomes. In the Potteries, as we have seen above in Chapter 3, significant proportions of the children employed tended not to be the children of potters, but the children of widows or of fathers in other occupations such as mining which would not be affected by a rise in real incomes for pottery-workers even if it had occurred.

Thus, unlike the factory movement in the textile districts thirty years earlier, the movement for the extension of factory legislation to pottery manufacture began in the Potteries as a movement of larger manufacturers who combined a genuine desire to improve conditions of health and education of children employed in the potteries with a realization of the impossibility of an agreement among manufacturers and an eye to their own interest in face of the loss of trade and the uncertainty due to the American Civil War. This coincided with the initiative of the school inspector and the example of previous legislation to produce a movement that was too strong to succumb to the changing opinion and active opposition of what became a substantial number of manufacturers or to the indifference of the majority of working potters.

Thus, contrary to accounts based on textiles which stress the opposition of industrialists dependent on female labour, and which emphasize working-class support for factory legislation,[113] the larger manufacturers in the Potteries supported protective legislation and the involvement of operative potters was minimal. Those potters who eventually expressed their opinions were men who argued against the legislation because they were in branches in which they would suffer a direct reduction in earnings. Family relationships have also played a key role in accounts of working-class support for factory legislation. Support has been seen as based on the separation of parents and children in the factory due to technological changes.[114] Others suggest that working-class support was

---

[113] Lown, *Women and Industrialization*, 214. S. Walby, 'Spatial and Historical Variations in Women's Unemployment and Employment', in L. Murgatroyd *et al.* (eds.), *Localities, Class and Gender* (London, 1985), 168.

[114] N. J. Smelser, 'Sociological History: The Industrial Revolution and the British Working-Class Family', *J. of Soc. Hist.* 2 (1967), 27–31.

based on a threat to already low family incomes which a universal ten-hour day would protect.[115] Finally, it is argued that working-class support for factory legislation was based on the patriarchal support of male trade unionists intent on keeping women out of the competition for jobs in an attempt to raise men's wages to the level of a 'family wage' which would support themselves and their families and protect the position of the 'male breadwinner'.[116] In the Potteries, family relationships played a role in the lack of working-class support for factory legislation. Even if Smelser were correct and the involvement of cotton textile-workers in the factory movement was at least in part an expression of their concern for their children, then the lack of involvement of working potters (except for the belated opposition of those branches in which men would suffer a direct reduction in earnings) should not necessarily be interpreted as lack of concern for their children. Again the fact that significant proportions of the children employed tended not to be the children of potters, but the children of widows or of fathers in other occupations, and that a relatively high proportion of children aged 8–12 employed had other family members including mothers employed, suggests that in general the employment of young children reflected family need rather than parental greed.

[115] M. Anderson, 'Sociological History and the Working-Class Family: Smelser Revisited', *Social History*, 3 (1976), 317–34.

[116] W. Seccombe, 'Patriarchy Stabilized: The Construction of the Male Breadwinner Wage Norm in Nineteenth Century Britain', *Social History*, 11 (1986), 55. The arguments are summarized in H. Bradley, *Men's Work, Women's Work* (Cambridge and Oxford, 1989), 45–6.

6

The Impact of the Extended Factory Acts on Families

1. Implementation

AN undercurrent of dissatisfaction accompanied the introduction of the Factory Acts to the Potteries during 1865 and 1866.[1] Robert Baker, HM Inspector of Factories, however, considered the dissatisfaction 'normal'. He wrote to the Home Secretary in 1864 that

> there exists on the minds of the manufacturers in the Potteries, the old feeling of 1833, as it was found in the textile districts when the Factory Act was introduced amongst them, that hands old enough to work full time, will not be procurable; which, evidently arises from a fear of trouble with respect to the schooling clauses, and of having to 'pay the school wage'.[2]

Baker's view was borne out, for after thirty months in operation he could quote a pottery manufacturer saying that 'nineteen-twentieths of the earthenware manufacturers were opposed to the Act when it was first introduced, myself among the number. I consider that nineteen-twentieths would now be unwilling to part with it'.[3] By this time even the Rector of Stoke 'with ineffable grace, has withdrawn all doubts he had about the education of the children employed'.[4] Moreover, in January 1867 a meeting in Wolverhampton looked to the Potteries as a successful example of the application of the Factory Acts and an argument in favour of their extension to the industries of South Staffordshire.[5]

The change in attitude of manufacturers in the Potteries towards the Factory Act was due partly to the manner in which the Factory Inspector implemented the Act and partly to the timing of its introduction, which corresponded with strikes in the ironworks and short time in the collieries, the end of the Civil War in the United States, and improvement in the pottery trade. The Factory Act in the Potteries changed from a

---

[1] See e.g. *SS* 18 Nov. 1865.

[2] PRO HO45/7570/2: Robert Baker to Sir George Grey, 27 Aug. 1864; also Baker expressed the same sentiment in his report to Grey, PP 1865, xx [3473], 479.

[3] PP 1867, xvi [3793], 412.   [4] Ibid.   [5] *SS* 26 Jan. 1867.

measure to be accepted or rejected to an accepted aspect of the structure of the trade and the community.

Robert Baker, the Inspector of Factories, personally supervised the introduction of the Act to the Potteries. He lived in Longton for four months, and believed that this procedure was necessary for the successful implementation of the Act:

the Factory Acts Extension Act received the Royal assent on the 26th of July 1864; and . . . on the 16th of August I went to the Potteries, having taken a residence there for a few months, under the conviction that, after all that had been previously advanced by the advocates for the Factory Act, or for the Mining Act, or for no Act at all, and after the final adoption of the Factory Act with such modifications as would provide for a gradual introduction of its clauses, if I wished to make it a success, it would be needful that, for a while I should live there. Because, first of all, I had to endeavour thoroughly to understand the Pottery system myself; and secondly, it seemed essential I should be present with the authority of my office and experience, personally to reply to questions put by anxious enquirers with respect to the anticipated interferences with a hitherto unrestricted labour, to allay fears, to suggest improvements, and to bring about conformity with the law by a gradual introduction of its provisions.[6]

Baker first contacted two principal firms, Wedgwoods and Mintons. With the help of M. D. Hollins, senior partner of Mintons and President of the Potteries Chamber of Commerce, Baker arranged a meeting of manufacturers, both members and non-members of the Chamber of Commerce. The meeting was a success and set in motion further meetings to draw up special rules for cleanliness and ventilation under a provision of the Act.[7] Baker also provided a handbook entitled 'The Factory Act Made Easy', and he told the manufacturers that 'he is quite prepared to extend a large measure of forbearance towards short comers at the outset'.[8]

Baker was careful to emphasize his leniency at the outset, for he and Capt. May, the Sub-inspector for the District, had to tread a fine line between establishing their authority and clarifying the law on the one hand, and avoiding the appearance of harsh imposition that might arouse opposition and encourage defiance of the still unpopular Act on the

---

[6] PP 1865, xx [3473], 478.

[7] PRO HO45/7570/2; Baker to Grey, 27 Aug. 1864. For the view of the hollow-ware pressers' union see, P. Anderton, 'A Trade Union Year: 1864—An Extract from the Transactions of the Executive Committee for the Hollow-ware Pressers' Union', *Journal of Ceramic History*, 9 (1977), 31–2.

[8] For an account of the meeting, see *SS* 27 Aug. 1864.

other. Baker, for example, finding evidence that 'night work was still practiced', reported that he 'felt this was a case for prosecution, and accordingly the firm was brought before the stipendiary magistrate; but I instructed the sub-inspector to withdraw the case, as it was the first, on condition that the practice should not be continued'.[9] Later in 1865 the sub-inspector brought a large number of summonses against 'manufacturers, parents, and workpeople of Longton. . . . From the crowded state of the Court, they seemed to excite considerable interest in the town'. May began by saying that

this was the first time he had summoned anyone for this offence [lack of a medical certificate as to age] in the Potteries. It having been stated that the regulations of the Factories Act had been somewhat harshly carried out, he was glad to state that he had been in the district eight months before he was compelled to take proceedings against anyone in Longton; and in those cases in which the offence was admitted he was willing that the defendant should be dealt with as leniently as possible.[10]

Although he was careful to emphasize his leniency and to bring cases against all three groups—manufacturers, parents, and workpeople—who were liable under the Act, it provoked a letter of outrage against the Factory Act in the *Sentinel* the next week from 'A Potter of Experience'.

When the question of Government interference was first introduced among us, there were many, like myself, who expected and desired (not the Factory Act to be forced upon us, but) that something might be done, compatible with the peculiarities of the trade, that would be a benefit to the district; but, alas! we have been, so far, lamentably disappointed, and so long as the iniquitous law continues in operation, are doomed to still greater disappointment.

I am sorry to use such an epithet in speaking of British legislation, but in my humble judgment, the spirit of the law, and the results of its administration, fully justify the appellation. Should any of your readers question this, I have only to refer them to the scene which presented itself in the Longton Police Court on Wednesday, the 19th inst., and as partially described by you in your issue of Saturday last—a scene such as I hope and trust will never again be witnessed in the Staffordshire Potteries. For respectable gentlemen to be arraigned at the bar, as so many criminals, on such trifles—made to be offences to be punished—at the will of a paid agent, employed by law for the purpose, with powers superior to the magistrate on the Bench who indeed has no discretion but to enforce the mandate of the Factory Law dictator, to me is an indignity and an insult which ought never to be tolerated in this boasted 'land of freedom and of justice'.[11]

---

[9] PP 1865, xx [3473], 492.   [10] *SS* 22 July 1865.   [11] *SS* 29 July 1865.

The meetings of manufacturers, the pamphlet, the appointment of certifying surgeons, and the image of leniency and symbolic prosecutions in order to clarify the law were sufficient to introduce the Act in general to the district. But the educational clauses were more difficult to implement. Baker compiled and circulated to manufacturers and the newspaper a list of schools in the Potteries willing to take half-timers,[12] but on 13 September 1864 he wrote to Sir George Grey from the Potteries

I find I shall have some difficulty in overcoming the Master Potters' prejudices against educating the short-time children. They are afraid of having to pay for it; and it unfortunately happens that the children for whom educational provision will have to be made, are just those that need it most, namely, the children of drunken fathers. Moreover, the masters have one valid plea against it, which I am not able to gainsay, 'that there are no schools available for this purpose, . . . for those which there are are full, and more school room is required; and that if it could be obtained, the higher class of working potters would not permit their children to associate in school with the lower class, a determination which is not without reason; for I am informed that many of these poorer children have the itch, and many are filthy.[13]

In order to meet the lack of schools and the reluctance of the 'higher class of working potters' to have their children in the same school as half-timers, Baker decided to establish a school financed out of his factory fines fund 'to which if [children] attend half-time, they may come in their potters' dresses'.[14]

Grey gave permission to establish a potters' school solely for children employed in the potteries at Longton. In addition, Baker emphasized how gradually he applied the education clauses, beginning 'first to familiarize the men with the half-day system of work, requiring only that the children should not work the other half, and then I intimated that after the 1st of January I should expect them to be sent regularly to school'.[15]

Baker's role in implementing the Act was praised by contemporaries in the Potteries, including the Rector of Stoke who asserted that 'no doubt the success of the Act arose mainly from the temperate and judicious way in which it had been introduced by Mr Baker'.[16]

In addition to the efforts of the Factory Inspector, fortuitous timing of the implementation of the Act also minimized opposition and facilitated the compliance of manufacturers and workpeople. According to the

---

[12] PP 1865, xx [3473], 528–30.
[13] PRO HO45/7570/3: Baker to Grey, 13 Sept. 1864.
[14] Ibid.   [15] PP 1865, xx [3473], 539.   [16] *SS* 26 Jan. 1867.

Sub-Inspector, 'at that time the ironworkers were on strike, and the collieries only partially at work; the demand for labour, also, was below the average, in consequence of the American war. The Act therefore could not have been introduced at a more favourable moment'.[17] With the end of the American Civil War 'came brisk and constantly increasing demand for our manufactures, until now the potting trade has arrived at a state of prosperity such as it has never experienced before'.[18] With this sharp increase in the demand for pottery it was in the interest of the manufacturers, workmen, and parents to accept the half-time system rather than avoid it by dismissing or withdrawing children from employment.[19] Thus, to meet the immediate increase in demand for pottery Baker reported that 'it is consequently the policy of the manufacturers, to add all the short-timers they can to their establishments, in order to increase the total number of workers, and thus make void the scarcity; or to supersede it by machinery, if they desire their trade to be still further extended'.[20]

2. Effects

Wages

The effects of factory legislation are difficult to isolate and measure. Concentrating only on the effects amenable to statistical analysis—wages and numbers employed, G. H. Wood writes

at the commencement some distinction must be made between the immediate and permanent (or at least, deferred) effects of Factory legislation. It is not easy to trace either of these, as other conditions may cause changes to take place which obscure the operation of the Acts. The immediate effects may be seen if we have evidence of the numbers and earning of operatives immediately before and after the date of the introduction of the changes demanded by a particular Act, but the abiding effects will have to be considered in relation to such forces as a change of prices, wars, strikes, fashions, and the like. Generally speaking, and 'if other things are equal', the difference in the rates of wages, and in the relative numbers employed between those obtaining immediately prior to the operation of an Act, and those obtaining three or four years after may be considered as due to its action.

Unfortunately in no case are these other things equal.[21] Wood finds the specific data on wages in the Potteries before and after the Factory Act

---

[17] PP 1866, xxiv [3622], 344.   [18] *SS* 18 Nov. 1865.
[19] PP 1866, xxiv [3622], 344–5.   [20] Ibid.
[21] G. H. Wood, 'Factory Legislation Considered With Reference to the Wages, etc. of the Operatives Protected Thereby', *JRSS* 65 (1902), 288.

of 1864 ambiguous, wages for some occupations moving up and others down,[22] and he does not present data on numbers employed in pottery manufacture before and after the Act.

However, other information from the Potteries survives which is pertinent to the question of the effects of the Factory Act. There is some evidence that it brought half-timers into day-school who would not have been attending otherwise and their school attendance was more stable than that of full-time students. In addition, contemporaries used it as a bargaining counter in wage negotiations and related it to the increasing proportion of women in the labour-force and their introduction into branches where they had not worked previously; the application of new types of machinery to several processes; the regularization of hours; a check on over-production; and an instrument of 'social control'.

Education

Before factory legislation was extended to the Potteries in 1864 there was complete disagreement among contemporaries about the meaning of statistics measuring, depending on their point of view, either the 'amount of ignorance' or the 'educational attainments' of children in the Potteries. At the same time there was surprising agreement about the general level of the statistics. According to the pessimistic 'Memorialists' only 72 per cent of working children could read while Longton manufacturers were delighted to find that 68 per cent of working children could read.[23] From a different perspective the 'amount of ignorance' calculated from the proportion of those marrying who signed the marriage register with marks in the Registrar General's Reports suggests that in 1860 65 per cent of the men who married in Stoke registration district signed the marriage register with their names rather than marks, compared with 74 per cent in England and Wales as a whole.[24] Thereby they lend some support to the Memorialists' pessimistic point of view.

Recognizing the difficulties with such statistics contemporaries also concentrated on other aspects of the state of education in the district, such as the small number of children 10 years and over who attended day-school. Although these figures too were justifiably criticized because they omitted Nonconformist schools and private schools that were not under government supervision, the pattern of one or two years at day-school before beginning to work at between 8 and 10 years of age coincides

---

[22] Ibid. 299–300.   [23] PP 1863, xviii, 418; *SS* 28 Nov. 1863.
[24] Calculated from PP 1862, xvii, 65. For a discussion of the limitations to these figures, see L. Stone, 'Literacy and Education in England 1640–1900', *Past and Present*, 42 (1969), 98–9.

with testimony from the Children's Employment Commission Report of 1842, and it suggests that a relatively high proportion of children attended day-school at some time in their lives, and after beginning work continued to attend Sunday school. Mary Ann Edwards, for example, aged 10 years, a cutter in William Adams and Sons factory in Stoke, told the Children's Employment Commissioner, 'I have worked ten months . . . can read, can't write; went to day school twelve months; go to a Sunday School now'.[25] Moreover, a clearer picture of the transition from day-school to work comes from an examination of the sample of the census enumerators' books for the parliamentary borough of Stoke-upon-Trent in 1861. It reveals that the proportion of boys employed jumps from 3 per cent of the 7-year olds, to 23 per cent of the 8-year olds, to 34 per cent of 10-year olds, and to 56 per cent of 11-year olds. At the same time there was a decrease in the proportion of boys in each age-group who were 'scholars'—from 74 per cent of boys 8 years old, to 52 per cent of boys 10 years old, to 32 per cent of boys 11 years old. Girls showed a similar pattern but with the jumps shifted about two years later. This pattern of a trade-off between employment and day-school also fits with other evidence from the 1861 census enumerators' books (Table 3.2) that indicates a relatively low proportion (19 per cent) of children aged 8–12 years old in the Potteries who were not listed either as in employment (27 per cent) or as 'scholars' (54 per cent).[26]

Competing with the employment of children in pottery manufactories were two alternative explanations of the educational condition of the district—a shortage in the supply of day-schools and the prevalence of Sunday schools. Some contemporaries argued that the supply of day-schools in the district was insufficient. The 1851 Education Census suggests that there were fewer schools, particularly public schools, in the Stoke-upon-Trent registration district (2.2 against 2.5 per 1,000 population in England and Wales), and that public schools in particular were more crowded than on average in England and Wales (see Table 6.1).

Furthermore, the Factory Inspector's efforts to initiate a school for half-time children lends support to this view. However, by 1870 voluntary agencies had provided large numbers of school places which in Hanley outstripped demand, so that Hanley's new school board predicted

[25] PP 1843, xiv, 258.

[26] Although the figures here are not directly comparable with Cunningham's, they suggest that the Potteries may be unusual in having high children's employment and a high proportion of 'scholars': see H. Cunningham, 'The Employment and Unemployment of Children in England *c*.1680–1851', *Past and Present*, 126 (1990), 143–5.

TABLE 6.1   *Number of Children per School: Stoke-upon-Trent
Registration District and England and Wales 1851*

	Public		Private	
	E&W	Stoke RD.	E&W	Stoke RD.
No. of children per school on the books	92	122	24	26
No. of children per school attending on 31 March 1851	73	98	22	23
Percentage attendance	79	80	92	89

Note:
According to the 1851 Education Census, 'private' schools were those which received all income from pupils or were run for a profit, while 'public' schools were those supported 'in any degree from other sources than the payments by scholars and which are established in any degree for other objects than pecuniary profits to the promoters'. Public schools included those supported by religious bodies, endowments, general, or local taxation: M. Goldstrom, 'Education in England and Wales in 1851: The Education Census of Great Britain, 1851', in R. Lawton (ed.), *The Census and Social Structure* (London, 1978), 225–6. There is reason to believe that the number of schools in the Census is an underestimate: see P. Gardner, *The Lost Elementary Schools of Victorian England* (London, 1984), 59–61.
Source: Calculated from PP 1852–3, xc, 218–19, 244–5.

at its first meeting that no large-scale building programme would be necessary.[27] Thus, the extension of factory legislation may well have indirectly encouraged continuing voluntary efforts.[28] These voluntary efforts came primarily from 'religious bodies'.[29] Pottery manufacturers rarely provided their own factory schools; there was a sharp separation between factory and school.[30] Those manufacturers who supported education worked within the institutions associated with voluntary schools. The Wedgwoods, for example, established and continued to provide funds for the British School in Etruria.[31] The Rector of Stoke noted that in contrast

[27] W. B. Nixon, 'Scholars Not Schools', Ph.D. thesis (Keele, 1982), 350.
[28] Voluntary efforts appear to have accelerated in e.g. Hanley after 1858 when seven new schools and 2,000 places were added: ibid. 59.
[29] PP 1852–3, xc, 360. Dupree 'Family Structure in the Staffordshire Potteries 1840–1880', D. Phil. thesis (Oxford, 1981), 308.
[30] *SS* 27 Dec. 1862.   [31] See above, Ch. 4.

with the manufacturing districts of Lancashire and Yorkshire, there are no schools established in connection with any of our large manufactories, and supported by the manufacturers for the education of children of people in their employ. I know of one exception, Mr C. Meigh's night school in Hanley.[32]

Some contemporaries in the Potteries also suggested that high attendance at Sunday schools accounted for low day-school attendance and made legislative restriction on children's employment unnecessary. Indeed, a complementary relationship between Sunday schools and factory employment existed in the Potteries. In Stoke registration district attendance at Sunday school on Sunday 30 March 1851 exceeded attendance at day-school on Monday 31 March 1851 by 19 per cent: 31 per cent more children were on the books as belonging to the Sunday schools than to the day-schools.[33] Further evidence of the complementarity between attendance at Sunday school and children's employment in pottery manufactories comes from the manufacturers' survey of Longton:[34] 79 per cent of the 439 boys and 87 per cent of the 405 girls employed in the forty Longton manufactories surveyed attended Sunday school. Testimony to the Children's Employment Commissioner also confirms this pattern.[35] The complementarity between work and Sunday schools was so well established in the Potteries that some participants in the discussion saw state intervention as an unnecessary alteration to the present situation. For example, Mr Hobson, a Longton manufacturer, commented that

he was sent to work very early, when he was seven years and four months old. He could read, but he could not write at the time, and the greatest part of the education he had, he received in Sabbath school. He was anxious for every child to be taught to read and write, as he knew something of the disadvantages of not being able to do so. He received influences for good in Sabbath school, and had since been industrious in that direction and had done something, and he believed others might do the same if they were disposed. It was to be feared that the greatest amount of suffering and ignorance arose from bad dispositions, and if education would do anything to mend man morally and physically, then by all means, let them have it, as he believed education would make them better if they could have it. There was the half-time system, the restrictive system, and the certificate system, but there was still another system by which they could have it, and which would not interfere with their manufactories at all (Hear, hear).[36]

---

[32] *SS* 17 Oct. 1863.   [33] PP 1852–3, xc, 242–5.
[34] See Dupree, 'Family Structure', 303, 309.
[35] PP 1843, xv, 242, 267.   [36] *SS* 10 Jan. 1863.

The immediate effect of the extension of the Factory Acts to the Potteries was to reduce the number of children under 13 years old employed in the potteries by half by January 1865. But, despite initial problems, the number of half-time children increased to 'about 2,500' in December 1866, and after the implementation of the last stage of the Act there were 2,951 in October 1867[37] or over three-quarters of the approximately 3,900 employed in 1864 before the implementation of the Act.[38] It was unlikely that these children would have been attending school at all without the indirect compulsion of the Factory Acts. In addition their attendance was more regular than that of full-time students.[39] A Longton clergyman, for example, testified that in his experience the half-time system 'had improved the attendance considerably'.[40] However, the number of half-timers made up a relatively small proportion (19 per cent at most) of the school-age population in 1871 who might have been half-timers.[41]

A related effect of the operation of the educational clauses of the Factory Acts in the Potteries was to prepare local opinion for the Education Act of 1870 and the formation of school boards. Prior to the Education Act the factory inspectors reported that in the Potteries the

only exception to the general well-working of the Factories Act is displayed in the neglect of the parents of half-timers to secure the regular attendance of their children at school. Stringent measures are needed, and should be put in operation, to insure compliance with this most salutary provision of the Acts.[42]

To demonstrate this conviction, the number of prosecutions against parents in the Potteries for neglecting to send children to school was exceptionally high for the six months ending 30 April 1870. In that period about two-thirds of the prosecutions were against parents, compared with 1864 and 1875 when about one-third of all prosecutions were against parents (see Fig. 6.1). There is no reason to suppose that there was a sudden change of behaviour on the part of parents. Instead, the temporary increase probably reflects the concerns of the inspector, and it suggests that he used his power of prosecution for political purposes to encourage local support for the Education Act and the formation of school boards.

---

[37] PP 1867, xvi [3794], 412; PP 1867–8, xviii [4010], 664.
[38] PP 1866, xxiv [3622], 344.
[39] Nixon, 'Scholars', 356.   [40] *SS* 10 July 1875.
[41] Calculated from figures in Nixon, 'Scholars', 51, 154, who reports 700 half-timers in Hanley and 6,183 children aged 5–12 years. Subtracting 2,500 as an estimate for those aged 5–7 years leaves approximately 3,700 children aged 8–12 years.
[42] *SS* 20 Nov. 1869.

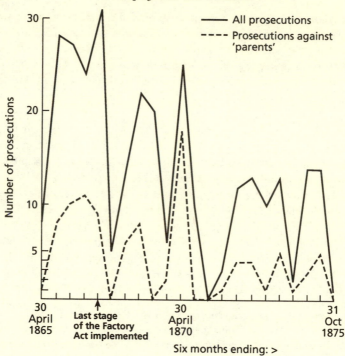

F IG. 6.1 Total Prosecutions and Prosecutions against Parents under the Factory Acts
Extension Act in the Potteries 1865–1875

Source: Factory Inspectors' Reports.

The Factory Act was also invoked during the elections for the Hanley
School Board a year later. Mr Powell, one of the candidates and a pottery
manufacturer, said that

he rejoiced that the School Board would be able to pass bye-laws which would
have the effect of compelling children to attend school, for his own experience of
the Factory Act taught him that if there was not some power beyond the influence of the parent, children did not go to school.[43]

Wage Negotiations

The effects of the extension of factory legislation to the Potteries were
not limited to their educational clauses. Contemporaries attributed to the
Factory Act increased wages for assistants, and workmen who required

[43] Ibid.

assistants used the Factory Acts as an argument for increasing their own wages. In November 1865 in its annual review of the trade, the *Sentinel* reported

hiring for the coming year has, in a general way, been affected very comfortably. In some instances—more particularly in those branches which are affected by the increased cost of child-labour caused by the operation of the Factory Act—advances have been willingly conceded by the masters. The only stand of any importance has been made by the oven men, who demand a rise of sixpence per day—making their wages 4s. 6d. per day. Some manufacturers have agreed to give the advance; and though the dispute is as yet unsettled a very general impression prevails that the men will gain their point.[44]

After 1870, in combination with the Education Act, the Factory Act provoked protest before Boards of Arbitration from branches in which workmen required assistants. One working man complained that 'after having got clear of the Factory Act they were overtaken by the Education Act with its amendments. . . . Again the price of juvenile labour was enhanced and again did that mean a reduction on the workmen's wages'.[45] The printers and transferers claimed advances before a Board of Arbitration in 1872 on the grounds that

we are now working for less remuneration than what we considered we deserved in the year 1836; and since the introduction of the Factory Act, we have been compelled to pay an advance for juvenile labour of from 30–40 per cent, which, taken in connection with the necessaries of life being much higher, make us altogether unable to meet the demands incumbent upon us—hence the cause of our appeal.[46]

The printers received an advance but other branches using children as attendants, flat-pressers, and handlers, did not, despite an estimated 10 per cent lowering of their wages due to a 100 per cent increase in attendants' wages since 1864.[47]

Before the Board of Arbitration in 1877 the hollow-ware pressers, a branch which did not require assistants, claimed an advance on the grounds of the restriction of their children's employment opportunities and thus the lowering of family incomes.

The legislation of the past 10 years (including the Factory Acts and other measures) have had peculiar force in the district by restricting child labour, for which

[44] *SS* 18 Nov. 1865. [45] *SS* 20 Nov. 1880.
[46] *SS* 16 Nov. 1872. [47] Ibid.

there was always a large demand, and throwing the entire maintenance of the family for a much longer period than formerly wholly upon the parents.[48]

Women in the Pottery Labour-force

Evidence of an increase in the proportion of the labour-force that was made up of women and girls, and by inference their use to compensate for the restriction on the supply of children, comes from the Factory Inspector's Report

> for want of a uniform application of restriction to works in the same neighbourhood, juvenile male labour for earthenware works has been both difficult to obtain and difficult to keep when obtained. And from this circumstance may have arisen a statement that has been somewhat current in the Potteries of girls being employed in those occupations which properly belong to boys.[49]

In 1875 before the Royal Commission on the Working of the Factory and Workshops Act there was testimony along the same lines concerning the increase of the employment of women due to the Factory Act.

> *Chairman*: Do you think there has been an improvement in the people since these acts came into operation?
> *Mayor of Hanley*: I think there has been an improvement physically, but not morally, because the sexes have been brought more together in the work places . . . the reason why there had been more mixing of sexes in workshops at factories, and which he considered had not tended to the moral improvement of the people, was owing to the fact that because of the requirements of the Factory Act the supply of boys had been narrowed, and workmen had been obliged to get female labour.[50]

Other evidence comes from the appeal of the printers and transferers before the Board of Arbitration in 1872.

> Mr Owen said there could be no question but that the printers experience great difficulty in getting women, who were now pushing for an advance of 10 per cent. . . . With the present prices, a printer had almost to go hawking round the country to get a woman to work for him.[51]

Although they are rough and they give no explanation, the published census figures show an increase in the proportion of females in the pottery labour-force from 31 per cent in 1861 to 35 per cent in 1871 (see Table 6.2). It is probable that the increase in demand for pottery after the end of the American Civil War accounts for this increase (see Fig.

---

[48] *SS* 17 Feb. 1877.   [49] Ibid.
[50] *SS* 10 July 1875.   [51] *SS* 16 Nov. 1872.

TABLE 6.2   *Female Workers as a Proportion of the Total Pottery*
Labour-Force: 1841–1891

| Year | Pottery Labour-force | | Females as a % of the total pottery labour-force |
	Females	Total	
1841	7,100	23,800	30
1851	10,700	34,300	30
1861	12,000	38,300	31
1871	16,000	45,300	35
1881	17,900	46,600	38
1891	21,800	56,600	38

Source: Armstrong, 'Occupation', in Wrigley (ed.), *Nineteenth Century Society*, 261.

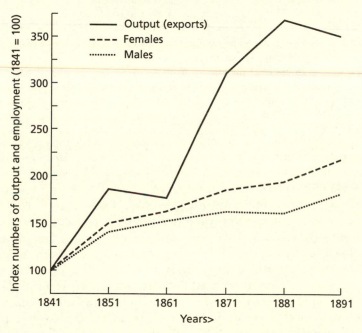

FIG. 6.2   Male and Female Employment and the Output of the Pottery Industry
1841–1891

6.2), though later, from the 1870s, fashions also changed towards hand-painted ware requiring increasing numbers of women as paintresses.

Labour-Saving Machinery

Another effect which contemporaries attributed to the Factory Acts, but which was also closely associated with the increase in demand, was the application of labour-saving machinery to pottery manufacture.[52] Although it is not possible to ascertain with any precision the extent to which the Factory Act encouraged the application of machinery to pottery manufacture, it probably reinforced tendencies in that direction, particularly for machinery for the preparation of clay. The pugmill especially was mentioned before the Board of Arbitration in 1877:

when labour was scarce they had found a difficulty in getting boys and girls to wedge clay. Workpeople refused to accept situations [with an employer] . . . when they knew he had no pug . . . [employers] had no doubt the wages of the attendants had been raised by the introduction of the Factory Act.

Mr Meir said that when the pug broke down at his place it cost the men 10*s*. a week for wedging clay. The charge for pugging was 1*s*. 3*d*. a week; so he calculated that the pug was an advantage to the men of 8*s*. 9*d*. a week . . . the extra help a man got from the pug made up for the loss of child labour. A good many men had their wives working with them, and it actually paid them to hire a nurse for their families.[53]

In many cases the operative of the pugmill machinery was a woman.[54]

In addition to the preparation of clay, other areas of pottery manufacture not previously mechanized were gradually mechanized from the mid-1860s. The restriction of the supply of child labour combined with a period of sustained high demand, unprecedented prosperity and high profits after the end of the American Civil War, followed by the need to reduce costs as selling prices fell in the later 1870s provided incentives.

During the first half of the nineteenth century pressing (the process by which pottery was made by pressing clay into plaster-of-paris mould and removing the mould after drying on a stove, to produce a cup, saucer, plate etc.) largely replaced throwing and turning as the method by which most pottery was produced. There were two distinct branches of pressers which manufacturers treated separately and which had distinct craft union organisations. Flat-pressers produced goods on a mould

---

[52] *SS* 18 Mar. 1865.   [53] *SS* 13 Jan. 1877.
[54] F. H. Botham, 'Working Class Living Standards in North Staffordshire 1750–1914', Ph.D. thesis (London, 1982), 375.

TABLE 6.3 *The Employment of Wives and Occupation of Husbands: Potteries 1881[a] (%)*

Husband's Occupation (%)	Wife's Occupation (%)			
	Pottery	Other	Not Empl.	All
Potter	[63]	[30]	*[29]*	[35]
	32	4	65	101 (331)
Miner	[11]	[8]	[14]	[13]
	15	2	83	100 (126)
Ironworker	[4]	[5]	[6]	[6]
	13	4	84	101 (56)
Labourer	[9]	[15]	[11]	[11]
	15	6	80	101 (103)
Other[b]	*[11]*	[40]	[37]	[33]
	6	5	89	100 (311)
Not Employed	[1]	[3]	[2]	[2]
	6	6	89	101 (18)
All %	99	101	99	100
(N)	(166)	(40)	(739)	(945)
	18	4	78	100 (945)

[ ] = column %
( ) = n
bold = the relationship between the categories is positive and significant at .05 level (Haberman's adjusted residual).
italics = the relationship between the categories is negative and significant at .05 level (Haberman's adjusted residual).
[a] Based on the sample of the census enumerators' books from the Potteries in 1881.
[b] 'Other' is a residual category which includes shopkeepers, tradesmen, professional men, etc.

which produced a profile of the inside of the ware, i.e. plates, saucers, cups and dishes. As we saw in Ch. 3, they were the largest single group of pottery-workers, accounting for 22 per cent of all male potters in the early 1860s.[55] Hollow-ware pressers produced jugs and ewers which had to be made in two halves, in two moulds and joined together afterwards. This was the second largest branch of pottery manufacture comprising 14 per cent of all male potters in the early 1860s. From the 1870s their

[55] They included three sub-branches which had distinct wage levels: saucer-makers (least well-paid); dishmakers (best paid); and plate-makers (middle range): Botham, 'Living Standards', 278–9.

numbers declined, slowly at first, but rapidly after 1900 as slip casting (in which irregular shapes were formed by pouring slip or liquid clay into plaster-of-paris moulds), often carried out by women, replaced hollow-ware pressing.[56] Pressing was entirely a hand process in 1860, although the jigger a machine that turned the mould was generally in use by the late 1850s (turned by a young boy or girl assistant). With the restriction of the supply of child labour steam power increasingly replaced jigger turners and turned wheels and lathes. The restriction of child labour also encouraged the gradual introduction of jollies (which fitted over the top of the jigger and enabled a mould of the outside of the ware to be pressed from the top onto the original mould which formed the inside of the ware) which had been too heavy to be turned by child labour[57] and required the employment of older, more expensive, assistants, or the wholesale introduction of steam power. As a result of the increasing use of steam power for turning machinery the physical strength required to make pottery was reduced and women could operate jiggers and jollies to produce small items such as cups and saucers just as effectively as men. There was no dramatic transformation of the industry; no complete branches of the industry were flung into technological unemployment. But relentlessly the relative wage earning position of the adult male potter was undermined as the premium on skill and strength was reduced.[58] The complexity of potters' wages increased rather than diminished with the widespread introduction of machinery during the period. The introduction was gradual so new piece rates existed alongside the old. Machinery also complicated the system of deductions and payment of attendants.

Thus, with the restrictions on children's employment, women not only replaced young children as assistants, but also the restrictions were one of the incentives for the increasing mechanization of areas in the potting or clay departments which in turn led to an undermining of the relative earning power of the adult male potter and to the influx of female labour into parts of the clay departments which had previously been male preserves and in which women had acted only as assistants.[59]

Hours and Output

Another effect attributed to the Factory Act and welcomed by manufacturers was the regularization of hours over a week. Baker, for example, reported to Grey in 1864 saying

[56] Ibid. 279.   [57] Ibid. 371.
[58] Ibid. 338   [59] Ibid. 275.

I see too that the masters are looking forward to the power which the Act will exercise over the hours of labour, as a means of inducing greater subordination among the adult workers; and the female workers are looking forward to the happy time, when they can be certain of being home to their domestic duties.[60]

In October 1865 Baker reported that the Factory Act in the Potteries 'has limited the hours of female, adolescent, and infant labour by a very considerable percentage over the ordinary and extraordinary hours of labour of preceding times, without diminishing production and with but a small temporary diminution of the rate of wages'.[61] He also reported that 'potters say they can and do produce as much under the Act as ever they did before, because they come earlier and lose less time'.[62] Furthermore, Colin Minton Campbell of Minton and Company testified that 'since the Factory Act, the quality of their ware has been improved; and they have less spoiled ware, since the greater regularity of work has put a stop to hurried production'.[63] In its annual review of the potting trade in November 1865, the *Sentinel* reported the general opinion that after twelve months in operation the Factory Act does not work 'altogether satisfactorily', but then admits that 'on the other hand, it has led to greater regularity of attendance on the part of the workpeople in the early part of the week'.[64] The Factory Act, however, did not complete the regularization of hours in pottery manufacture. In 1875 before the Board of Arbitration, a manufacturer complained of 'irregular working, including the general idleness on Mondays'.[65] On behalf of the workmen, William Eardly defended St Monday (the taking of an unofficial holiday on Mondays) by arguing that 'the flat-presser could not pursue his avocation six days per week on account of the unhealthiness of the work'.[66]

The effect of the Factory Act on total production is impossible to estimate, but on the basis of the number of new manufactories built and of new firms created since the introduction of the Act on 1 January 1865, Robert Baker argued that 'upon the whole, a pretty considerable increase has been established in the pottery trade since the restrictions came into force, which affords the strongest of all proofs that no commercial mischief has arisen to this manufacture from the operation of the law.[68] Moreover, the annual review of the potting trade in November 1865 saw the Factory Act as a check to over-production in the face of the increased demand from the American market following the end of the Civil War:

[60] PRO HO45/7570/2: Baker to Grey, 27 Aug. 1864.
[61] PP 1866, xxiv [3622], 377.   [62] Ibid. 349.   [63] Ibid.
[64] *SS* 18 Nov. 1865.   [65] *SS* 13 Jan. 1877.   [66] Ibid.
[67] *SS* 16 Nov. 1867.   [68] PP 1867, xvi [3794], 412.

'the application of the Factory Act to this district has curtailed our manufacturing power (only temporarily, however) some say to the extent of a fifth, [there is no] ground to fear over-production and that consequent glutting of the American markets which proved so disastrous in years gone by'.[69]

Social Control and Moral Reform

Finally, Robert Baker, the Factory Inspector, clearly saw the Factory Acts as an instrument of social control and moral reform, and he believed they would have that effect in the Potteries. He commented to Sir George Grey that 'I see too that the masters are looking forward to the power which the Act will exercise over the hours of labour, as a means of inducing greater subordination among the adult workers'.[70] In his summary of the operation of the Factory Acts in the Potteries after thirty months, Baker emphasized the benefits of the control they could provide:

what I wish to impress upon you is that, all factory labour, now-a-days more than ever, demands restriction, elementary education and supervision, both legal, medical and moral. The first to compel uniformity of time, whereby the second may raise the intellectual character of the artisans; and the third to protect their life and health, encourage virtue, and rescue the young from contaminating tendencies. Commerce seems to be growing faster than the population; and as the power of wages strengthens without the controlling influence of a well directed education, we may be certain of what the result will be, if that education is any longer neglected. My belief is that such labour may be as pure and as excellent and as obedient, as domestic labour, and perhaps more so, where the master wills a discipline, and enforces it.[71]

There is some testimony that the Act did have the effects which Baker prophesied; however, it is impossible to verify.

Mr Challinor, for example, speaking in favour of the Factory Act at the meeting in Wolverhampton considering the application of the Acts to South Staffordshire industries, emphasized in particular the moral reform it promotes: 'the application of the Act had led to a decrease of drunkenness, as the men could not now make up by overtime what they were accustomed to lose at the beginning of the week in drinking, and consequently they had to be more regular in their attendance during working hours'.[72] Furthermore, Baker asserted that the restriction and regulation of hours allowed more time for pursuits in the home.

[69] *SS* 16 Nov. 1865.   [70] See above p. 263.
[71] PP 1866, xxiv [3622], 379.   [72] *SS* 26 Jan. 1867.

Labour too is more regular, less hurried, and less protracted, by which latter advantage, the opportunities of domestic instruction of every kind are enlarged; whilst children that used to be precocious animals, are becoming obedient, docile, gentle and impressible with the lessons of divine truth. Can there be any stronger testimony given, than that now afforded, to the efficiency of the Factory Act, which under Providence has been applied to the Potteries; or can there be greater encouragement than these results show, to induce the legislature to carry the same work into other trades, in districts where it is even still more requisite, and in which equal usefulness under similar legislation may be anticipated.[73]

In addition to the regularization of hours during the week, the annual review of the potting trade in November 1867 attributed the uniformity of holidays to the Factory Act:

another [beneficial result of the introduction of the Factory Act into the district], which is 'looming in the future' is the reduction of the number of our annual holidays. Now that the working hours are shortened and men who are dependent on the assistance of women or children have no opportunity of making up for time lost in debauchery in the early part of the week by long days of slavery towards the end, and are consequently becoming more regular and steady in their labour, they do not need, nor can they afford, so much time for mere holiday making. . . . Messrs. Minton and Co. have dispensed with the Martinmas holidays, and their employees have been steadily at work during the week, altogether regardless of this ancient potters' festival. . . . A similar and equally commendable movement has originated at Tunstall, in the attempt to abolish the wakes holidays there and at Burslem, and to merge them in one general festival in the first week of August.[74]

Precedent

Whatever the effects of extension of the Factory Acts to the Potteries, the mere fact that they had been extended to pottery manufacture was in turn used as an argument in favour of the extension of the Acts to other industries. Baker concluded his summary of the result of thirty months of operation of the Act in North Staffordshire saying 'and thus it is we use again the same language precisely which was spoken of the textile works and workers years ago, with respect to the results of factory legislation among them; language that elicited such general satisfaction from the public, and which led to further steps in the same direction'.[75]

Steps in the same direction came quickly. In January 1867 there was a conference in Wolverhampton to discuss the recommendations of the

[73] PP 1866, xxiv [3622], 378.   [74] *SS* 16 Nov. 1867.   [75] PP 1867, xvi [3794], 413.

Children's Employment Commissioners which applied to the manufacturers of South Staffordshire and neighbourhood. The conference was
'influentially attended': those present included the Rector of Stoke, the
Stipendiary Magistrate and Mr Challinor from the Potteries, as well as
Baker. Lord Lyttleton, the chairman, opened the meeting, immediately
bringing up the example of the Potteries: 'he had no doubt that in some
way or other, the educational part of the Factory Acts ought to be
applied in the district, as it had been so successful in Lancashire and the
Staffordshire Potteries'.[76] The Earl of Lichfield added that

> They had only to go as far as the Potteries to see that the good which the system
> had done there was scarcely to be over-estimated, although educational results
> had not had time to show themselves. It protected the children from the cupidity
> of their parents and of their employers, and secured that they should be em-
> ployed only during a certain number of hours each day according to their age;
> and if it did nothing else, that was a great deal.[77]

Sir Lovelace Stamer, Rector of Stoke and initially an opponent of the
extension of factory legislation to pottery manufacture, admitted that he
was

> not at first a warm supporter of the Factory Act, . . . and it was only by slow
> degrees he had come to believe that the extension of the Factory Act to the
> Pottery district had been a blessing to that district . . . at first the clergy thought
> the acts defective or not applicable in several respects, . . . but he was glad now
> that the advice they tendered was not received.[78]

3. Conclusion

Although its effects were mediated through the state of trade, the extension of the Factory Acts to the pottery industry affected who was employed and at what ages and wages. Thus, in turn it affected family
employment patterns, family income, and the amount of time which
could be spent within the home.

In the Potteries, as in the cotton industry, the Factory Acts had the
immediate effect of reducing the number of children employed. Although
the pattern differed between boys and girls, there was a decrease overall
in the number of children aged 5–14 employed in pottery manufacture
from 17 per cent of the pottery labour-force in 1861 to 12 per cent in
1871.[79] Also, as a result of the Act there were approximately 2,700 children in school half-time. These children would have attended for one or

---

[76] *SS* 26 Jan. 1867.   [77] Ibid.   [78] Ibid.   [79] See above, Table 5.3.

two years before beginning work and attended Sunday school after beginning work. So, while attendance at school half-time did increase the time these children attended school, it probably did not bring children into school who had never been before, as the factory inspector claimed. The Act, however, was a first step, and it prepared local opinion in the Potteries for non-sectarian, compulsory education in the future.

In addition, the reduction in the employment of younger children in combination with the improved trade, led to increased wages for older assistants. This gave more money to adolescents at an age when it would have been more difficult than with younger children for parents to insist on the child contributing to the family income.

Moreover, as trade increased, expansion became dependent on the labour of women rather than young children, increasing both the number of women employed and their wages. This consequence in particular differs from the arguments which stress the role of protective legislation in the restriction and segregation of women's employment. After the introduction of the Factory Acts, rather than decreasing as might have been expected given the previous literature, the number and proportion of women employed in the pottery industry increased. In part this was due to changing fashions towards hand-painted ware, requiring increasing numbers of women as paintresses, but a large part was also due to the increase in the employment of women in their traditional areas as assistants in place of lower-cost child labour. At the same time, the functions of attendant labour changed with the advent of machinery encouraged by the restriction of low-cost child labour. Wedging or batting the clay might now be done by a pugmill machine rather than by an assistant or by the artisan himself, but the machine operative was in many cases a woman.[80] In addition, women began to move into areas in the clay departments which had previously been male preserves and in which women had acted only as assistants.

This in turn raises questions about the links between protective legislation and the spread of the 'breadwinner family' and fertility decline. Instead of encouraging the spread of 'breadwinner' families, the extension of protective legislation to pottery manufacture undermined the 'breadwinner' family headed by male pottery-workers, as their relative wage-earning position gradually slipped in relation to other groups and the number and relative wages of women in the industry increased over the last third of the century. Evidence of this tendency was already

---

[80] Botham, 'Standard of Living', 375.

apparent by 1881. The proportion of wives of potters employed in potworks increased from 21 per cent to 32 per cent in 1881, and there was no significant relationship between the employment of wives in pottery and husbands employed in other occupations (see Table 6.3, cf. Table 3.4 for 1861). Thus, by 1904 a female factory inspector reported that the Potteries was an area where well-paid men's employment was scarce and it was claimed that

a woman is looked upon as lazy unless she takes her share in contributing to the family income. In Staffordshire, the men and boys appear to be willing to do their part in the domestic work of the home, and it is no uncommon sight to find a man cleaning and sweeping, caring for the children and even putting them to bed on the evening when the women were engaged in family washing.[81]

Moreover, instead of protective legislation in the Potteries encouraging fertility decline by restricting the value of child labour (see Ch. 3), the male potters were among the occupational groups with the highest fertility.

Furthermore, at the same time that the Factory Acts were restricting the employment of children and young persons in the pottery industry, the iron industry in the region expanded and increased the competition for juvenile male labour. The introduction of protective legislation in the Potteries thus emphasizes both the importance of considering women and children together with other family members and the need to take a regional and 'community perspective'[82] rather than one based on a single industry or occupational group.

In addition, the extension of the Factory Acts to the pottery industry brought the central government into direct contact with the family, giving the state power over decisions regarding the allocation of time within the family. Although the inspector did not prosecute many parents, he now had the potential to intervene in relationships between parents and children employed in pottery manufacture.

Finally, the extension of factory legislation to the Potteries highlighted the high morbidity and mortality rates in the region and reflected the local structures of authority, their relationship with the state and the social assumptions within which individuals and families in the Potteries sought assistance for many of the problems they might face. We explore their sources of assistance and problems in Part Three.

---

[81] Quoted in M. Hewitt, *Wives and Mothers in Victorian Industry* (London, 1958), 193.

[82] M. Dupree, 'The Community Perspective in Family History: The Potteries during the Nineteenth Century', in A. L. Beier, D. N. Cannadine, and J. Rosenheim (eds.), *The First Modern Society: Essays in English History in Honour of Lawrence Stone* (Cambridge, 1989), 549–73.

PART III

Families and Social Welfare

7
Alternative Sources of Assistance?

A VARIETY of problems facing individuals and families in the Potteries have emerged in previous chapters. The relatively high levels of morbidity and mortality are particularly apparent. As we have just seen, in the discussions surrounding the extension of the Factory Acts to the Potteries, contemporaries were well aware of them. Other potential threats to family income and structure came from unemployment and desertion. In addition, there were problems associated with life-cycle stages, such as those of old age or young married couples, and there were day-to-day problems from the borrowing of potatoes to short-term child-care.

The purpose of this and the following chapter is to examine a functional aspect of family relationships—the part played by nuclear family members and kin in providing domestic and family help. In other words, to what extent did family relationships provide a source of assistance to individuals compared with other networks and institutions for meeting various problems in the mid-nineteenth century Potteries? What was the relationship between family relationships and other networks and institutions both in terms of the provision of assistance and in terms of encouraging individuals to maintain relationships with family and kin?

In order to approach these questions it will be necessary first to set out the historiographical context, second to describe the other networks and institutions which served as sources of assistance and which may have encouraged or sanctioned the maintenance of family relationships, and finally, in the following chapter, to take various 'problems' facing individuals in the Potteries between 1840 and 1880 and examine the ways in which inhabitants handled them.

1. Ways of Viewing the Relationship between Family Ties and other Sources of Assistance

Michael Anderson not only describes how family assistance filled the breach in welfare institutions in mid-nineteenth-century Preston, but he also carries the argument one step further and suggests that the

inadequacy of bureaucratic forms of assistance in combination with relatively great need explains why people in mid-nineteenth-century Preston
maintained relationships with family and kin.[1] From his perspective,
family relationships are seen as one among a number of mutually exclusive alternative sources of assistance; furthermore, apart from poor relief,
family relationships become the last line of defence against need. In other
words, individuals acted as if they turned to family relationships only
when other sources of assistance (e.g. friendly societies, employers, neighbours, trade unions) either did not offer the required assistance or the
assistance they did offer was exhausted.

Furthermore, in Preston according to Anderson individuals turned to
relatives for assistance not only because of the lack of alternative sources
of assistance, but also because non-family networks and institutions played
only a limited role in encouraging actors to maintain relationships with
family and kin as their sanctioning power was severely circumscribed
compared with that in rural society.[2]

There are several a priori reasons to question this perspective. First,
other sources of assistance may not have been as inadequate as they
appeared to be in Preston. Recently, proponents of the 'nuclear hardship' hypothesis suggest that in England at least since the sixteenth
century and probably earlier the 'collectivity'—friends, neighbours, church,
charitable institutions, and the village, town, or state—has been particularly important in providing support as an adjunct to the family system
based on the nuclear family, in which those marrying left their parental
households to form new households leaving individuals and nuclear families
vulnerable. In the nineteenth century the self-help of friendly societies
modified but did not transcend the importance of the collectivity, and
some argue that the Poor Law in the mid-nineteenth century was more
generous than the welfare state for the aged and for single-parent families.[3]
Furthermore, philanthropy within as well as between classes together with
churches were characteristic sources of assistance in nineteenth-century

---

[1] M. Anderson, *Family Structure in 19th Century Lancashire* (Cambridge, 1971), 137.
[2] Ibid. ch. 8.
[3] For a summary of this view, see: P. Laslett, 'Family, Kinship and Collectivity as
Systems of Support in Pre-Industrial Europe: A Consideration of the "Nuclear-Hardship"
Hypothesis', *Continuity and Change*, 3 (1988), 153, 164–7. D. Thomson, 'Welfare and the
Historians', in L. Bonfield, R. Smith, and K. Wrightson (eds.), *The World We Have Gained:
Histories of Population and Social Structure, Essays Presented to Peter Laslett* (London, 1986),
355–78; K. Snell and J. Millar, 'Lone Parent Families and the Welfare State: Past and
Present', *Continuity and Change*, 2 (1987), 387–422; D. Thomson, 'The Welfare of the
Elderly in the Past: A Family or Community Responsibility?', in M. Pelling and R. M.
Smith (eds.), *Life, Death and the Elderly: Historical Perspectives* (London, 1991), 194–221.

England, whose importance has tended to be underestimated in the historiographical tradition emphasizing the linear progression to increasing state action and the twentieth-century welfare state.[4] Recent emphasis is on the 'welfare mix' of voluntary, commercial, fiscal, state, and informal support, and their shifting boundaries.[5]

A second reason for scepticism is that instead of viewing family relationships and other organizations as alternative or substitute sources of assistance, they can be seen as complementary. Different sources of assistance, for example kin, neighbours, and institutions, perform different functions which cannot obviously be substituted for each other but which may be 'interwoven' or combined.[6] Furthermore, rather than competing with family relationships, other sources might reinforce family assistance.[7] For a given 'problem' more than one source of assistance might be called upon.

Third, it may be true with reference to rural society that the sanctioning power of non-family networks and institutions was sharply limited and as a result they played little role in encouraging actors to maintain relationships with family and kin. But such a comparison tends to lead to an underestimation of the extent to which alternative networks and

[4] F. K. Prochaska, 'Philanthropy', in F. M. L. Thompson (ed.), *The Cambridge Social History of Britain 1750–1950*, iii (Cambridge, 1990), esp. 359. H. McLeod, *Religion and the Working Class in Nineteenth-Century Britain* (London and Basingstoke, 1984). Id., 'New Perspectives on Victorian Working Class Religion: The Oral Evidence', *Oral History*, 14 (1986), 31–49; J. Obelkevich, 'Religion', in F. M. L. Thompson (ed.), *The Cambridge Social History of Britain 1750–1950*, iii (Cambridge, 1990), 311–56; J. Cox, *The English Churches in a Secular Society: Lambeth 1870–1930* (New York and Oxford, 1982), esp. ch. 3.

[5] M. A. Crowther, 'Family Responsibility and State Responsibility in Britain before the Welfare State', *Hist. J.* 25 (1982), 131–45; P. Thane, 'Essay in Revision: The Historiography of the British Welfare State', *Social History Society Newsletter*, 15 (1990), esp. 14; G. B. A. M. Finlayson, 'A Moving Frontier: Voluntarism and the State in British Social Welfare 1911–1949', *Twentieth Century British History*, 1 (1990), 183–206; M. Bulmer, J. Lewis, D. Piachaud, 'Social Policy: Subject or Object?', in eid. (eds.), *The Goals of Social Policy*, 7–15; A. Digby, *British Welfare Policy: Workhouse to Workfare* (London, 1989), esp. 8, 85, 90–1, 99, 127–8; N. Johnson, 'Problems for the Mixed Economy of Welfare', in A. Ware and R. E. Goodin (eds.), *Needs and Welfare* (London, 1990), 145–64; A. Ware, 'Meeting Needs Through Voluntary Action: Does Market Society Corrode Altruism?', in A. Ware and R. E. Goodin (eds.), *Needs and Welfare* (London, 1990), 203.

[6] M. Bulmer, *The Social Basis of Community Care* (London, 1987), 18–19, 23.

[7] In a later article Anderson demonstrates how a measure of state intervention such as old-age pensions can help sustain family relationships by preventing the elderly from becoming too dependent: M. Anderson, 'The Impact on the Family Relationships of the Elderly of Changes Since Victorian Times in Governmental Income-Maintenance Provision', in E. Shanas and M. B. Sussman (eds.), *Family, Bureaucracy and the Elderly* (Durham, NC, 1977), 36–59.

institutions encouraged individuals to maintain ties with family and kin in an urban area in the nineteenth century. A number of historians have argued recently that Christianity and the Christian churches had a more pervasive influence in the nineteenth century throughout British society, including in the working classes, than many contemporary observers and subsequent historians would allow. In addition, philanthropy which generally tended to operate through the home within and between all classes was characteristic of England in the nineteenth century.[8] Moreover, the comparison with rural society does not provide an approach to comparisons among different nineteenth-century industrial areas.

Thus, there are three aspects to investigate in the relationship between families and other institutions. One is the extent to which other networks and institutions provided assistance, to whom, and when. The second is the extent to which other institutions reinforced family relationships by sanctions or by the assumption that those receiving assistance were part of a nuclear family. And the third is the extent to which the family and other institutions directly provided assistance, either separately or together, for given problems. The first two topics are discussed in this chapter and the third in the following chapter.

'Problems' can be defined in two ways: (1) situations seen by participants as ones of great stress with which they cannot cope alone; (2) situations defined as potentially critical by observers which might require extra-familial assistance.[9] These are not mutually exclusive categories, but the second type will be the initial starting-point here. In either case it is necessary to make distinctions among problems. The importance of distinguishing among problems is apparent in work on twentieth-century Britain, which suggests that 'as the help that would be required becomes more demanding, there is a general and quite marked increase in the extent to which kin would be looked to'.[10]

Thus, the question is for which problems do individuals look to family and kin for assistance? Anderson also distinguishes among problems, but he asks a different question. First, he establishes that kin gave support for a particular problem, so the question is not whether kin provide help or not. Instead, he asks why such support was given, and his answer is that as the amount of help required to alleviate that problem increased, the more likely it was that the relationship would be 'calculative' or

[8] Prochaska, 'Philanthropy', esp. 360–6, 379–81, 393.

[9] J. C. Mitchell, 'The Concept and Use of Social Networks', in J. C. Mitchell (ed.), *Social Networks in Urban Situations* (Manchester, 1969), 256.

[10] J. H. Goldthorpe, *Social Mobility and Class Structure in Modern Britain* (Oxford, 1980), 154.

reciprocal. I shall ask the first question, and in so doing I hope to put Anderson's question into a different perspective. Therefore, in Section 3 below I take certain 'problems' (e.g. day-to-day, life-cycle stage, and the removal of a family's basis of support) and present evidence regarding the extent to which kin did or did not provide assistance, either alone or in combination with other sources of assistance. This approach offers a way of examining some of the differences and similarities between the Potteries and other nineteenth-century towns in the nature of the 'problems' and the ways in which inhabitants coped with them.

2. Alternative Networks and Institutions

What were some of the alternative networks and institutions in the Potteries which may have encouraged individuals to observe family obligations, and what was the nature of the assistance which these networks and institutions provided?

Neighbours, Friends, and Workmates

There is evidence that primary networks and groups—neighbours, friends, workmates—existed in the mid-nineteenth-century Potteries as in other working-class areas from Preston in the 1850s to pre-World War I London to Bethnal Green in the 1950s, which were 'sufficiently dense, complex and extensive and evoking sufficient commitment from residents'[11] to meet certain local needs within them and to apply some sanctions on family behaviour.[12] In the Potteries there were distinct clusters and communities of Irish and Welsh immigrants, but the relatively small amount of in-migration compared with Preston, for example, meant that it is likely that a smaller proportion of these networks were based on common origins outside the Potteries. Also, although Etruria is an example of an area where neighbours and workmates tended to be the same people, at the same time a large proportion of the Wedgwood workforce also resided in a variety of neighbourhoods outside Etruria. While there was some overlap between workmates and neighbours, it was not a dominant pattern.

Even where the neighbourhood alone seems to be the only link between

[11] P. Abrams quoted in M. Bulmer, 'The Rejuvenation of Community Studies? Neighbours, Networks, and Policy', *Sociological Review*, 33 (1985), 438.

[12] Anderson, *Family Structure*, 101–6; Bulmer, *Social Basis*, 76–80; E. Ross, 'Survival Networks: Women's Neighbourhood Sharing in London Before World War I', *Hist. Workshop*, 15 (1983), 4–27; M. Bulmer, *Neighbours: The Work of Philip Abrams* (Cambridge, 1986).

people, there is evidence[13] that neighbours had some knowledge about each other's behaviour and had a considerable amount of contact, though not always amiable; much of this contact was gender-specific. Neighbours were in a position to and did sanction the behaviour of individuals towards the family, especially nuclear family members, and neighbours were a source of assistance in certain circumstances.

Contact between neighbours could stem from the physical proximity of the houses alone. Mrs Walton, wife of a crate-maker, went next door when 'someone knocked at the wall'.[14] Mary Hanley remarked about a neighbour living 'a door or two' away that 'in our house we have heard her pommel the girl's head against the wall'.[15] And, Elizabeth Newton commented about her next-door neighbours that 'I could hear what took place in their house and have never heard the child beaten'.[16]

Moreover, neighbourhood knowledge and feeling extended further than next door. It is apparent from Chapter 2 that there was a considerable amount of endogamy within neighbourhoods. Furthermore, after Elizabeth Brammer committed suicide in her house in Hanley, it was reported that 'a gloom hangs over the neighbourhood at West Street and everybody seems surprised that Mrs Brammer thus destroyed her life as there appeared to be the greatest affection existing between her and her husband'.[17] Also, Fanny Lowndes was suspected of having given birth to an illegitimate child because she was a 'stranger' in the neighbourhood, although a neighbour knew her well enough after two weeks to be able to describe her as 'always a tidy wench' who 'used to go to work every morning'.[18] In addition, there were casual visits among neighbours. Mrs Hopkins happened to mention to a neighbour who came to her house one Sunday evening that her husband had heard a cry from the privy which sounded like a fowl. As a result of an investigation the body of a child was found.[19] Finally, contact among neighbours was not always amiable. One Saturday night in Hanley in 1874 Emily Hopley quarrelled with her neighbour, Ann Wilkinson, over Emily's boy. 'Bad language was used', and Emily alleged that Ann 'struck her on the side of the head, pulling some of her hair off'. Ann in turn said that 'if it had not been for the neighbours, she would have been murdered'.[20]

---

[13] The evidence is taken from six cases selected from my reading of the local newspapers from 1840–80 and from the autobiography of John Finney, which was described in detail in Ch. 4.

[14] *SS* 5 Mar. 1870. [15] *SS* 15 July 1871.

[16] Ibid. [17] *SS* 29 Aug. 1868. [18] *SS* 27 Jan. 1866.

[19] *SS* 20 Jan. 1866. [20] *SS* 24 Dec. 1874.

Neighbours not only had the knowledge of each other to intervene in each other's affairs, but particularly in cases of the 'ill-treatment' of children by parents, they did intervene. Samuel Cooke, a goods manager at Stoke station, was extremely annoyed with the cries he heard coming from the house next door. The cries sounded as though his neighbour 'was severely chastising his children or beating his servant'. Cooke first sent two men to the neighbour's house. The men 'inquired if any straw was wanted at the house, and upon being asked the reason for such a question, he replied, "Oh, we heard there had been some thrashing going on so we thought you might want some straw"'. When Cooke again heard cries from next door, he went to the neighbour's 'back door and kicked at it', and he said to the neighbour 'you are a d——d Irish fellow; if you will go into the street I will give you a good thrashing, and then spit upon a man like you'.[21] Another resident of the street claimed to have heard cries from the house 'to the alarm of himself and other neighbours . . . about 10 o'clock in the evening usually. On one occasion his wife was so much affected that she fainted'. The neighbour admitted 'that there seemed to be a feeling of malice in the street toward him'. He, however, attributed this to the fact that he and his wife' would not associate with the neighbours',[22] rather than their suspicion of ill-treatment of his children or servant. In another case the father of a 10-year-old girl was cohabiting with a woman named Eliza Williams. A neighbour had observed the woman's treatment of the girl. The neighbour described the girl as 'a very clean, industrious little girl. She was left in the care of a baby and had to clean up as well. Mrs Williams used to make her get the dinner ready and when she did not do so in time, Mrs Williams used to set agate, and beat and abuse the child shamefully'. The neighbour claimed that she used to go in and say to Mrs Williams, ' "Eliza, she is but a child, she is not a woman and cannot do so much." . . . I have said to the girl, "Polly, why don't you tell your father?" She used to answer "Because she would beat me worse." ' Finally, the girl and her brother told their father 'who falled out with the woman'. Subsequently, the girl committed suicide by jumping into an abandoned coalpit, and outside the place where the inquest was held 'a crowd was collected . . . and a strong feeling of indignation has been evoked by the suicide'.[23] Finally, neighbourhood indignation against Fanny Lowndes, who was suspected of infanticide, was so great that when she volunteered to go to the police station for a doctor's examination, the police sergeant had to warn her,

---

[21] *SS* 29 Aug. 1868.   [22] Ibid. 6.   [23] *SS* 15 July 1871.

saying 'if you go now, there will be some hundreds of people after us; you had better come up about six'.[24]

Neighbours' knowledge and readiness to intervene was limited, however. Elizabeth Brammer, for example, had lived in the neighbourhood twelve or fourteen years, but 'the neighbours state that Mrs Brammer was a very close minded woman and that if there was anything unpleasant between her and any of her relations she was not one who would have said anything about it'.[25] In the case of Fanny Lowndes, who eventually admitted giving birth to an illegitimate child, neither the neighbours nor her landlady noticed that she was pregnant. Even in the cases of ill-treatment of children, where neighbours seemed most likely to intervene, there were limits. When the neighbour observed the ill-treatment of the 10-year-old girl, she confronted the woman and encouraged the child to tell her father of her ill-treatment, but the neighbour did not take it upon herself to tell the father. Finally, workmates appear to have exerted more pressure on individuals to marry than neighbours alone. Elizabeth Brammer lived with her husband, a presser at Brownfields pottery, 'two or three years before she became his wife . . . her workmates having teased her about it, she at that time threatened that if he did not marry her she would do something worse.'[26]

Although it was probably rare for neighbours to take the initiative and intervene except over obvious and repeated ill-treatment of children, neighbours did provide short-term assistance for both mundane reasons and in crises. Emily Rowley, for example, sent the 10-year-old girl living with her to buy potatoes for herself and her next-door neighbour. Mary Ann Culverhouse knocked on the wall to summon the next-door neighbour when her mother collapsed and died from the shock of finding that Mary Ann had given birth.

The neighbourhood beerhouse could also serve as a focus for the provision of general assistance for neighbours and for transforming neighbourliness into friendship.[27] By 1880 there were 1,200 public houses in the district patronized by both men and women.[28] John Finney mentions that it did not take him long to make some new friends among his neighbours when he moved to Stoke. He describes meeting these neighbourhood

[24] *SS* 27 Jan. 1866.   [25] *Potteries Examiner*, 10 Apr. 1875.

[26] *Potteries Examiner*, 10 Apr. 1875, 8.

[27] For a discussion of distinctions between neighbours and friends and of the blurring of lines between them, see Bulmer, *Social Basis*, 76–8.

[28] E. E. Lane, 'Tunstall', in *United States Consular Reports Labor in Europe* . . . , 49th congress, 2nd Sess., House of Representatives, Ex. Doc. 54, pt. 1 (Washington, DC, 1885), 824, 829–31.

friends on Saturday and Monday nights at the 'Commercial Inn' kept by James Hobson, and he recounts how

they were an open-hearted and open-handed lot; ever ready to help the suffering in any form—sickness, distress, or whatever it was. A subscription list was always open for cases of urgent necessity, headed by James Hobson. Sam Swann, James Robinson . . . and others followed on, for we knew all calls for assistance were deserving ones.[29]

Churches, Chapels, and Sunday Schools

Organized religion was at least as pervasive as public houses in many neighbourhoods in the Potteries in the mid-nineteenth century. It has been argued that because the majority of the working class, apart from the Irish, did not attend church or chapel, organized religion did not directly influence the attitudes of individuals in the working class towards their obligations to family members.[30] Furthermore, organized religion has not been considered a significant source of assistance to members of the working class in industrial towns in Lancashire in the mid-nineteenth century.[31] Yet, historians have recently suggested that these negative views substantially underestimate the importance of organized religion within the working class. Evidence from oral history late in the century suggests that a higher proportion of the working class attended church or chapel fairly regularly than measures of attendance on a given Sunday favoured by contemporary middle-class commentators would indicate; furthermore more account should be taken of the influence of Christianity on those who seldom went to church.[32] The working class had their own approaches to religion, which were strongly practical and were concerned especially with maintaining standards of 'kindness' and 'decent behaviour' and with mutual aid.[33] Church activities included 'philanthropy which probably did more for the poor, and more humanely, than the poor law'.[34] To what extent did this situation prevail in the Potteries in the mid-nineteenth century?

[29] J. Finney, *Sixty Years' Recollections of an Etruscan* (Stoke-upon-Trent, 1903), 36.
[30] Anderson, *Family Structure*, 107.
[31] Ibid. 53. Anderson mentions churches only as a source of individual, not institutional, assistance. Churches are seen as a focus for primary networks of individuals who might provide assistance, but not as institutional sources of assistance.
[32] McLeod, *Religion*, 9–11, 15.
[33] McLeod, *Religion*, 11; Obelkevich, 'Religion', 341.
[34] Obelkevich, 'Religion', 345; see also, Cox, *English Churches*, ch. 3; McLeod, 'New Perspectives', 35.

T ABLE 7.1   *Attendance at Religious Services on 30 March 1851: Stoke-upon-Trent Parliamentary Borough, Preston, and England and Wales* (%)

	Maximum[a]	Minimum[b]	Approximate[c]
England & Wales	61	26	48
Stoke parl. borough	41	21	32
Preston	27	18	20

[a] Total attendances at all services as a proportion of the total population.
[b] Attendance at the service most numerously attended as a proportion of the total population.
[c] Two-thirds of the total attendances as a proportion of 85 per cent of the population after Joyce, *Work, Society and Politics*, 244.
Source: PP 1852–3, lxxxix, Census of Gt. Britain, 1851. Religious worship.

Attendance on Census Sunday 1851, 'a stormy, blustery day',[35] was lower in the parliamentary borough of Stoke-upon-Trent than in England and Wales as a whole (Table 7.1), no matter how attendance is calculated.[36] If registration districts, rather than the parliamentary borough, are taken as the units of analysis, the attendance in Wolstanton and Burslem (36 per cent) was higher than in Stoke-upon-Trent (30 per cent), but both were still lower than in England and Wales. When compared with attendance in Lancashire towns, attendance in the Potteries (32 per cent) fell in the middle between the high in Warrington (46 per cent) and the low in Preston (20 per cent).[37] Thus, about one-third of the population of the Potteries attended church or chapel on Census Sunday in 1851.

Yet, the influence of Christianity and Christian churches was more pervasive in the Potteries than the attendance figures indicate. As will be explored in more detail below, few escaped from exposure to religious ideas in Sunday schools. As a result, even non-church-goers went through at least one phase of active church involvement and did not necessarily cease to hold religious beliefs. Non-church-goers as well as church-goers with children sent them to Sunday school. Children at work in the painting rooms in potworks were reported as singing hymns at work. In 1842 the Children's Employment Commissioner commented that he had

[35] A. Curtis and E. Beech, *A History of the Wesley Methodist Church in Stoke-on-Trent for the years 1799–1851* (Stoke-on-Trent, 1974), 18.
[36] D. Thompson, 'The Religious Census of 1851', in R. Lawton (ed.), *The Census and Social Structure* (London, 1978), 251–2; Joyce, *Work, Society and Politics: The Culture of the Factory in Later Victorian England* (Brighton, 1980), 243–4.
[37] For attendance in Lancashire, see Joyce, *Work, Society and Politics*, 244.

TABLE 7.2 *Attendance on 30 March 1851 by Denomination: Stoke–upon–Trent Parliamentary Borough* (%)

Denomination	%
Church of England	32
Wesleyan Methodist	22
New Connexion Methodist	19
Primitive Methodist	9
Wesleyan Assoc. Methodist	4
Independents	6
Catholics	5
Other	3
(N = two-thirds of total attendances)	22,905

Source: see Table 7.1.

'often visited their rooms unexpectedly and been charmed with the melody of their voices'.[38] Furthermore, 86 per cent of all marriages in the Stoke-upon-Trent and Wolstanton registration districts in 1861 took place according to the rites of the Established Church or another Christian denomination.[39] In addition, Nonconformists, Anglicans, and Roman Catholics put great effort into providing places of worship in the Potteries throughout the nineteenth century, so that no area of the Potteries, as population increased and new areas developed, was without a church or chapel.[40] The Methodists alone increased their chapels from fifty-four to eighty-two between 1851 and 1882.[41]

The view that it was primarily those in the relatively prosperous groups that attended[42] also needs to be qualified for the Potteries. One estimate suggests that eight-tenths of the Sunday-school teachers in the Potteries in 1842 were 'of the working classes'.[43] Unlike Preston, where Anglicans (40 per cent) comprised the majority of attenders, in the Potteries Methodists were the majority of those who attended (see Table 7.2). The different varieties of Methodism offered a range of styles of worship and organization. The Wesleyans were more hierarchical, authoritarian, and 'respectable' and the Primitive Methodists more democratic,

[38] PP 1843, xiv, 216.   [39] PP 1863, xiv, 64.   [40] *VCH* viii, 277–8.
[41] IUP Population, x, 71, 'Census 1851: Religious Worship'; PP 1882, l, 336–7, 397–8.
[42] Anderson, *Family Structure*, 107–8; Thompson, 'Religious Census', 257–8.
[43] PP 1843, xiv, 223.

egalitarian, and less socially prestigious, though the differences in social backgrounds are less marked than was once thought as both groups spanned the middle-class, skilled, and semi-skilled working class. At the same time, it was equally true of all branches of Methodism that 'at its best . . . it was also a religion of family commitment, thrift and charity'.[44]

The strength of the Primitive Methodists is particularly significant. This sect originated in the moorlands to the north and east of Tunstall in the first two decades of the century. Tunstall became and remained a centre of the movement which, in the Potteries at least, retained its original working-class character.[45] Despite the move of worship from cottages to chapels and the decline of female preaching by the 1860s, this did not preclude sectarian practices and belief, much of which was rooted in the home and an attempt to reconcile rather than separate work and life and to protect domestic values and personal autonomy in work.[46]

Also, by the late 1860s in Hanley there was a population of about 2,000 Welsh, primarily colliers and ironworkers, who formed a chapel-centred community. A local newspaper report in 1877 commented

as they neither drink, nor fight nor hold much intercourse with the general population, it may be asked, how do they spend their time? The answer is that religion is the occupation, and—we were going to add—the recreation of their lives. Like all Welshmen, they are a chapel-going people. . . . The Welsh in Hanley are like the Welsh in Wales. They worship more regularly than Englishmen but they worship in chapel, not in church. There are four Welsh chapels in Hanley—a Presbyterian (i.e. Calvinistic Methodist), an Independent, a Wesleyan and a Baptist.[47]

In addition, the Irish in the Potteries, like their compatriots in Preston and the Welsh in Hanley, tended to form a close community with high church attendance. As we saw in Chapter 1, the number and homogeneity of the Irish in the Potteries aroused contemporary comment.[48] Furthermore, on census Sunday 1851 approximately 57 per cent of the Irish in the Potteries attended church.[49]

Thus, for those associated with organized religion, whether Methodists, the Welsh, or the Irish it could directly influence individuals to maintain

---

[44] D. Hempton, *Methodism and Politics in British Society 1750–1850* (London, 1987), 14.
[45] *VCH* viii, 277.
[46] D. Valenze, *Prophetic Sons and Daughters: Female Preaching and Popular Religion in Industrial England* (Princeton, NJ, 1985), 22–3, 33, 40–1, 47, 74, 274, 277.
[47] *SS* 3 Mar. 1877, 7.   [48] See above, 89.
[49] This figure is calculated on the basis that 3 per cent of the sample was born in Ireland and it assumes that all attenders at Catholic services were Irish.

family relationships both ideologically and as a community and way of life that might impose sanctions. Furthermore, these churches could serve as a focus for primary networks for working-class individuals to turn to as sources of assistance.

In addition, employers in the Potteries supported a variety of churches and chapels and some of the solidarity between employers and employees that appears in Joyce's study of Lancashire may have occurred. John Ridgway, the pillar of the New Connexion Methodists in Hanley, built a chapel with free pews with a Sunday-school room attached 'entirely for the use of his people, or any others that choose to attend'.[50] However, some employers used coercion, forcing those who would not agree to lose their jobs. 'Mr Spode compelled his men to give a weeks wages towards the rebuilding of the New Church. . . . Some of Spode's men left his employ rather than submit.'[51] Most employers appear to have left organized religious affiliation and participation to the free choice of their employees. When Spode approached Minton and urged him to compel his employees to contribute to the rebuilding, Minton 'declined exercising any compulsion and left the work people to obey their inclinations; some gave, but the majority did not'.[52] In testimony to the Children's Employment Commissioner in 1842 children from the same factory repeatedly attended different Sunday schools run by a wide variety of churches and chapels.[53] The superintendent of a painting room of women and girls at Messrs. Daniel and Sons' china works in Stoke commented that the children working in the same room with him 'are attendants at different places of worship'.[54] What seemed most important was the 'respectability' reflected in attendance at some Sunday school. Thus, in terms of organized religion, too, there appears to have been 'relative autonomy' between employers and families in the Potteries generally, as well as in Etruria, which reflected the large employers' non-sectarian attitude to the extension of factory legislation to the pottery industry in the early 1860s.

[50] PP 1843, xiv, 264.

[51] Minton MSS 277, 'Minton Notes', 8, Reminiscence on 25/3/1873 of Mr William Boulton, Minton employee.

[52] Ibid.

[53] e.g. children at Minton's and Boyle's attended the National Sunday School at Newcastle, Stoke Methodist (New) Connexion, the Ranters (Primitive Methodist), as well as many who did not specify a particular Sunday school. Children and young persons at Joseph Clementson's earthenware works in Shelton attended Bethesda (Methodist New Connexion) Sunday school and Sunday school at the Tabernacle (Independent) PP 1843, xiv, 241–9, 266.

[54] PP 1843, xiv, 256.

In addition, whether or not their membership was working class, there is evidence that churches and chapels in the Potteries contributed a substantial amount (£867 16s. 7d.) to the North Staffordshire Infirmary on 'Hospital Sunday',[55] thereby serving at least indirectly as a source of assistance. As a result of the collections, ministers could recommend individuals for admission to the Infirmary, according to Statute XLV of the Infirmary:

Collections—that the respective ministers who shall obtain and pay to this Institution congregational collections, amounting in each case to four guineas and upwards (be Governors for the year in which such payment shall be made and be entitled to vote and act as such for one year from date of payment) . . . shall, for every four guineas have the privilege of recommending one In-patient for the year, but confining their recommendations to residents in the respective parishes where such congregational collections shall have been made.[56]

The foregoing qualifies the picture of working-class non-attendance at church and chapel for the Potteries and raises the possibility of influence and assistance from organized religion for a larger proportion of the population in the Potteries than in Preston. But, as suggested above, it is through Sunday schools that religion seriously touched the lives of the majority of the working class.[57]

Sunday schools were far better attended than churches and chapels. In fact, the 'magnitude of enrollment was such that very few working class children after 1830 could have escaped at least a few years of Sunday school'.[58] The Potteries were no exception. A higher proportion of the population was enrolled in Sunday schools in the Potteries than in England and Wales.[59] Moreover, in the Wolstanton–Burslem registration district 94 per cent of the population aged 5–15 years were enrolled in a Sunday school. The comparable figure for the Stoke-upon-Trent registration district (62 per cent) is lower, but it is still higher than that for England and Wales as a whole (57 per cent). Although there were some

[55] *SS* 24 Dec. 1875, 8.

[56] 'Report of the General Annual Meeting of the Governors of the North Staffordshire Infirmary 1859–1860', in the possession of Dr Charles Webster, Director, Wellcome Unit for the History of Medicine, Oxford.

[57] Anderson does not mention Sunday schools.

[58] T. Laqueur, *Religion and Respectability: Sunday Schools and Working Class Culture* (London, 1976), 45.

[59] 13 per cent of the population of England and Wales attended Sunday school, compared with 22 per cent in Wolstanton and 15 per cent in Stoke-upon-Trent registration districts, PP 1852–3, xc, 218–19, 360.

Sunday-school scholars over the age of 15, thus lowering the proportion, it is still likely that most working-class children went to Sunday school for at least a few years in the Potteries.

The high Sunday-school attendance might be taken as an indication of a 'weakness' of the nuclear family, because one of the motives behind their establishment was the belief that the education of children could no longer remain the sole responsibility of parents. Sunday schools were necessary to perform functions that parents could not, or would not, perform. Yet, this was done partly in the hope that children in turn might 'serve as a moral advance force into the homes of their parents' and bring 'religion to their parents'. Moreover, Sunday-school teaching could cause bitter conflict within families with regard to adolescent conversion experiences or the child's attempt to impose religious observances, such as Bible reading, upon an unwilling family.[60] Nevertheless, parents were not coerced into sending children to Sunday school; instead they chose to send them, and in large numbers.[61] Although the church and chapel attendance figures show that they did not succeed in the intention that children would bring parents to chapel, Sunday schools were not meant to displace parents in the home. Instead, Sunday schools were complementary to family relationships, assisting rather than substituting. They helped children to cope with sickness and death, both through the content of the classes and through the relationship of the Sunday-school teacher and the students. It has been argued that parents sent their children to Sunday school to gain at low cost elementary education not available at home in a place that was part of the local community and the teacher was known to the parents. Sunday schools sustained a Christian culture symbolized by the Bible found in almost every working-class home. Although most Sunday schools taught reading and a small fraction, especially post-1840, taught writing, the emphasis in Sunday schools was on religious instruction, reading the scriptures, and moral regeneration.[62]

Furthermore, the teaching in Sunday schools tended to reinforce family values by condemning disrespect to parents and encouraging general values such as kindness. Moreover, in Burslem, for example, there was a sick and benefit society attached to one of the Sunday schools which

---

[60] Laqueur, *Religion and Respectability*, 15, 19, 166.   [61] Ibid. 119.

[62] Ibid. 148, 159–63, 166, 168; A. J. Field, 'Occupational Structure, Dissent, and Educational Commitment: Lancashire, 1841', in P. Uselding (ed.), *Research in Economic History: A Research Annual* 4 (1979), 263, 271, 275–6.

would both instil values of thrift and provide assistance.[63] In a Wesleyan Sunday school in Stoke there was a clothing fund to help poor scholars.[64] But, it was the Sunday-school teacher who could be an especially important source of assistance: 'the Sunday school theory is that every scholar is sure of a friend who will visit him in sickness, procure help for him in want, and to whom he may apply for advice in an emergency'.[65]

In 1842 the superintendent of Mount Zion (Methodist New Connexion) Sunday school in Stoke told the Children's Employment Commissioner that if children were absent 'they are visited at their homes by the teachers of the class to which they belong'. As there were twenty-three teachers for 128 boys in the Sunday school, or one teacher for every six boys, the teachers were likely to know the 'scholars' well.[66] Charles Shaw indicates the importance of a Sunday-school teacher in his autobiography in a particularly vivid passage[67] which Arnold Bennett used, giving further emphasis to the importance of the Sunday-school teacher, in *Clayhanger*. It is the Sunday-school superintendent, Mr Shushions, who rescues Darius Clayhanger and his family from the workhouse and literally puts the family back together. Moreover, he finds little Darius the job that is the beginning of his successful career as a printer.

The following afternoon he was forcibly reclothed in his own beautiful and beloved rags, and was pushed out of the Bastille, and there he saw his pale father and his mother, and his little sister, and another man. And his mother was on her knees in the cold autumn sunshine, and hysterically clasping the knees of the man and weeping; and the man was trying to raise her, and the man was weeping too. Darius wept. The man was Mr Shushions. Somehow, in a way that Darius comprehended not, Mr Shushions had saved them. Mr Shushions, in a beaver tall-hat and with an apron rolled round his waist under his coat, escorted them back to their house, into which some fresh furniture had been brought. And Darius knew that a situation was waiting for his father. And further, Mr Shushions, by his immense mysterious power, found a superb situation for Darius himself as a printer's devil. All this because Mr Shushions, as superintendent of a Sunday school was emotionally interested in the queer harsh boy who had there picked up the art of writing so quickly.[68]

[63] Laqueur, *Religion and Respectability*, 169, 172–5, 201, 214.

[64] Curtis and Beech, *Wesley Methodist Church*, 16.

[65] *Sunday School Teachers' Handbook* (1848), quoted in Laqueur, *Religion and Respectability*, 18.

[66] PP 1843, xiv, 275.

[67] C. Shaw, *When I Was A Child* (1st pub. London, 1903; repr. Firle, Sussex, 1977), 138–40.

[68] A. Bennett, *Clayhanger* (1st edn. London, 1910; Penguin edn., Harmondsworth, 1973), 45–6.

Friendly Societies

In the Potteries in the mid-nineteenth century, as in other areas of the country, friendly societies were important working-class organizations. Some were associated with religious denominations, others with individual workplaces, others with industrial groups, and others included members from a variety of occupational and industrial groups in the area; most were restricted to men, but there were two women's friendly societies and one which included both men and women members.

Friendly societies provided social life, as well as insurance against the costs of illness, accidents, death, and burials.[69] On a Monday evening in November 1860 in Hanley, for example,

the 'Good Samaritan Lodge' of the United Order of Free Gardeners, kept up their anniversary . . . at the Lamb Inn, Hanley. Supper was served up in Mr and Mrs Meigh's admirable style. The usual loyal and other toasts were duly honoured, the evening was spent very agreeably, interspersed with singing, music and dancing.[70]

During the same evening the members of St Andrew's Lodge of the Independent Order of Odd Fellows, Manchester Unity celebrated their twenty-fifth anniversary with a dinner, toasts, and entertainments. 'On the removal of the cloth . . . a number of toasts and sentiments were proposed and duly honoured, interspersed with songs, recitations etc.'[71] The same evening in Burslem the members and friends of the 'Court Victoria' of the Ancient Order of Foresters attended their annual dinner in the Court Room of the Town Hall. After 'a very excellent dinner prepared by Mrs Holmes of the Hop Poles' and four short addresses, 'the remainder of a very pleasant evening was spent in listening to the music of Mr Stubb's band and several songs and recitations'.[72]

Despite the dancing at the Good Samaritan Lodge's dinner, the social life of these societies tended to be for men, or in the case of the two small women's friendly societies, women only, and not for nuclear families. 'Social cohesion grew out of aspects of working class tradition that had survived the growing concern for the home.'[73] But, if the social occasions did not involve all nuclear family members, the benefits did. They were aimed at the support of the nuclear family, 'to make men better husbands

---

[69] P. Gosden, *Self-Help: Voluntary Associations in Nineteenth Century Britain* (London, 1973), viii, 2, 39–142; G. Crossick, *An Artisan Elite in Victorian Society* (London, 1978), 174–98.

[70] *SS* 17 Nov. 1860.   [71] Ibid.   [72] Ibid.

[73] Crossick, *Artisan Elite*, 192.

and fathers'.[74] In the Potteries in 1870, for example, the proposed Miner's Permanent Relief Society was criticized on the grounds that 'unmarried men with no families are not very eager to subscribe to a fund to leave a sum of £20 to their friends'.[75]

The important question is not whether or not they brought formal or informal sanctions on members with regard to family obligations; instead, membership in friendly societies should be seen as an expression of concern for family obligations. In this way these societies were not only substitutes or 'structured alternatives' to family assistance,[76] but also complementary, supportive, and reinforcing to family relationships. Nevertheless, it should be remembered that through friendly societies concern for obligations to one's nuclear family existed in a context of 'mutual support and collective strength without competitive exhortations of the individual' which distinguishes working-class from middle-class individualistic self-help.[77]

In the Potteries in the mid-nineteenth century there were societies which provided benefits in case of illness, accidents, death, burial, or a combination of these eventualities. What was the nature of these societies and how extensive was their membership?

Burial societies had the largest number of members. They paid a sum on the death of the member which was used to cover the cost of burial and thereby avoid a pauper burial. There were two large burial societies in the Potteries. The oldest was the Tunstall Benevolent Burial Society, established in 1839. By 1872 it had 17,545 members who contributed one half pence a week and who would receive benefits up to £5 10s. The investigator for the Royal Commission on Friendly Societies commented on the low cost of management, and he mentioned that 'the fewness of the lapses in this society is something remarkable and indeed unparalleled'. The cost of management was only 17 per cent of annual income, compared with about 30 per cent in large collecting societies. In 1869 less than 1.3 per cent of the members withdrew; in 1870 0.6 per cent withdrew; and in 1871 only 0.2 per cent of the members withdrew. Thus, the investigator pointed out that 'the society furnishes a striking refutation to the claims of the large Liverpool collecting societies that high salaries for collectors were necessary because of the extent of lapses by the contributors'.[78] The

---

[74] Quoted ibid. 193.   [75] PP 1874, xxii, pt. 2, 363.

[76] Anderson, *Family Structure*, 107.

[77] G. Crossick, 'The Labour Aristocracy and its Values: A Study of Mid-Victorian Kentish London', *Vict. Studies* 19 (1975–6), 322, 324, 326.

[78] PP 1874, xxiii, pt. 2, 365.

second burial society in the Potteries was the Burslem Mutual Burial Society established in 1841. It had nearly twice as many members as that in Tunstall (i.e. 33,762 members) in March 1872. The contribution for children under two years of age was 1*d*. a week for the first year and for those over two years the cost was 1*d*. a week for the first twenty-six weeks. For all others the contribution was a half pence a week collected fortnightly. The benefits ranged up to £6 at death.

The weekly contributions to friendly societies were higher than those to burial societies, but for the substantial minority of workers who could afford to, and chose to, joining friendly societies did provide some insurance against the costs of sickness, accident, and death, as well as burial. At a minimum they provided the member with a weekly allowance when sick and a funeral payment for his widow. They varied in quality, reliability, size of contribution, size of benefit, and criteria for membership, but the core of the movement formed around two types of registered societies: (1) the local courts or lodges of the national or regional affiliated orders; and (2) probably most important in the Potteries, the local societies with single branches or branches only within the Potteries and no external links.

There were lodges or courts of a number of national or regional affiliated orders in the Potteries in the early 1870s. In 1872 in the six towns of the parliamentary borough there were ten courts of the Ancient Order of Foresters with a total of 1,377 members; five lodges of the Manchester Unity of Odd Fellows with 567 members; three lodges of the Grand United Order of Odd Fellows with 107 members; five lodges of the Loyal Order of Shepherds with 328 members; and one lodge each of the Order of Druids and of the Free Gardeners.

In the Potteries, as Crossick found in Kentish London , local societies predominated in the 1840s and 1850s, giving way slowly to the affiliated orders. In the ten years between 1862 and 1872 the district secretaries of both the Grand United Order of Odd Fellows and of the Manchester Unity of Odd Fellows remarked that twenty years ago there were nearly a score of isolated societies in Burslem, but they had almost all died out. Nevertheless, there were still a number of local friendly societies and sick clubs in the six towns of the parliamentary borough in 1872. Moreover, a comparison between 1862 and 1872 shows that the affiliated orders grew, but in addition to, and not at the expense of, local societies. There were twenty registered societies, the largest of which was the North Staffordshire Provident Association, founded in 1847. By 1872 it had a total of 1,188 members in the six towns. It was, however, unusual, and the investigator for the Royal Commission on Friendly Societies singled it out for special notice. Not only did it have a graduated scale of payments and avoided meeting in public houses, but 'the peculiarity about this society is that sick pay is continued on the full scale throughout the sickness, no matter how long'.[79] The members were chiefly working potters, but also 'there is a fair average of other trades'.[80] The rest of the registered societies were sick clubs with benefits usually limited to one year. They had fewer members (about 20 to 150). Some of these had graduated scales for payments and some were dividing societies. There were two dividend societies in the Potteries, which operated on the principle of keeping a fundamental stock and only dividing the surplus beyond that. The New Friendly Dividend Society in Stoke, for example, had 104 members in 1872. They admitted no members past 30 years of age and the contributions were a uniform 1s. 10d. every four weeks and 1s. a year to the permanent fund, but they had no surplus to divide the previous year. The other dividend society, the Lily of the Valley Friendly Society, was also in Stoke. It had seceded from the Manchester Unity, and had 143 members and an average dividend of 14s. a year. Other societies did not divide the surplus and offered benefits of different sizes. The Wesleyan Mutual Provident Sick Society in Tunstall founded in 1847, for example, had 120 members in 1872. It admitted both men and women from the age of sixteen. They had graduated tables of contributions and benefits, but most members subscribed enough to obtain 10s. a week if sick. In contrast, the Stoke Commercial Friendly Society founded in 1828 had no graduated scale of contributions and the benefits were 7s. a week for six months and then 4s., with no man allowed to draw more than 52 weeks at 7s. in the whole of his life.

As well as conditions about the age of members, there were other criteria for membership in some societies. Some of the registered societies, such as the Catholic Brotherly Friendly Society in Cobridge and the Wesleyan Mutual Provident, restricted membership to those of the same religion. Apart from the two female friendly societies which had only women members and the Wesleyan Mutual Provident which had both men and women members, the societies were restricted to men only. Finally, however, apart from the North Staffordshire Railway Friendly Society with 900 members from among the porters, guards, fitters, signalmen, clerks, and engine-drivers, and the Miners' Permanent Relief Fund, most of the registered societies did not restrict membership to one trade.

---

[79] Ibid. 359.   [80] PP 1872, xxvi, 585.

There were, however, a large number of unregistered sick and burial clubs organized around the individual potteries, foundries, and mines. Although there are no membership figures for these societies, there is evidence that their membership was extensive.

> In the greater number of the workshops of the Potteries there are shop clubs, called there bank clubs; working at the bank being a local expression for a potter's work. They divide once a year, generally at Martinmas. They are managed by the men themselves, and there is no compulsion about joining them, though the men as a rule do so. . . . The Contribution was 3*d*. a week and 1*s*. entrance, payments fortnightly, a new hand comes into immediate benefit, and men are taken in at any age. The benefits are 6*s*. a week for 13 weeks, then half pay; for funerals there is a levy of 1*s*. a member. Sometimes the master subscribes to the club.[81]

Foundries had shop clubs and 'there are commonly pit clubs in North Staffordshire at the different collieries called ground clubs, which divide once a year. They are managed by the men in North Staffordshire, not as in South Staffordshire, where they are under the control of the masters'.[82] One ground club, for example, required a payment of 4*d*. a week for both sickness and accident benefits, 'but so much is there found to be in excess of what is required that at last year's end . . . a sum equivalent to 2*d*. a week was returned to the members, leaving 2*d*. a week as the net weekly payment.

The importance of sickness benefits and control by the men is illustrated by the resistance to the North Staffordshire Coal and Ironstone Workers Permanent Relief Society when it was founded in 1870. Initiated largely through the efforts of Sir Lovelace Stamer, the Rector of the Parish of Stoke-upon-Trent, it was copied chiefly from the Northumberland and Durham Coal Field Society. It grew out of a surplus from the subscriptions for the relief of the sufferers from a catastrophic explosion in 1866 at a Talk-o'-th'-Hill pit, in order to 'render these extraordinary appeals unnecessary'. But the society ran into considerable opposition, in part because the men suspected that the society was 'formed in the interest of the masters, who will then be relieved from their proper liabilities on the occurrence of accidents to the men in their employ'. Moreover, the contribution of 2*d*. a week was thought to be excessive for the benefits, which applied only to accidents in the mines and not to sickness.[83] Although the society had 803 members in 1872, at the tenth

---

[81] PP 1874, xxiii, pt. 2, 361.   [82] Ibid.   [83] PP 1874, xxiii, pt. 2, 363.

annual meeting in 1880 Sir Lovelace Stamer still commented that 'it had been a great surprise and regret to him that it was not taken up with the heartiness and warmth it deserved, and which had attended similar societies in other parts of the country'.[84] By the end of 1879 the number of members had more than doubled to 1,979. Nevertheless, they were 'almost entirely to be found in the north of the district, but the society had as yet made little progress in the collieries in the neighbourhood of Longton'. Still, he thought that 'its universal acceptance by the miners of North Staffordshire was only a question of time'.[85]

The absence of membership figures for the extensive but unregistered bank clubs, shop clubs, and ground clubs make it difficult to estimate the extent of friendly and burial society membership in the Potteries. The Consul for the United States based in the Potteries in the early 1880s reported that many of the working people in the district could 'by the aid of clubs and similar small insurances, save enough to tide over temporary misfortunes, such as sickness, loss of employment, etc., and for funeral expenses'.[86] Each of the three budgets of 'representative workmen and their families' which he gives includes a weekly subscription for the sick or burial club.[87] More quantitatively, the Registrar of Friendly Societies' annual returns can give a minimum estimate. The returns for two years, 1862 and 1872, in the Potteries suggest that in each year 16 per cent of the adult male population (i.e. men aged 20 and over) were members of registered friendly societies.[88] Even if this is less than the 23 per cent of occupied males aged 20 and over in Kentish London, it would be comparable with similar denominators. But this figure is certainly an underestimate of the extent of membership. A number of registered societies in the Potteries did not report their number of members and some societies did not send in returns every year. Most importantly, the membership of the unregistered societies in workplaces was extensive. Thus, despite the relatively low membership in registered societies, the probable extent of unregistered societies in the Potteries means that membership in some form of friendly society reached at least the level of 35–40 per cent of occupied males which Crossick found in Kentish London, and it must have approached the 50 per cent of adult males in Lancashire, the highest in the country. In the parliamentary borough of Stoke-upon-Trent 41 per cent of the population were members of a burial society in 1872 and 46 per cent of the population were members

---

[84] *SS* 3 Apr. 1880, 6.   [85] Ibid.

[86] Lane, 'Tunstall', 824.   [87] Ibid. 828–9.

[88] Calculated from membership figures in PP 1863, xxix, 562–8; PP 1873, lxi, 137–44.

of either a friendly society or a burial society. The figure again approaches that for Lancashire.

Moreover, there is evidence that the membership of friendly societies was drawn from the major occupational groups in the Potteries. The North Staffordshire district of the Ancient Order of Foresters had 2,060 members of which 1,083, or 53 per cent, were potters and glass-workers, 369, or 18 per cent, were miners, and there were 85 labourers and 65 brick-makers.[89] In addition, there is the evidence cited above that the 1,183 members of the North Staffordshire Provident Association were mainly potters, but also included members of other trades. Thus, the registered friendly societies, as well as the bank clubs, shop clubs, and ground clubs, were made up of working people in the major occupational groups.

To sum up then, membership in friendly and burial societies was extensive among working people in the major occupational groups in the Potteries in the mid-nineteenth century. Undoubtedly, for some individuals these societies provided an alternative to family relationships, but far more generally they provided benefits intended to assist family members with the costs of the member's burial, temporary illness, accident or, in one society, permanent illness.

The North Staffordshire Infirmary: 'A Gigantic Sick Club'

Appeals for support for the North Staffordshire Infirmary presented it as an institution that provided assistance which was complementary to, rather than a substitute for, that of families and other forms of mutual help in the Potteries. If, for example, the main income-earner in a family became ill and was cared for in the Infirmary, any savings or assistance from a benefit society would need to support only the family; it would not have to stretch to support the patient as well. The author of an article in the local newspaper described the Infirmary's role as follows

that the ills to which flesh is heir press with unusual severity upon the working classes no one will attempt to dispute. The benefit societies, dispensaries, and similar institutions for their mutual help in times of sickness which the more prudent section of the working classes have established, do much towards mitigating this severity. But there comes a time when the assistance afforded by the benefit society and the relief of the dispensary do not altogether meet the requirements of the case. The careful attention and nursing are needed which can rarely be obtained in even the more well-to-do-homes of the working classes.

[89] PP 1874, xxiii, pt. 2, 360.

Then it is that the merits and value of such an institution as the North Staffordshire Infirmary come to be recognised. Supposing the afflicted one to be the breadwinner of the family, the pittance allowed from the funds of the benefit society goes but a little way towards providing for the wants of a wife and family, to say nothing of procuring those extra comforts needed in times of sickness. The little hoard of money scraped together by years of honest toil is resorted to, and grim poverty stares in upon the little household. But a refuge is provided for the sufferer. The Infirmary opens its hospitable doors, the invalid's family manage to struggle along while he is being nursed and cared for without any cost to them, and ultimately, it may be he is restored to his family and to society, and the former are saved from the Workhouse.[90]

From its opening in 1819 the North Staffordshire Infirmary was housed in a two-storey building in Etruria not far from the Wedgwood works and directly across from the site of Earl Granville's ironworks and coal-mines. By 1855 with the noise, fumes, and smoke of the expanding ironworks and coal-mines and the increasing danger from subsidence 'from being one of the best it has become one of the worst situations in the district . . . all desirable prospect is gone; a foul bad atmosphere has succeeded and only noise, vapour and smoke remain for the music and solace of the inmates'.[91] Infirmary doctors pressed for a new building, and eventually, after a public appeal and considerable controversy over the site and ceremony over the laying of the foundation stone, the new building on Hartshill was opened in 1869.[92]

In the 1860s the Infirmary included an operating theatre, 117 beds for in-patients in men's and women's wards, fever wards, and a burns ward, as well as an out-patient wing. The staff was headed by a small number of unpaid honorary physicians and surgeons who had lucrative private practices, mostly in Newcastle. They were elected for life and the position enabled them to rub shoulders with wealthy trustees and patrons. They attended one day a week at the Infirmary and gave instructions to the paid house physicians and surgeons who saw to the day-to-day care of the patients.

During the 1850s the Infirmary had an average of 1,000 in-patients and between 4,000 and 5,000 out-patients per year (see Fig. 7.1). Although this is a large number in absolute terms, it is relatively small

[90] *SS* 24 Dec. 1875, 8.

[91] P. Anderton and W. E. Townley, *Doctors and Hospitals in the Region of the Potteries in the Mid-19th Century: A Selection of Documentary Evidence with a Commentary* (Madeley College of Education, Madeley, 1968).

[92] R. Hordley, *A Concise History of the North Staffordshire Infirmary and Eye Hospital from 1802-1902* (Newcastle, 1902), 17-32.

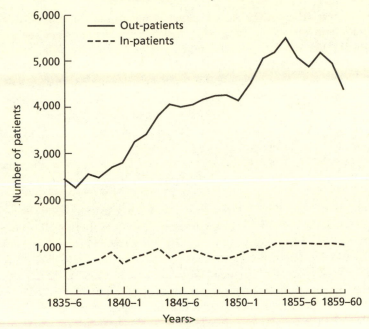

FIG. 7.1   Number of In-Patients and Out-Patients in the North Staffordshire
Infirmary 1835–1860

Source: Annual Reports of the North Staffordshire Infirmary 1836–1860

when it is compared with the population of the parliamentary borough (over 100,000 by 1861), which comprised only part of the potential population to be served.

The Infirmary kept the number of in-patients down partially by re-strictions on the types of ailments treated. The Infirmary provided as-sistance for individuals suffering from certain diseases, fevers, or accidents, but there were significant exceptions to the types of cases admitted. According to the General Laws of the Infirmary, admission as an in-patient was denied to women in an advanced stage of pregnancy, luna-tics, persons suffering from smallpox or Asiatic cholera, and those who were deemed incurable. Not only do the exceptions indicate the limita-tions of the Infirmary, but also the way in which they were handled probably served as an additional deterrent. In many cases where patients in such categories were inadvertently admitted to the Infirmary, the secretary of the Infirmary would send to the relieving officer of the Stoke-upon-Trent Poor Law Union to have the patients removed from the Infirmary to the workhouse hospital 'although they have never been paupers and no matter from what parish or by whom sent into the hospital'. The practice caused conflict with the Poor Law guardians in 1861, but it appears to have continued.[93]

The number of patients was also limited by the fact that both admission as an in-patient and treatment as an out-patient required that those treated either be subscribers or have a recommendation from a subscriber 'setting forth that, in the opinion of the subscriber who furnished it, I was "a proper object of charity" '.[94] An annual subscription of two guineas entitled the subscriber to recommend one out-patient at a time and one in-patient in the course of a year, and the scale continued from there.

The term 'subscriber', however, is misleading to the extent that it implies that the Infirmary was supported by the relatively large donations of individuals. Instead, it was financed by a combination of philanthropy and self-help. The majority of finance came not from individual 'subscribers' but from 'establishment subscriptions'. In 1859–60 32 per cent of the income of the Infirmary came from 'subscriptions' while 50 per cent came from 'establishment subscriptions'. These were subscriptions made up of the deductions of wages from workmen in a firm; when ill a workman acquired a recommendation for the Infirmary from the owner, manager, or foreman of the firm. One of the physicians described the Infirmary in 1864 as 'a gigantic sick club'.

It should be remembered that by the plan of 'establishment subscriptions', levied as a tax among the work-people, the Infirmary represents a gigantic sick club, and therefore the results arrived at respecting the physical condition of the artisans of the district, are of wider application than they would be in an Infirmary supported wholly by voluntary contributions, and therefore resorted to by the very poor only.[95]

There were seventy-one 'establishment subscribers' in 1859–60. They included pottery firms such as W. Adams and Sons (£42), William Brownfield (£65 10s.), W. T. Copeland (£83 15s. 5d.), W. Davenport (£51 8s. 11d.), J. Dimmock and Co. (£36 17s.1d.), Minton and Co. (£175 14s. 6d.), E. J. Ridgway (£42 18s. 6d.), and a very small subscription from J. Wedgwood and Sons (£8 9s. 5d.). They also included collieries such as Berry Hill Colliery, Oldfield Colliery, Stirrup & Pye Adderley Green Colliery; and ironworks such as the Ravensdale Forges, Cliffe Vale

---

[93] PRO. MH12/11465, 2 May 1861; 20 June 1861.   [94] *SS* 24 Dec. 1874.
[95] *Hansard*, 14 June 1864, 1723, Dr J. T. Arlidge to H. R. Grenfell, MP, 17 Feb. 1864.

Ironworks, and Stanier & Heath. The largest subscriber was the Shelton Colliery and Ironworks (£292 7s.) and the Shelton Bar Iron Works (£124 9s. 4d.). The carters at Etruria Wharf and the Locomotive and Carriage Department of the North Staffordshire Railway also had 'establishment subscriptions'.

One of the house physicians used statistics from the Infirmary and his own experience to discuss the extent of respiratory disease among potters and miners.[96] Thus, despite the relatively small numbers treated in the Infirmary compared with the total population of the area, the Infirmary did provide some assistance to potters, ironworkers, and miners for some of their most prevalent and severe ailments. For example, the medical report to the annual general meeting of the Infirmary commented on the increased number of 'cases of lung disease, mainly represented by chronic bronchitis, potter's consumption, and tubercular phthisis and involving long residence in the wards', and on the increase in serious fractures.[97]

Civic Subscriptions

In periods of acute unemployment and 'distress' relief funds were raised from subscriptions. Such funds provided a minimum of temporary assistance, usually soup and bread, to the desperate who could obtain a ticket. It is unclear precisely how extensive this practice was in the Potteries during the period, but such funds were organized in Hanley in the winters of 1847–8 and 1861–2.

In the winter of 1847–8 it was estimated that for several months at least half the workpeople of Hanley and Shelton were entirely out of employment and the remaining half were not employed for more than three days a week on average. In February and March 1848 relief was distributed 'to the distressed poor from a fund raised by subscription for that purpose'. But, by the end of March the fund was exhausted and although an attempt was made to renew it 'the distress pervades all classes, and what with the inability of those who would be willing and the backwardness of a few who might afford to subscribe, the utmost exertion will not avail to continue the relief more than two or three weeks longer'.[98] With the extensive distress and sensing the threat of insurrection, a meeting of the subscribers to the relief fund urged the Poor Law Guardians of Stoke-upon-Trent to provide outdoor relief.

[96] See above, 88–9, 226 n.53, 236–7.   [97] *SS* 23 Nov. 1872, 3.
[98] PRO. MH12/11462/9365, 30 Mar. 1848.

In the present most critical state of public feeling with sedition secretly but extensively instilled into the minds of the lower classes, and preparations being cautiously but certainly organized in these very townships to break out into insurrection so soon as circumstances seem to promise a successful result, it becomes a question of most immense importance how the present urgent distress may be best and speedily met. And it is our decided conviction that nothing can effect this so well and so properly as by granting outdoor relief from the parochial funds to those whose wants are caused only, and we trust temporarily, by the cessation of work. . . . Unless some immediate steps be taken to ameliorate the condition of the Parishioners the power of self-government will be weakened, the suffering ratepayers will be driven to the brink of desperation and the public peace alarmingly jeopardized.[99]

In the winters of 1860–1 and 1861–2 there were relief funds organized in Hanley. Relief was in kind—coals, soup, bread, and sometimes meat and clothing. Persons requiring relief were to make personal application to the relief committee and each case would be investigated by an officer appointed for that purpose. The clergy also distributed tickets. On one day during the first week of operation in January 1861, the Committee relieved 278 persons and families with '300 lbs. of bread and 400 qts. of soup. The bread to be provided by Mr George Ridgway and the Mayor'.[100] The number relieved eventually rose to 380 and the Committee continued into March, raising a total of £330.

One correspondent to the local paper presented a view of the objectives of such 'private' relief. It was not intended for the 'undeserving'. Instead, one of its objects was to keep families together, albeit those of the 'steady working man'.

By 'undeserving' I mean, of course, those not requiring relief. I do not mean those who through drunkenness or other vicious habits have impoverished themselves and their families—in the hour of need, we must not inquire into the causes but look at the facts as we find them, and who knows whether the very act of kindness may not be the means of reclaiming the poor creatures.

A few words as to selecting objects for relief and I have done. Everyone's heart must ache to enter the back streets and see there the scenes of want and destitution—the house without furniture, the grate without fire, the inmates without food or clothing. But to my mind these are not the cases for relief in these times. . . . The Poor Law should provide for these, and so it will if they go into the workhouse, and who would strive to keep them from such comparative comfort? They have no house to break up, and the mere feeling which exists

---

[99] Ibid: Special Meeting of the Ratepayers of Stoke-upon-Trent Union.
[100] HBRL. S/830: Hanley Relief Committee Minutes, 21.

against going into a workhouse ought not to be indulged; but for the steady workingman, suffering only from a temporary depression of trade, the workhouse is to be avoided. He can get no out-relief, and to go in he must sell his little furniture and break up his home; and when trade revives, he has the 'battle of life' to begin again, whereas a little help in the hour of need, and he would have got through.[101]

Employers

Employers were a source of direct assistance to employees in extraordinary circumstances. During the smallpox epidemic in Longton in 1871, for example, one pottery manufacturer commented that 'most of the manufacturers of the town had contributed to the support of workpeople who were suffering from smallpox; and he had not allowed a man of his who was suffering from the disease to go without his wages'.[102] In 1877 after a boiler explosion at the Ravensdale Ironworks belonging to Messrs. R. Heath and Sons killed ten men and injured twenty-three, the firm found coffins and paid the burial fees of those killed who were not members of a provident club at the works. The firm also made 'liberal provision for the necessities of widows and orphans. The sufferers have had all the medical assistance available, and nothing has been left undone that could be done to alleviate the pain and distress occasioned by the calamity'.[103] There is evidence that as a matter of course, Wedgwoods allowed workmen to draw on their wages in advance, in effect providing short-term loans.[104] At Minton's a workman remembered one of the masters would anonymously give assistance to workmen: 'He used often to take bottles of wine and other things as well as money to my father to take to different sick people, but always told him that he was never to let people know it came from him.'[105] But, in general, the pottery manufacturers, iron-masters, and coal-masters provided assistance, if at all, via institutions i.e. subscriptions or donations to relief committees and rates.

Trade Unions

It is unlikely that trade unions among potters, miners, or ironworkers in the Potteries in the mid-nineteenth century exerted formal or informal pressure on members to maintain family obligations. The actions of the unions, however, did incorporate the assumption that members had families

[101] *SS* 30 Nov. 1861. [102] *SS* 24 June 1871.
[103] *SS* 30 June 1877, 6. [104] See above, Ch. 4, p. 193.
[105] Minton MSS 277, 'Minton Notes', 2–4, Reminiscences on 28/7/1873 of Mr William Walker, Minton employee.

which were important to them. Arguments to raise wages or against cuts in wages, for example, were occasionally made in terms of the effects on the ability of the members to provide for their families.[106] Moreover, there is evidence that the large National Union of Operative Potters did not affiliate with Robert Owen's Grand National Trade Union in the early 1830s, in part because of opposition to his views on family life, marriage, and divorce.[107] Furthermore, union occasions could involve all nuclear-family members. Arriving at the North Staffordshire miners' gala in Hanley in April 1872, 'wives and children and sweethearts trooped along with the men, while bands of music did all that bands can do to raise inspiration amidst most gloomy adverses of the weather'.[108]

Unions of pottery-workers, miners, and ironworkers in the Potteries, however, were a source of assistance to members in a variety of ways in the mid-nineteenth century.

Pottery Workers. Unions among pottery workers were organized by the branches of the trade, even in the few years of the existence of industry-wide unions during the period.[109] The slip-makers, flat-pressers, hollow-ware pressers, mould-makers, printers and transferers, and engravers, for example, had their separate organizations with lodges in each of the towns, and these branch organizations remained after 1850 when the industry-wide organization dissolved, and they continued after another industry-wide organization emerged in 1883 as the National Order of Potters. Unions in the pottery industry had insurance schemes associated with them. In 1864 the Hollow-ware Pressers' Union subscription included 1*d.* per week for the provident fund which provided unemployment pay, and the union had plans to associate itself with a burial society.[110] The Ovenmen, Kilnmen and Sagger-Makers' Burial Society,

---

[106] H. Owen, *The Staffordshire Potter* (1st pub. London, 1901; repr. Bath, 1970), 322, 325, 331–2; e.g. the evidence of John Goodwin, potter's printer, before the Board of Arbitration, 1880, 'our wages are insufficient to meet our rents, rates, firing, insurance for sickness and death, religious and social charities, clothing for ourselves and families and twenty-one meals per week for parents and children', 328.

[107] F. Burchill and R. Ross, *A History of the Potters' Union*, (Hanley, 1977), 60–1.

[108] *SS* 6 Apr. 1872.

[109] See Owen, *Staffs. Potter*, 20, 48–9, 112; J. C. Wedgwood, *Staffordshire Pottery and its History* (London, 1913), 197–205; W. H. Warburton, *The History of Trade Union Organization in the North Staffordshire Potteries* (London, 1931), esp. 111–12, 168–76; and Burchill and Ross, *Potters' Union*, for accounts of the changes in union organization, size, and activities in the mid-nineteenth century. For one branch, the hollow-ware pressers, see Anderton, 'A Trade Union Year: 1864', 9–32.

[110] P. Anderton, 'A Trade Union Year: 1864—An Extract from the Transactions of the Executive Committee for the Hollow-ware Pressers' Union', *Journal of Ceramic History*, 9 (1977), 18–24, 26, 32.

inaugurated in 1864, had 1,200 members at the outset.[111] Apart from the Staffordshire Potteries Operative Flat Pressers' Society, which had a sick fund in 1871, unions in the pottery industry tended to leave the provision of sickness benefits to friendly societies or to bank clubs organized separately in each firm, rather than by branch. In general, in an industry prone to wage disputes, the unions concentrated on their primary function of negotiating wages and conditions of work. In 1864 the hollowware pressers, for example, attempted to impose a set of what they believed were appropriate piece-rates on one employer at a time, thereby concentrating union strength on a limited front and minimizing hardship among workers in the short run. The union also undertook a campaign against annual hiring agreements in which they supported men who gave one month's notice which under prevailing law left them liable to prosecution.[112] In this process the unions provided assistance to members in a variety of ways.

The potters created a remarkably strong union, the National Union of Operative Potters, in the early 1830s. 'The National Union of Operative Potters . . . was said in 1833 to have a membership of 8,000, probably a larger percentage of the workers eligible than any subsequent union before 1914.[113] In 1834–5 over 3,000 potters employed by ten large manufacturers in Tunstall and Burslem who refused to continue to pay union rates went on strike for fifteen weeks and won, largely due to financial support from the union subscriptions of those at work in the other Potteries towns. In 1836, during a combined strike and lockout lasting twenty weeks over the issues of 'good from the oven' and 'annual hiring', members were assisted with strike pay from both their own union and from workers' organizations in other areas, particularly Sheffield, which sent two-fifths of the £5,800 total sent for the union members. The assistance, however, was not enough to save potters from substantial losses; moreover, the Sheffield unions expected the potters' union to win and eventually to pay back the funds. However, the union broke up after the strike, and between 1837 and 1843 there was no general union of potters.[114]

In 1843 the United Branches of Operative Potters (UBOP) was established. Its founder William Evans advocated emigration as a solution to

---

[111] Ibid. 32.   [112] Ibid. 14, 27.

[113] R. H. Tawney, 'Introduction', in Warburton, *Trade Union Organization*, 12.

[114] R. Fyson, 'Unionism, Class and Community in the 1830s: Aspects of the National Union of Operative Potters', in J. Rule (ed.), *British Trade Unionism 1750–1850: The Formative Years* (London, 1988), 213–16; Burchill and Ross, *Potters' Union*, 65–74, 95.

unemployment in the pottery industry. Therefore, the union was associated closely with the Hanley Operative Potters' Emigration Society, a registered friendly society which Evans established in 1844. It was 'the first example of organized emigration linked to trade union objectives'.[115] The purpose of the society was to buy land and 'to locate on this land the families of British operative potters'.[116] The society succeeded in purchasing land in Pottersville, Wisconsin, and it assisted a handful of families to emigrate. But by 1850 the emigration society and the attempt to amalgamate the unions of the branches of the trade into one union had collapsed. After 1850 branch unions, a strong chamber of commerce, and vigorous efforts to introduce arbitration into disputes supplanted the UBOP and the emigration society. The extent of union membership after the strike of 1836 is not clear. The most prevalent view is that

10 per cent of the total operative class, in union, appears to have been in later years the high-water mark of pottery trades unionism. . . . Excluding female workers and males under eighteen years, as being unavailable for trades union membership, it would appear that only about one in four of the 'effective' male operatives have been members of their unions, even in the palmiest days of unionism during the last half century. Indeed, the potters have never had, since the Union of 1836, an organisation of such strength and completeness.[117]

Moreover, the return of the trade unions registered in the early 1870s lists numerous branch unions in the industry but few members.[118] Nevertheless, M. D. Hollins, a partner in Mintons, President of the Chamber of Commerce and an advocate of the new board of arbitration, indicated that a majority of working potters belonged to twelve or fourteen branch unions. These branch unions could co-operate with each other despite the absence of an over-arching union organization. Hollins testified to the Royal Commission on Trades Unions that, while it was completely up to the men how they selected their ten representatives on the board of arbitration, he was sure that their representatives would come from the unions.

[115] Burchill and Ross, *Potters' Union*, 85.
[116] Ibid. 86.   [117] Owen, *Staffs. Potter*, 334–5.
[118] These include: Printers' and Transferers' Amalgamated Trades Protection Society; United Kingdom Slipmakers' Trade Association; Staffordshire Potteries Trade Protection Society of the Engravers to China and Earthenware Manufactures; Staffordshire Potteries Operative Flat Pressers' Society; and Mould Makers' Trade Union. The slip-makers' society was reported to have 'broken up'; the printers' and transferers' society had the most members, at 850: PP 1875, xlii, 371–5.

I firmly believe, in fact I know, that the majority of the workpeople in the Staffordshire Potteries are connected with the union, and therefore it would be absurd to say that these men did not come with the cognizance of the unions of the different branches. There is a union in the Staffordshire Potteries for every branch of the trade, and it is no doubt through those unions that the representatives of each branch will be sent. . . . And has each branch its own separate union?—Yes.[119]

Thus, potters' unions existed in the mid-nineteenth century, and like other craft unions, they concentrated primarily on negotiations over wages and working conditions.[120] Some gave unemployment pay and burial society benefits, and the flat-pressers' society in 1871 provided sickness benefits. Moreover, in 1834–5 and 1836 the union provided members with assistance during the long strike and lockout, and in the 1840s the union assisted a handful of potters to emigrate.

Coal and Ironstone Miners. Before the formation of the North Staffordshire Miners' Association in 1870, industrial action was organized separately from sickness, accident, and death benefits in each colliery. Although there is conflicting evidence about their prevalence, it is clear that the range of methods of providing welfare benefits stretched from making a collection on Saturday night when a man had been injured, through ground clubs, to 'establishment subscriptions' to the North Staffordshire Infirmary.

The way in which they raise money in the north of the county is by the men giving their 6*d.* or 3*d.* or what they like, on a Saturday night, when a man has been injured. They do not pay anything if there is not a man ill. Is there not generally a colliery club?—No, very seldom. When John So-and-so is injured, it is told them, and one puts down his 6d and another puts down 3d and so on.[121]

They are generally supported in case of illness of accident, by field or ground clubs, or by other clubs in which there is always a provision for medical attendance; or where there is no such provision, they contribute to the North Staffordshire Infirmary.[122]

The North Staffordshire Infirmary [is] mainly supported by subscriptions from the workpeople; the colliers and miners are subscribers; the men pay 2*d.* a week,

---

[119] PP 1867–8, xxxix, 538–9.

[120] C. G. Hanson, 'Craft Unions, Welfare Benefits, and the Case for Trade Union Law Reform 1867–1875', *Econ. Hist. Rev.* 28 (1975), 245, 257.

[121] PP 1857, Sess. 2, xi, 710, Evidence of T. Wynne, Inspector of Mines for N. Staffs, 25 June 1857.

[122] PP 1857, Sess. 2, xi, 762, Evidence of R. Heath, Coal and Ironmaster, 2 July 1857.

and the boys under 15 pay 1*d*. a week; and that subscription entitles them, as a matter of right, to the infirmary, as in-patients or out-patients as the nature of the case may require . . . establishment subscriptions . . . also entitle them to similar assistance for their wives, children and stepchildren, under 14 years of age.[123]

Occasionally, these benefits were used in combination with assistance from the Poor Law guardians. Ironstone miners, for example, had field clubs which provided 6*s*. or 7*s*. a week to an injured man. If an injured miner who had a wife and young children and received money from his field club also applied to the guardians, they would consider that the man was himself provided for by the field club, but they would take the whole responsibility of supporting his wife and family.[124] The funds of field or ground clubs, however, were not used to assist miners during strikes or lockouts, according to a speaker at a miners' demonstration in Hanley in 1861, who urged the miners to form a union with lodges in each colliery on the model of the miners' union in Barnsley.

The one [proposed union] brought before them was certainly superior to any that had been tried in Staffordshire, in as much as it provided for accident as well as turnouts. . . . He made some remarks about the ground clubs, observing that the members did not know the state of the finances, not even the committee. Such clubs could make presents of £50 to some persons; they could give their £25 toward testimonials, but, men on strike, they could not receive a farthing benefit from them.[125]

Before the formation of the North Staffordshire District of the Amalgamated Association of Miners in late 1869, strikes and lockouts usually involved only one colliery at a time. Assistance during strikes and lockouts came from colliers in other collieries in the district, since a reduction in wages in one colliery could be the test-case for a similar reduction in collieries throughout North Staffordshire. Assistance also came from local inhabitants including potters. In the summer of 1842, for example, it was a strike of colliers working for W. H. Sparrow at Longton protesting against wage-cuts, followed by wage-cuts at Earl Granville's collieries a month later, that led to the formation of a central Committee of Operative Colliers, forcing turnouts in other collieries and the closing of potteries for lack of fuel and forming the prolonged industrial struggle

---

[123] PP 1857, Sess. 2, xi, 752, F. Wragge, manager of Lord Granville's collieries, ironstone mines and blast furnaces in N. Staffs.

[124] PP 1857, Sess. 2, xi, 725, Evidence of G. Baker, Chairman of Wolstanton-Burslem Board of Guardians, 30 June 1857.

[125] *SS* 22 June 1861.

preceding the Chartist riots in the Potteries in August 1842. The striking miners 'held a series of marches and meetings and sought moral and financial support from those still at work'.[126] At the same time the potters appeared content to have to stop work 'so that the rise asked by the colliers might be gained'.[127] In 1851, although the effects were not as widespread as in 1842, the 500 colliers at Earl Granville's pits struck because they received lower wages than other miners in the district and, unlike others, they had to pay for their own tools and the gunpowder necessary for their work. They were 'wholly dependent for support on the sympathy of the inhabitants of the surrounding towns, as there is no colliers' union in existence . . . Colliers employed at neighbouring pits and journeymen potters . . . have come forward to assist their brethren in toil by their subscriptions'.[128]

In 1861 the miners in Kidsgrove had been out on strike for nine weeks against a reduction in wages and during this period contributions from men in other collieries supported those on strike.

Kidsgrove had been made the leading place of the district. Various collieries around were working on this condition, that if the colliers at Kidsgrove have to submit to the reduction the other colliers would submit also. During the nine weeks during which the Kidsgrove men had been on strike, they had nobly supported them.[129]

During the strike of the Kidsgrove colliers, there was a demonstration of 6,000 miners in Hanley, 'the main object in view appearing to be the ultimate formation of a trades union to enable them to maintain a stand against any future attempts on the part of the masters to reduce their wages, as well as to improve their financial position generally'.[130] In addition, 'a collection [was] made to pay the expenses of the day, the surplus being devoted to the Kidsgrove turnouts' fund'.[131]

Thus, although there could be a high degree of organization among colliers in the North Staffordshire coalfield, as there was in 1842, there

[126] R. Fyson, 'The Crisis of 1842: Chartism, the Colliers' Strike and the Outbreak in the Potteries', in J. Epstein and D. Thompson (eds.), *The Chartist Experience: Studies in Working-Class Radicalism and Culture, 1830–1860* (London and Basingstoke, 1982), 197–200, 211.
[127] *N. Staffs. Merc.* 23 July 1842 quoted in Fyson, 'Crisis of 1842', 198.
[128] *Lever*, 1851, 277.   [129] *SS* 22 June 1861.   [130] Ibid.
[131] Ibid. Also, in 1865 there was a turnout of the men employed at the Pinnox Colliery, Tunstall and the men were 'well supported in their contest, both by their fellow workmen in the district and by the inhabitants generally of Tunstall and the neighbourhood; they consequently have been enabled, for some time past, to divide at the rate of 9s. per week per man, besides a weekly distribution of bread': *SS* 30 Dec. 1865.

was no permanent trade union. Until 1869 and the formation of the union and a separate organization, the permanent relief fund, assistance came from contributions to *ad hoc* relief funds for industrial action and for major disasters such as the explosion at Talk-o'-th'-Hill in 1866, which killed 99 men, from ground clubs at the individual pits and from subscriptions to the North Staffordshire Infirmary.[132]

The miners of North Staffordshire established a district of the Amalgamated Association of Miners at the end of 1869. At their gala in 1872 Thomas Halliday, president of the Amalgamated Union of Miners commented that

somewhere about three years ago they had not a union among them. Those who had worked and founded unions in other parts of the country had said that it was impossible to get a union in North Staffordshire, but through their own efforts and those of Mr Brown they were now second to no district in the Amalgamated Union of Miners.[133]

By May 1874 there were 9,000 financial members of the union in the North Staffordshire District. Although the basic function of the union was to negotiate about wages and conditions of work,[134] the union had a benevolent fund, providing assistance for widows and orphans and for men injured in accidents.

In 1873 the agent of the North Staffordshire Miners' Association told the Select Committee on Coal that

we have a widows' fund and an accident fund. Are these supported entirely by the men?—Yes. Do not the masters contribute anything?—As far as I am aware they do not contribute anything. How much do you pay for benevolent objects? —About four and one half pence per week; but it is optional to men whether they join or not. Is it a pro rata payment or is it a fixed payment?—It is a fixed payment of four and one half pence.[135]

---

[132] For a survey revealing the extensiveness of miners' self-help institutions throughout the country, see J. Benson, *British Coalminers in the Nineteenth Century: A Social History* (Dublin, 1980), ch. 7.

[133] *SS* 6 Apr. 1872.

[134] For a discussion of the distinction between friendly-society and trade-union functions, and evidence that the emphasis of unions was on their trade-union functions rather than friendly-society functions, see C. G. Hanson, 'Craft Unions, Welfare Benefits and the Case for Trade Union Law Reform 1867–1875', *Econ. Hist. Rev.* 28 (1975), 245. J. Benson, 'English Coalminers' Trade Union Accident Funds 1850–1900', *Econ. Hist. Rev.* 28 (1975), 410 also argues that 'unions never considered the provision of relief to be their major concern'.

[135] *SS* 31 May 1873, Report of the evidence of W. Brown, agent of the North Staffs. Miners' Association to the Select Committee on Coal.

Moreover, the benefit scheme was seen as a way of strengthening union organization. In May 1874 a demonstration of the Association resolved that

the time has arrived when all workmen in connection with the Amalgamated Association of Miners (N. Staffs. District) should become members of the Widows' and Orphans' Fund as by so doing it would become the means of strengthening the constitution of the said branch of the Association; and further it would secure its permanency and would add comfort to the fatherless and the widows.[136]

Of the 9,000 members of the union in May 1874, over 3,000 paid into the union's Widows' and Orphans' Fund. In addition, it appears that a number of lodges had sick funds which were probably the former ground clubs. They 'established sick funds in connection with the widow and orphans funds'.[137] In 1874 twenty-seven widows and over forty fatherless children were receiving support from the association.

Competing with the union's widows' and orphans' fund was the North Staffordshire Coal and Ironstone Workers' Permanent Relief Society.[138] Established in 1869, it had grown out of the relief committee and fund raised after the explosion at Talke in 1866. Although it was based on the Durham Miners' Permanent Relief Fund, which was one of the first permanent relief funds for accidents in the country, it had an uneasy relationship with the miners' union in North Staffordshire. In 1872 the chairman of the Relief Society remarked that

he was happy to say that the leaders of the Miners' Union had (indirectly, if not directly) approved of the society, that the opposition to the society which had been expressed had now been withdrawn, and that in some cases former opponents had become present advocates of the society's objects.[139]

Nevertheless, because of the use of benefit schemes to strengthen union organization, the union retained its own schemes. Moreover, the fixed payment of four and one half pence a week to the union's Widows' and Orphans' Fund was more attractive, though probably less actuarially sound,[140] than 2s. a week to the Permanent Relief Society. The number of members of the Permanent Relief Society hovered between 1,000 and 2,000 only reaching 2,000 in 1879. By 1877 twenty-four widows and fifty-two children were receiving relief from the Permanent Relief Society.

---

[136] Benson, 'Accident Funds', 406.   [137] *SS* 9 May 1874.
[138] Benson, 'Accident Funds', 403 implies that this society was associated with the union; but it was not.
[139] *SS* 6 Apr. 1872.   [140] Benson, 'Accident Funds', 407–9.

Ironworkers. The ironworkers in North Staffordshire had no separate union or branch of a union in 1865. Almost all of the puddlers, however, belonged to either the Brierley Hill (South Staffordshire) puddlers' union or to the Gateshead union. Some of the millmen were members of another union, but the majority (probably 75 per cent) of the iron-workers were underhands and labourers who were not in a union.[141] During a twenty-week strike in 1865 the puddlers employed at iron-works in North Staffordshire received a substantial amount of assistance from ironworkers in other parts of the country and from workmen in organizations in other trades.[142]

On the basis of a fall in the price of iron in June 1864, iron-masters in South Staffordshire, North Staffordshire, and North Yorkshire gave notice of a reduction in wages in December 1864. With the exception of the puddlers in North Staffordshire, the National Association of Iron-workers accepted the reduction. In an attempt to force the masters to withdraw the reduction in North Staffordshire, thereby providing a pre-cedent for other areas, the Ironworkers' Association supplied enough funds for the North Staffordshire Council to distribute sums varying from 6*s.* to 10*s.* per week to Union members on strike in North Stafford-shire. The masters retaliated in mid-March with a lockout in Stafford-shire and the North of England. The lockout stopped work for the non-union ironworkers as well as the union members already out on strike, and the tactic eventually broke the strike. Yet, before it ended the London Trades Council and Manchester trade unions had sent funds and plans were underway for emigration schemes to the United States and to Queensland, Australia. The assistance from other areas was tem-porary, and it only went to union members, but it was substantial.

Summary. Although funds were limited, often temporary, and did not prevent severe losses, fellow working men were an important source of direct assistance during major strikes for potters, miners, and iron-workers. In addition, the welfare benefits offered by the Amalgamated Association of Miners after its establishment in North Staffordshire in 1870, as well as the flat-pressers' benefit society and the potters' emigra-tion scheme should not be ignored, even though trade unions among potters, miners, and ironworkers in the Potteries in the mid-nineteenth century, as elsewhere, concentrated on their primary objective of nego-tiations over wages and conditions of work.

---

[141] PP 1867–8, xxxix, 112, Evidence of W. S. Roden to the Royal Commission on Trades Unions, 29 Nov. 1867.
[142] *SS* 21 Jan. 1865, 30 Dec. 1865. PP 1867–8, xxxix, 112–17. A. Birch, *The Economic History of the British Iron and Steel Industry 1784–1879* (London, 1967), 274.

The Poor Law

In the Potteries the Poor Law encouraged the maintenance of certain family relationships and obligations both by the sticks of legal sanctions and the deterrent effect of the policy of separation of family members in the workhouse, and by the carrot of out-relief. The Poor Law also provided a variety of types and amounts of assistance to different groups for varying periods of time. In some cases this assistance complemented family assistance, while in others it was a substitute for the inability of other family members to assist or the absence altogether of other family members. A focus of struggle for control between trade unions and manufacturers and tradesmen in the mid-1830s, the Poor Law guardians subsequently reached an accommodation between the humanitarian tendency and self-interest of the larger employers and the interests of smaller ratepayers, which while welcoming the central Poor Law authorities, also resisted certain policies and tempered the effects of the 'campaign against out-relief' in the 1870s.

Family Responsibilities: Legal Definitions, Policy Assumptions and Practice. The Poor Law placed on individuals the duty of maintaining parents, grandparents, children, and grandchildren.[143] Soon after the Parish of Stoke-upon-Trent came under the Poor Law Amendment Act at the end of March 1836, the Clerk to the Board of Guardians wrote to the Commissioners in London pointing out that the duty of children to support aged parents would be enforced. 'There is also another class of persons who having ample means would, rather than support their aged parents suffer them to become paupers, upon the Parish, but this is no longer permitted'.[144] Moreover, relieving officers brought cases of neglect before the magistrates in an attempt to enforce the laws. In January 1865, for example, John and William Barlow, brick-makers, were summoned for refusing to contribute to the support of their aged mother 'in consequence of which she became chargeable to the parish [of Stoke-upon-Trent]'.[145] As a result, an order was made for John Barlow to contribute 4s. per week to the union for his mother's maintenance. Similarly, in July 1865 Joseph Yates, a turner, was brought up on the charge of neglecting to support his wife and children 'hereby they had become chargeable to the Burslem and Wolstanton parish'.[146]

Nevertheless, the accounts of the Stoke-upon-Trent Poor Law Union indicate that relatives of paupers contributed relatively little. Out of a

---

[143] Anderson, *Family Structure*, 106–7; Crowther, 'Family Responsibility', 132–3.
[144] PRO. MH12/11458, 9 Nov. 1836.
[145] *SS* 21 Jan. 1865. [146] *SS* 22 July 1865.

total income of £10,672 in the half-year ending on Lady Day 1861, for example, only £18 17s. 2d. was received from 'Relatives of Paupers'.[147] The union received a similar amount in the six months ending at Michaelmas 1858.[148] As part of the 'campaign against out-relief' in the 1870s, however, the amount substantially increased. In 1876, £485 6s. was received from relatives in repayment of relief granted by the Stoke-upon-Trent Board of Guardians.[149] Yet, where a relative might have been able to pay, there were difficulties both with tracing relatives and with defining by statute the circumstances in which a given person should be expected to pay which limited the ability of the law to reinforce family obligations.[150] Furthermore, in some cases the relative was unable to pay. In the case of John and William Barlow mentioned above, for example, the relieving officer 'did not press for an order against William Barlow as he was a man in poor circumstances'. In any event, the Poor Law did make explicit the expectation that individuals would support close relatives, and it was important in extreme cases in enforcing the obligation.

The Poor Law guardians also attempted to reinforce nuclear family obligations and relationships positively by giving outdoor relief to the families of the sick and widows with children. For example, a member of the Stoke Board of Guardians in 1872 commented that it was the Board's policy to give outdoor relief to families in the case of sickness 'there having been a disposition not to break up the homes of families so circumscribed by requiring the parties to go into the workhouse'.[151] At a meeting of representatives of guardians in Staffordshire the chairman of the Stoke Board of Guardians led the successful opposition against the Local Government Board's suggestion that able-bodied widows with one or more children should not receive out-relief unless the children above one were sent to the workhouse, saying that 'the best possible place in which to bring children up was with their parents'.[152]

Administrative Structure and Expenditure. Two Poor Law unions covered the six Potteries towns in the mid-nineteenth century: Hanley, Stoke-upon-Trent, Fenton, and Longton were part of the Stoke-upon-Trent Union formed in 1836; Tunstall and Burslem became part of the new Wolstanton–Burslem Union formed in 1838.[153]

In 1836 the Stoke-upon-Trent Union was the first manufacturing

[147] PRO. MH12/11465.   [148] PRO. MH12/11464.
[149] *SS* 7 Apr. 1877, 7.   [150] Anderson, *Family Structure*, 107.
[151] *SS* 26 Oct. 1872, 6.   [152] *SS* 3 Feb. 1872, 6.
[153] The boundaries of the unions coincided with those of the registration districts of the same names, see Map. I.2.

area to be placed under a board of guardians according to the Poor Law Amendment Act,[154] and it will put the subsequent period into perspective to give a brief summary of the background to this early adoption. From 1816 the same area had been under the control of a select vestry. In 1832–3 the vestry erected a new workhouse, the Spittals; also, in 1832–3 the overseers' expenditure reached over £8,000 on out-relief and over £1,200 on workhouse relief. In an attempt to meet this expenditure there were five rates levied in one year. The following year a policy of retrenchment and administrative reorganization reduced the total amount spent on poor relief by nearly one-third. A salaried assistant overseer was given the power to appoint annually and pay the governor of the workhouse and the six collectors, subject to the supervision of the overseers and the select vestry.[155] The select vestry, however, was also elected annually. By 1835 its composition and policy had changed so that the salaried assistant overseer complained of the reversal of policy, and he attempted to thwart the new policy.[156] Furthermore, two of the officers were convicted of embezzlement, the cashier absconded, and 30 per cent of the rates collected were lost. Moreover, the potters' union (NUOP) declared its intention to take over the administration of relief and use rates to support industrial action. In the end it became impossible for the vestry to make decisions. In December 1835 a public meeting passed a resolution asking the Poor Law Commission to send an assistant commissioner to investigate. Both middle-class manufacturers, such as John Ridgway, and working-class ratepayers agreed. Rather than campaign against the principles of the 1834 Act the union strategy was to gain control of the new Board. The assistant commissioner arrived in the Potteries in March 1836 and by the end of the month the Stoke-upon-Trent Union had adopted the new Act.[157] The union urged the assistant commissioner to recommend a £6 qualification for membership of the board of guardians so that working-class guardians could be elected. Giving the impression that he agreed with this view, the assistant commissioner instead recommended a £20 qualification. The subsequent election resulted in the return of only one guardian reliably sympathetic to the union. The union's failure to take control of the board of guardians meant that when

---

[154] *VCH*, viii, 199.   [155] Ibid. 198–9.

[156] PRO. MH12/11458: Letter from G. T. Taylor, Assist. Overseer to W. T. Copeland, MP, 17 Oct. 1835.

[157] PP 1836, xxix, pt. 1, 401–3, Report of the Assistant Commissioner sent to investigate the affairs of the parish of Stoke-upon-Trent as a result of the resolution passed at the public meeting in Nov. 1835. See also, PRO. MH12/11458, 17 Oct. 1835; 25 Nov. 1835, and 10 Dec. 1835.

TABLE 7.3 *Poor Relief 1861: Stoke-upon-Trent Union, Wolstanton–Burslem Union, and England and Wales*

	Stoke[a]	Wolstanton[a]	Eng. & Wales[b]
Total Expenditure on Relief 1861–2	£8,688	£7,911	£5,779,000
Expenditure per Head of Pop. 1861	3s.	3s. 9d.	5s. 9d.
Paupers per 1000 pop. (inc. insane and vagrants)	51	56	43
% of outdoor paupers in the total no.	86	90	86

Sources:
[a] PP 1861, liii, 123–4, 160–1, 222–3, 284–5, 350–1.
[b] *Abst. of Brit. Hist. Stats.* 9, 410.

its funds were exhausted in the long strike of 1836–7 strikers could not receive relief from the guardians and the strike was defeated.[158]

By 1861–2 total expenditure on poor relief in the Stoke-upon-Trent Union was only slightly above the £8,000 which was spent on out-relief alone in 1832–3 (see Table 7.3). Expenditure per head of population in both the Stoke-upon-Trent Union and the Wolstanton–Burslem Union was below that of England and Wales, even though a higher proportion of the population in each of the two Unions was in receipt of relief than in England and Wales. Thus, in the Potteries more individuals were in receipt of relief in 1861–2, but less was spent on relief than in the country as a whole. These figures alone tell us little about the relationship between families and the Poor Law as a source of assistance in the nineteenth-century Potteries. Therefore, it is necessary to investigate the various forms of relief in more detail.

Forms of Relief: Indoor. The two unions in the Potteries were well provided with workhouse space for indoor relief. The select vestry of the Parish of Stoke-upon-Trent built the Spittals workhouse in 1832–3, and with the advent of the union in 1836, the building was altered to meet the requirements of the Poor Law commissioners. Its capacity was increased to 500 persons and by 1855 to 800 persons.[159] With the formation of the new Wolstanton–Burslem Union in 1838–9, a new workhouse

[158] Fyson, 'Unionism', 210–12.
[159] *VCH*, viii, 199–200; PRO. MH12/11463/449/5.

accommodating 400 persons was built at Chell near Tunstall; by 1861 it could hold 700.[160]

The well-known distaste for the workhouse was evident in the Potteries as in other areas of Britain in the mid-nineteenth century.[161] The author of a newspaper article about the Spittals Workhouse reflected the view, writing that 'amongst the lower classes of North Staffordshire the Workhouse is known as the "Bastille"—a circumstance not a little indicative of the light in which this institution is regarded by the class from which its inmates are mainly received'.[162] Moreover, out of thirty-two unemployed persons who received orders for admission to the workhouse when their applications for relief were brought before the Stoke-upon-Trent guardians on 14 June 1861, only twelve (or 38 per cent) 'availed themselves of the offer'.[163] Finally, Charles Shaw in his autobiography, *When I Was a Child*, provides a vivid picture of life in the workhouse at Chell in 1842. He, too, refers to it as the 'Bastille', and he describes how his family walked to the workhouse by a roundabout route in order to avoid notice. Amongst other things, he comments on the pain of the separation from his family, the harsh discipline, the cruelty of the other boys, and humiliation due to his workhouse clothes when he attended Sunday school the first Sunday after leaving the workhouse.

I had not yet the consciousness that the workhouse clothes and my having been to the workhouse had made such a difference. But I found out during the afternoon. No cry of leper, in the old days of Israel, could have put people more apart than I was apart from my old schoolfellows. In the afternoon they had become bolder. My clothes were pointed at, I was laughed at, jeered at, and I saw that I was clothed with contempt in their eyes . . . I knew now I was not as other children.[164]

Thus, it is probable that in the Potteries, as in Lancashire,[165] the workhouse was seen by most inhabitants as a refuge of last resort.

In many cases, however, the workhouse became a refuge, not because relatives were unwilling, but because they were unable, to provide assistance. In 1861, for example, Maria Leigh, an unmarried servant who was pregnant, applied to go into the workhouse for her confinement. Her father lived in Stoke, and although he was willing to keep her, he was

---

[160] *VCH*, viii, 130; PRO. MH12/11465, 9 Oct. 1861.

[161] Anderson, *Family Structure*, 137–8; for a judicious history of the workhouse within the Poor Law system which considers both officials and inmates, see M. A. Crowther, *The Workhouse System 1834–1929* (London, 1981; pbk, 1983).

[162] *SS* 24 Dec. 1875.   [163] PRO. MH12/11465.

[164] Shaw, *When I Was a Child*, 136–7.   [165] Anderson, *Family Structure*, 137–8.

unable because he was himself in receipt of relief from the guardians. Maria Leigh testified that

I asked my Father if he had told Mr Tilsley [relieving officer] he had a home for me. He said no, he did not object to take me but he had not the means to keep me. I then went to Stoke and . . . was admitted into Stoke workhouse and am now in the hospital.[166]

Forms of Relief: Outdoor. The workhouse was not the only form of relief under the Poor Law: the great majority of those in receipt of relief received outdoor relief.[167] In 1861–2 in the Stoke-upon-Trent Union 86 per cent of those in receipt of relief received out-relief; in the Wolstanton–Burslem Union the figure was 90 per cent (see Table 7.3, above). Out-relief took the form of a small sum of money (1 or 2 shillings) or income in kind (usually loaves of bread) or both. In the Stoke-upon-Trent Union out-relief was granted normally for reasons such as 'death of husband', 'sickness', 'deserted by husband', 'aged and infirm', 'wife's sickness', and 'old age'. Occasionally, it was granted to able-bodied men 'out of employ'.[168]

In some cases out-relief, unlike the workhouse, was seen not as a last resort to be considered only after assistance from family members was exhausted. Instead, out-relief was preferred. Instead of a constraint, recipients used it to construct their own line of action. The mother of John, William, and Ralph Beech, for example, preferred to receive out-relief of 1s. and a loaf weekly from the Wolstanton–Burslem Union rather than to reside with any of her sons. William was a brewer and the owner of several houses; John was a printer and beer-seller; and Ralph was a joiner earning 30s. per week. Each of them could afford to keep his mother, and each expressed willingness to pay the amount if she would live with one of them. But she refused their offer of a home, preferring relief from the union. The magistrates regretted that the case should have been brought before them, 'it might well have been arranged'. But they had no alternative, and they ordered the three sons to pay an amount each week towards her support.[169] Thus, the mother, whether deliberately or not, seems to have used the Poor Law to force her sons to support her

---

[166] PRO. MH12/11465: Deposition of Maria Leigh.

[167] D. Fraser, 'Introduction', in D. Fraser (ed.), *The New Poor Law in the Nineteenth Century* (London, 1976), 17–19.

[168] PRO. MH12/11465: From the list of applications for relief brought before the Guardians of the Stoke-upon-Trent Union at their meeting on Wednesday, 14 June 1861, see Table 8.2, below.

[169] *SS* 6 Apr. 1872.

without her having to reside with one of them. No matter what her motivation, however, the important point here is that resort to the Poor Law was not a last resort: she preferred out-relief to residence with a family member. Also, little stigma appeared to be attached to the receipt of outdoor relief in the case of sickness. In Longton, recipients spoke of it as 'my bit of pay' or 'my parish allowance' and claimed it as a matter of course after they had been ill for a week or so. One guardian charged that people regarded such relief from the parish as a 'pension', 'a sort of insurance society or sick club assistance'.[170]

Out-relief was intended to be a last resort before the workhouse for those entitled to it.[171] It was the relieving officer's job to ensure that an applicant had no other sources of assistance; and, it is probable that many applicants did see recourse to out-relief as a last resort. James Taylor, for example, was a cup-maker aged 33 living in High Street, Hanley with his wife and three children aged 4 to 8 and-a-half. He applied for out-relief under the Labour Test Order in February 1855, and the relieving officer reported that he 'pays rental of 2/– per week. Only worked one and a half days last month and cannot say when they are to begin again. He has no income from any source'.[172]

Whether or not out-relief was seen as, or in fact was, a last resort, it should not be considered a mutually exclusive alternative to family relationships as a source of assistance. Instead, resort to assistance from family members and from out-relief were closely related and they could exist simultaneously. Enoch Barker, aged 26, an ovenman living in Shelton, for example, had a wife and two children age 4 and 14 months. In February 1855 he applied for out-relief under the Labour Test Order, and the relieving officer noted that he 'lodges with father-in-law'. Titus Baddeley also applied for out-relief at the same time, and he and his

---

[170] *SS* 26 Oct. 1872, 6.

[171] PP 1837, xxxi, 198–9, 23 Nov. 1836: Letter from the Poor Law Commissioners to the Board of Guardians of the Parish of Stoke-upon-Trent: 'The law only provides parochial relief for those who are actually *destitute*, having no other resource than the parish. In every case of application, therefore, before granting any relief, the Guardians should be first assured that the applicant is in a destitute condition and has no other or adequate means of support than the parish. . . . In deciding as to the manner in which the relief should be afforded, and upon what terms, the Guardians should be governed by the following considerations: for all able-bodied applicants, relief in the workhouse is most in accordance with the spirit and provisions of the Poor Law Amendment Act; and the Commissioners consider, therefore, that no able applicant should receive out-relief so long as there remains room in the workhouse. Next to relief in the workhouse, out-relief in *kind* is best; and therefore, when the workhouse is full, at least three-fourths of the relief to the able-bodied should be given in kind.'

[172] PRO. MH12/11463/4834En/55.

family are described as 'lodges with his father Enoch Baddeley lately'. Not only did assistance from family members overlap with assistance from out-relief, but for persons in all categories of need normally entitled to out-relief, such relief was given on the assumption that it would be used in the nuclear family. Moreover, out-relief was seen as a way of preserving families. In 1841, 1848, 1855, and 1861–2 the guardians of the Stoke-upon-Trent Union urged the central Poor Law authorities to allow them to give out-relief to able-bodied men who were 'out of employ' through no fault of their own, but because of the lack of orders for pottery, particularly from the American market.

In March 1841 the present and past guardians of the Stoke-upon-Trent Union petitioned the House of Commons against the House's intended renewal of the 'vast powers of the Poor Law Commissioners for a period so long as ten years'. The petitioners approved of the principle of uniformity of administration, but they asked the House of Commons to allow a larger measure of discretion to the guardians in the application of outdoor relief:

experience as a Board of Guardians has shown your petitioners the necessity of the law being accommodated to the peculiar circumstances of Manufacturing Districts before it can attain the confidence and approbation of the people.

That the inhabitants of this Parish being chiefly employed in the manufacture of china and earthenware, a large part of which is exported have of late years suffered from fluctuations of trade which have subjected a considerable portion of the working class to great privations.

That in these seasons of distress we have found the Poor Law Amendment Act too severe in requiring such persons to pass through the test of going into the Workhouse. Many families having suffered the last extremity of wretchedness, rather than submit to such alternative and their objections being such as merit a most careful and kind consideration as will appear from the following facts. Families of this class are at such times in arrears of rent if they consent to go into the workhouse the landlord takes possession of the remains of their bedding and furniture and rents the house to others. They are then paupered for life and sink degraded into hopeless indifference to the future. In many cases the elder children are employed in manufactories and contribute in part to the subsistence of the family; if the parents are taken into the workhouse with their infant children the working boys and girls are deprived of parental protection, and of home. They are thrown upon the temptations of the world . . . If they are taken with their parents to the workhouse the burdens of the Parish are increased and they are prevented from learning a trade. Your petitioners [who] have therefore found themselves unable to enforce the strict provisions of the Amendment Act without injury both to the ratepayers and to the poor . . . want the House of Commons to allow a larger measure of discretion to the Guardians in the application of out-door relief, and that widows, orphans and working men suffering from a temporary stagnation of trade may be relieved from the rigours of the workhouse test.[173]

In late October of the same year the Board of Guardians petitioned the Poor Law Commission with resolutions asking to be able to continue to exercise their discretion and give outdoor relief to the able-bodied who were out of work.

Many industrious persons suffering from the temporary want of employment would have to give up their houses, sell their furniture, withdraw their children from their situations and be thoroughly pauperized whereas on the plan now adopted the parent has work found him at the workhouse and food with something to take home [,] when necessary the children keep their places and the family is kept in a state to embrace the first opportunity of getting employment and providing for themselves. That this Board has confined itself to giving outdoor relief to these and other special cases, such as sick, infirm and very old persons, the whole forming the exception to the general rule. And the Board is of the opinion that it has exercised a sound discretion in what it has done; and that while the plan it has adopted has given satisfaction to the poor, it has been equally for the advantage of the ratepayers.[174]

The Poor Law Commission was reluctant to allow the Board to give out-relief. The assistant commissioner sent to investigate argued that the guardians of the Burslem–Wolstanton Union were not giving out-relief to the able-bodied. Moreover, he pointed out the contrast between the petition and the guardians' position in 1836.

When this parish was first placed under a Board of Guardians . . . there was a strike amongst certain classes of workmen and a disposition to get into their control the poor rate to be used for the support of the strike. Amongst the manufacturers most to be injuriously affected by this were the Messrs. Ridgways and they were found to be the warmest supporters . . . and the most strenuous advocates for the strictest application of a workhouse principle. The state of things in Stoke has of late been changing. Instead of workmen wishing to quit the work by a strike and the masters anxious to retain them, the masters are anxious to reduce the number of their hands and the men are anxious to be continued in work. Hopes are entertained that the trade will revive and it is therefore desired that the workmen may not be so dismissed as not to be had when wanted but they might be kept in the parish ready for use when there shall be a demand for them. The depression in the trade is attributed to the state of the money market in America and none suffer from this more than the Messrs. Ridgway who have

---

[173] PRO. MH12/11459, 6 Mar. 1841: 'Petition to the House of Commons'.
[174] PRO. MH12/11459, 21 Oct. 1841: 'Petition to the Poor Law Commission'.

several manufactories, more, it is said than their capital is equal to; and the chief, if not the whole of whose trade is dependent upon America. Mr Ridgway is one of the Guardians and now the principal advocate and supporter of the outdoor relief system alluded to.[175]

Throughout November the guardians passed more resolutions in favour of outdoor relief and, despite the opposition of the Commissioners, they continued to give outdoor relief to the able-bodied. The Commission relented as long as the guardians submitted to them, for their sanction, a list of all the able-bodied who received outdoor relief.

During the twelve months preceding December 1847 the pottery trade was seriously depressed, and the guardians again requested the Poor Law Commission to suspend the Prohibitory Order so they could grant outdoor relief to the able-bodied.[176] In March 1848 a meeting of workpeople presented a memorial to the guardians requesting them to obtain land 'to employ the destitute poor upon', and they repeated this request in another memorial in May 1849. Lord Granville's ironworks were expected to close down partially, throwing many out of employ, and the guardians were 'continuing the Labour Test but the difficulty will be at what labour to employ them and how to raise money to meet the expenditure'.[177] On the resolution a Poor Law Commissioner commented that 'what the ratepayers ask is a matter wholly beyond the authority of those who have to administer the Poor Law . . . the commissioner absolutely prohibits doing what is asked'.[178] Distress became particularly acute in May.[179] Civic subscriptions 'have been entered into and a Bazaar is getting up in hopes of alleviating the distress'.[180] By July 1849 trade had revived and there were only two able-bodied recipients of out-relief in the Parish.[181]

Again in January and February 1855 trade was depressed and the guardians were determined to provide outdoor relief. They went so far as to warn the Poor Law Board that they felt 'so strongly the necessity of adopting the course that should the Poor Law Board decline to extend the outdoor Labour Test, this meeting cannot conscientiously carry out the Order of the Poor Law Board and they will feel it their duty to resign their offices of Guardians of the poor'.[182] The same view existed in Burslem where an official of the Poor Law Board went to the district and recommended sanctioning relief as long as work was done for it.

---

[175] PRO. MH12/11459, 22 Oct. 1841: W. J. Gilbert to the Poor Law Commission.
[176] PRO. MH12/11462/22629B/49.   [177] PRO. MH12/11462/9253/48.
[178] PRO. MH12/11462, 31 Mar. 1848.   [179] PRO. MH12/11462/12934/48.
[180] PRO. MH12/11462/14093/48.   [181] PRO. MH12/11462/21511/49.
[182] PRO. MH12/11463/5514En/55.

Again in November 1857 trade was depressed and the clerk of the guardians wrote to the Poor Law Board saying that the guardians considered the Board's order prohibiting out-relief to the able-bodied 'very harsh and arbitrary toward parties who are able and willing to work'. The Poor Law Board refused to suspend the prohibiting order because circumstances were not sufficiently bad, i.e. there were only 185 persons in the workhouse which could hold over 800. But the Board was willing to consider individual cases.[183]

In mid-February 1860 the chairman of the guardians wrote asking the Poor Law Board to allow the local board of guardians some discretion in distributing relief. The trade of the district was unusually good, but one firm, Messrs. Adams, suspended their works from 18 January. They employed about 500 hands. 'A great number of their workmen are in a destitute condition and are applying to our Board for relief'. The chairman urged the Poor Law Board to relax the rule that relief could only be granted to the able-bodied in the shape of an 'order for the workhouse', thus breaking up 'the homes of many an industrious man'. The local board of guardians devised specific plans for the operation of the Labour Test Order and the Poor Law Board approved such relief to able-bodied male paupers outside of the workhouse.[184] By the end of the first week of March most had obtained other employment.

At the time Mr Adams and Sons became bankrupt, their men were suddenly thrown out of employment. A day or two afterwards 109 men with their wives and families applied for and obtained relief (outdoor). When, however the outdoor labour test was brought to bear, and the 109 were allowed to go and work and take home provision for their families, only 45 went, and many of them worked only one day, showing that the majority could (when put under the outdoor labour test) obtain employment; but had the proper and best of all tests been applied there would not have been anything like the number accepted.[185]

In June 1861 the American Civil War depressed trade and the guardians again applied to the Poor Law Board for a suspension of the prohibiting order.[186] The Inspector who investigated found a great deal of distress particularly in Hanley, which depended on American orders. But he felt the distress was 'not so bad as I have known it upon former occasions. It is certainly not so bad as to make it advisable to suspend the prohibiting order'.[187] In the end he recommended that the Poor Law Board first urge the guardians to offer the workhouse, but then allow the guardians to

---

[183] PRO. MH12/11464/39039/57.   [184] PRO. MH12/11465, 11 Feb. 1860.
[185] PRO. MH12/11465, 15 June 1861: Relieving Officer Higgins's comments made to Inspector Doyle and Doyle's notes on a list of those receiving out-relief.
[186] PRO. 11465, 12 June 1861.   [187] PRO. MH12/11465, 15 June 1861.

implement the outdoor Labour Test Order. By September trade had become gradually worse. The guardians received a letter from a Mr Pankhurst, a Hanley pottery manufacturer dependent upon the American market. He wrote that he had not had work for his men for three months. 'I have in the past three months found them a little but the average is not more than 5/- a week and now I am obliged to stop altogether'. He went on to ask if anything could be done for them by the Parish in the form of outdoor relief until the trade revived. 'It is with very much regret and sorrow that I feel obliged to ask this for them—but necessity owns no law'.[188]

The Stoke guardians wanted not only to be able to apply the Labour Test Order, but also to give relief directly to the able-bodied. In October they approached the Burslem–Wolstanton Union suggesting that the two unions make a joint request to the Poor Law Board to relax the prohibiting order. The Burslem–Wolstanton guardians refused, saying that

Burslem was in as bad or perhaps even a worse state than Stoke and the difficulties of administrating the Poor Law were as great. Many painful cases had come before them; but exercising their judgment both in the interest of the poor and the ratepayers, they considered that the poorest of the population requiring parochial aid would be demoralized by putting aside the indoor labour test and that an unfair burden would be cast upon those who contributed toward the rates.[189]

By January 1862 there were seventy-seven cases of able-bodied men, most of whom had wives and families, to whom the guardians granted relief under the provisions of the outdoor Labour Test Order. In the next week there were eighty-three. The number rose to a high of 106 in the week ending 15 February, and it gradually declined until there were only eight cases in the week ending 23 April.[190]

Thus, despite the intention of the Law that the able-bodied should receive relief only in the workhouse, out-relief could become a source of assistance even for the able-bodied in the Stoke-upon-Trent Union. It was possible to make exceptions to the workhouse test not only for widows, deserted wives, orphans, the sick, and the aged, but also for the able-bodied during periodic crises when unemployment was so clearly not the fault of the workmen. Why did the Stoke-upon-Trent board of guardians attempt to persuade the central authority to suspend the order prohibiting outdoor relief to the able-bodied?

[188] PRO. MH12/11465, 5 Sept. 1861.
[189] PRO. MH12/11465, 9 Oct. 1861.   [190] PRO. MH12/11466.

The preservation of families was one explicit reason, but it was used in 1841 when it coincided with the self-interest of manufacturers, though not in 1836 when it did not. Some of the manufacturers whose workmen received relief were, or had been, guardians, including Ridgway and Adams. When they lacked orders, it was to their advantage to lay off workmen; however, it also was to their advantage for the workmen to be able to return to work as soon as trade revived. If the workmen had had to sell their furnishings and give up their housing to go into the workhouse for relief, it was unlikely they would have been willing or able to return to work quickly. The force of public opinion was a second reason for the guardians' actions. Some calamities were considered to be outside the control of the workmen and instead were seen to be inflicted upon the community as a whole. For example, it was acknowledged that the state of the money-market in the United States accounted for the depression in the pottery trade in 1841. Also, the outbreak of the American Civil War in April 1861 was recognized to be responsible for the sharp drop in pottery exports to the United States between June and December 1861 as the uncertainties of the early months of the war disrupted trade and the Union blockaded Confederate ports such as New Orleans which had been destinations for pottery exports; trade was diverted to Union ports and pottery exports to the United States began to recover in 1862 (see Fig. 5.1). Moreover, the force of public opinion on the guardians to provide assistance was further strengthened by the lack of other centres of pottery manufacture in the country, thus eliminating migration within Britain as a solution to unemployment.

These attitudes carried through the 1870s and shaped the Potteries guardians' responses to the Local Government Board's 'campaign against outdoor relief'.[191] At a series of conferences of representatives of guardians in Staffordshire in the 1870s the long-serving chairman of the Stoke board of guardians led the opposition to the abolition of outdoor relief and pointed out that 'very great hardships were endured by poor people who needed relief but who did not like to go into the workhouse. . . . applications for relief in the case of the manufacturing populations arose from the uncertain amount of wages received by them'.[192] In short, 'they must admit in a great many instances pauperism was a misfortune'.[193]

The number of recipients of outdoor relief in Stoke-upon-Trent declined in the 1870s, but the decline was considerably less than that in

---

[191] For the Local Government Board's attempt to restrict outdoor relief see e.g. Fraser, 'Introduction', 17; K. Williams, *From Pauperism to Poverty* (London, 1981), 96–107.
[192] *SS* 3 Feb. 1872, 6.   [193] *SS* 7 Apr. 1877, 7.

England and Wales as a whole. Between 1871 and 1876, the period of the
greatest reduction nationally, the number of recipients of outdoor relief
in Stoke-upon-Trent declined by 9 per cent compared with 33 per cent
in England and Wales.[194] During the year 1875–6 approximately 6 per
cent of the population of the Stoke-upon-Trent Union received outdoor
relief.[195] The Stoke guardians claimed that the Local Government Board's
suggested regulations as agreed at a conference of representatives of Staffordshire unions brought little change in their existing policy: 'The spirit
of the regulations suggested by the Conference had long been acted upon
by the Board, but it would be very advantageous to have them as a sort
of standing orders to guide the board in the distribution of outdoor
relief'.[196] In part this was the result of the Conference's agreement to
drop the suggested regulation of sending to the workhouse the dependent children of widows with more than one child in receipt of out-relief.
The chairman of the Stoke board had helped to reject this suggestion
at the Conference. The board also refused to adopt two of the nine
approved regulations regarding increased duties (and hence cost to the
union) for medical officers and relieving officers. The remaining regulations eliminated outdoor relief to able-bodied men and single women, to
families of men in gaol, and to deserted wives. The latter was controversial within the board in 1872 and in 1877 a new board of guardians
reversed the policy to allow discretion. Calling the failure to give outrelief
to deserted wives 'remarkably uncharitable' and pointing out that the
regulation 'was not law—merely an agreement come to by previous boards
of guardians not to do certain things', one guardian commented that
'such a regulation as that could only have been conceived by gentlemen
at a banquet badly served, when there was a paucity of wine and that
sour'.[197] Although the guardians spoke of more stringent investigation of
cases by medical and relieving officers and they enforced compulsory
payments by relatives of paupers more strictly, there is also evidence that
the board used its discretion in giving outdoor relief even to the able-
bodied. On 1 January 1875, 447 of those in receipt of outdoor relief were
'able' and only 'some of the able-bodied were temporarily disabled by
sickness'.[198]

The Burslem–Wolstanton board of guardians also appear to have
changed their policies little in the 1870s. They had one of the highest

---

[194] *SS* 7 Apr. 1877, 7; Williams, *Pauperism to Poverty*, 102.
[195] *SS* 7 Apr. 1877, 7. This is the total number of recipients for the year, not the number
in receipt of relief on 1 Jan. or 1 July.
[196] *SS* 16 Mar. 1872, 2.   [197] *SS* 28 July 1877, 6.   [198] *SS* 10 Apr. 1875.

proportions of all paupers on outdoor relief (92 per cent in 1870; 91 per cent in 1875; and 89 per cent in 1885) in the country at a period when some unions were below 30 per cent.[199] Keeping in mind the interests of the ratepayers, many of whom were working people and shopkeepers paying disproportionately high rates, the per capita expenditure on poor relief in the Burslem–Wolstanton Union was less than one-third the national average and among the lowest in the country.[200]

Thus, while the 'crusade against outdoor relief' appears to have had a comparatively small effect in the Potteries in terms of the number and groups relieved, the amount of relief given was small and often in kind and had to be applied for again every three months. Nevertheless, the guardians' did press for out-relief for the able-bodied and for other categories of those in need. In most cases this out-relief was not an alternative to, but was intimately related with family relationships. It was provided on the assumption that it would be given to a nuclear family if the recipient were part of one. And it often overlapped with assistance from family members.

The recipients paid a price for this assistance with regard to the autonomy within their families. The receipt of out-relief did not break up families, but the guardians could use it in an attempt to break into the autonomy of the family. First, in 1862 at the same time that the large employers were petitioning the Home Secretary in favour of the extension of the Factory Acts to the pottery industry on the grounds of the need to improve the education of children, the guardians adopted a condition requiring the children of those in receipt of out-relief under the Labour Test Order to attend school. 'Every child between six and twelve receiving relief shall be sent to some school approved by the Guardians and the Board will pay for each child on production of a certificate that the child was at school on days when the father was at work at the Spittals.'[201] Moreover, a month later the inspector from the Poor Law Board, commenting on the lists of those in receipt of out-relief, asked 'why so many children are reported as not going to school in conformity with the resolution of the Guardians'.[202]

Second, the guardians administered the Vaccination Act of 1867 which compelled parents to have their children vaccinated against smallpox three months after birth unless the parent could give a reasonable excuse for non-compliance. If convicted a parent was subject to a fine of 20s.

[199] PP 1876, lxiii, 43; PP 1910, li, 393; Williams, *Pauperism to Poverty*, 104–7, 159–60.
[200] PP 1876, lxiii, 43; Williams, *Pauperism to Poverty*, 170.
[201] PRO. MH12/11465, 28 Dec. 1861.   [202] PRO. MH12/11466, 23 Jan. 1862.

Opposition to this intervention between parents and children was so strong that one member of the Board of Guardians refused to have his baby vaccinated and was prosecuted. He defended his action on the grounds that he had a reasonable excuse. He cited the division of opinion among medical men in general, and the specific case of a medical man in the Potteries who knew of many cases of smallpox which were more severe after than before vaccination. Finally,

he took it that all the reasons which would be likely to sway his mind as a parent would be taken into consideration by his worship, and that his love for his child would be allowed to be some argument in justification of his having refused to submit it to the process of vaccination. The love which a father or mother felt for their children might be taken into consideration, and some allowance ought to be made for the prejudice entertained by many parents who had terrible experiences of the result of vaccination.[203]

3. Conclusion

This survey reveals a rich variety of networks and institutions in the Potteries between 1840 and 1880 in addition to the Poor Law which provided assistance for substantial numbers of individuals at different times for a variety of problems. This assistance often overlapped with, or substituted for, rather than competed with, assistance from family and kin. Furthermore, there were institutions and pervasive ideas which encouraged individuals to maintain relationships with family and kin.

Assistance was negotiated on a mutual-aid or philanthropic basis both within the working class—among neighbours, through trade unions, many churches, friendly, and burial societies—and between the middle and working classes—by some churches, employers, and through civic subscriptions. The North Staffordshire Infirmary combined working-class mutual aid and middle-class philanthropy. The feeling of relative independence of employees in the Potteries which the American Consul noted carried over into the sources of assistance, where employers tended to work through local institutions rather than all-encompassing factory paternalism.

I should generally describe the feeling between 'masters' and 'men' . . . as friendly but not cordial. On the part of the masters as kind and sympathetic but reserved, and on the part of the men as respectful, but independent. The workman . . . does not desire familiarity with him nor expect to be patronized by him.[204]

---

[203] *SS* 3 Apr. 1869.   [204] Lane, 'Tunstall', 825.

Any focus solely on the workplace of the separate industries would miss the civic, regional, and sometimes even wider context of much mutual aid and philanthropy as well as the Poor Law in the Potteries which frequently encompassed a variety of occupational groups.

Some networks and institutions offered a 'structured alternative' to family and kin relationships. For example outdoor relief under the Poor Law enabled an elderly woman to live apart from her grown sons, and some friendly-society benefits had the potential to provide a working man with income in the case of sickness. The Poor Law also provided assistance to those without family or kin or whose family and kin were unable to provide help. In general, however, assistance from these networks and institutions worked in conjunction with family assistance. These networks and institutions, including outdoor relief under the Poor Law, tended to supplement and complement, rather than compete with, family relationships.

The overt sanctions of neighbours and the Poor Law were limited in the influence they could exert on individuals to assist family members. Yet, the prevalent assumption from the friendly societies, trade unions, and Infirmary to the Poor Law, i.e. that individuals received assistance as part of a family, the self-interest of employers in keeping the families of their employees together through periods of underemployment and unemployment and sickness, and especially the pervasive influence of religion, meant that in the Potteries there were strong 'normative guidelines' encouraging the assistance of family and kin or, in other words, a morality that operated not on the basis of fixed rules specifying precisely what should be done in particular circumstances, but on how to work out what to do. They were shared ideas, related to but independent of material conditions and instrumental self-interest, about 'the proper thing to do' and influencing the 'public presentation of oneself and one's family' which individuals could draw upon when they negotiated about their needs and capacities to help in a particular situation.[205]

[205] J. Finch, *Family Obligations and Social Change* (Cambridge and Oxford, 1989), 213–17, 232–6, 240–2.

8

Solving Problems: Families and Others

HAVING surveyed some of the alternative networks and institutions in the Potteries, it remains to examine the part played by the nuclear family and other kin as a source of domestic or family help by considering a number of situations in which the individual or the nuclear family was unlikely to be able to cope without assistance from others. These crises ranged in magnitude along a spectrum from the day-to-day problems of borrowing an item of food when the supply suddenly ran out to those associated with life-cycle stages such as marriage, child-care, and old age, and finally to situations which involved the loss of a family's basis of support such as death, sickness, desertion, unemployment, or a strike or lockout.

'Problems' can be defined in two ways: (1) situations seen by participants as ones of great stress with which they cannot cope alone; (2) situations defined as potentially critical by observers which might require extra-familial assistance.[1] These are not mutually exclusive categories, but the second type will be the initial starting-point here. In either case it is necessary to make distinctions among problems. The importance of distinguishing among problems is apparent in work on twentieth-century Britain which suggests that 'as the help that would be required becomes more demanding, there is a general and quite marked increase in the extent to which kin would be looked to'.[2]

Thus, the question is to identify in which problem situations individuals look to family and kin for assistance? What is the role of other networks and institutions and what is their relationship with family assistance? Anderson also distinguishes among problems, but he asks a different question. First he establishes that kin gave support for a particular problem, so the question is not whether kin provide help or not.

---

[1] J. C. Mitchell, 'The Concept and Use of Social Networks' in J. C. Mitchell (ed.), *Social Networks in Urban Situations* (Manchester, 1969), 256.
[2] J. H. Goldthorpe, *Social Mobility and Class Structure in Modern Britain* (Oxford, 1980), 154.

Instead, he asks why such support was given, and his answer is that as the amount of help required to alleviate that problem increased, the more likely it was that the relationship would be 'calculative' or reciprocal. Others suggest that at least in rural areas and small towns during the mid-nineteenth century the collectivity, particularly the Poor Law, was more important for the elderly than assistance from family and kin. In addition, the alternative sources of assistance in the Potteries revealed in the survey in the previous chapter were not negligible and suggest that it would be useful to ask the first questions again about which problems individuals look to family and kin for assistance and what is the role of other networks and institutions and their relationship with family assistance. In the process Anderson's question of why family assistance is given and his answer to it can be seen in a wider perspective. Therefore, in what follows I take certain 'problems' (e.g. day-to-day, life-cycle stage, and the removal of a family's basis of support) and present evidence of the extent to which kin did or did not provide assistance, either alone or in combination with other sources of assistance.

This approach also offers a way to examine some of the differences and similarities between the Potteries and other nineteenth-century towns and rural areas in the nature of the 'problems' and the ways in which inhabitants coped with them. In particular, the relatively high mortality and morbidity rates and the relatively high employment in the Potteries helped to shape the needs and the capacities to meet them in the area.

1. Day-to-Day Problems

There is some evidence that for day-to-day problems such as acquiring an item of food, proximity was more important than kinship as a 'framework for reciprocation'. In an example cited above for a different purpose, Mary Rowley was sent to a shop for potatoes for her step-mother and their next-door neighbour who was not related. This service was low cost and likely to be 'mutually advantageous within a rather short time period'. If a reasonable level of reciprocation was not forthcoming within a comparatively short time-span the relationship could be terminated altogether. It is this context in which short-run calculative orientation toward assistance was evident.[3]

---

[3] M. Anderson, *Family Structure in 19th Century Lancashire* (Cambridge, 1971), 164.

2. Life-Cycle Stage Problems

The Elderly

In the Potteries as in Preston in 1851 families were a particularly significant source of support for the elderly. The contrast in co-residence patterns with the period since 1930 and with rural areas and small towns in the mid-nineteenth century is striking. Few of the elderly aged 65 and over lived alone in the Potteries (7 per cent) in 1861 and Preston (6 per cent) in 1851; in London in 1930, 30 per cent of those aged 65 and over lived alone and in 1976 39 per cent lived alone.[4] In the Potteries as in Preston over 80 per cent of those aged 65 and over lived with family or kin (see Table 8.1). In the Potteries in 1861 57 per cent lived with one or more children. This is considerably closer to the percentage in Preston (68 per cent) than to the picture of relatively little sharing with children which appears to have been the case in rural areas and small towns in the mid-nineteenth century, 'where time after time, for place after place, the percentage of elderly who lived with a child were found not to be above 40 per cent, with a few more per cent living with some other kin, especially grandchildren, nieces or brothers or sisters'.[5] Thus, in northern, urban, industrial areas such as the Potteries and Preston family and kin appear to have taken responsibility for the elderly, while the collectivity, particularly the Poor Law, which played such a central role in rural areas and small towns, was relatively less important.

In the Potteries the importance of family and kin may in part be due to the combination of relatively little need with a relatively large capacity for family care. In 1861 there were only 727 people aged 75 and over out of a population of over 100,000. Moreover, in the Potteries in 1861 it was more likely that an elderly person aged 75 and over would have had a female carer available than in England in the twentieth century. In the Potteries in 1861 the ratio of women aged 50–9 (those most likely to assume caring roles) to persons aged 75 and over in the population was 5 : 1, compared with ratios for England of 3 : 1 in 1901, 1 : 1 in 1976 and less than 1 : 1 in 1986.[6] Furthermore, in the Potteries in 1861 the aged do

[4] C. Gordon, *The Myth of Family Care? The Elderly in the Early 1930s*, The Welfare State Programme, Suntory-Toyota International Centre for Economics and Related Disciplines, London School of Economics, Discussion Paper no. 29, Apr. 1988, 26, 45.

[5] D. Thomson, 'Welfare and the Historians', in L. Bonfield, R. Smith, and K. Wrightson (eds.), *The World We Have Gained: Histories of Population and Social Structure, Essays Presented to Peter Laslett* (London, 1986), 364.

[6] For the figures from 1901 to 1986, see M. Bulmer *The Social Basis of Community Care* (London, 1987), 2.

TABLE 8.1 *Residence Patterns of Persons Aged 65 and Over by Marital Status: Preston 1851[a], Potteries Samples 1861 and 1881 (%)*

Living with	Married			Wid'd/single			All		
	Pres 1851	Pot. 1861	Pot. 1881	Pres 1851	Pot. 1861	Pot. 1881	Pres 1851	Pot. 1861	Pot. 1881
Married or widowed child	16	4	15	41	38	36	31	26	27
Unmarried child	47	41	34	29	21	14	35	28	23
Both married & unmarried child	—	7	8	—	1	8	—	3	8
Spouse only	37	37	32	8	12	13	13	13	11
Other kin only	—	11	12	22	28	29	5	12	13
No related person	—	—	—	—	—	—	—	—	—
As lodger	—	—	—	—	—	—	7	4	5
As servant	—	—	—	—	—	—	2	1	0
Takes in lodger	—	—	—	—	—	—	—	3	4
With servant	—	—	—	—	—	—	—	1	2
Alone	—	—	—	—	—	—	6	7	3
Workhouse	—	—	—	—	—	—	3	2	3
N	70	46	65	124	85	77	200	131	142

[a] *Source*: Figures for Preston from Anderson, 'Family Household and the Industrial Revolution', in M. Anderson (ed.), *The Sociology of the Family* (Harmondsworth, 1971), 86, and from *Family Structure*, 139, adjusted to include workhouse inmates.

TABLE 8.2   *Causes of Applications for Relief Brought before a Meeting of the Guardians of the Stoke-upon-Trent Union, June 1861*

Cause of Application	N	%
Death of husband	6	8
Sickness	18	25
of wife	1	1
of child	1	1
Deserted by husband	3	4
Deserted and sickness	1	1
Out of employ	21	29
Aged and infirm	8	11
Death of parents	1	1
Deserted by parents	1	1
Other (idiot, death of child, etc.)	11	15
TOTAL	72	97[a]

[a] The total % is less than 100 due to rounding.

not appear to have been a major burden for the Poor Law guardians. Only 11 per cent of the applications for relief brought before a meeting of the guardians of the Stoke-upon-Trent Union in June 1861 (see Table 8.2) were from the 'aged and infirm'. Because the aged made up such a small proportion of the applicants or recipients of outdoor relief, before the 'crusade against outdoor relief' in the 1870s the Stoke-upon-Trent guardians did not even mention let alone consider any changes in practice regarding outdoor relief to the aged in their discussions of the Local Government Board's regulations in 1872. While the aged in receipt of outdoor relief may have been affected by the general increase in scrutiny of relief applications and the increase in payments by relatives towards relief given, the effects were limited as there was no substantial change in residence patterns of the elderly in the Potteries between 1861 and 1881 (see Table 8.1). In 1881 58 per cent of those aged 65 and over resided with a child, compared with 57 per cent in 1861; in 1881 only 3 per cent of those aged 65 and over were in the workhouse, and in 1861 only 2 per cent were workhouse inmates.

The foregoing has treated those over sixty-five as dependants and their co-residence with kin as an indicator of dependence. Another indicator of dependence, or at least subordinate status within a household, is the relatively low headship rates compared with the early 1930s. In the Potteries in the mid-nineteenth century smaller percentages of both men and women aged 65 and over headed their own households than in London in 1930.[7] While dependence was undoubtedly the case for some, there is evidence to the contrary for others. In the Potteries in 1861 all of the married individuals over the age of 65 co-residing with 'other' kin (Table 8.1) were sharing their household with young, 'parentless' grandchildren. Thus, rather than being dependent, these older individuals were providing assistance.

Rather than relatively one-sided relationships of dependence or support, Michael Anderson stresses the reciprocity of the relationship between married couples and co-residing kin, particularly when the kin are older. His most striking evidence is the relatively high proportion of households with mothers employed and a child less than 10 years old which include a co-residing grandmother. This pattern, however, is not repeated as clearly in the Potteries, despite similar patterns of employment for some mothers outside the home.

Anderson found that in 14 per cent of the cases in which the mother worked and there was a child less than 10 years old (and in 17 per cent of the cases in which she worked in a factory), the household contained an unemployed grandmother. In contrast, in the Potteries in 3 per cent of the cases in which the mother worked and there was a child less than 10 years old (and in 4 per cent of the cases in which she worked in the pottery industry), the household included a grandmother (see Table 8.3). Furthermore, Anderson finds a sharp contrast between the 29 per cent of those mothers with a grandmother in the house and children under 10 who worked, while 58 per cent did not work; and the 12 per cent of those mothers without a grandmother in the house who worked and the 76 per cent who did not. No such contrast existed in the Potteries, where 20 per cent of those mothers with a grandmother in the house and children under 10 years worked and 17 per cent of those without a co-residing grandmother worked (see Table 8.4). Thus, there is no evidence from the Potteries that 'if a grandmother was in the household the mother was significantly more likely to maximize her earnings by working away from home'.[8]

Furthermore, in contrast to Preston, there was less tendency for a

---

[7] Of the males aged 65 and over in the Potteries sample 1861, 76 per cent were heads, compared with 92 per cent of those in London in the early 1930s; of the women aged 65 and over in the Potteries in 1861, 36 per cent were heads, compared with 57 per cent in London in the early 1930s; 56 per cent of all those aged 65 and over in the Potteries sample were heads, compared with 72 per cent of those in London in the early 1930s. For London, see Gordon, 'Family Care?', 24.

[8] Anderson, *Family Structure*, 141.

TABLE 8.3 *Residence Patterns of Mothers with Children less than 10 Years of Age by the Occupation of the Mother: Potteries Sample 1861* (%)

Household contains	Mother's Occupation		
	Pottery	Other	Not employed
Grandmother	4	3	3
Other kin	17	14	14
Lodger	9	14	18
No other person	71	70	65
N	82	37	630

TABLE 8.4 *Percentage of Mothers with a Child less than 10 Years of Age who were Employed, by Residence Pattern: Potteries Sample 1861* (%)

Household contains	% Employed	N
Grandmother	20	20
Other kin	18	107
Lodger	10	126
No other person	17	496

mother who worked in the Potteries to have someone outside the nuclear family (e.g. 'other' kin or a lodger) who co-resided and who could help with children. However, a slightly higher proportion of mothers who worked in the Potteries than those who did not work, had co-residing kin (Table 8.3).

Thus, fewer young children of women working in factories in the Potteries than in Preston were cared for at home by 'a close relative or a friendly lodger'. Nevertheless, it is probable that relatively more children in the Potteries might have been cared for by close relatives in the neighbourhood, so that Anderson's conclusion applied equally to the Potteries:

at a point in time, less than 2 per cent of all infant children in the industrial districts of Lancashire were being left with professional child minders. As a source of neglect and a factor affecting children's attitudes to their parents, then, working mothers were probably in fact of comparatively minor importance.[9]

There were other similarities and differences between the residence patterns of the elderly in the Potteries and Preston. In the Potteries, as in Preston, relatively few households contained two married couples of two succeeding generations. Married persons aged 65 and over tended to reside with their spouse only or with unmarried children, while widowed persons had a slightly greater tendency to live with married children. It is, however, apparent from Table 8.1 that the Potteries had a relatively small proportion of inhabitants over the age of 65 living with children, whatever their marital status, compared with Preston, and a relatively high proportion living with 'other' kin. The difference probably partially reflects the relatively high proportion of locally born inhabitants in the Potteries, and hence the probability that an individual had a greater variety of relatives present in the area. Nevertheless, despite these differences, it is probable that Anderson's calculation that approximately 67 per cent of persons aged 65 or over in Preston would have had a child alive[10] also applies to the Potteries. Therefore, if the presence of other relatives is added in the Potteries, it is possible to draw a conclusion similar to Anderson's for Preston. In other words, few old persons could not find one among their children or relatives prepared to house them in old age if they had children or relatives alive. The list of those who died in the explosion at Talke pits in 1866, for example, indicates that a substantial number of the men who were killed had supported dependent parents.[11]

Young Married Couples

In the Potteries there is evidence that family and kin were important sources of assistance for young married couples; however, the extent of the problems and hence the need for assistance differed from the circumstances in Preston.

The extent to which married couples in the Potteries in 1861 and in Preston in 1851 chose alternative patterns of residence at different periods of the life cycle was presented above in Table 2.7.[12] The residence patterns of those in LCS 1 reveal that a surprisingly high proportion of these childless, and probably for the most part newly married, couples co-resided with parents or other kin. The proportion is surprising because a far higher proportion of couples in the Potteries (76 per cent)

[9] Ibid. 74.   [10] Ibid. 140.   [11] *SS* 22 Dec. 1866, 8.   [12] See above, p. 113.

headed their own household than in Preston (44 per cent), and lower proportions in the Potteries than in Preston shared houses or lived as lodgers. Yet, roughly similar proportions of married couples (12 per cent in the Potteries and 15 per cent in Preston) resided in a household headed by kin (primarily parents). For couples with one child aged less than 1 year old (i.e. LCS 2) in the Potteries, co-residence with kin appears to have been even more important than for those with no children. Moreover, a higher proportion of couples in LCS 2 in the Potteries (16 per cent) than in Preston (10 per cent) lived with parents or other kin. Thus, despite the better supply of housing in the Potteries, a significant proportion of couples in the early stages of the life cycle were found residing with parents or other kin. It is a pattern which must also reflect the higher proportion of people in the Potteries who were born locally, for there probably were more parents or kin in the area with whom to reside. In addition, it suggests the functional importance of kin as a source of assistance.

To sum up, the co-residence patterns of the elderly in northern, urban, industrial areas such as the Potteries and Preston, in contrast to rural areas and small towns and to the twentieth century, suggest that family and kin were important sources of assistance. The collectivity, particularly the Poor Law, played a subsidiary role. The proportion of elderly people in the workhouses was small and the aged made up a relatively small proportion of the applicants for outdoor relief. At 1s. and a loaf per week in 1861 outdoor relief would not cover the approximately 2s. per week rent for a modest house, though there is a case which offers evidence that the elderly who preferred to live apart from their children could use outdoor relief under the Poor Law to extract payment from children. In Preston, short-run, instrumental reciprocity has been suggested as an explanation for the co-residence of the elderly with their children.

People phenomenally perceived this as a sphere where the maintenance of relationships led to a mutual increase of satisfaction in the form of fairly short-run and instrumental returns, regardless of other considerations, and that the prospect of these mutually advantageous returns was an important factor in the retention of the relationships.[13]

In the Potteries there were relatively few elderly people in relation to potential carers and there is evidence of a more complex pattern than

---

[13] Anderson, *Family Structure*, 139.

short-run, mutually advantageous returns. The figures regarding child-care in the Potteries, for example, do not provide evidence for short-run, instrumental reciprocity as a prime motive for couples in the Potteries taking in a parent. Long-term reciprocity, and one-sided dependence and the provision of support such as that for parentless grandchildren, also existed. Reciprocal assistance was one point along a continuum of relationships implied by patterns of co-residence. The older persons could be providing reciprocal assistance; they could be completely dependent; or they could even be rendering support. Furthermore, the evidence that co-residence with parents could be an important source of assistance for young married couples can be seen not only as a product of short-run mutual advantage, but also as part of the negotiations through which individuals built up relationships with family members over the long term which had a history 'stretching over many years in most cases, and . . . an anticipated future'. Ideally these interpersonal relationships within families would have been reciprocal but, depending on the negotiated needs and capacities at the particular time, they may have become asymmetrical and assistance may have been given without expectation of return.[14]

3. Removal of a Nuclear Family's Basis of Support

Death and Desertion

Early death rather than old age presented major problems in the Potteries in the mid-nineteenth century. In particular, the patterns of mortality left widows with dependent children and orphans, and removed children and infants from nuclear families. In coping with the effects of this pattern of mortality, the collectivity—burial and friendly societies and particularly the Poor Law—together with assistance from family and kin were important. Desertion, while not as final as death, raised some of the same problems, but the attitude of the Poor Law guardians and the collectivity more generally was ambivalent, leaving women and dependent children more reliant on kin.

In an area where the working conditions for men in the pottery industry exacerbated the effects of the generally smoky urban environment, resulting in a prevalence of lung disease, the relatively high death-rates

[14] J. Finch, *Family Obligations and Social Change* (Cambridge and Oxford, 1989), 240–2.

of men in their forties left substantial numbers of widows and dependent children. In contrast to England and Wales as a whole, widows and their children in the Potteries made up a substantial proportion of those receiving poor relief. Of those receiving outdoor relief in the Stoke-upon-Trent Union in 1875–6, 40 per cent were widows and dependent children, while in England and Wales as a whole 25 per cent of the paupers were widows and dependent children.[15] As mentioned in the previous chapter, the Stoke-upon-Trent guardians led the successful rejection in 1872 of the Local Government Board's suggested regulation restricting outdoor relief to widows with more than one child only if the children above 1 were sent to the workhouse. The local significance of this attitude with regard to keeping nuclear families together is apparent from the figures for recipients of outdoor relief in 1875–6, when 342 widows with more than one child had 1,151 children among them.[16] The guardians appeared to recognize the extent of the problem and that the widows and children were not responsible for their destitution.

Among other problems the death of a husband or wife raised the financial problem of paying for a funeral. In 1843 the average cost for artisans of a funeral was £5 for adults and £1 10s. for children.[17] Burial clubs, bank clubs, ground clubs, and friendly societies helped defray this cost for the relatively large proportion of the population who were members. For the victims of explosions, such as that at Ravensdale in 1877 or Talke Pits in 1865, the employer would pay the cost of a coffin.

In the case of major accidents such as that at Talke Pits the public subscriptions to a relief fund provided some assistance to widows and orphans. This relief was important, but most of the accidents resulting in the deaths of colliers involved only one or two persons. Hence their deaths, though cumulatively in one year reaching the number of those killed at Talke Pits, did not arouse the same scale of assistance. Some ground clubs and bank clubs provided assistance to widows and children, but the amount was a relatively small proportion of the former weekly wages, and even these small benefits lasted only temporarily for a few weeks or months.

Kin undoubtedly provided both financial and emotional assistance for many widowed persons: co-residence of widowed persons with kin gives some indication of this. In the Potteries, as in Preston, co-residence

---

[15] *SS* 7 Apr. 1877, 7; K. Williams, *From Pauperism to Poverty* (London, 1981), 103, 231, 233.

[16] *SS* 3 Feb. 1872, 6; *SS* 7 Apr. 1877, 7.   [17] *N. Staffs. Merc.* 30 Dec. 1843.

with kin provided a partial solution to the problem of long-term support for widowed persons by reducing necessary expenditures. In both the Potteries and Preston widows with unmarried children present in the household headed their own household. Unlike Preston, however, where widows in all age-groups above the age of 25 without dependent children tended to live with kin, the widows in the Potteries who lived with kin were predominantly those over the age of 65 without an unmarried child present (see Table 8.5). In the Potteries in all other age-groups above 25 years widows without an unmarried child present had a greater tendency to head their own household than in Preston. Widows who were less than 65 who headed their own households in the Potteries occasionally had a parentless grandchild or niece or nephew co-residing, even if they also had unmarried children of their own. Apparently these widows were able to support themselves, perhaps with the aid of outdoor relief, rather than depend on kin. Thus, these patterns suggest that widows in the Potteries, with or without co-residing unmarried children, tended to head their own household. Sometimes these households contained other kin who needed support or who might help support the household, often they contained lodgers who provided some income for the household. As a widow aged, or if a woman became a widow at an older age, she might continue to head her own household, particularly if she had an unmarried child present. But, to a greater extent as her age increased and her children married, she would not head her own household, but would live with a married child. In either case, the widow probably became increasingly dependent. In other words, the relationships indicated by the co-residence patterns were roughly correlated with the age of the widow. The younger the widow, the more support and mutual assistance she provided for those dependents co-residing with her. As her children grew older, the balance shifted, and she became more dependent on co-residing children, whether married or unmarried and whether or not she nominally headed the household.

For Preston where childless widows in all age-groups above 25 shared with kin it has been suggested that one reason why this pattern existed was that a childless widow would have been able to make some contribution to the household budget, and this is evidence for the 'instrumentality which seems to have been so important in these communities'.[18] In the Potteries, however, where the residence patterns of widows differed

---

[18] Anderson, *Family Structure*, 145.

TABLE 8.5 *Residence Patterns of Widows by Age: Potteries Sample 1861, Preston 1851* (%)

	<25 yrs.		25–44 yrs.		45–64 yrs.		65+ yrs.	
	Pot.	Pres.	Pot.	Pres.	Pot.	Pres.	Pot.	Pres.
Widows with unmarried children present:								
Live in								
own household	50	25	81	69	91	90	83	87
as kin	—	63	9	20	6	4	17	6
as lodgers	50	13	6	11	—	6	—	6
as servant	—	—	3	—	3	—	—	—
N	2	8	32	61	67	98	12	31
Widows with *no* unmarried children present:								
Live in								
own household	—	18	67	17	61	36	41	29
as kin	100	47	—	34	16	32	57	59
as lodgers	—	28	33	31	16	18	—	8
as servant	—	6	3	17	7	11	2	5
N	2	17	3	29	31	28	42	39

[a] Figures for Preston from Anderson, *Family Structure*, 145.

from those in Preston, they suggest that 'instrumentality' was less likely to have been a crucial factor in the Potteries and that there was a change over the lifetime of a widow from providing support for dependents from whatever sources to dependence on family and kin.

There were fewer widowers than widows in the Potteries, but they seem to have followed a pattern similar to that of widows, although widowers between 25 and 44 years of age without co-residing children tended to live with their parents.[19] Both widows and widowers in the Potteries headed their own households to a greater extent than in Preston and fewer lived in lodgings. Nevertheless, kin were important to widowed persons in the Potteries: 79 per cent of all widowed persons in the Potteries lived with an unmarried or married child, parents, or other kin, particularly siblings; only 12 per cent lived alone, 9 per cent lived as lodgers, and 2 per cent were in the workhouse.

Death also left orphans. Nearly 6 per cent of all children in the Potteries could expect to lose both parents before they were 15.[20] If some children were fairly grown up, they took responsibility for younger siblings. In the Potteries in 1861, for example, this seems to have happened to Sarah Wall, aged 18, the oldest of seven brothers and sisters living together. Where siblings were not old enough, however, the Poor Law was a source of assistance. At the meeting of the guardians of the Stoke-upon-Trent Union in June 1861, one child applied for relief due to 'death of parents'.[21] Nevertheless, the number of children in the census sample for the Potteries indicated as 'orphan' or 'adopted' who were parentless grandchildren, nieces, or nephews suggest that kin were particularly important in these circumstances.

A combination of reasons undoubtedly explains the willingness of kin to take in orphans. Some evidence from the Potteries suggests that the addition to family income may have contributed to the willingness of kin to take in orphans. The numbers are very small, but it is possible that boys aged 8 to 12 years without co-residing parents were more likely to be employed than those with parents; the difference is not as clear for girls.[22] This, however, might also reflect the greater likelihood that boys who were already employed may be those who had a greater likelihood of losing both parents.

Previous chapters have described the relatively high infant and child

---

[19] M. W. Dupree, 'Family Structure in the Staffordshire Potteries 1840–1880', D.Phil. thesis (Oxford, 1981), 410.

[20] See above, Ch. 2, p. 132.   [21] PRO. MH12/11465, 14 June 1861.

[22] Dupree, 'Family Structure', 412.

mortality rates in the Potteries in the mid-nineteenth century. The death of young children occurred with particular frequency.[23] If the child were an only child, the death may have had long-term implications by depriving the family of income if the children were employed or by depriving parents a source of assistance in their old age. But, in any case, the death of a child immediately required expenditure at least on a coffin, and even this expense could necessitate assistance from other institutions. On the death of one of his children, for example, a forgeman named Peter Lloyd applied for and received a coffin from the guardians of the Stoke-upon-Trent Poor Law Union in June 1861.[24]

Desertion, while not as final as death, raised some of the same problems arising from the removal of a nuclear family's basis of support. The law might be of some assistance, if the deserting party could be located. Thomas McKenzie, for example, was summoned for failing to obey an order made upon him for 'neglecting to maintain his wife and family', and the magistrate ordered him to contribute towards their maintenance.[25] Joseph Yates, a turner, was brought before the magistrate on the charge of neglecting to support his wife and children.[26] The Poor Law was one source of assistance for deserted families. Unlike widows, who tended to receive outdoor relief, deserted wives and their families tended to be relieved in the workhouse. At its meeting in June 1861 the guardians of the Stoke-upon-Trent Union received three applications with the reason stated to be 'deserted by husband', one 'deserted and sickness', and one case of 'deserted by parents'; each was given an 'order for the house'.[27] The attitude of the Stoke-upon-Trent guardians was ambivalent, as they gave up their discretion to give outdoor relief to deserted wives with dependent children for five years between 1872 and 1877. During this period the argument that the threat of the workhouse might be a deterrent against desertion, the fear that husbands and wives might be colluding, and the belief that even if there were no collusion families had to bear some responsibility for the 'misconduct' of their husbands found majority support. At other times, too, these were arguments that reflected ambivalent attitudes more generally towards deserted wives, though the guardians' belief that desertion was increasing—ten deserted

---

[23] See above pp. 86–90/136–7 for infant and child mortality rates. For attitudes towards the death of children and the influence of poverty on such attitudes, see D. Vincent, 'Love and Death and the Nineteenth Century Working Class', *Social History*, 5 (1980), 244–5.
[24] PRO. MH12/11465, 14 June 1861.
[25] *SS* 3 Apr. 1869.   [26] *SS* 25 July 1865.
[27] Table 8.2 and PRO. MH12/11465, 15 June 1861.

TABLE 8.6   *Residence Patterns of Persons Married but Spouse Absent:*
Potteries Sample 1861 (%)

Household status	<25 yrs.	25–44 yrs.	45–64 yrs.	65+ yrs
A. *Females*				
Head own hshld. or wife	13	33	64	—
Live as				
kin	38	28	14	—
lodger	25	18	14	—
visitor	6	10	—	—
servant	19	5	—	—
Workhouse or infirmary	—	5	7	—
N	16	39	14	0
B. *Males*				
Head own household	—	40	42	—
live as				
kin	33	10	8	100
lodger	67	30	33	—
Employee living in	—	5	8	—
Workhouse or infirmary	—	18	8	—
N	3	20	12	1

wives applied for relief during one week in Hanley in 1875—during their self-imposed ban on outdoor relief must have helped undermine support for the ban.[28]

Not all wives whose husbands were absent on census night 1861 were 'deserted', as husbands might have been absent for work-related and other reasons. But their residence patterns suggest that for wives aged 44 or less whose husbands were absent from the household on census night in the Potteries in 1861, residence with kin was important for some. Men whose wives were absent tended either to head their own households or live in lodgings (see Table 8.6).

Sickness

Sickness, like death, was a major problem for most individuals and families in the Potteries. They coped by a combination of assistance from

[28] *SS* 3 Feb. 1872, 6; 16 Mar. 1872, 2; 10 Apr. 1875; 28 July 1878, 6.

family and kin and from the 'collectivity' including friendly societies, the North Staffordshire Infirmary, and the Poor Law.

In 1868 at least one out of four working men in the Potteries was likely to be sick enough each year to require an application for sickness benefit, and the average duration of each illness was five weeks.[29] As described in the previous chapter, the North Staffordshire Infirmary relieved a family of nursing the sick or injured person if he or she could obtain a 'line' or suffered an accident and were not suffering from an excluded malady. But the Infirmary was 'not for long term invalids'. The benefits of sickness societies and friendly societies were also temporary, lasting a few weeks or months. The benefits were a small proportion of a normal weekly wage and they too, of course, were available only to members.

Thus, the Infirmary and benefit societies provided treatment or financial assistance only for maladies that were serious enough to qualify for a doctor's certificate and to lose a substantial amount of time from work, but which were not so serious as to cause long-term incapacity. For those who had no family, were not members of a sickness society, could not obtain access to the Infirmary, or who had a long-term illness, application for relief from the guardians was the only other institutional alternative: 28 per cent of the applications for relief to the guardians of the Stoke-upon-Trent Union in June 1861 were caused by 'sickness' of some kind (Table 8.2). Poor Law Medical Officers provided medications or 'extras' for the sick and most applicants received outdoor relief to fill the gap in income for themselves and their immediate families. As mentioned in the previous chapter there is evidence that recipients spoke of this as 'my parish allowance' or 'my 'bit of pay', and there was little stigma attached to it.

In general, however, families catered for their own sick or injured at home, and the Infirmary, sickness societies, and the Poor Law for the most part merely supplemented family assistance. Advertisements in the newspaper for patent medicines and home remedies suggest self-treatment or home treatment of minor ailments. Also, there is evidence that the more serious the illness or injury the more likely that relatives outside the nuclear family would provide aid. A local physician, for example, attributed the prevalence of smallpox in Longton in 1871 in part to relatives insisting on assisting the sick.

---

[29] *SS* 3 Apr. 1869. These figures are a minimum because they refer to members of the North Staffordshire Provident Association which had a relatively high subscription and required a medical examination for membership.

I attribute the prevalence of smallpox in Longton, in the first place to neglect in isolating early cases; next to the state of dirt and crowding in badly built and badly ventilated houses, aggravated by the folly and stupidity of relatives who go among the sick, and if not themselves attacked, become the means of conveying infection; also to a very considerable number of children and others not vaccinated at all, or where it had not been duly performed.[30]

After the Talke Pits explosion, to give a different example, a newspaper report included a remark about the arrival soon after the explosion on Friday of relatives of the injured.[31]

Unemployment

Although 1840–80 overall was a period of expansion for the pottery, coal, and iron industries, there were periodic depressions which resulted in short-time working and threw some out of work altogether. The pottery industry was sensitive to fluctuations in the American market in particular, and in 1842, 1848, 1855, 1861–3, and the mid-1870s this led to slumps. In addition, the closure of a firm such as Adams in 1860 or the blacklisting by an employer for union or political activities meant periods of transitional unemployment for individuals. Unions in the pottery industry provided some unemployment pay. Apart from the times when the guardians applied to the central Poor Law authorities to give able-bodied men relief outside the workhouse, the workhouse was the primary relief given. In 1861 all of those applying for relief because they were 'out of employ' received an 'order for the house' (Table 8.2), though there is evidence that the guardians gave outdoor relief to the able-bodied occasionally even in the 1870s. Relatives were particularly important as a source of assistance during periods of unemployment. The applications of the able-bodied for relief outside the workhouse indicated frequent sharing of residences with relatives. Charles Shaw's autobiography gives vivid testimony to the importance of assistance from a relative.[32] The family had little food; the children were without clogs and 'everything which could be turned into money or goods had to go'.[33] But, during this period the family had a visit from a young potter who was a distant relative.

[30] PP 1872, xvi, 106.   [31] *SS* 22 Dec. 1865, 7.
[32] C. Shaw, *When I Was A Child* (1st pub. London, 1903; repr. Firle, Sussex, 1977), 91–2.
[33] Ibid. 95.

He knew our family well, and though not related directly, he was so indirectly. He carried signs of being better off than most working potters, as he was, for he had some private means besides his weekly earnings . . . after this young visitor had been in the house a short time, and had heard the story of our need, I saw him put his thumb and finger down between his apron and his waistcoat. When he brought them back I saw a silvery gleam between his finger and thumb, and in a very few minutes I saw bread and butter on our table.[34]

This assistance did not save the family from the workhouse, but it did postpone it a little longer.[35]

Migration was an option for a few potters, but without other major centres of pottery production within Britain it was not an alternative available to many.[36] Thus, as the period of unemployment lengthened and the assistance of relatives was no longer able to suffice, families were forced to seek relief from the guardians or from civic relief funds.[37]

4. Conclusion

In the Potteries in the mid-nineteenth century family and kin were not demoted to a subsidiary role nor was it a 'golden age of family responsibility'. The foregoing survey of the several different kinds of problems and sources of assistance available to individuals for meeting those problems reveals some evidence that the more important and more long-term the problem, the more family and relatives provided assistance. Neighbours went to the market for items of food for each other, but it was relatives who assisted when smallpox struck or who came from afar to help those injured in the explosion at Talke Pits. In addition, the survey suggests that individuals frequently relied on a combination of sources of assistance with the family and the 'collectivity' supplementing support from each other. Where, as for the major problems for families in the Potteries caused by early death and sickness, there was recognition that the extent of need could exhaust family capabilities to assist and that the individuals and families were not responsible for their afflictions, there was an extensive network of private and public welfare agencies,[38] which in the Potteries included burial societies, ground and bank clubs, friendly

---

[34] Ibid. 92–3.   [35] See above, p. 313.   [36] See above, pp. 94–6.

[37] In June 1861 the largest number of applications for relief came from those who were 'out of employ', see above, p. 330.

[38] C. G. Hanson, 'Craft Unions, Welfare Benefits, and the Case for Trade Union Law Reform 1867–1875', *Econ. Hist. Rev.* 28 (1975), 245 and J. Benson, 'English Coalminers' Trade Union Accident Funds 1850–1900', *Econ, Hist. Rev.* 28 (1975), 401 make this point.

societies, employers, civic relief funds, and the North Staffordshire In-firmary. Even where support from family and kin was predominant, as in the co-residence of the elderly in the Potteries, outdoor relief from the Poor Law could supplement family support. Furthermore, this assist-ance can be seen as overlapping with and augmenting that of the nuclear family, relatives, and neighbours, as much as a mutually exclusive alter-native which weakened family relationships.

Second, the assistance of family and kin was particularly important in the Potteries as in Preston for life-cycle stage problems, especially those of the elderly. In contrast to rural areas and small towns of the same era, and the general position in the twentieth century, large proportions of the elderly co-resided with family or kin and few lived alone or in the workhouse. In the Potteries, however, patterns of co-residence differed from those in Preston in such a way as to suggest that the assistance given and received through family and kin was not necessarily mutual and characterized by immediate reciprocity.

Instead, relationships can be characterized along a spectrum from support through mutuality to dependence. Looking synchronically, the elderly in the Potteries, especially married couples over 65, occasionally supported co-residing, young, 'parentless' grandchildren; a few grand-mothers co-resided in households with children under 10 years of age, and a mother who was employed outside the home, suggesting a relation-ship of mutual assistance; but most grandmothers who co-resided did not live in such households, suggesting that dependence characterized the relationship. Looking diachronically, widows in the Potteries under the age of 65 tended to head their own household which contained not only their own unmarried children but also occasionally 'parentless' nieces, nephews, and grandchildren. Thus, younger widows tended to provide support for dependent children. As the widows grew older and the children became self-supporting the relationship gradually moved through mutuality to the reverse, with widows over 65 co-residing with and dependent on an unmarried or married child. Thus, there is evidence of long-term reciprocity and of relationships which offered little prospect of reciprocity such as those of the elderly supporting young 'parentless' grandchildren. And finally, although the co-residence of young married couples with parents was a common pattern in both the Potteries and Preston, it can be interpreted as part of the interpersonal negotiations through which people create a long-term history of relationships and shared understandings which shape the definition of needs and capacities for assistance in particular circumstances.

Conclusion

THIS investigation of the Staffordshire Potteries in the mid-nineteenth century has a number of wider implications. Many of the patterns of family employment, fertility, family standard of living, relations between firm and family, the advent and implications of factory legislation, and provision of social welfare differ from those of other areas of Britain. At the same time this investigation of the Potteries does more than show that patterns were different there from those in other British communities which have previously received attention. It suggests more generally the need for family historians to consider communities and regions rather than single occupations. Finally, the investigation extends general views of the maintenance and importance of family relationships in the face of the potentially disruptive processes of urbanization and industrialization.

First, although the analysis has to move quickly beyond the limits of the information in the census enumerators' books, the visibility of women's and children's factory labour and co-residence patterns in the census enumerators' books have made it possible to 'recognize and identify a plurality of competing family options extant within' a single region[1] and to pin-point certain differences between the Potteries and other areas of Britain. The unexpected variety of responses to employment opportunities in the Potteries provides evidence of variability in employment behaviour which sets up a more complex picture of how family decisions about earnings and fertility are made. Certainly the 'structural context'—social, demographic, economic, ideological, political—imposed constraints on behaviour, but the variations in patterns of family employment, fertility, and standards of living in the Potteries highlight the flexibility and relative autonomy of the nuclear family even in an area dominated by one industry, and the key position of women—as wives, mothers, daughters, and workers—in shaping the responses of families to their circumstances.

For example, the family employment patterns of pottery-workers described in Chapter 3 suggest that on the one hand, the wives and children aged 8–12 years of the great majority of potters, miners, and

---

[1] L. Stone, 'Family History in the 1980s: Past Achievements and Future Trends', *J. of Int. Hist.* 12 (1981), 82.

ironworkers did not work in the pottery industry or in other paid employment (except for the taking in of lodgers, particularly among miners' wives). On the other hand, some mothers and children aged 8–12 were employed in the pottery industry, and in these cases there was either no male head present in the household or, if present, the male head was not necessarily a potter, but may have worked in a variety of occupations. These family employment patterns suggest that there was a division between working-class families which cut across the main occupational groups within the Potteries and corresponded crudely to the division between 'rough' and 'respectable' cited in studies of other areas. Moreover, these family employment patterns, in which the children aged 8–12 years of male potters tended not to work in the potbanks, in turn explain in part the limited participation of pottery-workers in the movement for the extension of the Factory Acts to the pottery industry. The few protests there were came not from the widows and others whose family income would be reduced by the loss of children's earnings, but from male potters in the few sections that employed young children, as they would have to pay more for assistants. Thus, the extension of factory legislation did not directly affect most pottery-workers at first. John Finney fails to mention it at all in his autobiography.

Furthermore, the family employment patterns in the early 1860s changed over the second half of the century. They differed from those in 1881 and particularly from those in the years 1890–1914, when the wives and children of potters characteristically worked in the potbanks.[2] As the number and percentage of women in the pottery labour-force increased, they came disproportionately from the families of potters. By 1881 the percentage of wives and daughters of potters employed in the pottery industry increased while those of miners remained the same. These patterns reflect the increasing real wages of miners and declining real wages of potters during the period, competition from ironworks and mines for adolescent male labour, the introduction of technical changes, and the movement of women into formerly male occupations augmenting rather than displacing male labour, as well as changing tastes in pottery decoration requiring increasing numbers of paintresses.

Differences between conditions in the Potteries and other areas suggest differences in sets of needs and resources, which in turn had implications for the nature and extent to which alternative sources of assistance

[2] For the predominant pattern of employment of the families of male potters in the potworks in the period 1890–1914, see R. Whipp, *Patterns of Labour: Work and Social Change in the Pottery Industry* (London, 1990), 71–81.

to the family, such as the Poor Law, friendly societies, employers, and trade unions provided material assistance and exerted pressure on people to maintain family relationships at all costs. During the early 1860s the Potteries as a whole was an area of relatively good housing conditions and comparatively high wages and employment. Moreover, there were unusually low levels of population turnover and migration for pottery-workers, who tended to be locally born, though not for miners and ironworkers, who tended to have been born outside the Potteries in other centres of mining or ironworking. Nevertheless, despite general prosperity and relative geographical stability, the Potteries was also an area of exceptionally high mortality rates due to a combination of the conditions in the pottery industry and the general urban environment. Relatively few families in the Potteries were confronted with the problems associated with migration compared with many other nineteenth-century towns; and because of the higher proportion of locally born people in the Potteries, an individual might have had more relatives to call upon for assistance. The relatively high co-residence of elderly persons with family and kin in industrial areas such as the Potteries and Preston compared with rural areas and market towns may have been associated with the small numbers of elderly people both in absolute terms and in proportion to the rest of the population. Their small number relative to the number of women who were potential carers, the relatively high wages and employment, and the relatively low rates of outdoor relief for the elderly available from the local Poor Law guardians also influenced the level of co-residence. At the same time the relatively high mortality rates, particularly for male potters above 45 years suffering from respiratory diseases, may have been reflected in the high proportions of outdoor relief devoted to widows with children and sickness under the Poor Law in the area.

Second, the family employment and fertility patterns in the Potteries call into question the use of 'occupation' as a category with fixed prior characteristics which can be used as an explanatory variable. Instead, the social characteristics associated with occupations need to be seen as problematic. The family employment patterns in the Potteries reveal a mixing of occupations even among occupational groups such as miners and ironworkers, which are usually characterized as relatively homogeneous. They serve as a warning against assuming that it was the wives and children of men in the industry hiring women and children who worked in that industry. Although the largest proportion of women and children employed in the potteries were the wives, daughters, and children of male potters, there were substantial proportions of women and children employed who had husbands or fathers who were either dead or in other occupations. Moreover, the wives, daughters, and children of potters typically did not work in the potteries. Furthermore, in the long term over the second half of the century not only changes within the pottery industry but also changes in the local labour-market, including changing relative wages and increased demand for adolescent male labour from mines and ironworks, affected both the supply and demand for labour in the pottery industry.

In addition, the similarity in fertility in the Potteries among different occupational groups and the relatively high fertility in an area with relatively high married women's labour-force participation raise doubts about the use of 'occupation' not only as a category with fixed attributes, but also as a focus for analysis. In particular, it is plausible to argue that urban areas of mixed occupations were more typical of mid- and late Victorian Britain than homogeneous mining, iron, and textile areas; hence, studies of the fertility decline in nineteenth-century Britain have over-emphasized 'occupation' at the expense of studies of particular localities where it is possible to examine fertility behaviour in context.

Even for 'single occupation' communities, where the dominant industry did not employ women and children or where census enumerators' books are not revealing about women's employment or not available for the period in question, the inevitable presence of a service sector means that a community-based rather than an occupation-based methodology may be more appropriate. Such a perspective is also more useful for any study which approaches families as one of a number of sources of assistance—along with neighbours, the Poor Law, friendly societies, churches, trade unions, voluntary hospitals, and civic authorities—which individuals in nineteenth-century towns turned to in times of need. Apart from employers and trade unions, the institutions involved in the provision of social welfare in nineteenth-century areas, even those such as the Potteries where one industry was dominant, tended to be widely based across occupations. This approach quickly takes family history into the subjects and concerns of social history more generally. The more these are investigated the more important it is that the analysis of family structure itself is community-minded.

Third, the evidence in Chapters 2, 3, 7, and 8 indicated that members of the working class in the Potteries, as in Preston, in the mid-nineteenth century maintained relationships with family and kin. Moreover, the examination of Etruria in Chapter 4 suggested not only that individuals maintained family relationships, but also that nuclear families maintained a measure of autonomy. Relationships within the Wedgwood factory were not transferred directly to the families and village of Etruria.

The explanation for this persistence of family relationships, even from the perspective of the individual, however, is somewhat broader than that which Michael Anderson suggests. In part individuals maintained family relationships as Anderson argues because the family provided the only framework 'controllable by the working class, within which reciprocation could occur that was sufficiently defined to provide an adequate guarantee of assistance in crisis situations'. In other words, they were reciprocal relationships in which individuals received material and non-material assistance which they could not acquire elsewhere for problems such as finding a job, sickness, desertion, unemployment, or old age. Anderson emphasizes reciprocity on a short-term, calculative basis, but in the Potteries there is evidence of reciprocity negotiated between family members over the long term and even asymmetrical relationships with little prospect of reciprocity. In addition, as I illustrate above in Chapter 7, other institutions which provided assistance also encouraged individuals to maintain relationships with family and kin. Although institutional sanctions against individuals who neglected to assist family or kin were weak and easy to avoid, institutions such as friendly societies, burial societies, relief funds, infirmaries, and the Poor Law supplemented and complemented rather than replaced the assistance provided by family members to individuals, and thereby reinforced family relationships. To the extent that they provided a substitute for family relationships, it was usually to those who had no family or kin or whose family and kin were unable, though not necessarily unwilling, to assist. The extent to which they competed with and weakened family ties was minimal. Finally, the influence of ideology, particularly through Sunday schools, should not be neglected in an explanation of why individuals maintained family relationships in the Potteries in the mid-nineteenth century.

It is possible to restate these reasons in a way which allows one to move to a different level and consider the functions of and effects of family and kinship relationships as a structure or unit in relation to other institutions. Anderson's approach to the study of the family from the perspective of the individual allows no place for consideration of why the family provided certain benefits and other institutions offered other benefits. From the point of view of the individual, the context, including the division of labour among the family and other institutions, is fixed. The individual at different stages of the life cycle chooses relationships with an institution or a combination of institutions which provide him or her with most satisfaction. But the functions of families and other institutions are neither fixed nor are they the product of an inevitable progressive loss of functions by the family to other institutions. Instead, which institution provided what assistance (as well as which family members were employed) in a specific context was the product of a process of negotiation—of conflict and consensus. One way to illustrate this process is to categorize examples according to those reflecting consensus and those reflecting conflict between the family and other institutions. In the former, the members of families often took the initiative in seeking assistance from other institutions; in the latter, other institutions took the initiative and invaded the autonomy of the family and family members resisted.

When matrimonial or family disputes became irresolvable within the nuclear family, for example, family members took the initiative and resorted to an outside institution—the law—for assistance. In Hanley in 1874 'William Wedgwood ten years of age, was brought before the magistrates by his parents as an incorrigible boy, with whom it was impossible to do anything. On Monday morning, he stole 1s. 1d. The magistrates decided to send the boy to an industrial school, probably to Werrington'.[3] The large attendance at Sunday schools in the Potteries reflected a consensus among many working–class parents that they were unable to provide their children completely with what they saw as desirable moral or secular (at least reading and perhaps writing) education. This was not a one-way removal of functions from the nuclear family, however; instead, one aim of Sunday schools was for children to return to the family and be a good moral influence on parents.[4] Even if it did not work out thus in practice, the content of both Sunday–school and secular education tended to promote the observance of obligations to family members and reinforce the importance of the family. Similarly, subscription to the North Staffordshire Infirmary reflected the recognition on the part of many members of the working class in the Potteries that the nuclear family could not cope with all medical needs and their initiative in seeking assistance from an outside institution, the North Staffordshire Infirmary, which would supplement and reinforce the family assistance.

Occasionally other institutions attempted to invade families and met with considerable resistance. For example, in less religious families in

---

[3] *SS* 24 Dec. 1874.
[4] T. Laqueur, *Religion and Respectability: Sunday Schools and Working Class Culture* (London, 1976), 15, 19.

which an adolescent went through an evangelical conversion experience, there could be bitter generational conflict.[5] Refusal to have children vaccinated against smallpox and the resistance of some parents to the Factory Acts are other examples of the families in conflict with other institutions.

It has been suggested that one possible result of the maintenance of family and kin relationships in the nineteenth century was to strengthen working-class consciousness, rather than engendering false consciousness and promoting capitalist ideology. Jane Humphries argues that 'struggles around the family such as resistance to "in house" relief and the battle for the family wage unite families in class endeavours'.[6] Moreover,

heroic family loyalties undoubtedly sustained many individuals through the turbulent period of industrialization, and engendered a feeling of comradeship in oppression. This must have been important. Class solidarity does not materialize out of a sudden recognition by isolated individuals that their situation is shared and that though weak individually, they have collective power. It develops slowly over time as a result of real life experience. Rather than promoting individualism, the mutual dependence of the family could well point up class and community interest.[7]

The similarities in the patterns of family employment, fertility, and family income among the different occupational groups which emerged in Chapter 3 lend some support to the suggestion that the maintenance of family relationships promoted class and community, rather than individual, interests. Yet, it would be better to see family relationships as indeterminate—sometimes promoting individualism, sometimes promoting class and community interests, and sometimes promoting neither. Instead of a uniform result, it was the differences in family experience which differentiated otherwise homogeneous occupational groups. Whether or not the maintenance of family relationships promoted individualism or class and community solidarity, it reflects the lottery of birth and particularly death. Thus, in the Potteries, and perhaps elsewhere in England, in the mid-nineteenth century it was death rather than the factory or other institutions providing alternatives to family relationships which was most likely to break up families.

---

[5] Ibid. 166.

[6] J. Humphries, 'Class Struggle and the Persistence of the Working-Class Family', *Cambridge Journal of Economics*, 1 (1977), 254.

[7] Ibid. 255.

Census Taking in the Potteries

BECAUSE this thesis relies heavily on the census enumerators' books, it is appropriate to examine the process and reliability of census-taking in the Potteries in the mid-nineteenth century. The reliability of the census enumerators' books in general are discussed in the introduction to the published 1861 census returns and more recently in publications by P. M. Tillott and by Edward Higgs.[1] But the question remains whether there were any special, local peculiarities in the taking of the census in the Potteries in March 1851, April 1861, and April 1871 which might jeopardize the reliability of the returns.

Contemporary newspapers indicate that the taking of the census in the Potteries went smoothly each time. In 1851 a newspaper article announced the approaching census, stressed its importance, and described the census-taking process. After the enumeration the newspaper reported: 'from the extent of Stoke-on-Trent and its widely scattered population, the work of enumeration on Monday last, census day, was a task of considerable magnitude. It was, however, readily accomplished by the judicious division of labour'.[2]

In 1861 there was no mention of the census at all in the local newspaper before the returns were collected; and afterwards, the newspapers only reported the results. Indeed one wonders how an undertaking which affected every household could have no advance notice in the newspapers while articles on Garibaldi, Dr Livingstone, the secession of South Carolina, the death of the Second Duke of Sutherland, and the Hernanders and Elphinstone's Circus filled many columns. Moreover, without a newspaper announcement, how did people know what was happening when the enumerator knocked on the door? One can only suppose that 'Old Tamborine John', the Hanley Town Crier, who rode through the streets on a small pony and 'dressed like a yeoman of the Guard but with a hat like an admiral',[3] the memory of the last census ten years before, and the enumerator's explanations at the door must have been sufficient.

In 1871 the coming census received extensive coverage in the local press. Before the enumeration, articles emphasized the importance of filling out the schedules properly, and one even suggested additional instructions tailored to local readers:

---

[1] PP 1863, liii, 3. P. M. Tillott, 'Sources of Inaccuracy in the 1851 and 1861 Census', in E. A. Wrigley (ed.), *Nineteenth Century Society: Essays in the Use of Quantitative Methods for the Study of Social Data* (Cambridge, 1972), 82–113; E. Higgs, *Making Sense of the Census: The Manuscript Returns for England and Wales, 1801–1901* (London, 1989).

[2] *Staffs. Advert.*, 29 Mar. 1851.

[3] J. Finney, *Sixty Years' Recollections of an Etruscan* (Stoke-upon-Trent, 1903), 9.

printed with each schedule is a series of instructions for filling up the column headed
'Rank, Profession or Occupation'. In respect to this branch of the subject we take the
liberty to make a special addition to the lucid instruction of the Registrar-General, who
would perhaps be somewhat mystified by such occupations as 'flatpresser' and 'hollow-
ware presser'. The words 'in earthenware manufactory' or 'in china manufactory' or even
'in pottery' will make an infinite difference in the amount of information conveyed.[4]

Other articles described the local arrangements, the mechanics of census-
taking, and assured readers that the census 'has no connection whatever with
rates and taxes. There is nothing approaching a poll tax, and no one has anything
to dread from census inquiries'. Moreover, 'there is no conscription'.[5] After the
enumeration the local newspaper carried a lengthy report on census-taking in the
Potteries, giving a colourful description of the local proceedings and again leaving the impression of an essentially uneventful undertaking.[6] There were also
reports and letters to the editor from enumerators after the census-taking. One
enumerator reported that

among the curiosities from the census papers may be mentioned that one head of a
family . . . in the last column described himself as 'sound in wind and limb', his wife as
'all right', his eldest as a 'promising lad' and his youngest as having 'good eyes'. In the
occupation column opposite the name of the youngest who is twelve months old he had
written 'not able to decide'.[7]

Another enumerator reinforces the impression of a basically smooth census-
taking in the Potteries, when he writes 'I am convinced that an outsider would
never have credited that the census schedules would be so well and carefully
filled up as has been the case in 1871'.[8]

Thus, in 1871 contemporaries felt that census-taking in the Potteries had gone
well, and none mentioned any local peculiarities which might jeopardize the
reliability of the returns. In the absence of evidence to the contrary, it is possible
to assume that in 1851 and 1861 the process of census-taking was little different
from 1871.

Furthermore, the Whipple test on the age data for married couples in the
sample of the parliamentary borough and a check of ages and birthplaces of
people in the Etruria census enumerators' books in 1851 and 1861 (i.e. were they
recorded as ten years older and born in the same place in 1861 as in 1851)
confirm the impression of relative reliability.

The extent to which individuals when responding to the enumerator rounded
their ages to those ending in '0' or '5' can be estimated by the Whipple test.[9] This
test involves calculating the ratio of the sum of the returns of ages ending in '0'
and '5' to one-fifth of the total sum of returns. The ratios can be interpreted as
indicating the following qualities of age enumeration:

[4] *SS* 1 Apr. 1871.   [5] *SS* 8 Apr. 1871.
[6] *SS* 29 Apr. 1871.   [7] *SS* 15 Apr. 1871.   [8] Ibid.
[9] A. Armstrong, 'The Census Enumerators' Books: A Commentary', in R. Lawton (ed.),
The Census and Social Structure (London, 1978), 36–7.

100–104.9:	'highly accurate';
105–109.9:	'fairly accurate';
110–124.9:	'approximate';
125–174.9:	'rough';
175+:	'very rough'.

The ratio for husbands in the Potteries sample was 125.8, which suggests that the age enumeration was between 'approximate' and 'rough'. This, however, is not much different than the ratio of 120.4 which Armstrong found in his data for husbands in York in 1851. For wives in the Potteries the ratio is 113.2, which is somewhat better than the ratio of 129.0 for wives in York in 1851.

The consistency of the age data in the enumerators' books can be estimated by comparing the ages of individuals in one census with the age they report in the next census. In the Etruria enumeration district 62 per cent of the individuals who could be traced listed their ages as exactly 10 years older in 1861 than in 1851. This is somewhat more than the 53 per cent which Anderson found in Preston.[10] In both Etruria and Preston only 4 per cent gave ages that were more than 2 years greater or less than 10 years older, and 1 per cent were more than 5 years off.

The consistency of the birthplace information in the enumerators' books can be tested in the same way as the age data. Most of the differences between the two years were not important. Usually they were smaller or larger units or adjacent places with indistinct boundaries, such as Hanley in 1851 and Etruria in 1861, or Shelton in 1851 and Hanley in 1861. Approximately 8 per cent reported birthplaces that were different enough to make migrants into non-migrants and vice versa, but this figure is about the same as Anderson found in Preston.[11]

The Census Enumerators' Books Analysis: Procedure

A 1-in-15 sample was taken of all households in the census enumerators' books for the parliamentary borough of Stoke-upon-Trent in 1861.[12] The sample was a systematic sample with the initial case selected using a random-number table. It included 1,353 households (or co-residing groups), slightly more than the 1,241 co-residing groups in Anderson's sample of Preston. I copied, coded, and entered the data for analysis using SPSS on the University of Oxford and subsequently the University of Cambridge computer. Pre-coding, i.e. creating

[10] M. Anderson, 'The Study of Family Structure', in Wrigley, *Nineteenth-Century Society*, 75; also cited in A. Armstrong, 'Census Enumerators' Books', 36.

[11] Anderson, 'The Study of Family Structure', in Wrigley, *Nineteenth-Century Society*, 75; Armstrong, 'Census Enumerators' Books', 37.

[12] This procedure followed M. Anderson, *Family Structure in 19th Century Lancashire* (Cambridge, 1971), 19, 199 n.; id., 'The Study of Family Structure', in Wrigley, *Nineteenth-Century Society*, 56; and R. Schofield, 'Sampling in Historical Research', in Wrigley, *Nineteenth Century Society*, 151–63. The sample included quasi-institutions such as lodging houses. In addition, a 1-in-15 sample of the residents of institutions, e.g. workhouses, was taken for use when data for the whole population were required.

numerical summaries of information, was kept to a minimum to allow maximum flexibility in the original data-file for later analysis.

The age- and sex-distributions of the population in the parliamentary borough is not available in the published census. Nevertheless, the age- and sex-distributions of the sample were checked against the published tables for the six registration sub-districts which cover the parliamentary borough. Although the overlap of the boundaries is not exact, there is no reason to think that the additional area in the sub-districts but not in the parliamentary borough was unusual in any way. The distributions of the age- and sex-structure of the sample and the published tables for the sub-districts corresponded.

The main data-file, SAMPOTS, contained information on 1,353 co-residing groups and 6,707 individuals (excluding 64 'visitors'). From this main file two other files were created, using Fortran programs written by Clive Payne of the Oxford Social Science Faculty Computer Unit especially for this purpose. The first, MFCARDS, is a file of all 1,173 married couples in the sample. It includes individual information on the husband, wife, and children, if any, and on the household status of the couple (e.g. live as lodgers, kin, etc.). If the couple head the household, there is information about any lodgers, kin, or servants who might be co-residing. The second file, CHILDSM, is a file of all 775 children aged 8–12 years in the sample together with information about their co-residing fathers, mothers, and siblings, if any, and about the household status of the co-residing group in which they live.

The final file of data from the census enumerators' books is ETRURIA, a file of information on all of the co-residing groups and individuals in the census enumerators's book for Etruria in 1861.

When it came time to take a sample from the 1881 census enumerators' books, technological changes enabled me to type the information for the sample households directly from microfilm of the enumerators' books for the parliamentary borough of Stoke-upon-Trent into the computer. I took a 1-in-24 sample for 1881, which included approximately 6,000 individuals and 1,200 households.

Calculating Family Standards of Living for the Potteries Sample 1861: Procedure

The family standard of living was calculated for as many families as possible headed by married couples in the Potteries sample. The procedure used to calculate the family income component of the family standard of living was to match wage information with the sample of families headed by married couples taken from the census enumerators' books.[13] Thus, it was necessary first to

---

[13] The procedure used here follows that used by Anderson, *Family Structure*, 30–1. It is also similar to that used by J. Foster, *Class Struggle and the Industrial Revolution: Early Industrial Capitalism in Three English Towns* (London, 1974), 257–8, except in its treatment of lodgers and where Foster calculates the incomes of all wage-earning households and not just those headed by married couples.

estimate the 'normal' earnings, assuming a full week's work for all of the occupations where this could be ascertained with a reasonable degree of certainty.[14] Trade, clerical and middle-class occupations, as well as occupations that had highly variable earnings where no one figure for them could be assigned with any degree of reliability (e.g. dressmakers, laundresses) were excluded. The aggregate income of each nuclear family headed by a married couple where the income of all family members could be estimated from the figures for the earnings of the different occupations was obtained. Information was sufficient for incomes to be calculated for 78 per cent of the families headed by married couples in the Potteries sample.[15] Income from lodgers was ignored and it was assumed that co-residing children gave all their income to the family.

The minimum standard of family expenditure for each nuclear family headed by a married couple where the earnings of all family members could be estimated was based on Rowntree's scale of primary poverty expenditure as used by Anderson,[16] but adjusted for lower rents in the Potteries (see Table MA.1).

This scale differs from that used by Foster who followed Bowley in varying the food requirements by the age and sex of family members. The Rowntree scale assumes that all children regardless of age consumed 75 per cent of an adult diet. A comparison of the family expenditure of the same family, e.g. John and Mary Potts of Tunstall, with three sons aged 15, 11, and 1 month and two daughters aged 8 and 5 using the two methods results in a difference of 2/4 (the estimate by the Rowntree method is greater). However, this absolute difference depending on which method is used does not affect the relative difference within the sample when the same scale is used. It is the relative differences that are of concern here.

The resulting estimate of the minimum standard of family expenditure was

---

[14] Earnings in the different branches of the pottery industry were estimated from figures for North Staffordshire reported in the following: PP 1887, lxxxix, 508–9; PP 1863, xviii, 32, 46, 53–4, 56, 59–63; WMSS. 29241–6. W. H. Warburton, *The History of Trade Union Organization in the North Staffordshire Potteries* (London, 1931), 242–5; National Association for the Promotion of Social Science, *Report of the Committee on Trade Societies and Strikes* (London, 1860), 281; H. Owen, *The Staffordshire Potter* (1st pub. London, 1901; repr. Bath, 1970), 323; lists of able-bodied persons and their families who received out relief in 1855–8 found in the correspondence between the Guardians of the Stoke-upon-Trent Poor Law Union and the poor law commissioners in PRO MH12/11463. Earnings for miners and ironworkers were estimated from figures for North Staffordshire reported in: PP 1866, xiv, 535; PP 1887, lxxxix, 413–15, 427–8, 447. Wages for a wide range of occupations were estimated from the figures for Manchester in 1859 found in D. Chadwick, 'Rates of Wages', *JRSS* 23 (1860), 12–29; E. H. Hunt, *Regional Wage Variations in Britain 1850–1914* (Oxford, 1973), 30, 39–41 describes both the Potteries and Manchester as high-wage areas in 1850, so it seemed safe to use the Manchester figures without any adjustment. Estimates of servants' earnings come from T. McBride, *The Domestic Revolution* (London, 1975), 60.

[15] Cf. 55 per cent of the family units headed by married couples in Preston: Anderson, *Family Structure*, 31.

[16] Ibid. 201.

TABLE MA.1   *The Rowntree Scale of Primary Poverty Expenditure*
adjusted for the Potteries 1861

Family Composition	Food	Rent[a]	Sundries[b]	Total
1 man or woman	6/–	2/4	3/2	11/6
1 man, 1 woman, 1 child[c]	8/3	2/4	3/9	14/4
1 man, 1 woman, 2 children	10/6	2/4	4/4	17/2
1 man, 1 woman, 3 children	12/9	2/4	4/11	20/–
1 man, 1 woman, 4 children	15/–	2/4	5/6	22/10
increasing thereafter at a rate of 2/10 per child				

[a] The average of rents paid by families of 3 to 10 persons in the Stoke-upon-Trent
Poor Law Union 1855–8: PRO MH12/11463/.
[b] Heat, light, clothes, bedding, etc.
[c] Boys over 14 years old are counted as adults for food (i.e. 9*d*. is added to the cost of
food for each boy over 14).
Note: The table is adapted from Anderson, *Family Structure*, 201.

subtracted from the estimated income of each nuclear family. The results were
grouped in 8*s*. bands for Table 1.4 and Fig. 1.6. The results were also used in
calculations for Tables 3.12 and 3.13 and Fig. 3.3.

Marriage Register Analysis: Materials and Method

Regrettably, the Registrar General no longer gives researchers permission to use
the mid-nineteenth century marriage certificates which cover all marriages. For-
tunately, a high proportion of marriages in the Potteries took place according to
the rites of the Established Church, because Methodists (of which there were a
large number in the Potteries) were advised to marry in the Church of England.
In 1862 nearly 90 per cent of the marriages in the Stoke-upon-Trent registration
district and 82 per cent of the marriages in the Wolstanton–Burslem registration
district followed the rites of the Anglican Church, compared with 79 per cent in
England as a whole.[17] Thus, the proportion of marriages outside the Church of
England does not seem large enough to jeopardize unduly analyses using the
marriage registers from Anglican churches in the Potteries.

   The mid-nineteenth-century marriage registers contain a variety of information—date, age, marital status, occupation, and signature of the bride and groom,
and the occupation of the fathers of the bride and groom—which can throw light
on a wide range of questions. These include, for example, seasonality of marriage,
age at first marriage, remarriage, geographical horizons of marriage, literacy, and

[17] PP 1864, xvii, 72–3.

illegitimacy. Information from marriage registers from all of the Potteries towns is used at various points in the thesis with regard to such questions.[18] The registers used are named in the list of sources at the end.

Occasionally, a register contains unusually detailed information. The registers of Old Chapel and St Luke Wellington in Hanley, for example, give the street number as well as the street name for the addresses of the bride and groom at the time of marriage; the register of Christ Church, Tunstall indicates whether the bride or groom was illegitimate; the register of Holy Trinity, Sneyd in Burslem mentions whether the father of the bride or groom was dead; and the register of Holy Trinity, Northwood in Hanley gives the occupation of the bride at the time of marriage.

The primary purpose of this Appendix is to describe the use of the occupational information in the registers for two specific purposes: (1) to indicate the extent to which occupational groups were socially separate; and (2) to examine occupational change between generations. All entries in the four parishes covering Tunstall and most of Burslem including Cobridge were examined for a period of three years, 1860–2.[19] A total of 645 marriages were examined.[20] The information from the registers was copied without alteration on to forms. The analysis of the information on the forms was done by hand.

For the use of marriage as an indicator of the separation of occupation groups in Tables 3.9 and 3.10 I have followed Crossick and used the occupations of the fathers of grooms and brides rather than those of the marriage partners.[21] For widows, widowers, and where the groom was a soldier the occupation of the bride or groom (not the father's) was used.

The method used in Tables 3.11 and 3.7 to calculate the index of association followed the procedure described by Foster. The index of association 'measures how far the number of marriages which actually took place between different occupations exceeded (or failed to reach) the number that might have been expected had marriage between occupations been entirely random. The "random

[18] Part of twenty parishes overlapped with the parliamentary borough of Stoke-upon-Trent in 1861. Due to the vacancy of livings and the limited assistance of the Rector of Stoke-upon-Trent, I was not able to use the registers for five of the parishes. Two of these were peripheral, and I was able to use at least one register from each town. Stoke and Longton are the least well represented, while I was able to see registers for all of the parishes covering Tunstall and Burslem.

[19] These covered nearly the whole of the northern half of the parliamentary borough. It seemed preferable to concentrate this analysis on a coherent area covering two entire towns rather than to add information from other parishes which would not encompass entire towns due to the missing information from several parishes. Moreover, there is no apparent reason to think the patterns would differ substantially.

[20] Although this number is less than those used by Crossick and Foster, it is greater than the numbers used by H. McLeod, *Class and Religion in the Victorian City* (London, 1974), 294–5 and R. Dennis, 'Distance and Social Interaction in a Victorian City', *J. of Hist. Geog.* 3 (1977), 241.

[21] G. Crossick, *An Artisan Elite in Victorian Society* (London, 1978), 132.

expectation" of intermarriage between occupations A and B is calculated by multiplying the incidence of all occupation A sons and daughters in the total marrying population by the incidence of B sons and daughters (e.g. $1/10 \times 1/5$) and then multiplying by the total number of marriages for all occupations. This gives one the expected figure. The actual number of intermarriages is then divided by this. If precisely the same number of A sons and daughters married B sons and daughters as the "random expectation", then the index stands at unity (100 in the tables)'.[22]

[22] Foster, *Class Struggle*, 263.

Bibliography

The following bibliography includes items cited in the text and a selection of other relevant sources consulted.

A. MANUSCRIPT SOURCES

Public Record Office

RG 9. Census papers: population returns for 1861. Enumerators' schedules for Stoke-upon-Trent Parliamentary Borough.

RG11. Census papers: population returns for 1881. Enumerators' schedules for Stoke-upon-Trent Parliamentary Borough.

HO 107/2005. Census papers: population returns for 1851. Enumerators' schedule for Etruria.

RG 9/1935. Census papers: population returns for 1861. Enumerators' schedule for Etruria.

RG 10/2864. Census papers: population returns for 1871. Enumerators' schedule for Etruria.

RG 11/2724. Census papers: population returns for 1881 Enumerators' schedule for Etruria.

HO 45. Registered Papers. Correspondence of the Factory Inspectors.

MH 12. Poor Law Union Papers. Correspondence of the Poor Law Commission and the Poor Law Board with the Stoke-upon-Trent Poor Law Union 1835–64.

Horace Barks Reference Library, Stoke-on-Trent City Library, Hanley

Hanley Relief Committee Minutes 1861.
Hanley Rate Book 1862, 1865.
Marriage Registers:
　Hanley (Hope Parish), Holy Trinity.
　Hanley, 'Old Church'.

Keele University Library

Spode Company Papers.
The Wedgwood Papers.

University College of North Wales (Bangor) Library, Department of Manuscripts (now available at the Minton Archives, Royal Doulton plc, Minton House, London Road, Stoke-on-Trent)

Minton Company Manuscripts.

Marriage Registers: Staffordshire County Record Office

D/3229/6   Etruria, St Matthew (1849–69).
D/3463/1/19   Tunstall, Christchurch (1857–65).
D/3277/1/2/3   Longton, St James (1858–67).

Marriage Registers 1860–2 in Potteries Churches

Burslem, St John's.
Burslem (Sneyd), Holy Trinity.
Cobridge, Christ Church.
Fenton, Christ Church.
Hanley (Northwood), Holy Trinity.
Hanley (Wellington), St Luke's.
Shelton, St Mark's.
Stoke-upon-Trent, St Peter's.

Unpublished Theses

ANDERTON, P., 'The Liberal Party of Stoke-on-Trent and Parliamentary Elections 1862–1880: A Case Study of Liberal–Labour Relations', M.A. thesis (Keele, 1974).

BOTHAM, F. W., 'Working-Class Living Standards in North Staffordshire 1750–1914', Ph.D. thesis (London, 1982).

CLARKE, M. A., 'Household and Family in Bethnal Green, 1851–1871: The Effects of Social and Economic Change', Ph.D. thesis (Cambridge, 1986).

DENNIS, R., 'Community and Interaction in a Victorian City: Huddersfield 1850–1880', Ph.D. thesis (Cambridge, 1975).

DEWEY, J. A., 'An Examination of the Role of Church and State in the Development of Elementary Education in North Staffordshire Between 1870 and 1903', Ph.D. thesis (Keele, 1971).

DUPREE, M. W., 'Family Structure in the Staffordshire Potteries 1840–1880', D.Phil. thesis (Oxford, 1981).

GARRETT, E., 'Before Their Time: Employment and Family Formation in a Northern Textile Town, Keighley, 1851–1881', Ph.D. thesis (Sheffield, 1987).

GATER, S., 'A House of Long-Standing: A Study of Josiah Wedgwood and Sons in the Second Half of the Nineteenth Century', M.A. in Victorian Studies diss. (Keele, 1986).

HOLLEY. J., 'The Re-division of Labour: Two Firms in Nineteenth Century South-east Scotland', Ph.D. thesis (Edinburgh, 1978).

MOISLEY, H. A., 'The Potteries Coalfield: A Regional Analysis', M.Sc. thesis (Leeds, 1950).

NIXON, M. I., 'The Emergence of the Factory System in the Staffordshire Pottery Industry', Ph.D. thesis (Aston, 1976).

NIXON, W. B., 'Scholars Not Schools', Ph.D. thesis (Keele, 1982).

SZRETER, S., 'The Decline of Marital Fertility in England and Wales c.1870–1914', Ph.D. thesis (Cambridge, 1984).

TOWNLEY, W. E., 'Urban Administration and Health: A Case Study of Hanley in the Mid-19th Century', M.A. thesis (Keele, 1969).

Unpublished Papers

DRAKE, M., 'The Remarriage Market in Mid-19th Century Britain', a paper presented to the International Colloquium on Historical Demography, Kristiansand, Norway, 7–9 September 1979. ESRC Cambridge Group Library C/650.3.

DUPREE, M., 'Social and Economic Aspects of the Family Life-Cycle: Individuals, Households and the Labour Market in the Staffordshire Potteries During the Mid-Nineteenth Century', a paper presented at the Ninth International Economic History Congress, Berne, Switzerland, 25–9 August 1986, to be published in R. Wall and O. Saito (eds.), *Social and Economic Aspects of the Family Life Cycle: Europe and Japan, Traditional and Modern* (forthcoming, Cambridge University Press).

HOLLINGSWORTH, T. H., 'Illegitimate Births and Marriage Rates in Great Britain 1841–1911', a paper presented at the International Colloquium on Historical Demography, Kristiansand, Norway, 7–9 September, 1979. ESRC Cambridge Group Library C/651.2.

OBELKEVICH, J., 'Review of *Family Structure in Nineteenth Century Lancashire*', in possession of the author.

WALL, R., 'Employment Patterns and Family Structures: The Case of Early Nineteenth Century Bruges', unpublished paper in English available in the Library of the ESRC Cambridge Group for the History of Population and Social Structure; published in Dutch as 'Beroeps-en gezinstrukturen: Brugge in het begin aan de negentiende eeuw', *Handelingen van het Genootschap vor Geschiedenis*, 123, pts. 1–2 (1986), 29–60.

B. PRINTED SOURCES

1. Primary Sources

(a) Parliamentary Papers

The page numbers in the citations in the text refer to the page numbers of the volume rather than the page numbers of the command or sessional paper, unless otherwise noted.

1816, iii (397). Select committee on the state of the children employed in the manufactories of the United Kingdom. Minutes of evidence.

1831–2, xl (141). Parliamentary representation. Reports from the Commissioners on proposed . . . boundaries of boroughs, with plans.

1834, xx (167). Supplementary report of . . . Commissioners . . . [on] the employment of children in factories . . . Part II.

1836, xxix pt. 1 (595). Second annual report of the Poor Law Commissioners . . . with appendices.

1837, xxxi [546]. Third annual report of the Poor Law Commissioners . . . with appendices.

1843, xiv [431]. Children's Employment Commission. Appendix to the second report . . . Trades and manufactories; Part I, reports and evidence from sub-commissioners.

1843, xv [432]. ibid.; Part II.

1843, xxii [496]. Census of Great Britain, 1841. Enumeration abstract, pt. I.

1843, xxiii [497]. ibid. Age abstract, pt. I.

1844, xxvii [587]. ibid. Occupation abstract, pt. I.

1847–8, xxv [967]. Eighth annual report of the Registrar General of Births, Deaths and Marriages in England and Wales.

1849, xxi [1087]. Appendix to the ninth annual report of the Registrar General . . .

1852–3, lxxxv [1631]. Census of Great Britain, 1851. Population tables I, vol. I.

1852–3, lxxxvi [1632], ibid., vol. II.

1852–3, lxxxviii, Pt. I [1691], ibid. Population tables II, vol. I.

1852–3, lxxxviii, Pt. II [1691], ibid, vol. II.

1852–3, lxxxix [1690], ibid. Religious worship . . .

1852–3, xc [1692], ibid. Education . . .

1856, xiii [343]. Report of the select committee on masters and operatives . . .

1857, sess. 2, xi [241]. Report of the select committee on the rating of mines . . .

1857–8, xxiii [2415]. Introductory report by the Medical Officer of the Board of Health, esp. 'On the prevalence of certain diseases in different districts in England and Wales' by E. H. Greenhow, MD.

1860, xxix [2712]. Twenty-first annual report of the Registrar General . . .

1861, xvi (161). Third report of the Medical Officer of the Privy Council . . . 1860. Dr Greenhow's report on districts with excessive mortality from lung diseases.

1861, xviii [2897]. Twenty-second annual report of the Registrar General . . .

1861, liii [324]. Poor rates and pauperism. Returns.

1862, xvii [2977]. Twenty-third annual report of the Registrar General . . .

1862, l [3056]. Census of England and Wales 1861. Population tables, numbers, and distribution of the people, vol. I.

1863, xiv [3124]. Twenty-fourth annual report of the Registrar General . . .

1863, xviii [3170]. Children's Employment Commission (1862). First report of the Commissioners, with appendix.

1863, xxix (449). Annual report of the Registrar of Friendly Societies in England with appendix, for 1862.

1863, liii, Pt. I [3221]. Census of England and Wales, 1861. Population tables, ages, civil condition, occupations, and birthplace of the people, vol. II.

1863, liii, Pt. II [3221]. Census of England and Wales, 1861. General Report; with appendix of tables.

1864, xvii [3415]. Twenty-fifth annual report of the Registrar General . . .

1864, xxii [3414–I]. Children's Employment Commission. Third report of the Commissioners, with appendix.

1865, xiv [3562]. Twenty-sixth annual report of the Registrar General . . .

1865, xx [3473]. Reports of inspectors of factories . . . for half year ending 31st Oct. 1864. Report by Robert Baker for the nine months ending 31st Jan. 1865.

1866, xiii (449). Report of the Select Committee on master and servant . . .

1866, xiv (431). Report of the Select Committee on mines . . .

1866, xix [3712]. Twenty-seventh annual report of the Registrar General . . .

1866, xxiv [3622]. Reports of inspectors of factories . . . for the half year ending 31st Oct. 1865. Report of Robert Baker for the eight months ending 31st December 1865.

1867, xvi [3794]. Reports of inspectors of factories . . . for the half year ending 31st October 1866. Report of Robert Baker for the eight months ending 31st December 1866.

1867, xvi [3811]. Colliery explosions. Report made by Mr Wynne, inspector of mines, on the explosion at Talk-o'-th'-Hill . . . with evidence from the Coroner's inquest.

1867–8, xviii [4010]. Reports of inspectors of factories for the half year ending 31st Oct. 1867. Report of Robert Baker for the half year ending 31st Dec. 1867.

1867–8, xx [3972]. Report of the Boundary Commissioners for England and Wales (1868).

1867–8, xxxii [4059]. Report of the Royal Commission on the Marriage Laws.

1867–8, xxxix [3980–I]. Trade Unions. Fifth report of the Royal Commission on the organization and rules of trade unions . . . with minutes of evidence.

1872, xxvi [c. 514–I]. Second report of the Commissioners . . . into friendly and benefit building societies. Part II, evidence.

1872, lxvi, Pt. I [c. 676]. Census of England and Wales, 1871. Area, housing and inhabitants, vol. I.

1872, lxvi, Pt. II [c. 676–I]. ibid., vol. II.

1873, lxxi, Pt. I [c. 872]. ibid. Age, civil condition, occupation and birthplaces, vol. III.

1873, lxi (323). Annual report of the Registrar of Friendly Societies . . ., 1872, with appendix.

1874, xxiii, Pt. II [c. 996]. Friendly and benefit building societies. Reports of assistant commissioners . . . Staffordshire . . .

1875, xlii (469). Return of trade unions registered since 1871, names, numbers and capital.

1882, l (401). Return of the churches, chapels and buildings registered for religious worship in the registration districts of Great Britain.

1883, lxxviii [c. 3562]. Census of England and Wales, 1881. Area, houses . . ., vol. I.

1883, lxxix [c. 3563]. ibid., vol. II.

1883, lxxx [c. 3722]. ibid. Ages, condition as to marriage, occupation, birthplaces . . . vol. III.

1884–5, xvii [c. 4564]. Supplement to the forty-fifth annual report of the Registrar General . . .

1887, lxxxix [c. 5172]. Wage rates. 1830–1886. Return.

1917–18, xxxv [Cd. 8678]. Census of England and Wales, 1911. Fertility of Marriage, vol. XIII, pt. I.

1917–18, xxxv. ibid., vol. XIII, pt. II.

The following series of Parliamentary Papers were consulted and found useful. (Where an individual item in a series was referred to in an explicit citation in the text, the item is also listed above).

Half-yearly reports of the factory inspectors: 1865, xx; 1866, xxiv; 1867, xvi; 1867–8, xviii; 1868–9, xiv; 1870, xv; 1871, xiv; 1872, xvi; 1873, xix; 1874, xiii; 1875, xvi; 1876, xvi; 1877, xxiii; 1878, xx.

Annual reports of the Chief Inspector of factories: 1878–9, xvi; 1880, xiv; 1881, xxiii; 1882, xviii.

Annual reports of the inspectors of mines: 1857, xvi; 1857–8, xxxii; 1859, sess. 2, xii; 1860, xxiii; 1861, xxii; 1862, xxii; 1864, xxiv, Pt. I; 1865, xx; 1867, xiv; 1867–8, xxi; 1868–9, xiv; 1870, xv; 1871, xiv; 1872, xvi; 1873, xix; 1874, xiii; 1875, xvi; 1876, xvii; 1877, xxiii; 1878, xx; 1878–9, xviii; 1880, xv; 1881, xxv; 1882, xviii.

Annual reports of the Registrar General of births, deaths, and marriages for England, esp. those with information at the level of the registration district and sub-district: 1847–8, xxv; 1849, xxi (suppl.); 1857, sess. 2, xxii; 1857–8, xxiii; 1859, sess. 2, xii; 1860, xxix; 1861, xviii; 1862, xvii; 1863, xiv; 1864, xvii; 1865, xiii (suppl.); 1866, xix; 1867, xvii; 1867–8, xix; 1868–9, xiv; 1870, xvi; 1871, xv; 1872, xvii; 1873, xx; 1875, xviii, Pt. I; 1875, xviii, Pt. II (suppl.); 1876, xviii; 1877, xxv; 1878, xxiii; 1878–9, xix; 1880, xvi; 1881, xxvii; 1882, xix; 1883, xx; 1884, xx; 1884–5, xvii (suppl.).

Annual reports of the Registrar of Friendly Societies, 1860–2, 1868–72: 1863, xxix; 1864, xxxii; 1865, xxx; 1870, lxi; 1871, lxii; 1872, liv; 1873, lxi; 1875, lxxi.

(*b*) *Parliamentary Debates*

Hansard's Parliamentary Debates, 1864.

(*c*) *Acts of Parliament*

24 & 28 Vict. c. 48. Factory Acts Extension Act, 1864.

(*d*) *Newspapers*

The Birmingham Daily News, 1864.
The Lever, 1851.
The Morning Chronicle, 1850
The North Staffordshire Mercury, 1840–5.
The Potteries Examiner, 1871–80.
The Potters Examiner and Workman's Advocate, 1843–50.

The Staffordshire Advertiser, 1840–60.
The Staffordshire Sentinel, 1854–82.

(*e*) *Directories*

Jones, *Mercantile Directory of the Pottery District of Staffordshire* (1864).
Keates and Ford, *Annual Potteries and Newcastle-under-Lyme Street and Trade Directory* (1865–6, 1867).
Kelly and Co., *Post Office Directory of Birmingham, Warwickshire, Worcestershire and Staffordshire* (1860, 1872).
Kelly and Co., *Kelly's Post Office Directory of Birmingham, Warwickshire, Worcestershire and Staffordshire* (1880).
White, W., *History, Gazeteer and Directory of Staffordshire* (1834, 1851).

(*f*) *Poll-Books*

1841 Stoke-upon-Trent Parliamentary Borough. A list of electors and how they polled at the contested election . . . William Salt Library, Stafford.
1859 Poll-Book, ibid.
1862 Poll-Book, ibid.
1865 Poll-Book, ibid.

(*g*) *North Staffordshire Infirmary*

Annual Reports 1833–60. Courtesy of Dr Charles Webster, at the Wellcome Unit for the History of Medicine, Oxford.

(*h*) *United States Consular Reports*

LANE, E. E. 'Tunstall', in *United States Consular Reports Labor in Europe . . .*, 49th Congress, 2nd Sess., House of Representatives, Ex. Doc. 54, Pt. 1 (Washington, 1885). [On microfilm in the British Library.]

2. Secondary Sources

ABRAMS, P., *Historical Sociology* (Ithaca, NY, 1982).
ANDERSON, M., *Family Structure in Nineteenth Century Lancashire* (Cambridge, 1971).
——'Introduction', in M. ANDERSON (ed.), *The Sociology of the Family* (Harmondsworth, 1971).
——'Family and Household in the Industrial Revolution', in M. ANDERSON (ed.), *The Sociology of the Family* (Harmondsworth, 1971).
——'Standard Tabulation Procedures for the Census Enumerators' Books 1851–1891', in E. A. WRIGLEY (ed.), *Nineteenth Century Society: Essays in the Use of Quantitative Methods for the Study of Social Data* (Cambridge, 1972).
——'The Study of Family Structure', in E. A. WRIGLEY (ed.), *Nineteenth Century Society: Essays in the Use of Quantitative Methods for the Study of Social Data* (Cambridge, 1972).

—— 'Marriage Patterns in Victorian Britain: An Analysis Based on Registration District Data for England and Wales 1861', *J. of Fam. Hist.* 1 (1976), 55–78.

—— 'Sociological History and the Working-class Family: Smelser Revisited', *Social History*, 3 (1976), 317–34.

—— 'Review Essay: The People of Hamilton, Canada West, Family and Class in a Mid-19th Century City', *J. of Fam. Hist.* 2 (1977), 139–49.

—— 'The Impact on the Family Relationships of the Elderly of Changes Since Victorian Times in Governmental Income-Maintenance Provision', in E. SHANAS and M. B. SUSSMAN (eds.), *Family, Bureaucracy and the Elderly* (Durham, NC, 1977), 36–59.

—— *Approaches to the History of the Western Family 1500–1914* (London, 1980).

ANDERSON, O., 'The Incidence of Civil Marriage in Victorian England and Wales', *Past and Present*, 69 (1975), 50–87.

ANDERTON, P., 'A Trade Union Year: 1864—An Extract from the Transactions of the Executive Committee for the Hollow-ware Pressers' Union', *Journal of Ceramic History*, 9 (1977), 9–32.

—— and TOWNLEY, W. E., *Doctors and Hospitals in the Region of the Potteries in the mid-19th Century: A Selection of Documentary Evidence with a Commentary* (Madeley College of Education, Madeley, 1968).

ARLIDGE, J. T., *On the Mortality of the Parish of Stoke-upon-Trent* (Hanley, 1864).

—— *On the Diseases Prevalent Among Potters* (London, 1872).

—— *The Hygiene, Diseases and Mortality of Occupations* (London, 1892).

ARMSTRONG, W. A., 'The Use of Information About Occupation', in E. A. WRIGLEY (ed.), *Nineteenth Century Society: Essays in the Use of Quantitative Methods for the Study of Social Data* (Cambridge, 1972).

—— *Stability and Change in an English County Town: A Social Study of York 1801–1851* (Cambridge, 1974).

—— 'The Census Enumerators' Books: A Commentary', in R. LAWTON (ed.), *The Census and Social Structure* (London, 1978).

ASLIN, E. and ATTERBURY, P., *Minton 1798–1976: Exhibition, Victoria and Albert Museum, August–October 1976* (London, 1976).

BARCLAY, G. W., *Techniques of Population Analysis* (New York, 1958).

BATKIN, M., *Wedgwood Ceramics 1846–1959: A New Appraisal* (London, 1982).

BEAVER, S. H., 'A Geographical Agenda for North Staffordshire', *N. Staffs. J. of Field Studies* 3 (1963), 1–16.

—— 'The Potteries: A Study in the Evolution of a Cultural Landscape', in *Presidential Addresses Delivered to the Institute of British Geographers* (London, 1964).

BECKER, G. S. 'A Theory of the Allocation of Time', *Economic Journal*, 75 (1965), 493–517.

—— *A Treatise on the Family* (Cambridge, Mass., 1981).

BELL, C. and NEWBY, H., *Community Studies: An Introduction to the Sociology of the Local Community* (London, 1971).

BELL, C. and NEWBY, H., FIRTH, R. and HARRIS, C., 'Review Symposium on M. YOUNG and P. WILMOTT, *The Symmetrical Family*', *Sociology*, 8 (1975), 505–12.

BENNETT, A., *Clayhanger* (1st edn., London, 1910; Penguin edn., Harmondsworth 1973).

BENSON, J., 'English Coalminers' Trade Union Accident Funds 1850–1900', *Econ. Hist. Rev.* 28 (1975), 401–12.

——*British Coalminers in the Nineteenth Century: A Social History* (Dublin, 1980).

BEST, G. F. A., *Shaftesbury* (London, 1964).

——*Mid-Victorian Britain 1851–1875* (rev. edn., St Albans, 1973).

BIRCH, A., *The Economic History of the British Iron and Steel Industry 1784–1879* (London, 1967).

BLAUG, M., 'The Empirical Status of Human Capital Theory: A Slightly Jaundiced Survey', *J. of Econ. Lit.* 14 (1976), 827–55.

BOOTH, P., 'Herbert Minton: Nineteenth Century Pottery Manufacturer and Philanthropist', *Staffordshire Studies*, 3 (1990–1), 65–85.

BOTT, E., *Family and Social Network* (New York, 1971; 1st pub. 1957).

BOWEN, W. and FINEGAN, T. A., *The Economics of Labor Force Participation* (Princeton, NJ, 1969).

BRADLEY, H., *Men's Work, Women's Work* (Cambridge and Oxford, 1989).

BULMER, M., 'The Rejuvenation of Community Studies? Neighbours, Networks and Policy', *Sociological Review*, 33 (1985), 430–48.

—— *Neighbours: The Work of Philip Abrams* (Cambridge, 1986).

——*The Social Basis of Community Care* (London, 1987).

——LEWIS, J. and PIACHAUD, D. (eds.), *The Goals of Social Policy* (London, 1989).

BURCHILL, F. and ROSS, R., *A History of the Potters' Union* (Hanley, 1977).

CAIRNCROSS, A., 'Economic Schizophrenia', *Scot. J. of Pol. Econ.* 5 (1958), 15–21.

CALHOUN, C. J., 'History, Anthropology and the Study of Communities: Some Problems in Macfarlane's Proposal', *Social History*, 3 (1978), 363–73.

——'Community: Toward a Variable Conceptualization for Comparative Research', *Social History*, 5 (1980), 105–29.

CANNADINE, D. N., 'The Present and the Past in the English Industrial Revolution 1880–1980', *Past and Present*, 103 (1984), 131–72.

CELORIA, F., 'Ceramic Machinery of the 19th Century in the Potteries and in Other Parts of Britain', *Staffs. Arch.* 2 (1973), 11–48.

CHADWICK, D., 'Rates of Wages', *JRSS* 23 (1860), 12–29.

CLELAND, J. and WILSON, C., 'Demand Theories of the Fertility Transition: An Iconoclastic View', *Pop. Studies* 41 (1987), 5–30.

COALE, A. J. and WATKINS, S. C. (eds.), *The Decline of Fertility in Europe* (Princeton, NJ, 1986).

COLEMAN, D. A., 'The Geography of Marriage in Britain 1920–1960', *Annals of Human Biology*, 4 (1977), 101–32.

COLLIER, F., *The Family Economy of the Working Classes in the Cotton Industry 1784–1883* (Manchester, 1964).

COOK, K. S. (ed.), *Social Exchange Theory* (London, 1987).

COX, J., *The English Churches in a Secular Society: Lambeth 1870–1930* (New York and Oxford, 1982).

CRAFTS, N. F. R., 'A Cross-Sectional Study of Legitimate Fertility in England and Wales, 1911', *Research in Economic History*, 9 (1984), 89–107.

—— *British Economic Growth During the Industrial Revolution* (Oxford, 1985).

—— 'Duration of Marriage, Fertility and Women's Employment Opportunities in England and Wales in 1911', *Pop. Studies* 43 (1989), 325–35.

CROMWELL, V., 'Interpretations of Nineteenth Century Administration: An Analysis', *Vict. Studies* 9 (1966), 245–55.

CROSSICK, G., 'Review of *Self-Help: Voluntary Associations in 19th Century Britain*', *Vict. Studies* 18 (1974–5, 238–40).

—— 'The Labour Aristocracy and its Values: A Study of Mid-Victorian Kentish London', *Vict. Studies* 19 (1975–6), 301–28.

—— *An Artisan Elite in Victorian Society* (London, 1978).

CROWTHER, M. A., *The Workhouse System 1834–1929* (London, 1981; pbk., 1983).

—— 'Family Responsibility and State Responsibility in Britain Before the Welfare State', *Hist. J.* 25 (1982), 131–45.

CUNNINGHAM, H., 'The Employment and Unemployment of Children in England *c.* 1680–1851', *Past and Present*, 126 (1990), 115–50.

CURTIS, A. and BEECH, E., *A History of the Wesley Methodist Church in Stoke-on-Trent for the Years 1799–1851* (Stoke-on-Trent, 1974).

DARWIN, E., *A Generation of Family Letters*, i (Cambridge, 1904).

DAUNTON, M. J., *House and Home in the Victorian City: Working-Class Housing 1850–1914* (London, 1983).

DAVENPORT, D. P., 'Duration of Residence in the 1855 Census of New York State', *Historical Methods*, 18 (1985), 5–12.

DAVIDOFF, L., 'The Separation of Home and Work? Landladies and Lodgers in 19th and 20th Century England', in S. BURMAN (ed.), *Fit Work for Women* (London, 1979).

—— 'The Family in Britain', in F. M. L. THOMPSON (ed.), *The Cambridge Social History of Britain 1750–1950*, ii (Cambridge, 1990), 71–129.

—— and HALL, C., *Family Fortunes: Men and Women of the English Middle Class 1780–1850* (London, 1987).

DEANE, P. and COLE, W. A., *British Economic Growth, 1688–1959* (Cambridge, 2nd edn., 1969).

DEGLER, C., 'Women and the Family', in M. KAMMEN (ed.), *The Past Before Us: Contemporary Historical Writing in the United States* (Ithaca, NY and London, 1980), 308–26.

DENNIS, N., HENRIQUES, F., and SLAUGHTER, C., *Coal is Our Life: An Analysis of a Yorkshire Mining Community* (1st edn. London, 1956; 2nd edn., London, 1969).

DENNIS, R., 'Intercensal Mobility in a Victorian City', *Trans. Instit. Brit. Geog.* NS 2 (1977), 349–63.

—— 'Distance and Social Interaction in a Victorian City', *J. of Hist. Geog.* 3 (1977), 237–50.

—— *English Industrial Cities of the Nineteenth Century* (Cambridge, 1984).

DENVIR, J., *The Irish in Britain* (London, 1892).

DICKENS, C., 'A Plated Article', *Household Words*, 5 (24 Apr. 1854), 117–21.

DIGBY, A., *British Welfare Policy: Workhouse to Workfare* (London, 1989).

DRAY, W. H., 'Holism and Individualism in History and Social Science', in *The Encyclopedia of Philosophy*, iv (London and New York, 1967), 119–29.

DUPREE, M., 'The Community Perspective in Family History: The Potteries during the Nineteenth Century', in A. L. BEIER, D. N. CANNADINE, and J. ROSENHEIM (eds.), *The First Modern Society: Essays in English History in Honour of Lawrence Stone* (Cambridge, 1989), 549–73.

DUTTON, H. I. and KING, J. E., *'Ten Per Cent and No Surrender': The Preston Strike, 1853–1854* (Cambridge, 1981).

EDWARDS, M. M. and LLOYD-JONES, R., 'N. J. Smelser and the Cotton Factory Family: A Reassessment', in N. B. HARTE and K. G. PONTING (eds.), *Textile History and Economic History: Essays in Honour of Julia de Lacy Mann* (Manchester, 1973).

ENGELS, F., *The Condition of the Working Class in England*, trans. W. O. HENDERSON and W. H. CHALONER (Oxford, 1958).

EVERSLEY, D. E. C., 'Exploitation of Anglican Parish Registers by Aggregative Analysis', in E. A. WRIGLEY (ed.), *An Introduction to English Historical Demography* (London, 1966).

FIELD, A. J., 'Occupational Structure, Dissent and Educational Commitment: Lancashire, 1841', *Research in Economic History*, 4 (1979), 235–87.

FINCH, J., *Family Obligations and Social Change* (Cambridge and Oxford, 1989).

FINER, A. and SAVAGE, G. (eds.), *Selected Letters of Josiah Wedgwood* (London, 1965).

FINLAYSON, G. B. A. M., 'A Moving Frontier: Voluntarism and the State in British Social Welfare 1911–1949', *Twentieth Century British History*, 1 (1990), 183–206.

FINNEY, J., *Sixty Years' Recollections of an Etruscan* (Stoke-upon-Trent, 1903).

FLINN, M. W., 'Introduction', in M. W. FLINN (ed.), *Report on the Sanitary Condition of the Labouring Population of Great Britain* (Edinburgh, 1965).

FLOUD, R., THANE P., and ANDERSON, O., 'Debate: The Incidence of Civil Marriage in Victorian England and Wales', *Past and Present*, 84 (1979), 146–62.

FOSTER, J., *Class Struggle and the Industrial Revolution: Early Industrial Capitalism in Three English Towns* (London, 1974).

FOX, A., *A Sociology of Work in Industry* (London, 1971).

FRASER, D., 'Introduction', in D. FRASER (ed.), *The New Poor Law in the 19th Century* (London, 1976).

FRIEDLANDER, D., 'Demographic Patterns and Socioeconomic Characteristics of the Coal-mining Population in England and Wales in the 19th Century', *Econ. Dev. and Cultural Change*, 22 (1973), 39–51.

FRIEDMAN, G., *The Anatomy of Work: The Implications of Specialization* (London, 1961).

FYSON, R., 'The Crisis of 1842: Chartism, the Colliers' Strike and the Outbreak in the Potteries', in J. EPSTEIN and D. THOMPSON (eds.), *The Chartist Experience: Studies in Working-Class Radicalism and Culture, 1830–1860* (London and Basingstoke, 1982), 194–220.

——'Unionism, Class and Community in the 1830s: Aspects of the National Union of Operative Potters', in J. RULE (ed.), *British Trade Unionism 1750–1850: The Formative Years* (London, 1988), 200–19.

GALENSON, D. W. and LEVY, D. S., 'A Note on Biases in the Measurement of Geographic Persistence Rates', *Historical Methods*, 19 (1986), 171–9.

GARDNER, P., *The Lost Elementary Schools of Victorian England* (London, 1984).

GARRETT, E., 'The Trials of Labour: Motherhood versus Employment in a Nineteenth-Century Textile Centre', *Continuity and Change*, 5 (1990), 121–54.

GATER, S. and VINCENT, D., *The Factory in a Garden: Wedgwood from Etruria to Barlaston—the Transitional Years* (Keele, Staffordshire, 1988).

GAY, P. W. and SMYTH, R. L., *The British Pottery Industry* (London, 1974).

GEERTZ, C., 'Thick Description: Toward an Interpretive Theory of Culture', in C. GEERTZ, *The Interpretation of Cultures* (New York, 1973).

GELLNER, E., 'Reply to Mr Watkins', in P. GARDINER (ed.), *Theories of History* (Glencoe, Ill., 1959).

——'Holism versus Individualism in History and Sociology', in P. GARDINER (ed.), *Theories of History* (Glencoe, Ill., 1959).

GERGEN, K. J., GREENBERG, M. S., and WILLIS, R. H. (eds.), *Social Exchange Theory and Research* (London, 1980).

GIBSON, W., *The Geology of the Country Around Stoke-upon-Trent* (London, 1925).

GIDDENS, A., *Central Problems in Social Theory: Action, Structure and Contradiction in Social Analysis* (London and Basingstoke, 1979).

GODDEN, G. A., *Ridgway Porcelain* (London, 1972).

GOLDIN, C., 'Female Labor Force Participation: The Origin of Black and White Differences 1870–1880', *J. of Econ. Hist.* 37 (1977), 87–108.

GOLDSTROM, J. M., 'Education in England and Wales in 1851: The Education Census of Great Britain, 1851', in R. LAWTON (ed.), *The Census and Social Structure* (London, 1978), 224–40.

GOLDTHORPE, J. H. (in collaboration with C. LLEWELLYN and C. PAYNE), *Social Mobility and Class Structure in Modern Britain* (Oxford, 1980).

—— LOCKWOOD, D., BERKHOFER, F., and PLATT, J., *The Affluent Worker in the Class Structure* (Cambridge, 1969).

GORDON, C., *The Myth of Family Care? The Elderly in the Early 1930s*, The Welfare State Programme, Suntory-Toyota International Centre for Economics and Related Disciplines, London School of Economics, Discussion Paper no. 29 (Apr. 1988).

GOSDEN, P., *Self-Help: Voluntary Associations in Nineteenth Century Britain* (London, 1973).

GRAY, R. Q., *The Labour Aristocracy in Victorian Edinburgh* (Oxford, 1976).

—— *The Aristocracy of Labour in Nineteenth-Century Britain* (London, 1981).

GRIFFITHS, S., *Griffiths' Guide to the Iron Trade*, new edn. with intro. by W. K. GALE (1st edn., 1873; new edn., 1967).

GRONAU, R., 'The Intrafamily Allocation of Time: The Value of the Housewife's Time', *Amer. Econ. Rev.* 63 (1973), 684–91.

HAINES, M. R., 'Fertility, Marriage and Occupation in the Pennsylvania Anthracite Region 1850–1880', *J. of Fam. Hist.* 2 (1977), 28–55.

—— 'Fertility, Nuptiality, and Occupation: A Study of Coal Mining Populations and Regions in England and Wales in the Mid-19th Century', *J. of Int. Hist.* 8 (1977), 245–80.

—— 'Industrial Work and the Family Life Cycle 1889–1890', *Research in Economic History*, 4 (1979), 289–356.

—— *Fertility and Occupation: Population Patterns in Industrialization* (London, 1979).

—— 'Social Class Differentials during Fertility Decline: England and Wales Revisited', *Pop. Studies* 43 (1989), 305–23.

HAJNAL, J., 'Age at Marriage and Proportions Marrying', *Pop. Studies* 7 (1953), 111–36.

HALL, R., *Women in the Labour Force: A Case Study of the Potteries in the Nineteenth Century*, Department of Geography and Earth Science, Queen Mary College, University of London, Occasional Paper no. 27 (London, 1986).

HANSON, C. G., 'Craft Unions, Welfare Benefits, and the Case for Trade Union Law Reform 1867–1875', *Econ. Hist. Rev.* 28 (1975), 243–59.

HAREVEN, T., 'Family Time and Industrial Time: Family and Work in a Planned Corporation Town 1900–1924', *J. of Urban Hist.* 1 (1975), 365–89.

—— 'The Laborers of Manchester, New Hampshire, 1912–1922: The Role of Family and Ethnicity in Adjustment to Industrial Life', *Labor History*, 16 (1975), 249–65.

—— 'Family and Industrialization', *Daedalus*, 106 (1977), 57–70.

—— *Family Time and Industrial Time: The Relationship Between the Family and Work in a New England Industrial Community* (Cambridge, 1982).

—— 'The History of the Family and the Complexity of Social Change', *Amer. Hist. Rev.* 96 (1991), 95–124.

—— and MODELL, J., 'Urbanisation and the Malleable Household: An Examination of Boarding and Lodging in American Families', *Journal of Marriage and the Family*, 35 (1973), 467–79.

—— and VINOVSKIS, M., 'Marital Fertility, Ethnicity and Occupation in Urban Families: An Analysis of South Boston and the South End in 1880', *J. of Soc. Hist.* 8 (1975), 69–93.

HARRIS, C., 'Review Article: Sociology and the Family', *Sociology*, 10 (1976), 355–9.

—— (ed.), *The Sociology of the Family: New Directions for Britain* (Keele, 1979).

—— *The Family and Industrial Society* (London, 1983).

—— 'Kin Rights and Kin Duties', *Times Higher Education Supplement* (1 Dec. 1989), 18.

HARRISON, B., 'State Intervention and Moral Reform in Nineteenth Century England', in P. HOLLIS (ed.), *Pressure From Without in Early Victorian England* (London, 1974).

HARTWELL, R. M., *The Industrial Revolution and Economic Growth* (London, 1971).

HAYDEN, A., *Spode and His Successors* (London, 1925).

HEATH, A., *Rational Choice and Social Exchange: A Critique of Exchange Theory* (Cambridge, 1976).

HEDLEY, J., 'Mines and Mining in the North Staffordshire Coal Field', *T. N. of Eng. Inst. of Min. Eng.*, 2 (1854), 242–55.

HELD, D., and THOMPSON, J. B. (eds.), *Social Theory of Modern Societies: Anthony Giddens and His Critics* (Cambridge, 1989).

HEMPTON, D., *Methodism and Politics in British Society 1750–1850* (London, 1987).

HEWITT, M., *Wives and Mothers in Victorian Industry* (London, 1958).

HICKS, J., *The Theory of Wages* (London, 1932).

HIGGS, E., 'Women, Occupations and Work in the Nineteenth Century Census', *Hist. Workshop*, 23 (1987), 59–80.

—— *Making Sense of the Census: The Manuscript Returns for England and Wales, 1801–1901* (London, 1989).

HILEY, M., *Victorian Working Women: Portraits From Life* (Boston, Mass., 1980).

HIRSCH, F. and GOLDTHORPE, J. H. (eds.), *The Political Economy of Inflation* (London, 1978).

HOLLEY, J., 'The Two Family Economies of Industrialism: Factory Workers in Industrial Scotland', *J. of Fam. Hist.* 6 (1981), 57–69.

HOPPIT, J., 'Counting the Industrial Revolution', *Econ. Hist. Rev.*, 2nd ser., 43 (1990), 173–93.

HORDLEY, R., *A Concise History of the Rise and Progress of the North Staffordshire Infirmary and Eye Hospital from 1802–1902* (Newcastle, 1902).

HOWE, A. C., *The Cotton Masters 1830–1860* (Oxford, 1984).

HOWER, R. M., 'The Wedgwoods—Ten Generations of Potters', *J. of Econ. Business Hist.* 4 (1932), 665–90.

HUDSON, P., 'The Regional Perspective', in P. HUDSON (ed.), *Regions and Industries: A Perspective on the Industrial Revolution in Britain* (Cambridge, 1989), 3–38.

—— (ed.), *Regions and Industries: A Perspective on the Industrial Revolution in Britain* (Cambridge, 1989).

—— and LEE, W. R. (eds.), *Women, Work and Family in Historical Perspective* (Cambridge, 1990).

—— *The Industrial Revolution* (London, 1992; repr. with corrections, 1993).

HUMPHRIES, J., 'Class Struggle and the Persistence of the Working-Class Family', *Cambridge Journal of Economics*, 1 (1977), 241–58.

—— and RUBERY, J., 'The Reconstitution of the Supply Side of the Labour Market: The Relative Autonomy of Social Reproduction', *Cambridge Journal of Economics*, 8 (1984), 331–46.

HUNT, E. H., *Regional Wage Variations in Britain 1850–1914* (Oxford, 1973).

HUNT, R., *Mineral Statistics of the United Kingdom 1855–1881* (London, 1855–82).

HUTCHINS, B. L. and HARRISON, A., *A History of Factory Legislation* (Westminster, 1903).

JEVONS, H. S., *The British Coal Trade* (1st pub. London, 1915; Newton Abbot, 1969).

JEWITT, L., *Life of Josiah Wedgwood* (London, 1865).

JOHN, A. V. (ed.), *Unequal Opportunities: Women's Employment in England 1800–1918* (Oxford, 1986).

JOHNSON, N., 'Problems for the Mixed Economy of Welfare', in A. WARE and R. E. GOODIN (eds.), *Needs and Welfare* (London, 1990), 145–64.

JOHNSON, R. C., 'A Procedure for Sampling the Manuscript Census Schedules', *J. of Int. Hist.*, 8 (1978), 515–30.

JONES, G. Stedman, 'Working-Class Culture and Working-Class Politics in London 1870–1900: Notes on the Remaking of a Working Class', *J. of Soc. Hist.* 7 (1974), 460–508.

Journal of Family History, special issue (incorporating nos. 1–3), 12 (1987).

JOYCE, P., 'The Factory Politics of Lancashire in the Later Nineteenth Century', *Hist. J.* 18 (1975), 525–53.

—— *Work, Society and Politics: The Culture of the Factory in Later Victorian England* (Brighton, 1980).

—— 'Work', in F. M. L. THOMPSON (ed.), *The Cambridge Social History of Britain*, ii (Cambridge, 1990), 131–94.

KATZ, M., 'Review Essay: Family Structure in 19th Century Lancashire', *J. of Soc. Hist.* 7 (1973–4), 86–92.

KETTLE, R., *Music in the Five Towns: 1840–1914* (London, 1944).

LAQUEUR, T., *Religion and Respectability: Sunday Schools and Working Class Culture* (London, 1976).

LASLETT, P., 'Mean Household Size in England since the Sixteenth Century', in P. LASLETT and R. WALL (eds.), *Household and Family in Past Time* (Cambridge, 1972), 125–58.

—— 'Introduction', in P. LASLETT, K. OOSTERVEEN, and R. M. SMITH (eds.), *Bastardy and its Comparative History* (London, 1980).

—— 'The Character of Familial History, Its Limitations and the Conditions for its Proper Pursuit', *J. of Fam. Hist.* 12 (1987), 263–84.

—— 'Family, Kinship and Collectivity as Systems of Support in Pre-Industrial Europe: A Consideration of the "Nuclear-Hardship" Hypothesis', *Continuity and Change*, 3 (1988), 153–75.

LAWTON, R., 'Mobility in Nineteenth Century British Cities', *Geog. J.* 145 (1979), 206–24.

LEES, L., *Exiles of Erin: Irish Migrants in Victorian London* (Manchester, 1979).

LEIBENSTEIN, H., 'An Interpretation of the Economic Theory of Fertility: Promising Path or Blind Alley?', *J. of Econ. Lit.* 13 (1974), 457–79.

LEVINE, D., 'Industrialization and the Proletarian Family in England', *Past and Present*, 107 (1985), 168–203.

—— *Reproducing Families: The Political Economy of English Population History* (Cambridge, 1987).

LEWIS, J. (ed.), *Labour and Love: Women's Experience of Home and Family 1850–1940* (Oxford, 1986).

LICHFIELD, R. B., 'The Family and the Mill: Cotton Mill Work, Family Work Patterns and Fertility in Mid-19th Century Stockport', in A. S. WOHL (ed.), *The Victorian Family: Structure and Stresses* (London, 1978).

LITWAK, E. and SZELENYI, I., 'Primary Group Structures and Their Functions: Kin, Neighbours, and Friends', *Amer. Sociol. Rev.* 34 (1969), 465–81.

LLOYD, CHRISTOPHER, *Explanation in Social History* (Oxford, 1986).

LLOYD, CYNTHIA B. (ed.), *Sex Discrimination and the Division of Labour* (London, 1975).

LOCKETT, T. A., *Davenport Pottery and Porcelain 1794–1887* (Newton Abbot, 1972).

LOWN, J., *Women and Industrialization: Gender at Work in Nineteenth-Century England* (Cambridge and Oxford, 1990).

LUKES, S., 'Methodological Individualism Reconsidered', *Brit. J. of Sociol.* 19 (1968), 119–29.

MCBRIDE, T., *The Domestic Revolution* (London, 1975).

MACFARLANE, A., *The Family Life of Ralph Josselin: An Essay in Historical Anthropology* (Cambridge, 1970).

—— 'History, Anthropology and the Study of Communities', *Social History*, 2 (1977), 631–52.

—— *The Origins of English Individualism* (Oxford, 1978).

MCKENDRICK, N., 'Josiah Wedgwood: An Eighteenth Century Entrepreneur in Salesmanship and Marketing Techniques', *Econ. Hist. Rev.* 12 (1960), 408–33.

—— 'Josiah Wedgwood and Factory Discipline', *Hist. J.* 6 (1961), 30–55.

—— 'Josiah Wedgwood and Thomas Bentley: An Inventor-Entrepreneur Partnership in the Industrial Revolution', *Royal Historical Society Transactions*, 5th ser., 14 (1964), 1–33.

—— 'Josiah Wedgwood and Cost Accounting in the Industrial Revolution', *Econ. Hist. Rev.* 23 (1970), 45–67.

—— 'The Role of Science in the Industrial Revolution: A Study of Josiah Wedgwood as a Scientist', in M. TEICH and R. M. YOUNG (eds.), *Changing Perspectives in the History of Science* (London, 1971).

—— 'The Victorian View of Midland History: A Historiographical Study of the Potteries', *Midland History*, 1 (1971), 34–47.

McKENDRICK, N., 'Review of J. Thomas, *The Rise of the Staffordshire Potteries*', in *Midland History*, 2 (1972), 55–8.

——'Home Demand and Economic Growth: A New View of the Role of Women and Children in the Industrial Revolution', in N. McKENDRICK (ed.), *Historical Perspectives: Studies in English Thought and Society in Honour of J. H. Plumb* (London, 1974), 152–210.

McLEOD, H., *Class and Religion in the Victorian City* (London, 1974).

——'Review of *Family Structure in 19th Century Lancashire*', *The Local Historian*, 11 (1974), 167–8.

——*Religion and the Working Class in Nineteenth-Century Britain* (London and Basingstoke, 1984).

——'New Perspectives on Victorian Working Class Religion: The Oral Evidence', *Oral History*, 14 (1986), 31–49.

MACLEOD, R., 'Statesmen Undisguised', *Amer. Hist. Rev.* 78 (1973), 1386–405.

MALTBY, B., 'Easingwold Marriage Horizons', *Local Pop. Studies* 2 (1969), 36–9.

——'Parish Registers and the Problem of Mobility', *Local Pop. Studies* 6 (1971), 32–43.

MANDLEBAUM, M., 'Societal Facts', in P. GARDINER (ed.), *Theories of History* (Glencoe, Ill., 1959).

MANKOWITZ, W., *Wedgwood* (Prague, Paris, and London, 1966; 1st pub. London, 1953).

MARSHALL, G., *In Praise of Sociology* (London, 1990).

——NEWBY, H., ROSE, D., and VOGLER, C., *Social Class in Modern Britain* (London, 1988).

MARSHALL, J. D., 'Colonisation as a Factor in the Planting of Towns in North West England', in J. DYOS (ed.), *The Study of Urban History* (London, 1968).

MATHIAS, P., *The First Industrial Nation: An Economic History of Britain 1700–1914*, 2nd edn. (New York and London, 1983).

MEADE, R., *The Coal and Iron Industries of the U.K.* (London, 1882).

MEDICK, H. and SABEAN, D. W. (eds.), *Interest and Emotion: Essays on the Study of Family and Kinship* (Cambridge, 1984).

MEIKLEJOHN, A., 'Health Hazards in the North Staffordshire Pottery Industry, 1688–1945', *J. Royal Sanitary Institute* 66 (1946), 516–25.

——'A House-Surgeon's Observations on Bronchitis in North Staffordshire Pottery Workers in 1864', *British J. of Industrial Medicine* 13 (1956), 211–12.

——'The Successful Prevention of Silicosis Among China Biscuit Workers in the North Staffordshire Potteries', *British J. of Industrial Medicine* 20 (1963), 255–63.

——'The History of Occupational Respiratory Disease in the North Staffordshire Pottery Industry', in C. N. DAVIES (ed.), *Health Conditions in the Ceramic Industry* (Oxford, 1969), 3–14.

MITCHELL, B. R. and DEANE, P., *Abstract of British Historical Statistics* (Cambridge, 1962).

MITCHELL, J. C., 'On Quantification in Social Anthropology', in A. L. EPSTEIN (ed.), *The Craft of Social Anthropology* (London, 1967).

—— 'The Concept and Use of Social Networks', in J. C. MITCHELL (ed.), *Social Networks in Urban Situations* (Manchester, 1969).

MOCH, L. P., FOLBRE, N., SMITH, D. S., CORNELL, L. L., and TILLY, L. A., 'Family Strategy: A Dialogue', *Historical Methods*, 20 (1987), 113–25.

MOISELY, H. A., 'The Industrial and Urban Development of the North Staffordshire Conurbation', *Trans. Instit. Brit. Geog.* 17 (1951), 151–65.

MORGAN, A. H., 'Regional Consciousness in the N. Staffs. Potteries', *Geography*, 27 (1942), 95–102.

MORGAN, D. H. J., *The Family, Politics and Social Theory* (London, 1985).

MURGATROYD, L., SAVAGE, M., SHAPIRO, D., URRY, J., WALBY, S., WARDE, A., and MARK-LAWSON, J. (eds.), *Localities, Class and Gender* (London, 1985).

NARDINELLI, C., 'Child Labour and the Factory Acts', *J. of Econ. Hist.* 40 (1980), 739–55.

—— *Child Labour and the Industrial Revolution* (Bloomington and Indianapolis, Ind., 1990).

National Association for the Promotion of Social Science, *Report of the Committee on Trade Societies and Strikes* (London, 1860).

NIXON, M., 'Sources Towards a History of the North Staffordshire Pottery Industry in the 18th and 19th Centuries', *Business Archives*, 38 (1973), 47–66.

OBELKEVICH, J., 'Religion', in F. M. L. THOMPSON (ed.), *The Cambridge Social History of Britain 1750–1950*, iii (Cambridge, 1990).

OUTHWAITE, R. B., 'Population Change, Family Structure and the Good of Counting', *Hist. J.* 22 (1979), 229–39.

OWEN, H., *The Staffordshire Potter* (1st pub. London, 1901; repr., Bath, 1970).

PARKERSON, D. H., 'How Mobile were Nineteenth-Century Americans?', *Historical Methods*, 15 (1982), 99–109.

PARSONS, T., *The Structure of Social Action* (Glencoe, Ill., 1949; 1st edn. New York and London, 1937).

PATTERSON, G. (ed.), *Penkhull 1851: An Analysis of the Census Returns* (Stoke-on-Trent, 1972).

PEEL, R. F., 'Local Intermarriage and the Stability of Rural Population in the English Midlands', *Geography*, 27 (1942), 22–30.

PELLING, M. and SMITH, R. M., 'Introduction', in M. PELLING and R. M. SMITH (eds.), *Life, Death and the Elderly: Historical Perspectives* (London, 1991), 1–38.

PERKIN, H., *The Origins of Modern English Society 1780–1880* (London, 1969).

PERRY, P. J., 'Working-Class Isolation and Mobility in Rural Dorset 1837–1936: A Study of Marriage Distances', *Trans. Instit. Brit. Geog. 46* (1969), 121–41.

PFISTER, U., 'Work Roles and Family Structure in Proto-industrial Zurich', *J. Int. Hist.* 20 (1989), 83–105.

PLECK, E., 'Two Worlds in One: Work and Family', *J. of Soc. Hist.* 10 (1976), 178–95.

POOLEY, C., 'Residential Mobility in the Victorian City', *Trans. Instit. Brit. Geog.*, NS 4 (1979), 258–77.

PRIESTLEY, J. B., *English Journey* (London, 1934; edn. 1968), esp. 203–34.

PROCHASKA, F. K., 'Philanthropy', in F. M. L. THOMPSON (ed.), *The Cambridge Social History of Britain 1750–1950*, iii (Cambridge, 1990).

REES, A., *The Economics of Work and Pay* (London, 1973).

REID, D., 'The Decline of St Monday 1766–1876', *Past and Present*, 71 (1976), 76–101.

REILLY, R., *Wedgwood*, ii (London, 1989).

REYNOLDS, J., *The Great Paternalist: Titus Salt and the Growth of Nineteenth-Century Bradford* (London, 1983).

RICHARDS, E., 'The Industrial Face of a Great Estate: Trentham and Lilleshall, 1780–1860', *Econ. Hist. Rev.* 27 (1974), 414–30.

ROBERTS, E., 'The Working-Class Extended Family: Functions and Attitudes 1890–1940', *Oral History*, 12 (1984), 48–55.

——*A Woman's Place: An Oral History of Working-Class Women 1890–1940* (Oxford, 1984).

—— *Women's Work 1840–1880* (Basingstoke and London, 1988).

ROSE, S. O., ' "Gender at Work": Sex, Class and Industrial Capitalism' *Hist. Workshop*, 21 (1986), 113–31.

—— *Limited Livelihoods: Gender and Class in Nineteenth Century England* (Berkeley, Calif., 1991).

ROSS, E., 'Survival Networks: Women's Neighbourhood Sharing in London Before World War I', *Hist. Workshop*, 15 (1983), 4–27.

ROSTOW, W. W., *The Stages of Economic Growth: A Non-Communist Manifesto* (Cambridge, 1960).

RUGGLES, S., *Prolonged Connections: The Rise of the Extended Family in Nineteenth-Century England and America* (Madison, Wis., 1987).

SAMUEL, R., 'Workshop of the World: Steam Power and Hand Technology in Mid-Victorian Britain', *Hist. Workshop*, 3 (1977), 6–72.

SCHOFIELD, R., 'Sampling in Historical Research', in E. A. WRIGLEY (ed.), *Nineteenth Century Society: Essays in the Use of Quantitative Methods for the Study of Social Data* (Cambridge, 1972).

SCHULTZ, T. W. (ed.), *Economics of the Family: Marriage, Children and Human Capital* (London, 1974).

SCOTT, J., 'The History of the Family as an Affective Unit', *Social History*, 4 (1979), 509–19.

—— 'Women In History: The Modern Period', *Past and Present*, 101 (1983), 141–57.

——and TILLY, L., 'Women's Work and the Family in Nineteenth Century Europe', *Comparative Studies in Society and History*, 17 (1975), 36–64.

—— *Women, Work and Family* (London, 1978).

SECCOMBE, W., 'Patriarchy Stabilized: The Construction of the Male Breadwinner Wage Norm in Nineteenth Century Britain', *Social History*, 11 (1986), 53–76.

—— 'Starting to Stop: Working-Class Fertility Decline in Britain', *Past and Present*, 126 (1990), 151–88.

—— *Weathering the Storm: Working-Class Families from the Industrial Revolution to the Fertility Decline* (London and New York, 1993).

SEN, A. K., *Choice, Welfare and Measurement* (Oxford, 1982).

—— *Resources, Values and Development* (Oxford, 1984).

SHAW, C., *When I Was a Child* (1st pub. London, 1903; repr., Firle, Sussex, 1977).

SHRYOCK, H. S. and SIEGEL, J. S., *The Methods and Materials of Demography*, ii (Washington, DC, 1973).

SMELSER, N. J., *Social Change in the Industrial Revolution: An Application of Theory to the Lancashire Cotton Industry 1770–1840* (London, 1959).

—— 'Sociological History: The Industrial Revolution and the British Working Class Family', *J. of Soc. Hist.* 1 (1967), 17–35.

SMITH, D. S., 'Family Strategy: More than a Metaphor?', *Historical Methods*, 20 (1987), 118–20.

SMITH, ROGER, 'Early Victorian Household Structure: A Case Study of Nottinghamshire', *Int. Rev. of Soc. Hist.* 15 (1970), 69–84.

SMITH, R. M., 'Fertility, Economy and Household Formation in England over Three Centuries', *Population and Development Review*, 7 (1981), 595–622.

SNELL, K. and MILLAR, J., 'Lone Parent Families and the Welfare State: Past and Present', *Continuity and Change*, 2 (1987), 387–422.

SPREAD, P., 'Blau's Exchange Theory, Support and the Macrostructure', *Brit. J. of Sociol.* 35 (1984), 157–73.

STACEY, M., 'The Myth of Community Studies', *Brit. J. of Sociol.* 20 (1969), 134–47.

STONE, L., 'Literacy and Education in England 1640–1900', *Past and Present*, 42 (1969), 69–139.

—— *Family, Sex and Marriage in England 1500–1800* (London, 1977).

—— 'Family History in the 1980s: Past Achievements and Future Trends', *J. of Int. Hist.* 12 (1981), 51–87.

STUART, D. G. (ed.), *The Population of Central Burslem 1851 and 1861*, Department of Adult Education University of Keele Local History Occasional Paper no. 2 (Keele, 1973).

SUTHERLAND, G., 'Recent Trends in Administrative History', *Vict. Studies* 13 (1970), 408–11.

TAWNEY, R. H., 'Introduction', in W. WARBURTON (ed.), *The History of Trade Union Organization in the North Staffordshire Potteries* (London, 1931).

THANE, P., 'Essay in Revision: The Historiography of the British Welfare State', *Social History Society Newsletter*, 15 (1990), 12–15.

THIRSK, J., 'Family Life Among the Gentry', *Times Higher Education Supplement* (28 Oct. 1977), 16.

THISTLETHWAITE, F., 'The Atlantic Migration of the Pottery Industry', *Econ. Hist. Rev.* 11 (1958), 264–78.

THOMAS, J., *The Rise of the Staffordshire Potteries* (Bath, 1971).

THOMAS, K. V., 'The Changing Family', *Times Literary Supplement* (21 Oct. 1977), 1226–7.

THOMAS, M. W., *The Early Factory Legislation* (London, 1948).

THOMPSON, D., 'The Religious Census of 1851', in R. LAWTON (ed.), *The Census and Social Structure* (London, 1978).

THOMPSON, E. P., 'Time, Work-Discipline and Industrial Capitalism', *Past and Present*, 38 (1967), 56–97.

—— '"Rough Music": Le Charivari Anglais', *Annales ESC* (Economies, Societies, Civilisations), 27 (1972), 285–312.

—— 'Happy Families', *New Society* (9 Sept., 1977), 499–501.

THOMSON, D., 'Welfare and the Historians', in L. BONFIELD, R. SMITH, and K. WRIGHTSON (eds.), *The World We Have Gained: Histories of Population and Social Structure, Essays Presented to Peter Laslett* (London, 1986), 355–78.

—— 'The Welfare of the Elderly in the Past: A Family or Community Responsibility?', in M. PELLING and R. M. SMITH (eds.), *Life, Death and the Elderly: Historical Perspectives* (London, 1991), 194–221.

TILLOTT, P. M., 'Sources of Inaccuracy in the 1851 and 1861 Census', in E. A. WRIGLEY (ed.), *Nineteenth Century Society: Essays in the Use of Quantitative Methods for the Study of Social Data* (Cambridge, 1972), 82–113.

TILLY, L., 'Demographic Change in Two French Industrial Cities, Anzin and Roubaix, 1872–1906', in J. SUNDIN and E. SODERLUND (eds.), *Time, Space and Man: Essays in Microdemography* (Stockholm, 1979), 107–32.

—— 'Beyond Family Strategies, What?', *Historical Methods*, 20 (1987), 123–5.

—— and COHEN, M., 'Does the Family Have a History? A Review of Theory and Practice in Family History', *Social Science History*, 6 (1982), 131–79.

—— SCOTT, J., and COHEN, M., 'Women's Work and European Fertility Patterns', *J. of Int. Hist.*, 6 (1976), 447–76.

VALENZE, D., *Prophetic Sons and Daughters: Female Preaching and Popular Religion in Industrial England* (Princeton, NJ, 1985).

Victoria County History of Stafford, ii and viii.

VINCENT, D., 'Love and Death and the Nineteenth Century Working Class', *Social History*, 5 (1980), 223–47.

—— *Bread, Knowledge and Freedom: A Study of Nineteenth-Century Working Class Autobiography* (London, 1981).

WALBY, S., 'Spatial and Historical Variations in Women's Unemployment and Employment', in L. MURGATROYD, M. SAVAGE, D. SHAPIRO, J. URRY, S. WALBY, A. WARDE, and J. MARK-LAWSON (eds.), *Localities, Class and Gender* (London, 1985), 161–76.

WALL, R., 'The Age at Leaving Home', *J. of Fam. Hist.* 3 (1978), 181–202.

—— 'Work, Welfare and the Family: An Illustration of the Adaptive Family Economy', in L. BONFIELD, R. SMITH, and K. WRIGHTSON (eds.), *The World We Have Gained: Histories of Population and Social Structure, Essays Presented to Peter Laslett* (Oxford, 1986), 261–94.

WARBURTON, W. H., *The History of Trade Union Organization in the North Staffordshire Potteries* (London, 1931).

WARE, A., 'Meeting Needs Through Voluntary Action: Does Market Society Corrode Altruism?', in A. WARE and R. E. GOODIN (eds.), *Needs and Welfare* (London, 1990), 185–207.

WARRILLOW, E. J. D., *History of Etruria 1760–1951* (Hanley, 1954).

——*A Sociological History of the City of Stoke-on-Trent* (Stoke-on-Trent, 1960).

WATKINS, J. W. N., 'Ideal Types and Historical Explanations', in H. FEIGL and M. BRODBECK (eds.), *Readings in the Philosophy of Science* (New York, 1953).

——'Historical Explanation in the Social Sciences', in P. GARDINER (ed.), *Theories of History* (Glencoe, Ill., 1959).

WEATHERILL, L., *The Pottery Trade and North Staffordshire 1660–1769* (Manchester, 1971).

——*The Growth of the Pottery Industry in England, 1660–1815* (New York and London, 1986).

WEBER, M., *The Theory of Social and Economic Organization*, ed. T. PARSONS, Free Press edn. (New York, 1964).

WEDGWOOD, H. and WEDGWOOD, B., *The Wedgwood Circle 1730–1897* (London, 1980).

WEDGWOOD, J. C., *A History of the Wedgwood Family* (London, 1908).

—— *Staffordshire Pottery and its History* (London, 1913).

WHIPP, R., 'Labour Markets and Communities: An Historical View', *Sociological Review*, 33 (1985), 768–91.

——'"A Time to Every Purpose": An Essay on Time and Work', in P. JOYCE (ed.), *The Historical Meanings of Work* (Cambridge, 1987), 210–36.

——'Women and the Social Organization of Work in the Staffordshire Pottery Industry 1900–1930', *Midland History*, 12 (1987), 103–21.

——'Work and Social Consciousness: British Potters in the Early Twentieth Century', *Past and Present*, 119 (1988), 132–57.

—— *Patterns of Labour: Work and Social Change in the Pottery Industry* (London, 1990).

WILLIAMS, K., *From Pauperism to Poverty* (London, 1981).

WILLMOTT, P., *Kinship and Urban Communities: Past and Present*, The Ninth H. J. Dyos Memorial Lecture, Victorian Studies Centre, University of Leicester (Leicester, 1987).

WILSON, C. and WOODS, R., 'Fertility in England: A Long-Term Perspective', *Pop. Studies* 45 (1991), 399–415.

WOOD, G. H., 'Factory Legislation Considered With Reference to the Wages, etc. of the Operatives Protected Thereby', *JRSS* 65 (1902), 284–324.

WOODMAN, H. D., 'Comment', *J. of Econ. Hist.* 37 (1977), 109–12.

WOODS, R., *Population Analysis in Geography* (London and New York, 1979).

—— and SMITH, C. W., 'The Decline of Marital Fertility in the Late Nineteenth Century: The Case of England and Wales', *Pop. Studies* 37 (1983), 207–25.

Woods, R., 'Approaches to the Fertility Transition in Victorian England', *Pop. Studies* 41 (1987), 283–311.

Wrigley, E. A., 'Reflections of the History of the Family', *Daedalus*, 106 (1977), 71–86.

——'Population History in the 1980s', *J. of Int. Hist.* 12 (1981), 207–26.

——and Schofield, R. S., *The Population History of England 1541–1871: A Reconstruction* (London, 1981).

—— *Continuity, Chance and Change: The Character of the Industrial Revolution in England* (Cambridge, 1988).

Young, M. and Willmott, P., *The Symmetrical Family* (Harmondsworth, 1973).

Index